Practices of Freedom

The shift from government to governance has become a starting point for many studies of contemporary policy making and democracy. *Practices of Freedom* takes a different approach, calling into question this dominant narrative and taking the variety, hybridity and dispersion of social and political practices as its focus of analysis. Bringing together leading scholars in democratic theory and critical policy studies, it draws upon new understandings of radical democracy, practice and interpretative analysis to emphasise the productive role of actors and political conflict in the formation and reproduction of contemporary forms of democratic governance. Integrating theoretical dialogues with detailed empirical studies, this book examines spaces for democratisation, institutional design, democratic criteria and learning, whilst mobilising the frameworks of agonistic and aversive democracy, informality and decentred legitimacy, in cases from youth engagement to the Israeli-Palestinian conflict.

STEVEN GRIGGS is a Reader in Local Governance in the Department of Politics and Public Policy at De Montfort University, Leicester. His work draws on political discourse theory, examining environmental policy, community participation and local governance. His publications include *The Politics of Airport Expansion in the United Kingdom* (with David Howarth, 2013), as well as articles in the *British Journal of Politics and International Relations* and the *Journal of Political Ideologies*. He is co-editor of *Critical Policy Studies*.

ALETTA J. NORVAL is a Professor of Political Theory in the Department of Government at the University of Essex. A leading democratic theorist, she draws inspiration from the agonistic tradition, as well as from a wider range of theorists, to understand and analyse processes of the articulation of democratic demands, the formation of democratic subjectivities and the institutionalisation of a democratic ethos. Her publications include *Aversive Democracy* (Cambridge University Press, 2007) as well as articles in the *American Political Science Review* and *Ethics and Global Politics*. She is consulting editor of *Political Theory*.

HENDRIK WAGENAAR is a Professor of Town and Regional Planning in the Department of Town and Regional Planning at the University of Sheffield. He publishes in the areas of urban governance, citizen participation, prostitution policy, administrative practice, complexity theory and interpretive policy analysis. His publications include *Deliberative Policy Analysis* (with Maarten A. Hajer, Cambridge University Press, 2003) and *Meaning in Action* (2011).

Practices of Freedom

Decentred Governance, Conflict and Democratic Participation

EDITED BY

STEVEN GRIGGS
De Montfort University, Leicester

ALETTA J. NORVAL
University of Essex

HENDRIK WAGENAAR
University of Sheffield

CAMBRIDGE
UNIVERSITY PRESS

CAMBRIDGE
UNIVERSITY PRESS

32 Avenue of the Americas, New York NY 10013-2473, USA

Cambridge University Press is part of the University of Cambridge.

It furthers the University's mission by disseminating knowledge in the pursuit of education, learning and research at the highest international levels of excellence.

www.cambridge.org
Information on this title: www.cambridge.org/9781107056107

© Cambridge University Press 2014

First published 2014

Printed in the United States of America

A catalogue record for this publication is available from the British Library.

Library of Congress Cataloguing in Publication data
Practices of freedom: decentred governance, conflict and democratic participation / [edited by] Steven Griggs, Aletta J. Norval, Hendrik Wagenaar.
   pages   cm.
Includes bibliographical references and index.
ISBN 978-1-107-05610-7 (hardback)
1. Freedom.   2. Democracy.   I. Griggs, Steven, 1962–   II. Norval, Aletta J.
III. Wagenaar, H.
JC585.P675   2014
323.44–dc23   2013037542

ISBN 978-1-107-05610-7 Hardback

Contents

List of Contributors   *page* vii

Acknowledgements   xi

1   Introduction: Democracy, Conflict and Participation
    in Decentred Governance   1
    STEVEN GRIGGS, ALETTA J. NORVAL
    AND HENDRIK WAGENAAR

2   Governance-Driven Democratization   38
    MARK E. WARREN

3   Deliberative, Agonistic and Aversive Grammars of
    Democracy: The Question of Criteria   60
    ALETTA J. NORVAL

4   Designing Democratic Institutions for Decentred
    Governance: The Council of Europe's *Acquis*   85
    VIVIEN LOWNDES AND LAWRENCE PRATCHETT

5   Assessing the Democratic Anchorage of Governance
    Networks   108
    EVA SØRENSEN AND JACOB TORFING

6   Learning through Contested Governance: The Practice
    of Agonistic Intersubjectivity   137
    JOHN FORESTER

7   Decentred Legitimacy in the New Community
    Governance   155
    STEPHEN CONNELLY

8   Designing 'the Political' in (and out of) Neighbourhood
    Governance   176
    HELEN SULLIVAN

9   Participatory Governance in Practice   199
    THERESE O'TOOLE AND RICHARD GALE

10 The Agonistic Experience: Informality, Hegemony and
    the Prospects for Democratic Governance   217
    HENDRIK WAGENAAR

11 Insurgent Citizenship: Radicalism, Co-optation and
    Neighbourhood Geopolitics among the Palestinian
    Citizens of Haifa, Israel   249
    JOSEPH LEIBOVITZ

Bibliography   277

Index   309

Contributors

STEPHEN CONNELLY is a Senior Lecturer in the Department of Town and Regional Planning at the University of Sheffield. Prior to his appointment in 2002, he worked as a development practitioner and researcher in India, Sri Lanka, Eritrea and Sudan. His research centres on questions about the relationship between policy norms promoting 'collaboration' and substantive goals of sustainability, democracy and welfare provision. His recent work extends the investigation of legitimacy and representation into the domain of local welfare service integration and decentralisation. He has published widely, including articles in *Urban Studies*, *Planning Practice and Research* and the *Journal of Rural Studies*.

JOHN FORESTER is a Professor of City and Regional Planning at Cornell University. His work explores practice-focused oral histories to study issues of power, conflict and organising in domains of urban studies. A collection of his favourite 'profiles of practitioners' appears in his book, *Planning in the Face of Conflict* (2013); teaching materials are assessed analytically in his *Dealing with Differences: Dramas of Mediating Public Disputes* (2009).

RICHARD GALE is a Lecturer in Human Geography at Cardiff University, and his research interests lie at the intersection of geography and sociology. Richard's main areas of research include ethnic and religious segregation, place and the politics of identity, religion and urban governance, and ethnicity and political participation. To date, his primary contributions have been to debates in the geographical study of planning, religion and Islam in the United Kingdom and the political engagement of young people of minority ethnic heritage. He has recently published, with Therese O'Toole, *Political Engagement among Ethnic Minority Young People: Making a Difference* (2013).

STEVEN GRIGGS is a Reader in Local Governance in the Department of Politics and Public Policy at De Montfort University. His work draws on political discourse theory, examining environmental policy, community participation and local governance. His publications include *The Politics of Airport Expansion in the United Kingdom* (with David Howarth, 2013), as well as articles in the *British Journal of Politics and International Relations* and the *Journal of Political Ideologies*. He is a co-editor of *Critical Policy Studies*.

JOSEPH LEIBOVITZ is a Senior Policy Advisor at the Ministry of Research and Innovation, Government of Ontario. His research has focused on comparative urban political economy, regional economic development, European urban and regional governance and the politics of citizenship in contested cities. He received a PhD in geography from the University of Toronto and held academic appointments at the University of Glasgow and the University of Edinburgh. His work has been published in journals such as *Urban Studies,* the *International Journal of Urban and Regional Research, Space and Polity* and *Ethnopolitics.*

VIVIEN LOWNDES is a Professor of Public Policy at the University of Nottingham. She has conducted major research projects on citizen participation, partnership governance, local political leadership and central/local relations. Her current work focuses on faith engagement in public policy and local governance. Vivien has published widely in journals such as *Public Administration, Policy and Politics* and the *Urban Affairs Review*. She has recently published *Why Institutions Matter: The New Institutionalism in Political Science* (with Mark Roberts, 2013). She is a co-editor of *Political Studies*.

ALETTA J. NORVAL is a Professor of Political Theory in the Department of Government at the University of Essex. A leading democratic theorist, she draws inspiration from the agonistic tradition, as well as from a wider range of theorists, to understand and analyse processes of the articulation of democratic demands, the formation of democratic subjectivities and the institutionalisation of a democratic ethos. Her publications include *Aversive Democracy* (Cambridge University Press, 2007) as well as articles in the *American Political Science Review* and *Ethics and Global Politics*. She is a consulting editor of *Political Theory*.

THERESE O'TOOLE is a Senior Lecturer in Sociology at the University of Bristol. Her research interests are in the fields of governance, political activism, ethnicity, religion and young people. Her latest book, with Richard Gale, is *Political Engagement among Ethnic Minority Young People: Making a Difference* (2013). In 2009, she was awarded an AHRC/ESRC grant to lead a project on Muslim Participation in Contemporary Governance, and in 2011, an AHRC Knowledge Exchange grant to fund Public Spirit, an online forum on religion and public policy for academics, policy makers, politicians, practitioners and faith and community activists.

LAWRENCE PRATCHETT is the Dean of the Faculty of Business, Government and Law and a Professor of Politics at the University of Canberra. He was a member of the Council of Europe's expert working party on the Future of Democracy in Europe. His research is focused especially on local democracy and the changing notions of citizenship and democratic participation that new technologies and differing forms of governance initiate. Most recently, he has published on issues of citizenship in the age of the Internet (with RabiaKarakaya-Polat).

EVA SØRENSEN is a Professor of Public Administration and Democracy in the Department of Society and Globalization at Roskilde University. Her main research interests are questions related to how public institutions develop over time in order to meet new governance tasks and ambitions, and the impact of these changes on the perceptions of the involved actors and the general capacity of the public sector to provide effective, democratic and innovative governance. Her publications include *Interactive Governance: Advancing the Paradigm* (co-authored with Jacob Torfing, B. Guy Peters and Jon Pierre, 2012), as well as articles in *Planning Theory* and the *American Review of Public Administration*.

HELEN SULLIVAN is a Professor of Public Policy and the Director of the University of Melbourne's School of Government. Her research examines the theory and practices of contemporary governance focusing on popular modes of state-society interaction such as collaboration and 'active' citizenship, and exploring how they are constituted and expressed. She has published widely on these topics, including the books: *Working Across Boundaries* (2002); *Power, Participation and Political Renewal* (2007); and *Hybrid Governance in European Cities*

(2013). Her current research projects include the 'Citizens' Agenda', an exploration of the relationship between social media, journalism and citizen participation in Australian electoral politics.

JACOB TORFING is a Professor in Politics and Institutions in the Department of Society and Globalization at Roskilde University. His research interests include network governance, democracy, governance reforms and the role of politicians, administrators and citizens in reinvigorating local democracy. His most recent books in English include *Theories of Democratic Network Governance* (co-edited with Eva Sørensen, 2007) and *Interactive Governance: Advancing the Paradigm* (co-authored with B. Guy Peters, Jon Pierre and Eva Sørensen, 2012).

HENDRIK WAGENAAR is a Professor of Town and Regional Planning in the Department of Town and Regional Planning at the University of Sheffield. His research investigates urban governance, citizen participation, prostitution policy, administrative practice, complexity theory and interpretive policy analysis. He has published widely in journals such as the *American Review of Public Administration*, *Public Administration Review* and *Urban Studies*. His books include *Deliberative Policy Analysis* (with Maarten A. Hajer, Cambridge University Press, 2003) and *Meaning in Action* (2011).

MARK E. WARREN holds the Harold and Dorrie Merilees Chair for the Study of Democracy at the University of British Columbia. He is especially interested in democratic innovations, civil society and democratic governance, and political corruption. Mark is author of *Democracy and Association* (2000), editor of *Democracy and Trust* (Cambridge University Press, 1999) and co-editor of *Designing Deliberative Democracy: The British Columbia Citizens' Assembly* (Cambridge University Press, 2008). His work has appeared in journals such as the *American Political Science Review*, the *American Journal of Political Science* and *Political Theory*.

Acknowledgements

It is often the case that the origins of academic volumes can be traced back to one timely conversation between colleagues or a single intervention from the floor at a workshop. This is not the case for this volume. This book has emerged over a number of years from multiple conversations with numerous colleagues at conferences, panels, workshops, doctoral seminars and reading groups. Many of these conversations took place at the annual Interpretive Policy Analysis conference, where thoughts were triggered, claims discussed and perspectives nurtured within a community of scholars themselves engaged in critical accounts of democratic governance. Academic scholarship is a collective endeavour and this book rightly bears testament to that.

We would like, however, to make a few special mentions. We thank colleagues at the Institute of Local Government Studies at the University of Birmingham, who helped to support this project in its initial stages. Other conversations took place at the European Consortium for Political Research (ECPR) Joint Sessions in Nicosia in 2006, and the five days of lively debates and interventions from participants, a number of whom are represented in this volume, helped to bring together the themes of this edited collection. The Centre for Theoretical Studies at the University of Essex also kindly hosted a two-day seminar on democratic governance, giving us another opportunity to revisit with contributors our key arguments and claims. These different forms of support and the intellectual spaces they offered us contributed significantly to the framing of the arguments set out in the following pages.

Yet books do not come together through intellectual effort alone. The final stages of the production of the manuscript were made possible by the financial support provided by the Department of Government at Essex University and the Department of Politics and Public Policy at De Montfort University. At the same time, we benefitted from the work of Peter Josse, who undertook the initial copy-editing of the manuscript, and from the administrative support provided by Suzanne Walker. Our special thanks go to them both.

Finally, we wish to thank our contributors. Through the long process of bringing this volume together, they kept with us, offered us fruitful comments and insights and engaged throughout with the aspirations of this volume.

1 | Introduction: Democracy, Conflict and Participation in Decentred Governance

STEVEN GRIGGS, ALETTA J. NORVAL
AND HENDRIK WAGENAAR

The Shift from Government to Governance?

New canonical beliefs in government enter our collective understandings through compelling narratives of inescapable pressures for social, political and economic change. These narratives typically speak of 'ruptures with the past'. While they list the failings of traditional policy instruments to address new complexities, they extol the promise of new organisational forms and strategic approaches. They give policymakers and practitioners assurances of solutions and 'road maps' through which they can navigate the confusing events that are deemed to frustrate their everyday activities. Of course, any new claims of orthodoxy are inevitably open to charges of simplification and the undue aggregation of complex and distinct practices. The struggle to impose such dominant narratives arguably rests on the capacity of their proponents to construct credible claims to uniformity across diverse practices and contexts. However, accusations of simplification and alike should not detract from recognition of how far new ideas held in 'good currency' are inevitably tied to the work of government. For, as Rose (1999, 8) notes, the practices of government are 'both made possible by and constrained by what can be thought at any particular moment in our history. To analyse the history of government, then, requires attention to the conditions under which it becomes possible to consider certain things to be true – and hence to say and do certain things'.

Recognising this intertwining of the activities of thought and government, we suggest that we are now faced with a new orthodoxy encapsulated in the narrative of the 'shift from government to governance' (Frederickson 2007; Chhotray and Stoker 2009; Bellamy and Palumbo 2010). This governance narrative has become an indispensable point of departure for many inquiries into the contemporary practices of policymaking. At the same time, it has attracted substantive praise for its analytical move away from the 'narrow' confines of government to the 'broader' concerns of governance interactions (Rhodes 2000), 60–1, with Guy Peters going so far as to suggest that a focus on governance rather than government obliges 'the discipline of political science to recapture some of its roots by focusing more explicitly on how the public sector, in conjunction with private sector actors or alone, is capable of providing direction and control to society and economy' (Peters 2011, 63).

Here, so the story goes, in the absence of both a 'formal chain of command' and any explicit directive role for public agencies, government itself has become 'merely one amongst many actors' who populate shifting networks of more or less collaborative or competitive stakeholders, who come together to define and work towards a shared public purpose (Sørensen and Torfing 2004, 7–8; see also Klijn and Koppenjan 2012; Lewis 2011). We now inhabit, it is claimed, a 'networked polity' in which the blurred boundaries between state and civil society have produced new processes of horizontal decision making and collaborative modes of governing between public, private, voluntary and community actors (Hajer and Wagenaar 2003). Accordingly the art of government has become that of 'steering not rowing', recast in terms of 'regulation', 'enabling', 'facilitation' or indeed 'network management' and 'metagovernance'. Policymaking, it is alleged, is best characterised as the processes of 'negotiated social governance' (Hirst 2000), 'societal governance' (Kooiman 2000), 'interactive governance' (Edelenbos 2005; Torfing et al. 2012), 'network governance' (Marcussen and Torfing 2007) or 'new public governance' (Osbourne 2010). In fact, Klijn (2008a) ultimately claims that 'governance is more or less the new consensus' (p. 11), marking the 'transition … from a situation where public actors handle problems mostly through vertical steering … to a situation of horizontal steering, where policy outcomes are, sometimes perforce, realised in cooperation with a large variety of public, private and semi-private organisations' (pp. 9–10).

As we have suggested, orthodoxies are by definition broad caricatures or 'ways of seeing'. Indeed, the very popularity of 'governance' owes much to its ambiguity (Peters 2011, 63). Too often it has come to operate as a 'nebulous catch-all' (Dean 2007, 1) or 'useful substitute and analogue' (Rose 1999, 16) for the bewildering and often contradictory range of strategies and tactics deployed in regulating, administering and managing organisations, localities, nation states and international organisations (Rose 1999, 15–16; see also Hirst, 2000, 14–19). Microeconomic narratives have for example interwoven explanations of governance into neoliberal accounts of public sector reform, in which allegedly irresistible pressures for change – be it globalisation, escalating competition between states or 'global cities' (Sassen 2001), the growing mobility of capital and finance, mounting critiques of bureaucratic inefficiencies, and, lately, the need to reduce mounting budget deficits – compel states to subject their public sector to principles of market rationality (Bevir 2003, 201). Typically in such accounts, governance, Bevir (2003) suggests, becomes associated with the efficiencies of marketisation, competition, contracting out and budgetary rationalisation as judgements of 'good' or 'bad' governance rest heavily on the adoption of new public management strategies which emulate the alleged rationality and efficiency of corporate management (Rose 1999, 16). Framed as such, governance becomes the expression of a neoliberal political rationality which extends market-inspired forms of political-economic governance into social relations (Larner 2000).

In fact, in his critical assessment of the concept of governance, Offe asks whether governance is best understood as an empty signifier, suggesting that its 'unresolved polysemy' permits 'its protagonists to connect it to all kinds of positive adjectives and to embed it in a harmonizing rhetoric' (2009, 557). Echoing such concerns, we do not seek therefore to impose any rigid uniformity or consistency on what we have characterised as a governance orthodoxy. Governance narratives draw on overlapping and distinct traditions, often conflating work on policy networks, inter-organisational service delivery and implementation, and network management (Klijn and Koppenjan 2012, 588–89).[1] They have evolved over time, opening up avenues for analytically distinguishing ever more refined variants and 'generations' of approaches to governance (Sørensen and Torfing 2007). Indeed, in the field of network governance, Lewis argues that despite the development of more or less 'coherent definitions' in recent critical assessments of the field, there 'remains less agreement on whether it is merely useful as a metaphor, a method, an analytical tool, or a theory' (Lewis 2011, 1221).

---

[1] For a discussion of the critical distinctions between the literature on policy networks and governance networks, see Blanco, Lowndes and Pratchett (2011).

However, while we recognise that many different perspectives on the practices of governance exist, it is difficult to deny the 'broad consensus' which surrounds the alleged benefits of governance as a new process or mode of governing across advanced liberal democratic societies, one which involves complex processes of co-operative horizontal decision making and engages large numbers of interactive stakeholders in bottom-up participative networks (Brugnoli and Colombo 2012, ix; Klijn 2008b). New ethical politics and value pluralism, a general discontent among citizens with the institutions of representative democracy, the increasing prevalence of 'wicked issues' facing policymakers, and the fragmentation and weakened control of state institutions (in part a result of the devolution of control to local and societal actors) have, it is widely accepted, all conspired to produce new demands, new spaces of politics and new challenges for government. The privileged 'solution' to such challenges lies in the recognition by government of its interdependency with other actors, not least its reliance on the mobilisation of resources at the disposal of others (Hajer and Wagenaar 2003). Networks and collaborative decision making, it thus follows, promise a practice of social and political co-ordination that is both more participatory and inclusive of multiple stakeholders, and more co-operative and negotiated than hierarchical or market alternatives (Jessop 2003, 101; Koppenjan and Klijn 2004, 9). Indeed, the patterns of mutual dependency that incite collaboration mean that policymaking becomes 'an issue of interaction where the actors with a stake in the problem must manage to co-ordinate their perceptions, activities and institutional arrangements' (Koppenjan and Klijn 2004, 9).

Such normative and managerial appeals increasingly exercise a particular hold on the minds and practices of policymakers, with public managers interpreting networks not only as a tool to advance their short-term policy goals but also often as a means to address the limits of representative democracy (Jeffares and Skelcher 2011). Take for example the rhetoric of a 2005 policy report from a large municipal agency in the Dutch city of The Hague, representative of countless such policy statements from local and national administrations in Western Europe. The report, which announces the introduction of 'area-based governance' across the city, reproduces the underlying narrative of the shift to governance, recognising the constraints on hierarchical government in its assertions that 'as the acceptance of government as self-evident authority declines ... government increasingly runs into the limits of what it can or cannot regulate and influence'. Indeed, the authors of the report invoke a number of 'steering principles which [they] also want to employ with all relevant actors in the city and the region' (Gemeente Den Haag 2005, 5).[2] In so doing, they articulate mechanisms of network governance, invoking 'steering principles' such as 'giving space to citizens and organisations', 'effective partnerships' and 'deconcentration and integrality'. What is fascinating about this report is that it is not about substantive problems, such as housing, education or crime, but about the introduction of a new mode of governing to allegedly better tackle such substantive issues. As such, it reproduces the overriding normative appeal of governance that suggests that disputes and bargaining over resource allocation will be mediated best in networks by recognising the ties of mutual dependency that unite stakeholders and that underpin an effective politics of exchange (Koppenjan and Klijn 2004).

This particular governance orthodoxy thus offers both analytical and normative anchors in its claims that policy is made and ultimately should be made within self-organising networks of interdependent policy actors 'based on continuing dialogue and resource-sharing to develop mutually beneficial joint projects and to manage the contradictions and dilemmas inevitably involved in such situations' (Jessop 2003, 101). Yet, with the boundaries between state and civil society said to be increasingly blurred, more dystopic versions of networked governance raise the spectre of a 'hollowed out' state (Rhodes 1994; Stoker 2011). This dispersion of government acts as a bridge to microeconomic narratives of governance. The microeconomic or neoliberal doctrine, as we suggest earlier in this chapter, implies the delegating of a wide array of governing tasks to a host of societal actors, although it continues to proffer centrally orchestrated prescription and advice to guide the conduct of individual citizens (Rose and Miller 1992; Dean 1999). Similarly, network governance privileges the co-ordination of collective activities through the interactions of more or less self-governing groups of public and private actors (Rhodes 1996, 2000; Peters and Pierre 2000; Sørensen and Torfing 2009).

In fact, the explanatory capacity and normative connotations of orthodox governance accounts of policy-making are increasingly

---

[2] The report is titled, characteristically, 'People Make the City'.

contested (Hysing 2009). Such contestations bring out the inherent tension between the logic of control and the logic of collaboration which resides in the two faces of governance. One significant line of critique charges the governance literature (of the collaborative stripe) with wrongly directing our attention away from the continued role of the state and government (Dean 2007, 1), a charge that also emanates from those governance scholars who seek to maintain state-centric interpretations of network management (Peters and Pierre 2000). The hierarchical state, it is argued, has not disappeared but has merely changed tactics (Marsh et al. 2003; Bell and Hindmoor 2009). Instead of centralised steering through vast, sectorally organised state bureaucracies, it now regulates indirectly through audit regimes, partnerships and networks, and market mechanisms (Moran 2003; Fuller and Geddes 2008; Griggs and Sullivan 2012). For example, Davies characterises partnership working in the United Kingdom as a mode of government through hierarchies of collaboration. Indeed, he argues that the ideology of network governance represents a key element of neoliberalism, while drawing attention to the continued presence of a hierarchical and coercive state (Davies 2002, 2007, 2011). Similarly, Lowndes and Sullivan (2004) label community participation and stakeholder dialogue as the 'new corporatism', fuelling concerns that networks and practices of participation are ridden with power imbalances (Griggs and Howarth 2007). Governance thus masks in these perspectives new technologies, practices and rules of governmentality, including centrally orchestrated prescription and advice, active citizenship, and co-production which guide the conduct of individual citizens (Rose and Miller 1992; Dean 1999, 2007; Rose 1999). These latter critiques point towards a regime of 'culture governance' which privileges rule through capacities of self-government (Dean 2003, 117; see also Bang 2003, 2004). As the critique goes, in neoliberal societies even citizens who choose to engage in democratic participation cannot escape being co-opted by a dominating state.

Paradoxically, as with many prevailing orthodoxies, 'governance' is both simultaneously all-pervasive and discredited. But even those who seek to challenge this orthodoxy too often continue to construct their problematisations of contemporary democratic policymaking through the well-used lens of governance. In so doing, they run the risk, whatever their intentions, of reproducing governance-inspired a priori assumptions about the shifting practices of government. Equally, however, we have to be wary of simply substituting one orthodoxy for another and, in the process, exchanging one set of constraining assumptions for another. In this volume we argue for the pursuit of a *critical* engagement with practices of government, asking 'whether the inherited languages of description and reflection are adequate to the task' (Tully 2008a, 19). Our critical engagement does not accept dominant languages and conceptualisations of existing practices at face value, but, drawing inspiration from the work of James Tully (2008a, 25) starts with a 'provisional language of description' that surfaces the existing practices and problematisations of governance as a first step towards generating alternative democratic practices and processes. We position this volume in terms of a critical, performative approach to politics, governance and public policy, one that takes the variety, hybridity and dispersion of practices of governance in contemporary society as its focus of analysis.[3]

Practices of Governance and Practices of Freedom

To develop our argument, let us take a brief aside to consider the remarkably sophisticated, critical approach to governance advocated by the political theorist James Tully (2008a, 2008b). His starting point is to recognise that any critical inquiry begins with an engagement with the multiple practices of governance *and* of freedom that go beyond the traditional practices of the representative democratic nation state, which he calls 'capital "G" Government' (2008a, 21). Drawing on Foucault, Tully argues that as power relations are 'exercised over an agent who is recognised and treated as a partner who is free, from the perspective of the governed', practices of governance cannot be divorced from practices of freedom. Differently put, any exercise of governance or power – and obviously the two go hand in hand – brings with it a diversity of potential reactions, or practices of freedom. Relations of governance do not act on wholly 'unfree or passive bodies' and, and as such, they do not constitute subjects without the 'mediation of their own thought and action' (2008a, 23).

Against this background, Tully (2008a, 22–23) identifies three characteristics of any form of government. Firstly, he focuses on the

---

[3] For a discussion of the hybridity of governance practices across different localities, see Skelcher, Sullivan and Jeffares (2013).

language games through which governors and governed come together as partners to coordinate activities, define problems and solutions, and negotiate modes and practices of government. Secondly, he emphasises the 'web of relations of power', the diverse technologies and strategies through which individuals and groups directly or indirectly govern the conduct of others – 'actions that aim to structure the field of the possible actions of others'. Finally, he points to the 'practical identity' of a form of government which becomes embedded over time as governors and the governed acquire a 'habitual way of thinking and acting within the assignment relations and languages of reciprocal recognition'.[4]

However, as we argued earlier in this section, Tully does not posit that being 'subject' to one particular form of government dictates 'the self-consciousness and self-formation of the governed down to every detail' (2008a, 23). Rather, he identifies three general cases of practices of freedom that accompany practices of governance. Individuals and groups can co-operate and follow the 'rules' of existing practices, although through the reproduction of existing practices they will modify those very practices. The work of local stakeholders in The Hague to give shape to area-based policymaking in their neighbourhoods is an example of this first practice of freedom (Duiveman et al. 2010). However, the governed might equally contest the existing rules of dominant practices, but do so within existing language games and institutional channels and procedures. The activities of youth representatives in the young people's forums analysed in the chapter by O'Toole and Gale in this volume are an example of this second practice of freedom. Finally, when such institutional strategies are either not open to the governed or fail, individuals and groups can 'exit' such relations of domination or contest them through a strategy of struggle and transformation. Bottom-up initiatives of citizens in disadvantaged neighbourhoods who take charge to improve long-festering problems in their immediate environment are an example of this third practice of freedom (Wagenaar and Specht 2010; Specht 2012).

This 'provisional language of description' brings to the surface the existing orthodoxies within which the art of government is articulated, enabling us to view such frames as 'one historically specific ensemble of forms of government and practices of freedom among many, rather

---

[4] So far, Tully's argument closely follows the governmentality literature (Rose and Miler 1992; Dean 1999).

than as the comprehensive and quasi-transcendental framework' (Tully 2008a, 25). Indeed, it is armed with such a provisional language that we question and seek to explore understandings of what we call *decentred governance*. This term does not just indicate, as we earlier described, that policymaking under the influence of processes of marketisation and decentralisation is in many societal sectors distributed over a wide range of institutional actors, with state institutions no longer holding a monopoly on decision making or implementing power. Instead, it captures how the process and outcomes of collective problem solving in contemporary liberal societies are the result of the involvement of many actors, across traditional boundaries of state and civil society, who, from the informal, everyday, experiential space they occupy in society, act upon the *meaning* they ascribe to particular problems and their proposed solutions (Wagenaar 2011, 75–80). Decentredness thus points towards a larger role for contingency in understanding governance, the foregrounding of struggle and resistance (Norval 2009a), and, most importantly, a redrawing of the very category of governance as also including a wider range of expressions, such as citizen initiatives and social movements, and a wider range of issues as being part of the 'agenda'. 'The important thing', as Bevir puts it, 'is that we begin to think of governance as the contingent product of political struggles embodying competing sets of beliefs' – and practices, as we will argue (Bevir 2003, 208; Wagenaar 2012).

Understanding Decentred Governance

Accepting the notion of decentredness has a number of important implications for our understanding of contemporary governance and democracy. Firstly, and following Tully, actors introduce a wide range of beliefs, understandings, allegiances, interests, routines and action preferences into the spaces in which collective problem solving takes place. Governing is thus deeply pluralistic (Wagenaar 2011, ch. 10). This, as Gerry Stoker argues, makes both the practices of governance and our understanding of them unabashedly political. 'Politics matters', he says, 'because there are conflicts and differences of perspective in society about what to do, what resources to collect for public use and how those resources should be spent'. One cannot escape politics simply because all judgement in public affairs is inevitably partial and limited (Stoker 2006, 5). However, the notion of 'politics' has itself different meanings. Broadly speaking we distinguish between a conventional and a radical meaning of politics. As it is more conventionally understood, politics is about settling inevitable conflicts of interest in the public domain, similar to Stoker's definition above. A radical notion of politics, however, sees politics as *constitutive* of the issues, interests and identities of its protagonists (Laclau and Mouffe 1985; Connolly 1991; Wenman 2003). Politics in this sense is not the domain of specialists or restricted to moments when conflict is inevitable. Rather, the antagonisms and power differentials which define political identity are everywhere. Politics is thus potentially ubiquitous, often operating far removed from 'official' policymaking institutions.

Secondly, a theory of decentred governance emphasises its practical, situated nature. While talk and exchange of arguments are a key part of it, the whirl of organisational routines, practical judgements, subjective voices, personal histories and improvisational practices are equally important. For the countless administrators, elected officials, street-level bureaucrats, professionals, activists and ordinary citizens who are involved in struggling with collective problems, governance is, above all about 'intervening' in practice. We have barely begun to fathom what an interventionist approach to politics, governance and public policy might look like. Although Lasswell, in his original formulation, envisioned a problem-oriented policy analysis, from the very start it has defined itself in a thoroughly modernist vein (Bevir 2010) as a science of representations in the service of the reigning governing elite, and, despite its emancipatory rhetoric, embracing the economic, managerial doctrine of the times. Epistemology resonates with power here (Hajer and Wagenaar 2003, 17). For an actionable version of policy analysis we need to look elsewhere, for instance, towards dialogical and poststructuralist approaches to policy analysis and public policy mediation (Glynos and Howarth 2007; Griggs and Howarth 2012, 2013; Howarth and Griggs 2012; Wagenaar 2008; 2011, chap. 8), or to the ontological politics of material semiotics (Law 2007; Latour 2005). Leibovitz's chapter on the possibilities and contradictions of Arab activism in urban development in Haifa and Wagenaar's chapter on the citizens of Dortmund's efforts in addressing the prostitution problem in their neighbourhood, explore the articulation of political claims and conceptions of citizenship by neighbourhood groups at the local level.

Thirdly, decentredness is about meaning. Decentredness does not merely denote the dispersion of collective decision making throughout society, or the functional differentiation of mutually dependent and complementary actors in policy networks, but rather the contingent construction of meaning by actors who face all sorts of challenges and dilemmas (Griggs and Howarth 2013; Howarth and Griggs 2012; Bevir 2003, 209). A decentred approach to governance emphasises agency as it thinks of institutions, societal problems, policy networks and democracy as created and sustained by actors who, operating within large societal frames (Rein 1983; Schön and Rein 1994), traditions (Bevir and Rhodes 2003, 2006) or hegemonic discourses (Griggs and Howarth 2013; Howarth and Griggs 2012), struggle with dilemmas and dislocations (Glynos and Howarth 2007, 110–11).

Privileging the contingent construction of forms of governance, rules and policy practices, as well as the political struggles of different agents in and through the policy process, prompts us to consider understandings of hegemony and how particular practices become institutionalised (or not). Here the work of David Howarth (2009, 2013) and others, who build on the neo-Gramscian perspectives of the Essex School of poststructuralist discourse theory,[5] offers critical insights into the practices of governance and freedom, and how agents may reproduce or seek to contest established rules and policy practices. On the one hand, hegemony can be understood, Howarth (2009, 310) argues, as a particular mode of governance. In this sense it allows us to analyse how, through a mixture of consent, compliance and coercion, particular norms and practices exercise a hold over a group of actors. On the other hand, hegemony, Howarth (2009, 317) suggests, can also be conceptualised as a political practice that 'captures the making and breaking of political coalitions'. This 'twin face' of hegemony draws our attention to how groups and movements, in challenging particular institutionalised or sedimented orders, will seek to link together or draw equivalences between different sets of demands for radical change or reform through constituting political boundaries that draw oppositions between insiders and outsiders (Howarth 2009, 317–20).

---

[5] For further discussion of the Essex school of poststructuralist discourse theory and its approach to hegemony, see Laclau and Mouffe (1985); Howarth and Stavrakakis (2000); Norval (1994, 1996); Torfing (1998, 1999).

of critical explanation'. Importantly, their approach is to reconstruct the different logics that underlie a social or political phenomenon. It starts from the presumption that although crucial, the contextualised self-interpretation of actors need to be supplemented with an analysis of logics that seek to capture 'the point, rules and ontological preconditions of a practice or regime of practices' (2007, 165). They distinguish between social, political and fantasmatic logics, and recognise the 'constructed and political character of social objectivity' (2007, 166) and the importance of locating policies in wider discursive contexts.

To sum up, the notion of decentredness goes beyond the surface meaning that collective decision making is 'distributed' over a wide array of actors and sites in contemporary governance. It has at least three additional meanings. Firstly, by employing a decentred account of governance, we acknowledge the deep pluralism of the public domain. This implies that we embed our understanding of changing patterns of government firmly in the domain of the political. Secondly, a decentred account of governance shifts the emphasis to the way that actors make sense of the world around them. An appeal to 'objective' institutional structures, 'natural' rational preferences, or 'obvious' functional interdependencies between actors in networks frontloads our explanations of governance with the very assumptions we try to prove. Instead, in a decentred approach, governance is the emergent outcome of actors who struggle to make sense out of the world in which they move. Finally, sense making is not just the application of beliefs or understandings to confusing circumstances. Instead, we find our way in the world by acting on the problem at hand. This acting is partly driven by understandings and meanings as they are embedded in everyday practical routines and sedimented, hegemonic discourses, and partly by improvisations when routines fall short because of dislocations. A decentred account of governance, in other words, requires that we can explain governance as the result of the interaction between people's practices and the larger discursive, hegemonic conditions with which they operate, and which they may contest. In short, taking the decentredness of democratic governance seriously requires that we examine situated practices of new forms of political engagement and analyse how shared meanings and institutional rules and norms emerge to 'make sense' of complex policy problems, considering how they privilege or constrain different (democratic) spaces within the policy process. It is to this challenge of providing an account of decentred democratic governance which grasps fully its political, interpretive, and performative nature that we turn in the remainder of this Introduction. We first say a few more words about the understandings of practice that informs many of the contributions to this volume, before setting out in greater depth our understanding of radical pluralism. We then turn to our engagement with theories of radical democracy.

The Primacy of Practice

People do not only make sense of the situations which confront them by reflecting upon them within the context of traditions, belief systems, or ideologies. They also move about in the world in a more or less effective way by acting upon the situation at hand. Most of the time this acting takes the form of enacting routines; largely self-evident, habitual ways of accomplishing everyday tasks. We participate in a meeting, write a policy memo to our line manager or head of department, hold an annual appraisal interview with one of our employees, or assess a proposal for an evaluation study we requested. We rarely give the initiation and execution of these tasks a second thought because we are experienced policy actors deeply socialised into the world of public administration. We can put this differently by saying that people engage in *practices*.

Now, the term 'practice' is on the way to becoming one of the most inflated concepts in contemporary social science. We insert the term when we want to demonstrate our awareness that we understand that people do not just cognise about the world but also act in it. However, just paying lip service to action will not do. With the concept of 'practice' we bring into play a conceptual apparatus, a mode of inquiry, even an ontology (Law 2007, 16), with its own assumptions, logics, and coherence, which radically differs from the standard, epistemology-driven world view which has permeated social science, and in general the institutions with which we attempt to know and control the world (Taylor 1995; Cook and Wagenaar 2012). To appeal to practice means that we open ourselves up to different, more dialogical methods of research and conceptions of meaning (Wagenaar 2011, chap. 8). The nature and limited space of this Introduction does not allow for an exposition of the philosophy of practice and performative approaches to democratic governance that does any justice to it.[6] Without touching on too much specificity, we summarise a performative account in three premises. The first, at the same time the most obvious and most far-reaching, is the primacy of interventionism. This is the insight that reality – that is, the environment that we live and move about in and that rubs and brushes against us from all sides, and that we overwhelmingly experience as 'out there', largely independent from ourselves – is a product of our ongoing practical engagement with the world (Law 2009, 1; Cook and Wagenaar 2012). The second premise concerns temporal emergence. This is the insight that the constraints and affordances of the outer world come to us only through our experience of them in emergent time. The significance of temporal emergence is that two key elements of a practice account that are necessarily connected to each other in the sense that they bring each other into being – time and experience – are folded into it. The third premise regards the interpenetration of the human and the material in the way we act on and understand the world (Pickering 1995; Law 2007; Pickering and Guzick 2008).

With respect to the analysis of democratic governance, performativity thus requires that we pay close attention to the intricate 'choreographies of practice' with which we accommodate the resistances that our interventions throw up, produce provisional solutions to the problem at hand, and, temporarily at least, stabilise reality (Law 2009, 13). Democracy, as we have seen, is fundamentally about intervening in the world to make things better; to improve a situation that falls short of its ideal (Norval 2007, 2012). The contributions to this book demonstrate the viability of an actionable approach to radical, decentred governance. In his chapter, Forester puts forward an 'interventionist', or as he calls it, a critical-pragmatist approach to governance. Norval, in her chapter, articulates a conception of analysis that seeks to make visible sites of intervention and practices of freedom, as they are conceptualised in different contemporary accounts of democratic politics. Connelly's account of the political construction of legitimacy in 'local'

---

[6] For a good introduction, see Schatzki (1996). Bourdieu (1977) is a classic, but his take on practice is rather idiosyncratic. Law (2007) is an excellent introduction to material semiotics and Actor Network Theory. Wagenaar and Cook (2003) discuss the importance of practice for policy analysis. Wagenaar (2011) continues this exploration in his book on interpretive policy analysis. Some of the insights in this section are based on chapters 4, 9 and 10 of that book.

neighbourhoods, as well as Sullivan's study of the constitution and contestation of the rules and norms of governance, and O'Toole and Gale's practice-based assessment of participatory governance, each describe the acts of citizen activists in actionable, pragmatic and forward-looking terms, with insight and understanding emerging in the give and take between interventions and the resistances these evoke. What makes this conception of governance radical is that the struggle is not only about overt interests. Instead, the movements described in these chapters challenge deep-seated assumptions about the problem at hand, they struggle to define new social identities, and they defy and attempt to reformulate the rules of the game. What we see here is an expansion of our taken-for-granted repertoire of democratic governance through the deployment of practices of freedom. This is a theme, the all important relationship between decentred governance and democracy, which we address in our final two sections. Let us begin by exploring further our understanding of politics and radical pluralism.

Bringing the Political Back in: Acknowledging the Deep Pluralism of Contemporary Society

What the conventional and radical understandings of politics have in common is the acknowledgement that the world of public affairs is deeply pluralistic, although they do not share an understanding of pluralism. As we saw earlier in this Introduction, while the former treats plurality as given – 'the fact of pluralism' – the latter focusses on processes of pluralisation (Connolly 1995). Putting such debates to one side for the moment, this acknowledgement of pluralism shatters any hope for unitary solutions in policymaking. With unitary solutions we refer, for example, to those decision-making algorithms whose economic logic results in 'the one best solution' (Stokey and Zeckhauser 1978), rigorous 'evidence-based' studies whose purported scientific authority cannot but sway policy-makers, 'best practices' which can be applied in widely different policy contexts, or interpretive studies which reveal the 'real' interpretation of a policy problem. Pluralism, instead, suggests that the world refuses to be organised under one overriding external principle, whether it is a scientific epistemology, a universal moral principle, or a rational politics beyond power and doctrine.

There is a logical connection between the acknowledgement of pluralism in public affairs (not self-evident) and the necessity – inevitability if one prefers – of politics as the prime mechanism of social coordination (equally non self-evident). As Waldron argues in introducing his now-famous conception of the 'circumstances of politics':

The prospect of persisting disagreement must be regarded, I think, as one of the elementary conditions of modern politics. Nothing we can say about politics makes much sense if we proceed without taking this condition into account. We may say ... that disagreement among citizens as to what they should do, as a political body, is one of the circumstances of politics. It is not all there is to the circumstances of politics, of course: there is also the need to act together, even though we disagree about what we do ... the circumstances of politics are a coupled pair: disagreement wouldn't matter if people didn't prefer a common decision; and the need for a common decision would not give rise to politics as we know it if there wasn't at least the potential for disagreement about what the common decision would be. (1999, 153–54)

Since the early days of Bentleyan group theory, the conventional argument about politics is that it is, realistically speaking, the only way out of the conundrums that are posed to us by conflicts of value and interest and structural differentials of power (Dahl 1961; Lindblom 1965). Contemporary notions of politics go a long way to overcome some of the well-known problems of standard group theory: an arid procedural conception of politics as the give and take between interest groups whose identity is taken as given and which act on a priori preferences; an 'empty' conception of the state as the arbiter between competing interests groups; and a one-dimensional conception of power. In its modern understanding, however, politics is seen as going beyond compromise to allow for the collective production of value by wide and shifting alliances of actors beyond institutionalised interest groups. One of the most articulate formulations of this modern notion of politics is by Gains and Stoker:

Politics is about getting interests to come together and take account of each other. These interests may be reconciled, but not bound by a new, jointly discovered consensus. The preferences associated with interests are malleable; shaped as they are by norms and values and the context of what is achievable. This definition also places power at the centre of politics, a share in the collective decision is granted according to the interest's importance in social welfare. Those that control key resources are likely to have increased decision-making clout and whilst the basic principle of democracy – granting each affected by a decision a say in that decision – is formally met, it does so in the context of a real world understanding of power. Accommodation is achieved in a variety of ways: sometimes by mutual understanding driven by deliberation but often through hard bargaining, vague specification of outcomes, the use of rituals and symbols and the exercise of hegemonic influence. Politics is driven not by mutual admiration but rather by the necessity of pursuing a common purpose in an interconnected world where one cannot choose one's neighbours. (2008, 17–18)

As we have argued, one of the strengths of this conception of politics is that politics is no longer the exclusive domain of the state or of a class of specially trained experts. Politics is 'distributed' (Flinders 2004) across groups, issues, formats (Web 2.0) and sites. Also, the repertoire of political communication has broadened. Much political communication is of the questionable top-down, spin control type, but under the influence of the requirement to work effectively 'across boundaries' (Sullivan and Skelcher 2002) communication has moved beyond bargaining and compromise to include deliberation and forms of accommodation (Wagenaar 2006, 2007; Forester 2009; Innes and Booher 2010). As a result, actors who engage in this kind of interactive, participative politics discover that their interests are not fixed but shaped by the encounter with the realities of the problem at hand and the perspectives of other actors (Warren 1992; Wagenaar and Specht 2010). Contemporary politics is an expression of a richer, more inclusive form of democratic association.

Finally, this is a realist notion of politics. The relentless laws of negative unintended consequences are built into the sheer complexity and diversity of the public domain. At the same time, some problems are higher on the political agenda than others, inequality is endemic to the system, some actors have easier access to the corridors of power than others, and it is exceedingly difficult to form effective alliances of actors to work on problems which are unpopular with the business and policy elites (Stone 2005). In fact, one of the most promising directions in which the modern conception of politics is developing is civic capacity theory. While, for the moment, no more than a loose set of empirical observations and mid-level generalisations, it shows how alliances of public officials, enlightened administrators and citizen activists are able to make a difference in highly policy-resistant problems in exceedingly unpromising situations (Stone et al. 2001; de Souza Briggs 2008).

Nevertheless, this modern conception of politics suffers from a number of problems. First, despite the centrality of the principle of democratic equality, it also operates on a surprisingly dystopian view of citizen participation (Stoker 2006, chap. 9; Gains and Stoker 2008, 24). The usual theoretical arguments against participation (the free-rider problem, socially biased representation, the lack of social capital in disadvantaged neighbourhoods, the denial of diversity, and problems with accountability) are brought forward, conveniently neglecting the by-now extensive empirical literature that successful democratic participation is possible despite these problems (Mathews 1999; Fung and Wright 2003; Boyte 2004; Fung 2004; Avritzer 2009; Specht 2012). There is an element of institutional bias in this participatory dystopia. While mature representative democratic institutions are the standard by which participatory experiments are judged (Norval and Abdulrahman 2011), participation is surprisingly varied, ranging from state-sponsored multi-stakeholder initiatives, via bottom-up, 'uninvited' citizen participation and social entrepreneurship, to militant activist movements. Again, we are only beginning to understand how this participatory variety can contribute to collective problem solving in complex post-industrial societies.

The second problem with the modern approach to politics is its restricted conception of power. The argument is well known and need not be articulated here: standard pluralism takes power in its repressive, first, and at best, agenda setting, second dimension. However, power also operates at the level of self-evident, linguistically sedimented, understandings and has a productive, performative aspect, bringing whole social configurations into being (Lukes 1974). More important is the conclusion that this is no mere theoretical exercise but goes to the heart of a fuller, more inclusive understanding of the role of politics in governance. The different dimensions of power operate alongside one another. By neglecting the taken-for-granted aspects of power, we miss the hegemonic aspects of modern governance, the fact that certain topics or solutions have no standing within the political debate. Think of the food consumption problem and its ramifications for public health and the climate problem; or, for that matter, the climate problem itself; or the role of investment banking in the destabilisation of the financial world and the economy; or the effects of income inequality on a wide range of social pathology. These are immense and urgent problems that allow for only a very partial and restricted set of problem definitions and solutions.

Radical pluralism is more sensitive to these hidden, taken-for-granted aspects of power and seeks to develop mechanisms and modes of analysis to make these visible, as Norval argues in her contribution to this volume. Again the argument is well known: radical pluralism operates with a different, more ontological notion of pluralism. Radical pluralists foreground the element of difference and contingency in politics. It takes politics as constitutive of the issues, interests and identities of its protagonists (Laclau and Mouffe 1985). The ontological notion of pluralism has two momentous implications for our understanding of politics, in that it puts both political identity and contingency at the centre of our conception of politics. Political identity, per definition, is precarious and open-ended (Connolly 1991, 2011). Even seemingly stable, institutionalised, taken-for-granted configurations are constantly prone to dislocation and challenge (Laclau 1990, 39). Hence, the emphasis is not simply on the constitutive character of pluralism but, equally important, on processes of pluralisation (Connolly 2005; Norval 2010). As a result, politics is not restricted to a particular domain of expertise but is ubiquitous and truly decentred in our society. Practically speaking, it brings into the remit of governance a whole range of problems and practices which challenge the hegemonic assemblages of liberal representative democracy.

Finally, radical pluralism confronts us with strong ethical challenges. While all democratic theory has an intrinsic ethical calling, radical pluralism not only foregrounds and problematises the ethical dimension of democracy, it also squarely places it within democracy's essentially contested nature. The argument goes as follows: when all political positions, all forms of social identity, are the outcome of the interplay of difference, when there is an 'impossibility of closure of any identity or structure' (Norval 2007, 39), we do not have recourse to a priori principles or beliefs (Christian values, rationality, utility maximisation, Western ideals of the Enlightenment) to settle conflict arising from these differences. Not only are such first principles themselves discursively constituted 'subject positions', but the appeal to such principles or beliefs as the ultimate, self-evident grounds for the rightness of a position is itself a wilful, an ultimately unilateral, act of power within an open, contingent, discursive field. Clearly, at times, people manage to agree, but consensus is *also* the outcome of a process of articulation, an outcome that is attained by having reached a position or having settled on an identity at the exclusion or suppression of other positions or identities. Mouffe goes as far as to call a 'non-coercive consensus' a 'conceptual impossibility' (2000, 33). She argues that we should be talking of 'conflictual consensus' instead. Be that as it may, the importance of this claim is that it raises a serious challenge, namely the moral challenge of how to live and work together in a world of deep and infinite disagreement. Differently put, what is required is an ethos of pluralisation (Connolly 1995). But, how does this challenge our understanding of democratic governance? We set out our response to this question in the section that follows.

Democracy as Practices of Governance and Freedom

Contemporary democratic theory is replete with attempts to supplement our existing representative institutions. One only needs to think here of the proliferation of deliberative mechanisms such as citizens' juries or consultation forums to supplement these institutions, particularly at local and regional level. The main reasons for seeking to develop such alternatives consist of the perceived lack of legitimacy of electoral institutions; their distance from the voters they are supposed to represent; the consequent loss of interest in the normal, ongoing, regular practice of elections; their inability to represent the concerns of younger voters and issues considered to be marginal to the electoral process; and their capacity to address the growing interactions of the global and the local, amongst others, amongst others. In short, there is a lot of talk of the malfunctioning, or even a crisis, of these representative institutions. The turn to deliberative forms of democracy followed in the wake of this perceived crisis in our traditional representative institutions. It is particularly noticeable that the second generation of deliberative theorists – including thinkers such as Mark Warren, Iris Marion Young, James Bohman, Simone Chambers and John Dryzek – situate their respective analyses explicitly in this context and present various versions of deliberative theory as a response to these problems. Bohman, for instance, notes that 'globalization asks us to be morally and politically innovative, to expand the limits of our previous ideals and institutions and to produce wider variations of them than are currently available' (1999, 193).

There is a similar impetus in recent work on the new forms and politics of representation, all of which emphasise the need to think critically and creatively in our engagement with new demands and their representation, which often occur in non-traditional sites and through non-traditional means (Warren and Castiglione 2006; Barnes, Newman and Sullivan 2007). In this, these studies follow an important trajectory of radical democratic thinking, which shuns armchair theorising in favour of engaging with the problems raised by the need for a richer, more expansive and participatory democratic politics. In so doing they also move away from the excessive rationalism for which theorists such as Habermas have long been criticised, towards a wider, more open conception of deliberation and publicness that can accommodate cultural identities, voices and social roles beyond that of the 'private person'. It is in the area of developing a critique of traditional, aggregative forms of democracy and supplementing it with additional, alternative mechanisms of representation that the most innovative work has been done by deliberative theorists. Whilst much of this work remains rife with problems concerning the precise relation between deliberative institutional mechanisms – such as deliberative polls, citizens' juries, deliberation days and so on – and more traditional representative institutions, this does not detract from the imaginative attempts to think through, in practice, what an emphasis on deliberation might imply for democratic institutions and norms. Indeed, these second-generation theorists have equally imaginatively worked through what norms we might need in these novel institutional domains as functional equivalents of the democratic norms of accountability and authorisation (Warren and Castiglione 2006). In this volume, Warren critically examines the emerging domain of governance-driven democratisation and its democratic potentials and challenges, whilst Sørensen and Torfing investigate criteria for assessing the democratic anchorage of governance networks.

Within the remit of Tully's distinction between practices of governance and practices of freedom, we would argue that the thrust of deliberative theory is to *articulate* democratic norms of governance via an expansion both of the character of deliberation and of participation. It is also for this reason that deliberative work has proven to be attractive to policy analysts and practitioners alike. Given that it explicitly raises questions and provides imaginative answers concerning the need to expand not only the pool of participants in the democratic process but also the sites of participation, this is not surprising. However, despite this interest and the obvious advantages of a (more) deliberative approach to democratic activities, questions relating to the relation between deliberation and democracy have continued to surface. Early commentators such as Sanders and Kohn raised questions regarding the voice that predominates in the public conversation proposed by deliberative thinkers and in so doing, have also been critical of the impact of a conception of democracy predicated on the need to achieve or work towards consensus. In contrast to deliberative approaches, much work emanating from the radical pluralist tradition has tended to emphasise less the norms of conduct in such institutions and the form of the institutions themselves than the very activity of critical engagement with these and more traditional sites of democratic participation (Norval 2009b). Kohn summarises this shift in emphasis, arguing that it is not that there is no place for deliberation, but rather that:

[T]here is something more crucial at stake in democracy. Realizing abstractions such as reciprocity, equality, and opportunity is usually a process of historical struggle rather than theoretical consensus. This struggle does not take place primarily on the abstract terrain of language, but at the concrete sites of resistance, the literal, symbolic, and imaginary barricades, forums, and fortresses where people mount challenges to currently hegemonic visions of collective life. (Kohn 2000, 426)

Kohn's statement accords with our emphasis on the paramount role of practice and discursive struggles in decentred governance (the third implication of accepting decentred governance). Alongside analysis of the hegemonic visions of collective life, we also need to give attention to the conditions of possibility of challenging those visions, and to the role of different actors in putting forward their own solutions to collective problems. By implication, they thereby put forward their unique claims towards more inclusive and richer forms of democratic governance. If seen in this manner, the emphasis shifts from a concern with formulating the norms of activities to thinking more clearly about how such norms are realised, institutionalised, resisted and challenged. This, in our view, entails an aspect change in the movement from a deliberative to a radical conception of democracy (Norval 2007, chap. 3) Both Norval and Sullivan, in their respective contributions to this volume, investigate these issues further and work through examples of how this might occur in practice. Similarly, Lowndes and Pratchett in their discussion of institutional design bring to the fore the ongoing iteration of meanings and practice.

As is the case with deliberative theory, there are many versions of radical-pluralist-inspired approaches to democracy. For our purposes it is important that, broadly speaking, radical approaches foreground the political in characterising democracy. Just as in debates on governance, debates on democracy have considered just how deep contestation runs. Radical pluralists generally take the view that contestation runs all the way down, up to and including the principles of the constitution itself (Tully 2008a, 199). Once the primacy of politics is established, as we saw, it is important to rethink all the dimensions of democratic politics theoretically. Hence, thinkers such as Connolly, Mouffe and Laclau have drawn on different resources and provided divergent answers to the way in which they characterise the relations between participants in the process of democratic contestation (rather than participation). Connolly (1995), for instance, draws on Nietzsche, Foucault and Deleuze, and emphasises an ethos of abundance and generosity. Mouffe (2000) takes her inspiration from the German political theorist Carl Schmitt and focuses attention on the need to transform relations of enmity and antagonism into relations of agonistic respect. Laclau (2005), on the other hand, has continued to emphasise the central role of antagonism in the constitution of demands. Norval (2010, 2011, 2012), drawing on Ralph Waldo Emerson and Stanley Cavell, argues for a democratic politics of receptivity.

Let us look at these in more depth. Mouffe's solution to the problem of contestation is 'agonistic pluralism': the transformation of a politics of antagonism into one of agonism. Antagonism she defines as a struggle between enemies (out to eradicate each other). By contrast, agonism is a struggle between adversaries: 'somebody whose ideas we combat but whose right to defend those ideas we do not put into question' (2000, 102). As we have noted earlier, in her view, we need to aim for a 'conflictual consensus' (2000, 103). Such a consensus necessarily and unavoidably excludes some positions (in that sense the consensus is hegemonically constructed), but, as Wenman emphasises, 'the terms of that exclusion are perpetually renegotiated' (2003, 182). According to Mouffe, this is exactly what agonistic pluralism is and should be about: an ongoing confrontation of different conceptions of citizenship. In contrast to Mouffe, Connolly's ethos of pluralisation focuses more on micro-processes of self-making. Key to Connolly's theory of pluralism is the anxiety that is produced in established identities by new forms of social identity. As we are living in a world in which new claims and new social identities appear on the scene in ever-faster succession, he sees the confusion and anxiety this generates as the central challenge of pluralism. To counteract this alleged tendency towards reciprocal existential resentment, he suggests what he variously calls an ethos of 'agonistic respect', an 'ethic of cultivation', or a 'generous ethos of engagement' (1991, xxii).

Connolly's ethos of engagement has an individual and a public dimension. Individually it amounts to an attitude of welcoming openness, or as he calls it, 'gratitude' towards the irrepressible abundance and fullness of life. This personal attitude of receptiveness is tempered by 'agonistic respect' and 'critical responsiveness'. This is the public, dialogical, dimension of Connolly's pluralist ethos. Agonistic respect is projected as a strategy to negotiate and include difference and to incorporate them into one's own identity. It is a 'civic virtue that allows people to honour different final sources, to cultivate reciprocal respect across difference and to negotiate larger assemblages to set general policies (somewhat similar to the articulation of hegemonic blocs)' (1991, xxvi). There is an undeniable element of realism in this vision of a democratic attitude that is simultaneously agonistic and respectful. It promulgates an active engagement with public life (as against the more inert and passive tolerance of liberalism, which Connolly thinks is insufficient to counteract the dangers of pluralistic resentment), while also recognising the need for a certain measure of distance and privacy (as in agonism) (1991, xxvi). However, the final element in Connolly's ethos is an attitude of 'critical responsiveness'. Where agonistic respect fits a situation where established groups vie with one another, critical responsiveness fits a situation in which new groups, new identities, try to obtain a place in the political arena. A problem arises when their values, beliefs, and action preferences are so incompatible with those of the established identities that they are automatically considered illegitimate, wrong, or worse. In the spirit of an ethos of cultivation, the element of responsiveness signifies an openness and receptiveness to new ways of life, new ideas and outlooks that may result in a questioning and reorganisation of one's own identity. The critical element is an effort to safeguard that the newcomer promises to support, or at least not harm, the spirit of pluralism (1991, xxix).

Norval elaborates on the confusion around disagreement and difference. Citing Connolly, she portrays democracy as a necessary tension, a 'productive ambiguity' between governance and disturbance (2007, 55). Democracy is eternally poised between stability and disruption, between its own glorification and its own undoing. As Norval (2007) argues, it is intrinsic to democracy that it will always fall short of its own high standards. The intrinsic fallibility of democracy places the individual in a complex ethical position. If we do not embrace a radical rejection of democracy because of its imperfections (a common reaction which nowadays expresses itself in alienation and cynicism towards everything political or in the currently fashionable, right-wing, ethnophobic populism), we have no alternative left but to take responsibility and try to repair the imperfections or undo the shortcomings. Democracy constantly has to be rediscovered (Norval 2007, 175). Following Cavell, Norval calls this an ethos of non-teleological perfectionism, one that seeks to criticise and animate our existing institutions, with a view to change and challenge them, so addressing the risk that our democratic institutions may become fossilised and sclerotic (Norval 2007, 175). This has echoes with Connolly's 'generous ethos of engagement' and his 'critical responsiveness', but with an important added ingredient: an analysis of the role imagination plays in the fostering of alternative ways of doing things (Norval 2012).

What is at stake in the works of all of these thinkers is a conception of radical democracy that gives a pride of place to what Tully calls practices of freedom. Let us recall the three general cases of practices of freedom suggested by Tully. They include, 'acting otherwise', where practices in accord with norms and rules result in often unnoticed modifications; problematisation of rules of the game and existing norms, through deliberation, negotiation, problem solving and reform; and finally, refusal of existing norms and practices of governance, resulting in resistance and confrontation (Tully 2008a, 23–24). Hence, while deliberative theorists are interested in elaborating the norms that ought to govern such practices, agonistic democrats think about the historical conditions of possibility – to use a term from Foucault – of contestation, as a vital element of practices of democratic governance. Hence, they are interested, not so much in institutional forms, but in the modalities of subjectivity that are engendered by both practices of governance and of freedom; in the manner in which norms come to be established and 'normalised'; and the ways in which such hegemonic norms become and remain subject to contestation. Radical pluralism in the context of decentred governance, in other words, views spaces and forms of contestation as contingently instituted, sometimes deeply sedimented, but always re-contestable.

Now, there is a risk of simply viewing the aspect change brought about by poststructuralist interventions as something that adds to the deliberative picture of democracy, without simultaneously altering any dimension of that picture in any significant respect. This would be mistaken. While the aim of developing an account of democracy that can take in these and other aspects of democracy is a laudable one, it cannot be done without alteration of the accounts that are party to such an articulation. We cannot pursue this argument in full here. Suffice it to note that one of the aims of this book is precisely to contribute to a conversation which might have the effect of furthering this aim. However, this cannot be done without also shifting the very *framing* of the account of democracy present in the deliberative picture, as Rancière would argue (Norval 2012). Whilst both deliberative and poststructuralist accounts of democracy take issue with an aggregative conception of democracy that reduces democracy to periodic elections and a set of institutional rules, there nevertheless remains an important difference between these two traditions in the status it accords the liberal democratic model. Deliberativists, more than agonists, remain tied to liberal democracy and autonomy as an ideal, to be emulated in expanded domains of democratic participation. In so doing, it runs the risk of simply not considering a whole range of practices of freedom that are crucial to the extension and deepening of democracy today. To put it differently, deliberative conceptions of democracy treat liberal forms of democracy and their extensions as *the* model of democracy as such. Radical pluralists such as Connolly, Norval, Kohn, Wenman and Laclau, in different ways, argue that one needs to challenge the view that democracy takes one and only one form: a liberal democratic one. This challenge allows one to make visible the *grammar* of democracy as a practice of claim making and contestation that is not bound by any a priori institutional form (Norval 2007).

Reframing Democracy

Radical pluralists have long recognised that liberal democracy is but one form or embodiment of democratic practices, and one that is not without its tensions. However, this is not a view held by all theorists of democracy. To the contrary, dominant theorists of deliberative democracy, such as Habermas, refuse both the idea that there is a tension between liberalism and democracy, and that we should think of liberal democracy in terms of the historical articulation between two distinctive traditions.[7] In contrast to this view, theorists such as Macpherson, Bellamy, Mouffe and Laclau have argued that we need to aware of the historical tensions between the traditions of liberalism (rights) and democracy (popular sovereignty), because a lack of awareness of these tensions might also blind us to the extent to which, in contemporary liberal democracies, the liberal tradition has tended to trump democracy. Hence, both theoretically and politically these theorists have argued that it is necessary to challenge this uneven relation and to *democratise* liberalism (even as we also need to liberalise democracy). To be blind to the irresolvable tension between these historico-political traditions is to risk uncritically accepting our contemporary practices as the only form they may legitimately take. This was already recognised by C. B. Macpherson well before the genealogical turn in political theory. In *The Life and Times of Liberal Democracy*, he argued that historical comparison was crucial to sensitise us to the particularity and historical specificity of what we hold to be universal and unchangeable (1977, 7). This, indeed, remains the task for us today, for without this historical sensibility we are unable to engage critically with what appears to be an unchallengeable good: the promotion of liberal democracy as if it is democracy tout court.

It is precisely in this context that Tully's situating of the terms 'governance' and 'government' in the historical context of the seventeenth-century use of the terms, is illuminating. 'Governance' and 'government' as terms referring to multiple and overlapping ways of governing individuals and groups, became narrowed over time to refer to formal public practices of governance of the representative democratic, constitutional nation-state (Tully 2008a, 21). As we have argued earlier, policy analysis, political science and political philosophy

---

[7] For a critical discussion of the co-constitutivity thesis, see Bonnie Honig (2007).

have traditionally concerned themselves almost exclusively with government in the narrow sense, and hence have tended to exclude and ignore all those wider relations of governance through which individuals and groups are subjected and constituted as actors and political agents. A similar process has occurred with respect to democracy. The term democracy, Tully argues, 'which formerly stood for *any ad hoc assembly of people in negotiation*, came to be associated with "representative democracy" in the late eighteenth century by "ingrafting" ... representation upon democracy' (Tully 2008a, 155–56). The process of transforming 'democracy' into 'representative democracy' historically displayed features not dissimilar to what we are witnessing today. Prior to the eighteenth century, 'democracy' was used routinely 'as a term of abuse to refer to the "people" assembling together and demanding a direct voice in the specific manner in which they were governed'; democracy was condemned as 'popular, contentious' and as ill-suited to modern conditions (Tully 2008b, 55). Macpherson characterised this as a particularly *liberal* fear of the masses. There is an important sense in which the exclusive institutional focus is blind to the very way in which its framing of democracy already excludes a whole range of practices of freedom and of contestation from the remit of practices that ought to be considered by democratic theorists. Treating democracy as a matter of formal rules, norms and procedures – we have democracy (and the same goes for human rights) where the correct procedures are in place, inscribed in the constitution – important as they are, risks neglecting the fact that democracy, at root, consists of a practical ethos of questioning and collective problem solving. It is here that radical pluralism and the pragmatist conception of democracy meet (Dewey 1954).

Treating democracy as *practical* and *processual*, but not procedural, allows one to focus on the extent to which it is constituted in and through practices; how it is always incomplete, in process.[8] Although more or less institutionalised forms of rule may develop from it, rule formation is not conceived of as the telos of democracy. Seen in this way, attention needs to be given to practices of

---

[8] See Owen (2001) and Norval (2007). The incompleteness of democracy is not here understood in the Habermasian sense of the unfinished project of modernity. Rather, we draw on Derrida's account of democracy-to-come (Norval 2007). Our conception of democracy is also close to Dewey's notion of democracy as public-making. (Dewey 1954; Mathews 1999).

contestation, claim making and negotiation that are not reducible to, nor occur in the sites associated with traditional representative democratic institutions, expanded or not (Norval 2009b). Although struggles in and over democratic institutions are crucial, democracy cannot be limited to these. Democracy exists even in the absence of such institutions. Democratic contestation concerns *claims* to assert control over the way one is governed; it is a performative *ethos* of questioning, responding, negotiating, challenging and disruption. This ethos focuses on the activities of citizen-subjects, who are not satisfied to let others speak for them, the practices with which they question the ordering of prevailing institutions and techniques of governance. Democratic activity, on this reading, does not presuppose the existence of elaborate systems of rules and law embedded in particular institutional forms. To put it differently, people are not democrats by virtue of the existence of institutions, laws and rights, but they become so in exercising their capacities for questioning, affirming, negotiating and contesting the regimes and micro-practices of governance that shape and limit their lives – all this guided by an 'ethics of cultivation', which fosters an attitude of agonistic care for difference (Connolly 1991, 10–11).

Now, if democracy is conceived of in this extensive sense, then support for and the deepening of democratic practices and activities must take the form of attentiveness to the specificities of the actual practices, traditions and forms of contestation characteristic of a particular society or location. Critical practices do not take a singular form, and the forms of subjectivity they inspire necessarily also vary widely. On this view, one cannot seek to prejudge either the sites where democracy may erupt or the actors who may engage in such activities. This is a crucial point and it requires reflection on the unevenness of the political terrain, including questions concerning the relation between state and non-state actors, or institutional forms and everyday informalities. Finally, attentiveness of this sort should also lead one to give consideration to the very processes through which democratic demands are formed and expressed and the way in which such practices of claim making are constitutive also of the identities of the individuals and groups involved in them (Laclau 2005). The formation of democratic forms of subjectivity, fostered and cultivated in and through contestatory practices, is crucial to any serious project of democratisation and cannot be attended to as an afterthought. In conclusion, one way to summarise our argument is to suggest that practices of governance and practices of freedom always go hand in hand. The democratic practices of freedom – of questioning, contestation and even disruption – do not follow from laws and institutions, but precede them always and challenge them in a spirit of agonistic respect. Democratic practices of freedom are in principle everywhere available, are not limited to specific actors and sites, and may sometimes but not as a matter of course be sedimented into rules, which are in turn, also always, open to further contestation, deformation and challenge.

The Contributions to This Book

We began this introduction by calling for a critical engagement with the plural and dispersed practices of governance. Each of the contributions in this volume responds in different ways to this call. The first part of the volume investigates how we might reconsider questions of institutional design within the context of our understanding of democracy as both practical and processual. Mark Warren opens our analysis with a critical exploration of governance-driven democratisation. He argues that it is primarily in the domain of the front-line practices of government that democratic norms are now being fostered and implemented. These emerging policy spaces, Warren suggests, present opportunities to redefine peoples and boundaries, while opening up new paths for participation and deliberation, as well as new forms of representation. However, he does advocate caution alongside such optimism. Governance-driven democratisation remains elite-driven. Its orientation towards policy-driven issues also hampers the development of broad political programmes. Warren thus concludes that there is a pressing need to develop middle-level theory that can guide 'local' analyses and critical assessments of this emerging landscape of governance-driven democratisation.

Following this recognition of the importance of developing mid-range theory that can foster critical engagement with democratic practices, Aletta Norval sets out a poststructuralist perspective on the criteria for thinking about the design of democratic institutions and the practices of freedom they encourage and that emerge in response to them. Drawing on Wittgenstein, she questions the view that criteria are structurally separate and separable from the judgements we make, linking them instead to practices of freedom. This, she argues, directs our attention back to the emerging practices in which we engage, but not without simultaneously allowing us to reflect on the character of those practices, the demands and responsibilities that are inherent in democratic practices and the conditions under which such reflection becomes possible. Norval thus seeks to articulate a contextual account of criteria, which nevertheless suggests that we are able to reflect back on our activities, so drawing out the grammar of these democratic practices. This poststructuralist perspective, as Norval acknowledges, privileges in our understanding of democratic practices the processes of contestation, claim making and competing demands.

Taking a more institutionalist approach, Vivien Lowndes and Lawrence Pratchett then discuss the strategy of 'indirect design', examining how the Council of Europe operates through its *acquis* (the explicit and implicit body of knowledge established in its treaties and other publications) to shape the design of democratic institutions in a wide range of political and cultural contexts. They argue that the strength of the *acquis* lies in its clear value base and its promotion of the principle of 'variable geometry'. However, its weaknesses as a design strategy relate to its linearity (which limits iteration and reversibility) and to enforceability (the balance between incentives and sanctions). They conclude their argument by noting that the challenge of indirect design involves the creative sequencing of different democratic devices (aggregative, negotiative and deliberative) in different contexts (Saward 2003) – rather than any specific choice between competing 'models of democracy'.

We close this first half of the volume with an examination by Eva Sørensen and Jacob Torfing of how we measure the democratic anchorage of governance networks. Efforts to determine the democratic impact of governance networks, they assert, must be based on a concrete, empirical measurement of their actual functioning. They thus formulate a series of indicators for measuring the democratic anchorage of governance networks in four anchorage points: (1) metagoverning politicians, (2) stakeholder organisations, (3) broader citizenry, and (4) democratic norms and rules within the network. These indicators measure the degree to which governance networks are democratically controlled, representative, accountable and accessible in ways applicable to governance networks. This exercise calls for a reconsideration and redefinition of what these democratic core values imply and how they can be institutionalised. Sørensen and Torfing conclude with a discussion of the role that metagoverning public authorities must play in promoting the democratic anchorage of concrete governance networks and hence for ensuring that governance networks become a benefit for and not a threat to democracy.

This examination of how we might start to measure democratic anchorage leads us into the second half of the volume, in which we analyse the emergence, constitution and contestation of norms and rules in different policy contexts. We begin by investigating the practices of dispute resolution with John Forester who captures the lessons that might be drawn from the 'practical wisdom' of mediators of public disputes. The work of mediators, Forester argues, demonstrates how practical agreement between parties with deep value differences can be possible despite their rhetoric to the contrary, with parties learning about each other and revising their opening demands as they learn. Indeed, reflecting upon the lessons of such practices for the design and development of democratic institutions, Forester argues that early stages of successful processes involve careful convening of the parties to enable mutual recognition not agreement, to enable surprise rather than confirmation of stereotypes, and to enable identification of both joint vulnerabilities and opportunities to learn.

In his discussion of situated legitimacy and deliberative politics, Stephen Connelly addresses how legitimacy operates as a political value in processes of community participation. He argues that as a prerequisite for making normative judgements, we can and should understand how legitimacy is constructed in specific processes by actors in neighbourhoods and by those affected by their deliberations. Developing Beetham's analysis of legitimacy as resting on the three dimensions of consent, legality and justifiability (Beetham 1991), he applies this to local situations through an analysis of the discourses and practices which establish, sustain and challenge the legitimacy of actors and processes across the three dimensions. He then deploys this framework to analyse the processes through which neighbourhood 'development trusts' sustain (or not) their legitimacy as they mediate between state and community in many British regeneration programmes. Such analysis provokes unsettling wider questions about how we can come to normative judgements about the legitimacy of institutions and actors, and how (or indeed whether) we can distinguish between 'authentic' and 'selfish' participation.

Against this background, Helen Sullivan critically examines recent experiments to redesign governance institutions by implementing neighbourhood working across local authorities in the United Kingdom. In recent times, 'neighbourhoods' have become a policy panacea for many central and local governments, promising officials and politicians the positive-sum outcome of democratic renewal, more responsive public services and greater community cohesion. However, drawing primarily on research into the operation of five neighbourhood initiatives across two English cities, Sullivan demonstrates how such experiments in institutional design cannot be divorced from the contingency and 'messiness' of politics, conflicting interpretations and agency. Importantly, she foregrounds the extent to which even apparently democratic rules and norms, which are often bound up with the practices and procedures of representative democracy and consensual decision making, can inhibit community engagement and work against the development of more radical democratic designs of neighbourhood governance. As such, her analysis makes visible the political character of what are often presented as 'neutral', 'non-political' rules of participation through an exploration of the competing ideas underpinning neighbourhood initiatives, the ways in which procedural rules and norms enable or constrain deliberation, and the conflicts between actors seeking to embed, resist or subvert proposed rules and norms. Attempts to minimise conflict are, Sullivan concludes, misguided both because of its inevitability and its significance in shaping adversarial identities and opening up opportunities for more robust and meaningful deliberation.

Continuing our focus on the different meanings and values that actors attach to the new political spaces of co-governance, Therese O'Toole and Richard Gale follow on with an empirical exploration of the impact of participatory governance initiatives and inclusion projects that target young people, especially black and minority ethnic young people, at local and national levels. Indeed, deploying de Certeau's concepts of 'strategies' and 'tactics', they suggest that participative governance initiatives can potentially create new political spaces, particularly for those groups with little prior organisation or power within local democratic institutions. But there is a need for practice-oriented assessments of how state and civil society partnerships play out, once they have been entered into. Specifically, O'Toole and Gale suggest that young people who have entered into state-sponsored youth schemes can have a degree of success in reconfiguring the terms on which they interact with the state, achieving thereby a partial fashioning of their own agendas and creating a political space for young people that did not previously exist. These are dependent both on the agency of the young activists themselves, as well as on the particular institutional arrangements in place for their participation.

In his chapter, Hendrik Wagenaar explores the intricate relationships between public administration, informality, freedom, power and democracy. He argues that informality, the informal modes of organising space, livelihood and citizenship, which are generally regarded by governing elites as a lesser social practice, should be seen as spaces of freedom and possibility. They offer, in his view, alternatives to the official order, in which new understandings and practices are hatched and from which new, creative solutions to intractable urban problems may emerge. Analysing a citizen-led initiative in response to the nuisance created by street prostitution in one neighbourhood in the German city of Dortmund, Wagenaar argues for a conception of agonistic democratic governance that focuses on and addresses problems arising from the constantly shifting alliances of actors, each with different capacities, skills and responsibilities, and, no less important, different interests, experiences, identities and perspectives. Significantly, he foregrounds citizens' 'informal' practices and subvention of power as instances of agonistic freedom, the 'practices of freedom' from which new democratic forms emerge. The recognition of these practices of freedom, Wagenaar suggests, allows us to go beyond the two usual forms of democratic participation, bottom-up participation and governance-driven democratisation, opening up the prospect of a transformative form of collaborative, participatory urban governance, which he dubs 'civic capacity'.

Finally, drawing our attention to contexts of heightened ethno-politics and cultural diversity, Joseph Leibovitz closes the volume by investigating the patterns and dynamics of Israeli–Palestinian neighbourhood mobilisation in the so-called 'mixed city' of Haifa. He couples institutional theories of ethnic mobilisation with urban regime analysis to offer a powerful analytical tool to investigate the intersection of place-based (neighbourhood) activism and the political construction of identities and their mobilisation, demonstrating how the unpacking of the techniques of governance – facilitated by urban regime analysis – provides a useful inroad into normative discussion of representation and participation in urban politics. Indeed, Leibovitz highlights how discourses and regimes of urban governance tend to structure expectations and outcomes around the appropriateness of certain political strategies of claim making. At the same time, he points to the importance of understanding the subtle ways through which community activists can generate effective oppositional strategies, capable of enhancing local democracy and social rights.

2 | *Governance-Driven Democratization*

MARK E. WARREN

Introduction

We are witnessing a new and important development in the history of democracy: policymaking and administration are moving into the front lines of the project of democratization. On the face of it, this development comes as something of a surprise to those who have viewed democratization as the mission of class agents and social movements, or as a matter of establishing and reforming electoral processes and the rule of law. Who would have thought that policy and policymaking – the domain of technocrats and administrators – would move into the vanguard of democratization? And yet it is in this domain – and not in electoral democracy – that we are seeing a rebirth of strongly democratic ideals, including empowered participation, focused deliberation and attentiveness to those affected by decisions. I shall refer to these developments as *governance-driven democratization*. That is, the norms of democracy are now being fostered, implemented and sometimes institutionalized through practical, front-line practices of government, motivated by administrators who find they need to forge partnerships with those their policies affect in order to plan, regulate, build, administer or govern. The resulting forms of governance are often ad hoc and sometimes novel, and they make use of variety of techniques for consultation, co-operation, learning, deliberation and co-governing.

In this chapter I argue that as 'government' becomes 'governance', the resulting forms of collective action often have the potential to satisfy the norms of democracy better than do other forms, such as electoral democracy. That said, I am not arguing that governance-driven democratization is replacing (or should replace) other forms and spaces of democracy – such as electoral democracy, public sphere discourse, social movement and advocacy democracy. To the contrary, it is likely that governance-driven democratization is developing within political vacuums that result from incapacities of electoral democracy to respond to citizens who increasingly demand responsiveness, and do so within increasingly complex societies (Rosanvallon 2011). Innovations in electoral democracy continue to develop, albeit slowly, no doubt because most potentials of this form have been achieved (Cain, et al. 2003a). At the same time, as an institutional form, electoral democracy is overtaxed: it cannot accomplish much of the political work that needs to be done within complex, postmodern, highly differentiated societies, primarily because these societies generate numerous high-capacity agents that can be regulated and engaged but not directly governed (Warren 2003). Indeed, in every developed democracy 'government' itself is highly differentiated into multiple layers, branches, agencies and departments. From the perspective of governments – or any large collective organization for that matter – these developments can produce political gridlock, or they can be harnessed through *governance*, the term I use (following the introduction to this volume) broadly to denote the functions of governing as well as more narrowly to denote the style of governing that works though collaborations of multiple agents, both inside and outside government. Thus, the term *governance-driven democratization* denotes both the functional problems of governing within complex societies, as well as the more specific strategies of engaging those subject to government decisions and actions that may have democratic consequences.

Although the forces promoting governance-driven democratization are growing most rapidly within electoral democracies, they are probably driven by broad social and economic developments that are independent of electoral democracy as we know it. In China, for example, experiments in governance – many of them genuinely democratic, most not – are developing very rapidly, despite the authoritarian rule of the Communist Party (He 2006, He and Warren 2011). The likely reason is functional: in China as elsewhere, fast-paced economic developments tend to generate social capacities for opposition and co-operation in ways that are similar to those in the developed democracies. These forces generate demands for more 'political' work: new forms of security for a newly mobile labour force, contract law, transparent regulatory regimes, negotiations with the 'newly rich' representing a growing tax base and so on. These pressures alone may hold potentials for democratization in ways that are quite autonomous from the regime-level democratization with which we are more familiar.

As a final point of introduction, it is worth noting that the term 'democratization' in *governance-driven democratization* should not be understood as indicating that all governance is democratic or even potentially democratic. Rather, the term provides a normative frame, drawing attention to the possibility that governance represents a relatively new and potentially deep trajectory of democratic development. The term is analytic, insofar as it denotes a domain of political experiments that may have democratic potentials. It is normative, insofar as it draws attention to processes of governance that have democratic potentials, by which I mean that they increase the chances that those potentially affected by collective decisions will have some chance to influence those decisions (Fung 2013). But it is not descriptive: as an empirical matter, domains of governance make use of many kinds of processes that are not democratic and some which are harmful to democracy – as my analysis below will suggest.

In this chapter, I first locate the domain of governance-driven democratization in relation to other spaces and domains of democratic politics. Second, I suggest several reasons why the domain of governance-driven democratization has become so dynamic in the last couple of decades. Third, I identify four characteristics of the governance-driven democratization, each of which specifies a dimension of democratic promise and potential limitation: it emerges as a response to democratic deficits. It tends to be elite-driven or instigated. It is typically de-linked from electoral democracy. And it brings into existence constituencies as a consequence of the potential impact of policies.

These characteristics of governance-driven democratization bring with them several specific democratic opportunities, although each is accompanied by challenges. Most strikingly, governance-driven democratization can engage constituencies of those affected by issues or policies, thus expanding democracy beyond electoral constituencies. In addition, governance-driven democratization often involves specific and direct empowerments of those affected – empowerments that are often more effective and extensive than voting. And governance-driven democratization promises new kinds and forms of political representation, often with ordinary citizens representing other ordinary citizens. Closely related, because governance-based processes involve people in advice or decision making who are not professional politicians, they can also enable forms of deliberation that would otherwise be undercut by the strategic features of campaigns, elections and party politics. Finally, governance-driven democratization can harness the potentials of civil society for knowledge, organization, energy and creativity for government policymaking and decision. At the same time, I shall emphasize, each of these potentials comes with potential challenges and dangers to democracy. But if these challenges and dangers are identified, institutions can be designed that will mitigate them – for we are now in a period of democratic experimentation – helping to push governance along the pathways of greater democracy.

The Domain of Governance-Driven Democratization

Governance-driven democratization names only one kind of political space among many, and its opportunities and challenges have much to do with the space it occupies within encompassing systems of political institutions, social organizations, and political practices (see Table 2.1). In one dimension, we can think of politics (and thus possible sites of democracy) as being located primarily within the state, within society, or within the economy. The significance of these distinctions is that they capture the fact that developed societies make collective decisions and organize collective actions in three basic ways: (1) through administrative power organized through the state, (2) through norms expressed and organized through the associations of civil society, and (3) through money organized by markets (Habermas 1987). As societies differentiate along these lines, represented by the rows in Table 2.1, so we should expect politics to differentiate as well. State and state-like entities such as the European Union (EU) remain the ultimate locus of politics. That said, as states and governments develop, they also internally differentiate – increasingly decentralizing and deconcentrating powers to lower forms of government, as described in the Introduction to this volume (see also Ansell and Gingrich 2003a), while ceding key structural powers to more encompassing structures, as in the case of the EU, and in other ways to trade and security organizations. Of most importance here, however, is the internal differentiation within constitutional regimes between the legislative, judicial, and administrative functions of the state. With the increasing complexity of governance, legislatures tend to limit themselves to legislating broad policy goals, while directing agencies to develop the necessary administrative rules and laws to achieve these goals (Ansell and Gingrich 2003b). Legislation in the developed democracies – and some newer democracies, such

Table 2.1. *Domains of democracy*

Domain focus	Institutionalized		Non-Institutionalized
	Centred	Devolved, reflexive	
State: Representative democracy	Elected representatives, Parties, interest groups, corporatist representation		Political protest, demonstration, public discourse and influence, networks
Direct democracy	Referenda, town meetings		Political protest, demonstration, public discourse and influence, networks
Non-elected institutions (agencies, courts)	Public hearings, deliberative stake holder rule-making, citizen juries, town-hall meetings	Devolved and deconcentrated administration, citizen use of courts enabled by legal standing	Political protest, demonstration, public discourse and influence, networks
Society		Devolution of public functions to associations	Political protest, demonstration, public discourse and influence, networks; Democracy within associations
Economy		Collective bargaining, stakeholder representation, workplace democracy	Direct action, boycotts, social entrepreneurship

as Brazil – very often comes with directives for 'public,' 'stakeholder,' or 'community' engagement. These directives anticipate that processes of program creation are themselves political, with potential impacts that cannot be foreseen in the legislation, and which exceed the relatively modest political capacities of legislative bodies in any case. In addition, judiciaries have become much more involved in the development of policy, particularly as related to rights-based standings of citizens that are relatively new in the EU and in countries such as Canada, and recently politicized in countries such as the United States (Cichowksi and Stone Sweet 2003). Finally, because we have seen an increase in direct democracy in the form of referendums in most of the developed democracies, we should distinguish between representative and direct democracy. Although there are some exceptions, governance processes are usually directed toward what Rosanvallon (2011, chap. 10) calls 'proximity' to specific constituencies, and so will tend to lack the encompassing features of directly democratic devices such as referendums or the open town meetings found in the states of New England.

Developed societies also differentiate state from civil society and economy, each of which operates with distinctive media, and each of which produces distinctive kinds of politics. Civil societies, the domain of purpose-built associations, have developed at a healthy pace over the last few decades, so much so that the developed democracies are now densely populated with non-profit organizations and voluntary associations. The functional importance of these sectors for governance and democracy is that they support public spheres of opinion formation, enable representation of marginal groups, provide public goods, as well as goods that fall outside of electoral attentiveness, enable organization outside of government and the state on behalf of social agendas, provide alternative means for delivering public goods, and form capacities for citizenship (Warren 2001). Civil societies function as the social infrastructure of the politics of networks, protest, resistance, and public opinion formation and discourse. And, finally, developed societies make use of markets to organize most of their economically productive activities. Capitalist societies transfer, as it were, large numbers of public decisions to organizations responding to markets (Lindblom 2002), producing the politics of direct action, social entrepreneurship, boycotts, as well as enabling the organization of consumer demand for public goods and purposes.

In a second dimension, represented by the columns in Table 2.1, we can distinguish between institutionalized politics, such as occurs through elections and political parties, and non-institutionalized politics of the sort exemplified by new social movements and civil society organizations. The significance of this distinction is that the success of democracy depends both on the existence of protected space for non-institutionalized forms of politics, such as protest and public debate, as well as political institutions that are sensitive enough to the 'output' of non-institutionalized politics to formulate these outputs into collective agendas and decisions (Cohen and Arato 1992, Habermas 1997: chaps 7–8). In order to account for the de-centring impact of liberal-democratic governance on decision making, we should also distinguish between 'centred' forms of institutions, and 'reflexive' forms (Teubner 1983). Centred institutions receive input, process it, issue authoritative decisions, and then organize collective actions. Representative institutions such as legislatures combined with executive agencies operate in this manner. Reflexive institutions develop the conditions under which parties to a conflict can work out their differences and monitor solutions more directly. An example would be laws establishing collective bargaining, since they serve to equalize the powers of labour relative to management and define fair processes, but do so without deciding or imposing outcomes. The effect of reflexive institutions is to devolve and decentre sites of collective decision and action – one of the key strategies pursued by the developed societies to manage political complexity.

Combining these dimensions in Table 2.1 gives us a rough map of the potential spaces within which democratic norms and practices might exist, from direct action in the economy, discourse and demonstration in public spheres, to the more traditional politics of elections, political parties and interest groups. The circled cells identify the domain within which governance-driven democratization is a possibility – that is, within the domain of non-electoral institutions of government, of both the older, centralized variety as well as the newer decentred and reflexive kind. It is within this domain that we are seeing a rapid development of what are often called 'citizen engagement' and 'public engagement' processes – that is, everything from the from the public hearings and mandatory public comment periods that emerged after WWII, to the stakeholder meetings that began to spread in the 1980s, and to newer consensus conferences, town-hall meetings, citizen juries, citizen assemblies, deliberative polling, on-line dialogues, deliberative planning, participatory budgeting, study circles, planning cells, collaborative learning, and even participatory theatre (Fung 2003, 2006; Hajer and Wagenaar 2003; Parkinson 2006; Gastil 2008; Smith 2009). There are, most probably, between one and two hundred named and branded processes. Typically, these processes use the languages of participation, collaboration, citizen engagement, and deliberation; they are designed for particular policy problems; they bypass the formal institutions of democracy, and they do not involve protest, lobbying, or obstruction.

In drawing this map, I want to make what may be an obvious point. The domain of governance-driven democratization has certain characteristics that will limit the kinds of democratization that can occur here, but also bring possibilities that cannot be gained in other domains. We could think about this map using an ecological metaphor: we need to identify the characteristics of the species so we can identify its niche, comparative advantages, and vulnerabilities. Importantly, as in any ecology, both the existence and the potentials of governance-driven democratization work in conjunction with other spaces of democratization. Thus, for example, without the public critique and obstruction potentials generated within civil society, governments would have fewer incentives to practice 'public engagement'. And were legislatures structured to handle high levels of political complexity, there would be less institutional demand for new governance processes.

Understanding the potentials of this domain requires specifying not only its location, but also those characteristics that are most relevant to its democratic potentials. As I suggested earlier, four characteristics seem particularly important. First, governance-driven democratization is a response to democracy deficits. Second, it tends to be elite-driven. Third, its evolution is often de-linked from electoral democracy. Fourth, it has an important capacity to bring into existence dynamic, serial, and overlapping peoples and constituencies based on the 'all-affected' principle rather than pre-defined and static territorial constituency.

With respect to the first characteristic, governance-driven democratization makes most sense as a response to deficits in standard electoral representative democracy (Pharr and Putnam 2000). There is a lot of political work in today's societies that electoral democracy is unable to accomplish. Part of this story is a functional one: the capacities of political institutions are being outstripped by the development of the societies in which they are embedded. With respect to policymaking and implementation, the general outlines of the story are well known. Under the standard model of democratic self-rule, of course, citizens elect representatives who then make policy on their behalf. When they are able to form a government, they legislate goals and means, and then pass these broad directions over to administrators, who then further develop and execute policy. But the linkages that should establish democracy are broken at almost every step: territorial electoral constituencies do not match issue constituencies, which are increasingly non-territorial (Bohman 2007). Even when issues match territorial constituencies, electoral processes only roughly reflect citizen preferences, and they do so in highly aggregated, information poor ways. Legislatures tend to have very low policymaking capacities, and so pass most decisions to executive agencies, which are then often left to guess what constituents want or how to respond to affected groups. These problems are multiplied by forces that work against electoral democracy, including monied influence, corporatism, and bureaucratic power and inertia (Bobbio 1987). And passing policy development and implementation over to bureaucratically organized executive agencies also has limitations: rule-based hierarchy tends to limit upward and horizontal flows of information, and they are unresponsive to direction either from the top or from constituents. The use of administrative power is often as likely to generate new administrative incapacities as to result in legitimate and effective administration (Gormley 1989).

Then add to this picture of institutional incapacity several broad facts of social and economic development. Today's societies are enormously complex, not just technically, but also politically. Although it was technical complexity that bothered earlier generations of democratic theorists from Schumpeter through Sartori, it is political complexity that is especially challenging for the standard model (Beck 1997). The causes of political complexity fall into several categories. One is the intensification and globalization of markets, migration, security regimes, environmental issues and the like. Globalization threatens the relevance of territorially-based electoral democracy, simply because the reach and impact of collective decisions and the structures they engender far exceed the organization of constituencies. As Bohman (2007) aptly puts it, the 'chains of affectedness' generated by collective decisions are now often so long that standard democratic mechanisms of collective decision making have little relevance. Even when decisions are made by democratic institutions, they are often disconnected from those they affect, who may be separated by great distances of space and time. Naturally, the greater the distance from democratic inclusions, the less democratic legitimacy accompanies the decision, and the more likely it is to generate (rather than address) political complexity.

Another trend is the general post-modernization of culture, particularly in the developed world (Inglehart and Welzel 2005). Generation by generation, people are becoming less deferential to authority and to hold values that are more democratic (Dalton 2007). This trend can be conceived as having two facets. One is a general distrust and often disaffection from the formal institutions of democracy. Among the developed democracies these effects vary by country, with Denmark on one extreme and the US on the other. But the trends are detectable in almost every developed democracy, and are now well-documented (Newton 2008). But at the same time, citizens are more likely to volunteer for causes, they are more interested in self-government, and they are keenly attentive to their powers over their own futures. They are increasingly likely to demand specific, even individualized performances from government in health, education, and other services (Rosanvallon 2011, chaps 10–12). These trends are not necessarily contradictory: though citizens are increasingly critical of government, patterns of activism and association outside of the traditional channels of political participation suggest not so much disaffection, but rather disjunctions between the collectivities that make decisions and citizens' capacities to control the social relations that affect their lives (Norris 1999).

We find a related trend in the rapid development of dense civil societies. Today's societies are increasingly populated by groups with resources – not just wealth and market power, but also social movements, cultural and ethnic groups, and groups that arise spontaneously in response to issues and policy initiatives. The developed democracies are populated by associations, organizations, and networks which are growing exponentially, not only in numbers of associations, but also in the relative size of civil society sectors (Warren 2001). Advocacy groups take up and frame almost every imaginable cause. They perform key democratic functions insofar as they articulate the preferences of citizens and support the public spheres through which public opinion is developed and conveyed to policymakers. But they also tend to overwhelm the capacities of electoral institutions to absorb and aggregate political demand, often producing political gridlock (Cain et al. 2003a).

At the same time, there is a parallel and closely related trend for civil society to absorb some of this demand through increased political and organizational capacity. Civil society organizations have increasingly developed their own expert capacities, enabling them both to challenge and to partner with governments and sometimes corporations (Fischer 2009). Some of these developments are by design: over the last few decades, the developed democracies have rapidly and uniformly adopted sunshine and freedom of information laws (Cain et al. 2003b). In addition, governments have increasingly organized information in ways that are broadly available to publics, which enables groups to engage much more effectively in advocacy, monitoring, and co-operation than in the recent past.

From a political perspective, these trends do not add up to anything like the crisis of democracy or legitimation predicted on both the left and right in the 1970s, when these trends started to become clear (Crozier, Huntington, and Watanuki 1975; Habermas 1975; cf. Offe 1984). The reason is that there are many points of adjustment and deflection in the developed democracies, so broad legitimation pressures do not show up as a general system crisis. Rather, they show up issue by issue and policy by policy, in protests over airport expansions, medical coverage, poverty issues, GMO regulations, forest management, struggles over neighbourhood development, energy pricing, and so on. So rather than general institutional or system level crises, we have something like pluralized challenges to governability, driven by functional incapacities of government agencies, as well as overlapping or competing jurisdictions, and failures by governments to anticipate and address spill-over consequences and linkages among issues (Beck 1997). Viewed as a whole, these trends suggest why much of the interesting innovation in democracy and democratization has moved into the domains of administration and policy.

The second characteristic of governance-driven democratization follows from these observations. If a previous recent wave of democratization could be said to reside in the development of civil society and the public sphere driven by citizen activists, this next arena – governance-driven democratization – is very much about the responses of those with positions of power within governing organizations. What is most remarkable about the last decade or so is the interest policymakers have taken in new democratic processes, with the active encouragement of a now large industry of consultants and democratic process entrepreneurs, such as America Speaks, Deliberative Polling, and Citizen Juries. The broadly functional reason is that policymakers are on the front lines of this new pluralized ungovernability. They find the legitimacy generated by electoral democracy does not necessarily carry over to issue-segmented constituencies (Rosanvallon 2011). The reasons for these weaknesses of electoral democracy, as suggested earlier, have to do with disjunctions between (a) electoral constituencies and the constituencies of policies, (b) the low information carried by elections and the high information requirements of policymaking, and (c) divergences between the relatively exclusive mechanics of electoral systems and the inclusive effects of policies – that is, their effects fall upon electoral winners and losers alike. Each of these disjunctions increases the possibility that any given policy will generate opposition that derails the capacities of policymakers to plan and implement policies. They will often find that legislative direction fails to equip them with information and enforcement capacities that are sufficient to their tasks. Such capacities often only can be expanded by engaging with advocates – most notably in the areas of environmental policy and urban planning, but also in labour policy, public health, and many other issue areas. And, finally, if policymakers fail to anticipate problems, formal democracy remains powerful enough to impose solutions, but often in ways that are clumsy and costly – as with the cases of medical research tissue-banking in the United Kingdom and stem-cell research in the United States (Mackenzie and Warren 2012). For these reasons, policymakers increasingly speak the language of trust, collaboration, public engagement, and dialog, in part to avoid the alternative politics of opposition, protest, gridlock, and imposed solutions. There is, no doubt, no overall plan or strategy to shift discourses from those centred on contestation to those emphasizing co-operation. Rather, the strategies are piecemeal, each responding to the failures of the general legitimacy generated by winning elections to translate into the policy-specific legitimacy necessary to address policy problems. Viewed from a distance, however, a pattern emerges: policymakers and administrators are working issue by issue, policy by policy, constituency by constituency, to generate legitimacy 'locally' in ways that compensate for the weak linkages between electoral legitimacy and policy development and implementation – a pattern Rosanvallon (2011) calls the 'legitimacy of proximity'.

The third characteristic of governance-driven democratization follows this pattern: it is often de-linked from electoral democracy. The logics that drive governance-driven democratization are related to policy development, planning, and administration rather than to the global legitimacy of elected governments. That said, elected governments have become increasingly aware that electoral legitimacy does not translate into policy-specific legitimacy. Thus, legislation in the developed democracies has for some time – beginning in the post-war period but picking up speed in the 1980s – directed agencies to establish processes for 'public input' or required 'community representation' during policy development. Initial forays into governance-driven democracy were timid and inadequate, consisting in required public hearings or public notice and comment periods during administrative rule-making. More recently, governments have provided for bolder initiatives: in the mid-1980s, for example, when the Oregon State Legislature was faced with the task of prioritizing Medicaid coverage – state administered health care insurance for those who fall below the poverty line – it decided it lacked the legitimacy and capacity to develop an approach. Instead, it legislated a public process, run by a non-profit organization called *Oregon Health Decisions*, which it tasked with the problem of prioritizing the medical conditions to be covered by the Medicaid programme (Kitzhaber 1993). Although the process has attracted many critics, its importance here is that it marked an early instance in which a formal elected body created a supplementary democratic process to generate a broadly legitimate framework for the distribution of publicly-funded health care. In a more recent case, the '21st Century Nanotechnology Research and Development Act of 2003' (U.S.) directed the implementing agencies to develop 'mechanisms such as citizens' panels, consensus conferences, and educational events, as appropriate' (Goodin and Dryzek 2006, 241). These kinds of developments suggest that governance-driven democratization can be *supplementary* to electoral democracy – shoring up its functional weaknesses.

This de-linking from electoral democracy is also evident in the emergence of governance-driven democratization in places where competitive, multi-party democracy does not exist at all. In China, the Communist Party has been actively encouraging new 'consultative' and 'deliberative' processes, particularly in local government. In a now-famous experiment in Zeguo township in Wenling City, for example, officials used deliberative polling to set annual budget priorities (Mo and Chen 2005). The process was so popular that city officials found they could not go back to the old ways, for fear of generating protests. While broad data is not available, some areas in China exhibit an impressive density of these new ways of conducting politics. In Wenling City from 1996 to 2000, for example, more than 1,190 deliberative and consultative meetings were held at the village level, 190 at the township level, and 150 in governmental organizations, schools, and business sectors (Wenling Department of Propaganda 2003, 98).

The Chinese case suggests that the conditions for governance-driven democratization are broader than deficits in electoral democracy (He and Warren 2011). In China, attention to governance appears to be driven by a development agenda, combined with the tendencies of development to produce multiple actors with credible capacities for opposition. The Chinese Communist Party is, no doubt, hoping that these democratic experiments will head off regime democratization in the Western sense, while – like their Western counterparts – they hope to generate legitimacy, policy by policy, in ways that will replace the long-bankrupt Maoist ideology. Whether the Party will be successful remains to be seen. The point here, however, is that the China is a limiting case: if governance-driven democratization shows up here, it cannot be attributed to regime democratization, and we should look for causes that are rooted in pluralization, contestation, and social capacities unleashed by social and economic development rather than by pressures for electoral democratization or reform. Indeed, from the perspective of governance complexities rooted in economic and cultural complexities, the case of China is more comparable to the developed democracies than to the less-developed electoral democracies, its authoritarian regime notwithstanding.

Fourth, it follows from the policy-focused nature of governance-driven democratization that constituencies may come into existence in ways that are quite distinct from electoral democracy. In electoral democracy, 'the people' are those who live within the boundaries of a state, and they are represented (typically) through territorial constituencies. Territorial constituencies, however, limit the reach of democracy whenever the collective issues and decisions that affect people fail to coincide with those territories, as is the case with many economic, environmental, and security issues. Likewise, peoples defined by one territory often make decisions that off-load costs or damages onto people outside of their constituency, in such a way that decisions made through formally democratic means can produce domination among peoples (Bohman 2007). Governance-driven democratization is less bound by the territorial constitution of peoples. 'Peoples' are, in effect, brought into existence in response to issues, and often dissolve when issues are resolved (Warren 2002, 689–90). And, indeed, legislation often directs agencies to engage 'stakeholders' when they develop policy – a term often understood to encompass organized interests and advocates, but which should be construed as pertaining to all who are potentially affected by the policy, whether organized or not. Such constituencies are dynamic, overlapping, issue-focused, and serial. Individuals may belong to many distinct 'peoples' at any given point in time, in ways that are potentially more adaptable to the 'all affected' principle of democracy than are territorial constituencies (Fung 2013). In this way, governance-driven democratization can involve democratic responsiveness well beyond the kinds enabled by territorially-based democratic systems.

This sketch of the governance-driven democratization landscape suggests two broad judgements. The first is critical: if the democratic potentials of governance-driven democratization are to be captured, we shall need to be clear that these forms of democracy have inherent limitations. In this domain of government-driven democratization, for example, agendas are typically elite-defined, and policy-driven issues often make it difficult to encompass full political programs in the way that coherent political parties can within legislatures. Protest and opposition are ill-suited to the form, although without these possible obstructions there would be fewer incentives for policymakers to devise new forms of democracy. And although the discourses of 'citizen participation' and 'public engagement' are ubiquitous within this domain, the laws of size and scale work here as in every other domain, limiting the numbers of people that can be simultaneously involved in deliberations and decisions. Participatory claims are inevitably exaggerated, and can even function ideologically, to obscure what may be, in fact, very undemocratic processes (Warren 1996, 2008a).

The second broad judgment, however, is positive: if we view governance-driven democratization as a response to the rise of advocacy, social movements, and civil society more generally, we may be witnessing a transformation of democracy as dramatic and important as the rise of mass, electoral democracy in the nineteenth century (Warren 2003). Part of the work of democratic theory involves expanding our imaginations about these possibilities and opportunities while framing their limitations.

I see at least five distinct kinds of opportunities opened by governance-driven democratization. Viewed as a whole, these developments promise to (1) alter definitions of peoples and boundaries, (2) open new venues of direct participation, (3) alter forms of representation, (4) inject new forms of deliberation into government, and (5) harness the enormous collective capacities of civil society.

The first opportunity I have already indicated. Because governance-driven democratization is not tied to statically-defined electoral constituencies, it has the potential to include all those affected by an issue. Because constituencies are defined by issue rather than territory, it is possible to draw democratic processes closer the 'all-affected' principle – the basic norm of democracy that says that those affected by a collective decision should have some influence over the decision (Goodin 2007; Fung 2013). This quality is an effect of the drivers of governance-driven democratization: the specific issues and policies that can provoke those affected into forming a constituency. This quality of governance-driven democratization is the democratic side of the elite-led nature of the area. Though elite constitution of peoples is not, on the face of it, a particularly democratic way of defining peoples, within the broader ecology of electoral institutions, advocacy, and social activism, we could look at elites as intermediaries in an on-going process of constituency formation that is potentially more responsive to those affected by issues than territorially-defined electoral constituencies can be (Saward 2010). This dynamic is, perhaps, one of the most important of the trajectories along which contemporary democracies can develop: it brings with it the potential to cross boundaries for the sake of inclusion, as well as the capacity for rapid, flexible responsiveness to new issues and emerging publics.

Of course, the challenges and dangers are part of the same package. Without electoral mechanisms of accountability and operating under mandates that are often vague, elites have discretion in how they define relevant constituents when they devise 'public engagement' processes. Elite discretion can produce at least three kinds of dangers to democracy. First, elites can frame agendas in ways that simply fail to capture the issues, and in so doing fail to include the relevant constituencies. Second, because elites are often responding to opposition, they are often most responsive to well-organized interests rather than to all of those affected, thus biasing constituency definition toward those with wealth, education, and power (Fung 2003). Third, if elites open processes to all those who are interested, processes of self-selection bias toward the intensively interested and well-organized, and bias against the unorganized, as well as against latent public goods (Dalton et al. 2003; Dietz and Stern 2009). So the democratic challenges here will be to conceive and devise recursive agenda-setting and constituency definition processes that approximate the all-affected principle. One important innovation that addresses these concerns are government partnerships with organizations that specialize in democratic processes that anticipate and target affected but unorganized publics. On behalf of the City of New Orleans, for example, America Speaks organized a series of deliberative events entitled 'The Unified New Orleans Plan', focused on a plan to rebuild New Orleans in the aftermath of the hurricane Katrina (America Speaks 2009). America Speaks faced the challenge that many of the residents of New Orleans had dispersed to other cities. In response, the organization publicized and conducted events across the country. Its methodology included recruiting segments of populations that were likely to be underrepresented in participatory venues.

A second opportunity is in the area of empowerment. Whereas voting for representatives is a limited and non-specific form of empowerment, many of the new governance-driven processes promise to empower participants directly and specifically – an ironic potential, since empowerment often builds on elite capacities to define agendas precisely and narrowly enough to lead to decisions. But this democratic opportunity typically comes with an imbalance between elites and participants: the elites who generate processes are often operating under powers formally granted by states, and they have the benefit of this kind of authority. In contrast, the democratic legitimacy of ad hoc citizen engagement and public participation processes is often unclear, primarily because participants are unelected, and particularly when a body is unrepresentative of those affected by decisions, as will often occur in cases of open processes into which participants self-select. In addition, the authority of these new bodies is likewise ambiguous, particularly if they compete with the authority of elected representatives. So, in fact, most new processes are advisory rather than empowered. The challenges here will have to do with conceiving forms of empowerment that are consistent with electoral democracy, and which can, perhaps, generate different and yet democratically robust forms of legitimacy. The challenges are not insurmountable: the Canadian provinces of British Columbia and Ontario, for example, recently constituted citizens' assemblies on electoral reform. These processes were empowered to set electoral reform agendas in the form of referendum questions, which not only focused public debate and deliberation, but also left the final judgement to voters. So the legitimacy of the assemblies was underwritten and complemented, as it were, by direct democracy (Warren and Pearse 2008; see also Cutler and Fournier 2007). Another case of a process that empowered affected constituencies is documented by Fung: under a design imposed by the State of Illinois legislature in the late 1980s, Chicago public schools are now run by school-level committees of parents and teachers. These committees have significant powers of resource deployment in response to school-specific needs and problems. Results, however, are measured by the Chicago Public Schools, thus ensuring that these new 'democratic' bodies are, in fact, responding to those most affected by their decisions – that is, the students attending the school. This institutional design combines decentralized empowerments with centralized accountability (Fung 2004).

A third opportunity is in the domain of representation. These opportunities are, of course, linked to the problem of constituency. But they are worth highlighting in their own right. Democracy entrepreneurs often use the language of 'participation' and 'engagement' to describe these processes. In my view, democratic theorists should be focusing more closely on representative relationships, since the fact remains that most people do not participate in these processes (Warren 2008a). What makes many of these processes distinctive is that representatives are not professional politicians: a few citizens represent (or claim to represent) other citizens. They are usually selected or self-selected rather than elected. What matters most from the perspective of democratic representation is that selection processes result in a body that includes the interests, values, views, and opinions of those potentially affected, as well as has the capacity for considered advice or decisions that represents the affected.

From the perspective of democratic representation, governance-driven democratization involves two kinds of challenges. The first kind results from open processes into which individuals self-select. Policy decision makers often dread open processes, which can provide public stages for those with axes to grind. As one-off events, such processes can often be quite destructive, sometimes devolving into shouting matches, failing to produce actionable proposals, and increasing public cynicism about 'politics'. From a democratic perspective, because open forums have self-selected participants, they often fail to represent those affected by decisions. A second kind of challenge is closely related: policymakers increasingly convene 'stakeholder' meetings, seeking to engage groups and interests potentially affected by policies. For strategic reasons, policymakers often gravitate toward those stakeholders with obstruction potential – that is, those sufficiently organized or otherwise powerful enough to create governance problems if they are not at the table. By default, those stakeholders without organization or other resources for voice or pressure are left out of the processes, undermining the democratic representativeness of the process. In both kinds of cases, selection processes tend to be biased in favour of those with intense preferences and high levels of organizational resources. Their effects are undemocratic to the extent that these kinds of interests crowd out the interests of affected but unorganized populations. In general, increasing opportunities for political participation tends to bias 'voice' in favour of the well-organized (Cain et al. 2003a). Thus, a key challenge for democratic theorists will be to identify alternative forms of representation that would balance these tendencies, and then figure out why elites should want to adopt them (Saward 2010). But the very fact that governance-driven democratization is elite-led provides opportunities for such correctives. Processes can be designed for the purposes of democratic representation in the initial selection process: random selection and targeted recruitment of participants are two devices that can be used to correct representative biases that are typically part of open forum and stakeholder processes.

A fourth opportunity offered by governance-driven democratization is that of deliberative leadership by ordinary citizens of a kind that exists neither in the electoral arena nor in the less structured sphere of public discourse. In electoral democracy, deliberation is often undercut by the strategic features of campaigns, elections, and party politics. Public sphere deliberation runs the gamut of possibilities, and is essential to public opinion formation. But public discussion is often poorly linked to the incremental learning, problem-solving, and sustained attention necessary for policy decisions. Both limitations can be mitigated by designed 'minipublics', of which deliberative polls, consensus conferences, planning cells, citizens' assemblies, citizens' parliaments, and processes such as those devised by America Speaks (2009) are examples. Minipublics are de-linked from both the strategic elements of electoral politics and from the unfocused elements of broad publics (Goodin and Dryzek 2006; Warren and Pearse 2008; Fishkin 2009; Smith 2009, chap. 3; Mackenzie and Warren 2012). Well-designed and well-facilitated, minipublics can capture the innovative and progressive capacities of deliberation, and often do so in ways that are broadly representative of public interests. The key challenge here has less to do with designing high deliberative quality into minipublics – we mostly know how to do that. The challenges have to do with linking minipublics back to broader publics. Learning and deliberation transforms participants from citizen representatives into public opinion vanguards that may become as distant from public opinion as any other kind of representative (Chambers 2009).

The final class of opportunities has to do with the key role that governance-driven democratization innovations can play in connecting state power to civil society – a point that returns to the basic thesis, namely, that the rise of governance-driven democratization has much to do with the functional incapacities of electoral democracy in complex societies. Again, the way I am constructing the thesis, governance-driven democratization is a response to the increasing strength and pluralism of society, reflected in its increasingly self-conscious and organized characteristics. That said, connections between civil society and state operating through electoral democracy, as I have suggested, are often abstractly global, low on information, and non-specific. In contrast, connections working through advocacy and social movements are important for pressure, but often lead to political gridlock. Governance-driven democratization might be viewed as stepping into the breach: when processes are well-designed, they enable governments can capture the potentials within civil society for organization, information, energy, and creativity (Hajer and Wagenaar 2003; Gastil 2008; Smith 2009). Examples are now legion, in social and medical services, urban planning, environmental issues, community development, policing, public schools, and other policy areas. I see the challenges from a democratic perspective in two areas. First, governments can co-opt civil society organizations in such a way that they lose their capacities to represent their constituencies. Selective inclusion can develop into new kinds of exclusive and informal corporatist structures (Van Til

2000, chap. 6). Second, civil society capacities are unevenly distributed, in such a way that any general policy to, say, deliver services in
co-operation with civil society organizations, is likely to favour those
areas and segments of society where civil society is robust (Warren
2001, chap. 7).

In conclusion, I am not making an argument so much as drawing
attention to an emerging landscape, which I am calling *governance-
driven democratization*. If there is an argument, it is both optimistic
and cautious, very much in keeping with the overall approach of this
volume. On the optimistic side, there are radically democratic potentials in this emerging phenomenon. 'Governance' can inject into modern societies and government democratic ideals that have been thought
to be impossible in large scale, complex, mass societies: more citizen
participation, more government responsiveness, better representation,
and more deliberation (Warren 2002). On the cautious side, these are
potentials, not necessities. For this reason, we shall need to approach
this emerging landscape with a critical eye: we need to look at these
emerging institutions and practices, and ask about their immanent
potentials. To identify these potentials, we will need to use a two-step
strategy of analysis. The first involves abstracting democratic norms in
such a way that they are not necessarily identified with any particular
set of institutions. We should not identify democratic norms with any
specific political mechanisms, such as elections, majority rule, deliberation, or even participation. These institutions and practices are ways
and means, not ends. Rather, in keeping with the overall message of
this volume, we should identify as 'democratic' any set of arrangements
and practices that enables collectivities to make common decisions
that support the self-development and self-government of individuals.
The second step will involve looking for ways in which democratic
norms find life in new institutional forms, and to keep an open mind
about how these might evolve into practices that contribute to self-
development and self-government – including those new institutions
devised by policymakers in response to political and policy gridlock
(Fung 2007; Smith 2009).

There is also a more specific kind of theoretical task. Sorting out the
good from the bad in these policy-defined arenas of governance means
that we will need to develop a somewhat complex middle-level body
of theory to help guide more 'local' analyses and critical assessments –
particularly those that might distinguish more from less democratic

innovations. So we need to develop approaches that will allow us to assess the fit between processes and issues (see, e.g., Warren 2001; Fung 2007; Gastil 2008; Smith 2009). What kinds of processes are likely to generate better rather than worse outcomes – more legitimacy, justice, or effectiveness, say – given the characteristics of the issues and the constraints of time and money? We are not starting from scratch – we have much general knowledge about democratic mechanisms such as voting schemes, kinds of representation, and deliberative procedures. We also now have a lot of specific knowledge about the effects of various combinations. We know, for example, that combining experts with lay citizens over time within a deliberative context can overcome many of the constraints of technical complexity. We know that processes which allow citizens to self-select will bias the process toward organized, high-resource interests, and that random selection can produce a closer approximation of informed public opinion. We have detailed knowledge of particular designs, such as the British Columbia Citizens' Assembly or 21st Century Town Hall Meetings. We know that 'enclave deliberation' may reinforce undesirable kinds of prejudice (Sunstein 2002, chap. 1). But we do not yet have the theoretically-organized knowledge that would allow us to begin with an issue and a set of goals, and then conceive processes that are appropriate to the demands of the issues and the desired normative outcomes. Were we to develop this kind of knowledge, we would then be able to recommend institutional designs that would increase the chances that the process will maximize democratic processes and outcomes for any given issue. We would then be able to deliver specific assessments about what counts as a better or worse process from the perspectives of democracy – or, if we wish, from any other normative perspective, although this is the one I have developed here. In short, if I am right that governance-driven democratization is now one of the most dynamic vectors of progress in democratization, issue-focused policy development will have moved to the front lines of democratic reform and innovation.

Deliberative, Agonistic and Aversive Grammars of Democracy: The Question of Criteria

ALETTA J. NORVAL

Introduction

In recent years the United Kingdom has witnessed a spate of cases where members of religious communities have challenged local authorities, education providers and the state to allow them to display symbols of their faith in schools, places of employment and public services sites. This reflects a wider politicization of religious symbols, of buildings and of the activities that define public life, in Europe and in the United States. One such case is that of Shabina Begum (Halpin 2005; Goldrich, 2006),[1] a student at Denbigh High School in Luton, who challenged her school's dress policy. As a result of a Court of Appeal ruling that she was unlawfully excluded from her school for wearing traditional religious dress, she won the right to wear to lessons a jilbab (which leaves just the face and hands exposed), only to see the House of Lords reverse this decision in 2006.[2] At the time, Shabina Begum called the Court of Appeal's decision 'a victory for all Muslims who wish to preserve their identity and values despite prejudice and bigotry'. She blamed the school's initial decision on

---

[1] For a summary of the case, see McGoldrich (2006, chap. 6). There are several other examples of cases in the United Kingdom dealing with the question of religious dress in schools, as well as other high-profile cases of workers challenging companies on their right to display religious symbols. See the case of Eweida v British Airways plc (2010) concerning a dispute between BA and an employee about uniform policy.

[2] 'Denbigh's uniform policy allows girls to wear a skirt, trousers or shalwar kameez, comprising a loose tunic and trousers, and to cover their heads with headscarves. Miss Begum had worn the shalwar kameez since entering the school at the age of 12. But in September 2002 she and her brother, Shuweb Rahman, told Stuart Moore, an assistant head, that she had switched to the jilbab. Miss Begum believed that the kameez did not comply sufficiently with Islam's requirement for women to dress modestly. She now attends another school which permits the jilbab.' (Halpin 2005)

hostility to Muslims after the September 11 terrorist attacks. 'As a young woman growing up in a post-9/11 Britain, I have witnessed a great deal of bigotry from the media, politicians and legal officials', she said (Halpin 2005). 'This bigotry resulted from my choice to wear a piece of cloth, not out of coercion, but out of my faith and belief in Islam. It is amazing that in the so-called free world I have to fight to wear this attire.' (Halpin 2005) In reaching its decision, the Court of Appeal argued that she had been denied the 'right to education and to manifest her religious beliefs' when her high school excluded her for wearing the jilbab. The school had argued, in its defence, that the jilbab contravened its uniform policy. That policy had been agreed by governors at the school – where 79 per cent of pupils are Muslim – and with local Muslim organizations. Initially the High Court decided in the school's favour. But this ruling was overturned by the Court of Appeal, which stated that Denbigh High had breached the Human Rights Act. Lord Justice Brooke said that Miss Begum, 16, had been unlawfully excluded. The school had a right to set a uniform policy but nobody in the previous ruling had considered that Miss Begum also had a right recognized by English law. The onus was on the school to justify any interference with that right. Lord Justice Brooke called on the Department for Education and Skills to issue guidance to schools on complying with their obligations under the Human Rights Act. Responses to the decision, not surprisingly, varied widely. The Secondary Heads Association expressed its disappointment. Martin Ward, the deputy general secretary, said: 'The ruling is not at all clear in what will be expected.... It states that schools have a right to uniform policies but students also have a right to disregard them.' (Halpin 2005) David Hart, general secretary of the National Association of Head Teachers, said that the ruling had enormous ramifications for any school whose pupils wanted to wear traditional dress for religious reasons. 'This is a legal minefield and heads and governors urgently need guidance from the DfES,' he added (Halpin 2005).[3] Denbigh High said in a statement that it had lost on a technicality. It insisted that its uniform policy took account of the cultural and religious sensitivities of pupils. The Muslim Council of Britain said that the decision was a 'very important ruling on the issue of

---

[3] Reference to the Begum case is included in the 2007 'Guidance to schools on school uniform related policies', Department of Education and Skills (20 March 2007).

personal freedom'. Iqbal Sacranie, the secretary-general of that organization, said: 'Many other schools have willingly accommodated
Muslim schoolgirls wearing the jilbab.' (Halpin 2005)

There is no doubt that these sorts of challenge raise important
questions for contemporary European and Western societies in a
myriad of policy settings, where inclusiveness and participation are
the keywords shaping interactions among the relevant parties. In the
United Kingdom there is a certain sense of crisis as to how to address
these issues. Dominant discourses organizing community relations,
such as that of multiculturalism, have come under fire, and successive governments have been grappling with new forms of engagement with alienated and marginalized communities (New Labour,
for instance, through their 'community cohesion' programme; and
more recently, the Coalition Government through their 'big society'
programme). In this search for new solutions, sites of consultation
and participation have proliferated, and they display all the strengths
and pathologies now commonly associated with innovative forms
of non-hierarchical governance. Quite apart from the absence of
codified rules and regulations shaping participation and domains of
power, as noted by Hajer (2003), issues of representation, accountability and legitimacy arise in the context of governance-beyond-the-
state (Warren and Castiglione 2006; see also Warren's contribution
to this volume). While promising greater participation, forms and
mechanisms of representation are often woefully inadequate, failing
to engage the relevant communities and their representatives. In a
context where constituencies are in the process of formation, where
they are not based upon any simplistic predetermined communities
of identity or interest, serious problems are posed for democracy.
How does one ensure that all communities and groups with an interest in a particular problem are represented when it is not clear what
the boundaries of such communities are? Assuming that the mere
presence of a group in a participatory process is not sufficient, how
can one ensure equality of participation once the relevant communities are represented? Once engaged in this process, how does one
further facilitate what Sanders (1997) has called 'epistemic equality',
the ability to be heard by dominant groups?

In this chapter I critically examine contemporary democratic theory
with a view to establish what light it may throw on some key aspects
of these problems, marked as they are by what Jeremy Waldron (1999,

1–4) has called 'the circumstances of politics'.[4] These issues arise on the 'input' side of democracy, where questions of the legitimacy of processes of democratic decision making are approached from a processual perspective (Goodin 2003, 9). Seen from this vantage point, the legitimacy of decisions rests crucially on getting the process right. Contemporary theories of democracy have developed against a common backdrop of dissatisfaction with aggregative mechanisms for reaching decisions (e.g., voting), and have focussed on the need to supplement more traditional mechanisms by new suggested modes of reaching decisions. Despite this common background problematic, different alternatives have been put forward by *deliberative* and *poststructuralist* theorists of democracy respectively. Here I am not concerned to rehearse what are a familiar set of recommendations, objections and counter-objections between these approaches.[5] Instead, I will focus on what I think is one of the key issues shaping these exchanges, namely that of the *criteria* we use in evaluating our democratic practices in and beyond the policymaking process. The issue of criteria seems to me to lie at the heart of disagreements between these approaches. I will suggest that a focus on criteria may offer us a way of bringing into sharper relief what is at stake in these debates. In so doing, I will also seek to problematize the sharp division between the rationality and context-independence of our criteria of judgement on the one hand, and an emphasis on the presence of power relations in the establishment of any and all criteria on the other. It is precisely this division that has tended to confound debate and has led to stalemates in thinking productively about the ways in which we make our

---

[4] Waldron explains these circumstances in the following way: 'The prospect of persisting disagreement must be regarded, I think, as one of the elementary conditions of modern politics. Nothing we can say about politics makes much sense if we proceed without taking this condition into account. We may say ... that disagreement among citizens as to what they should do, as a political body, is one of the circumstances of politics. It is not all there is to the circumstances of politics, of course: there is also the need to act together, even though we disagree about what we do.... [T]he circumstances of politics are a coupled pair: disagreement wouldn't matter if people didn't prefer a common decision; and the need for a common decision would not give rise to politics as we know it if there wasn't at least the potential for disagreement about what the common decision would be' (Waldron 1999, 153–4).

[5] I have dealt with the convergences and divergences between these approaches more extensively in *Aversive Democracy* (Cambridge: Cambridge University Press, 2007).

evaluative judgements and think about the fostering of democratic subjectivity and the creation of open, critical participatory processes that can sustain practices of freedom.

The Question of Criteria: What Is at Stake?

At stake here is the question of how and on what grounds we evaluate our ongoing political practices. What matters here whether contemporary democratic theory gives us (and ought to give us) guidelines that can inform the development of critical participatory processes. As we have argued in the Introduction to this volume, such processes are at their most powerful when they are approached from the perspective of viewing them as practices of freedom. Critical participatory processes, in this sense, could be understood as means of acting on, developing and contesting the range of possibilities of thinking and acting arising in response to practices of governance (Tully 2008a, 24). Assuming one starts from the proposition that democratic theory should provide a horizon of possibilities and facilitate the creative development of our imagining a diversity of forms for practices of freedom, a number of diverging options present themselves here. One can develop a set of idealized criteria, removed from any concrete and specific set of practices; alternatively, criteria may be drawn from and developed out of such practices.[6] One could also start with a set of ontological propositions concerning the

---

[6] There is a wide range of possible positions on the question of abstraction and idealization. O'Neill (1997, 419) argues, for instance, that abstraction is necessary and unobjectionable, whereas idealization is not. Whilst acknowledging that idealizations may be of great help in theory-building, O'Neill contends that it is particularly problematic in the case of practical reasoning, 'whose aspiration it is to fit the world (to some degree) to certain conceptions or principles' (ibid.). Laclau (2000, 76) holds a broadly similar position on the necessity of abstraction, although his deconstructive reading clearly takes distance from O'Neill's. Two further sets of partially overlapping distinctions may be drawn into the fray here. The first concerns the manner in which one justifies political principles. Here Laden's distinction between a theoretical and political approach to justification is relevant (2001, 16). In the case of the former, what justifies political principles is 'the soundness of the theorists' reasoning', whereas according to the latter, what matters is whether political principles are ultimately endorsed 'in some suitably defined sense' by 'actual people acting politically in actual societies'. The second is Mason's distinction between reasons for accepting and reasons for implementing a political principle; the former is epistemic and depends on the quality of reasons offered, while the latter is a matter of moral justification, and raises issues of legitimacy (Mason 2010, 665).

political world and set out to develop criteria from these propositions. In what follows I explore different aspects of these possibilities and how they relate to deliberative and poststructuralist approaches to democracy respectively. In so doing, I seek to delineate the different aspects of practices of freedom that are made available by these approaches and, further, I seek to develop a set of tools that will allow us to reflect critically on these practices and the possibilities they open up.

The Status and Implications of Criteria in Deliberative Accounts

In drawing upon Habermas, deliberativists tend to rely on procedures to ensure the rationality and legitimacy of decisions. As Habermas (1997, 147) puts it, 'the free processing of information and reasons, of relevant topics and contributions is meant to ground the presumption that results reached in accordance with correct procedures are rational'. As a result, the focus of theorizing is on the conditions under which processes of decision making can be deemed legitimate. In this respect, the stipulation of discourse rules provides seemingly clear guidance. For instance, it allows theorists and practitioners of democracy to argue that a decision will be democratic if and only if:

> No one with the competency to speak and act is excluded from the process.
> Everyone is allowed to question or introduce any assertion they wish, while also expressing their attitudes, desires and needs.
> No one is prevented, by internal or external coercion, from exercising these rights.

These rules make explicit that under conditions of democratic deliberation:

> We must treat each other as equal partners.
> Individuals must be given the space to speak.
> We must listen to each other, and justify our positions to one another.

Moreover, it seems possible to ascertain in practice whether these guidelines are being followed, and thus whether any particular process in fact measures up to the standards of democratic practice specified in the model. For instance, in her book *Reasonable Democracy,*

Chambers fleshes out these conditions by spelling out what is entailed by the conditions of universality, rationality and the requirement of reciprocity respectively. Chambers (1996, 197–98) argues that the *condition of universality* means:

> There should be no barriers excluding certain people or groups from debate.
>
> As many voices as possible should be heard; hence, the requirement of a high level of participation.
>
> Practically, one has to ask whether any groups have been systematically excluded; whether there are organizations and movements through which the public can voice its opinion, and whether there is a high level of interest and involvement on the part of all those affected.[7]

Chambers (1996, 202) further suggests a set of positive and negative specifications to ensure that the *condition of rationality* (being persuaded by the force of the better argument) and non-coercion obtain:

> Agreement must be autonomous.
>
> Overt coercion, bribery and threat of force are excluded.
>
> Hence, the conditions under which deliberation takes place:
> - must exclude both internal and external coercion, and
> - should emphasize the need for critical reflection and evaluation.

Finally, the *requirement of reciprocity* (Chambers 1996, 208–9) means that we must assess how close we come to maintaining respect and impartiality. Asking the following questions may be of help in this respect:

> To what extent do participants approach disputes discursively as opposed to strategically?
>
> Are the indicators of 'sincere acting' by participants – including consistency in speech, consistency in speech and action, and coherence – present?
>
> Are the indicators of respect and impartiality – including acknowledgement of the moral status of opposing views, a cultivation of openness, and starting from the point of view of reaching possible agreement – present?

---

[7] For a critical discussion of the all affected principle, see David Owen (2012).

The ideal of proceduralism aspired to by deliberativists aims to ensure equality between citizens, since it seeks to give 'everyone equal standing to use their practical reason in the give and take of reasons in dialogue'. Such ideal conditions, Bohman (1997, 323) points out, 'form an *independent standard* in light of which we can judge whether the outcome of actual democratic deliberation is legitimate'.[8]

Now, even though the criteria set out within the deliberativist approach seem to be incontrovertible, they have in fact proven to be rather controversial, containing more specificity than (could be) acknowledged by an approach that explicitly aspires to a de-contextualized status. They have also proven to be more difficult to realize in practice than seems to be the case at first glance.[9] Quite apart from the practical, empirical difficulties of realizing this model, it has been criticized, inter alia, for working with an overly rationalistic and disembodied conception of subjectivity, and for ignoring the impact of material inequalities on the ability of participants to partake as equals in dialogue. More recently, and particularly relevant to our case, is the discussion around the use of religious language and the impact of religious world views on such public dialogue. In a world in which there are increasing demands to express aspects of religious identity in public, the limitations placed on such engagement by deliberative models are potentially serious.[10]

While my aim here is not to rehearse these criticisms in any detail, it is worth our while to pause for a moment to consider what light the criteria set out above may throw on the admittedly rather broad set of questions posed at the outset of this chapter. It does seem that these criteria would work rather well in conditions where relevant groups are clearly identifiable and where they share ways of interaction. If the groups are clearly identified and they are not too disparate in outlook,

---

[8] Emphasis added. It should be noted that Bohman is critical of several aspects of this account.

[9] There is now a growing debate on the respective roles of 'ideal' and 'non-ideal' theory in light of the development of principles of justice and democracy. See, for instance, Mason (2010); Simmons (2010); Valentini (2009); Robeyns (2008).

[10] This issue cannot be addressed in full here. While deliberativists have shifted their position somewhat recently, it remains one which subordinates religious discourse to the strictures imposed by deliberative politics. This is particularly evident in the continued demand that one can only learn from one's religious counterparts insofar as they are able to express their demands 'in a generally accessible language' (Habermas 2006, 15; Chambers 2007, 216).

in capacities and in material circumstances, it is quite likely that these criteria will provide us with a clear set of guidelines for equality of participation. However, as noted above, things are rather more difficult in the context of inequality – including both material (Fraser and Honneth 2003) and epistemic (Sanders 1997) – where groups are marginalized (Norval 2010), and where groups do not express their demands in a purified secularist language, not to speak of situations in which those to be represented do not form clearly predefined communities.[11]

However, my aim here is not simply to rehearse these criticisms, but also to think about the status attributed to criteria on this account. In this respect it is important to note that there are (at least) two aspects of the Habermas-inspired account that have the potential to muddy the waters, so to speak. The first concerns the fact that Habermas (1997, 287) sets out to develop a reconstructive sociology of democracy, which chooses its basic concepts in such a way that it can identify 'particles and fragments of an "existing reason" already incorporated in political practice', however distorted these may be. The question remains as to the degree to which such particles of existing reason can be shown to be purely rational and hence decontextual.[12] And second, democratic deliberation involves a *mixture* of different aspects of practical reason – pragmatic, ethical and moral – that, according to Bohman (1996, 206), form 'a complex discursive network which includes argumentation of various sorts, bargaining and compromise, and political communication for the purposes of the free expression of opinions'. Hence, even though the proposed procedures aim for a rational and context-free status, this is rarely achieved, and, as I have argued earlier in this chapter, as much is acknowledged by numerous deliberativists today. Hence, one should think, at the very least, about the sources of these difficulties. Is it merely a question of getting the

[11] Here the poststructuralist literature is particularly relevant in its focus on the formation of subjectivity, rather than the assumption of identity.

[12] For Habermas (1975, 107–08), rational discourse is 'a form of communication that is *removed from contexts of experience* and actions and whose structure assures us: that the bracketed validity claims of assertions, recommendations, or warnings are the exclusive object of discussion; that participants, themes, and contributions are not restricted except with reference to the goal of testing the validity claims in question; that no force except that of the better argument is exercised; and that, as a result, all motives except that of the cooperative search for truth is excluded' (emphasis added).

movement from theory to practice right (an application problem) or is the source of difficulty located at a deeper level, in the very conception of a politics that aims at a very demanding and some would argue rarified form of rational engagement?

Poststructuralism and Criteria

Poststructuralists, on the whole, have tended to shun accounts that attempt to develop idealized norms of conduct, emphasizing that such procedures run the risk of ignoring the presence of power relations in the development of such norms. For instance, Butler (1997, 134) argues in this respect that the conditions of intelligibility of expression 'are themselves formulated in and by power, and this normative exercise of power is rarely acknowledged as an operation of power at all'. Laclau and Mouffe similarly argue in their works that any social objectivity is constituted through acts of power (cf. Laclau 1993). For our purposes, it is important to determine the consequences of this emphasis on the constitutive character of the political, while noting that it also is an ontological claim. Several different possibilities are opened up here. One could argue, following the assertion of the ever-present character of power relations, that any and every norm that is articulated is nothing but a 'cultural' or 'contextual' norm, specific and relevant *only* to the context in which it first emerged and is articulated. In this case, we would end up with a communitarian approach in which norms would have relevance only for the community in which they originated. This clearly entails a denial of the possibility of context-transcendent norms, with all the attendant political problems associated with such a position.[13] On the other hand, one could argue that even if every norm is always already contaminated by particularity, there is also discernable in it a process of universalization – a movement beyond particularity – which frees one from the limits of a pure contextualism. The latter is indeed the strategy followed by poststructuralists such as Laclau and Mouffe in the articulation of their overall theoretical framework. Even more importantly, their understanding of

---

[13] While I do not argue for a conception of criteria and norms that are completely context-independent, I do not think that a conception of norms that completely denies transcendence is either theoretically plausible or politically productive.

the political and of subjectivity and democracy is deeply informed by a set of strong ontological presuppositions, which ultimately facilitates this movement of universalization.[14] This is a feature shared by others, such as Connolly (1995, 1–9), who argues for thinking about politics in terms of ontopolitical interpretation (Howarth 2008). This ontological emphasis, Connolly suggests, questions approaches that privilege epistemology and wrongly assumes access to criteria of knowledge that are ontologically neutral. As he (1995, 5) puts it: 'every interpretation of political events … contains an ontopolitical dimension'.

If we turn to democracy more specifically, poststructuralist accounts tend to have two specific sets of features. Firstly, they are inclined to emphasize the *historicity* of democracy. In this respect, Laclau and Mouffe, following Lefort (1981) repeatedly emphasize the historical horizon (the French Revolution) within which claims and demands for democracy first arose and from which they have been extended. Secondly, there is an emphasis on the place of contingency in their accounts of the political (and by extension of democracy). From this acknowledgement of contingency, further conclusions regarding political and democratic subjectivity are drawn. Laclau (2000, 49) characterizes the consequences of the emphasis on contingency, especially for thinking about subjectivity, in the following manner:

[O]n the side of the 'active subject of history' we find only ultimate contingency. But the problem then arises: *where* and how is that subject constituted? What are the places and logics of its constitution which makes the actions that subject is supposed to perform compatible with the contingent character of this intervention?

In other words, once we are on the terrain of contingency, 'nothing is guaranteed', and everything is at stake: the question of the emergence of subjectivity is opened up and the contours and the boundaries of what can be regarded as 'common space' is put into question.

---

[14] It should be noted here that we are talking of universalization, which for Laclau (1996) is a process and not a given. Zerilli (1998, 4) notes that Laclau's account 'offers both an alternative to the binarisms spawned by the "return" to the universal (for example, false universalism/true universalism) and a trenchant critique of the original binary couple itself (universalism/particularism)'.

One of the distinctive consequences of this emphasis on contingency is that while it specifies a set of ontological guidelines, it is not prescriptive about the 'ontic' features of democratic politics. Instead, it suggests that both the sites of conflict and the character of political subjectivities are contingent. *That* they are contingent is not in question. However, *what form* they will take and *where* they arise depend on the particular articulation given to it, and this in turn depends upon the character of existing and available political discourses and traditions.

With this it is clear that we have already moved quite some distance from the proceduralism of deliberative approaches to democracy, where the issues of the constitution of democratic subjectivity and of a common space of argument do not even arise. In poststructuralist accounts the emphasis is no longer on specifying the rules of democratic deliberation under idealized conditions. While still very much to do with the 'input' side of democracy the focus has shifted to a range of deeply political and contingent processes, including:

The emergence of democratic demands.
The articulation and universalization of demands.
The constitution of subjectivity in these processes.

Once we focus on these processes, the question concerning criteria is posed differently. Theorists such as Connolly, Rancière, Butler, and Laclau and Mouffe are not concerned with the specification of evaluative criteria in isolation from these processes. Hence, if anything, their position(s) regarding criteria could be characterized as *processual* and *pragmatic*. (I return to this assessment shortly.) The criteria for thinking critically about democracy that may be gleaned from their work are often left *implicit* in their accounts, and may have to be formulated explicitly by those interested in drawing them out. However, if this strategy is followed, one has to be clear about what one is doing in so formulating implicit norms explicitly. Before going into this important question in more detail, I will briefly look at some of the features of their treatment of democracy, which lend themselves to such formulation. Let us first turn to Rancière's account of democracy as the eruption of egalitarian claims, before outlining Laclau and Mouffe's joint and respective accounts of democratic subjectivity.

The Emergence of Claims: Rancière

Deliberativists, I have argued, focus on the structure and requirements of argumentation within deliberative settings. Hence, they assume the existence of a common space in which arguments can be made and heard. Rancière, on the other hand, is interested in what is required for such shared spaces – in which all reasons and demands may be heard – to be instituted or to appear in the first place.[15] Thus, it is crucial to note that we cannot assume that such spaces are already in existence (Norval 2007). Moreover, we cannot assume that they can be 'created' from within the existing order. For Rancière, the existing order (what he calls the order of the police) needs to be challenged, and in the process, a new space of commonality needs to be constituted between those already 'counted' and those 'who do not count', who are excluded. As a consequence, democracy – which for Rancière (1999, 57) always takes the form of *disagreement* – concerns a *dispute* over the object of the discussion, over the capacity of those who are making an object of it, and the world in which it features as an object. What is at stake here is precisely the possibility of the emergence and constitution of a space as a shared space. The making visible of what was previously unseen – a wrong – is the polemical moment of democracy. Thus, democracy is *not* characterized as a regime/way of life or a set of rules and procedures. Rather, it is an *interruptive* moment, in which new subjects and new spaces of commonality come into existence.

Returning to our earlier example, namely the case of the demand by a school girl to wear a jilbab to lessons in a school whose dress policy was decided in consultation with the relevant community. Bracketing for a moment the difficulties faced by Habermas on the incorporation of religious demands, seen from a perspective that specifies context-independent norms, the ensuing dispute is simply a matter of whether particular rights – the right to education and to manifest religious beliefs – are applicable in a particular case. However, it is possible to regard this dispute not as simply about the application of a right, but as a demand that exposes a wrong. Her demand disrupted accepted practice, even in predominantly Muslim UK schools, and exposed a

---

[15] I discuss different aspects of Rancière's work in greater detail elsewhere. See, Norval (2012, 2009).

wrong, that of alleged discrimination against Muslims women, especially felt after 9/11. Drawing on Rancière thus sensitizes us to the fact – and we can read these as criterial statements – that:

> We cannot assume that all is already in place (in our liberal societies).
>
> We need to be alert to the fact and continued possibility of exclusion, which is necessarily present in political society and is not visible from within the existing order.
>
> We need to be aware of the fact that spaces of engagement emerge only as a result of a process of contestation.
>
> Hence, we cannot in advance list subjectivities in need of inclusion.
>
> As a result, we need to be attentive to the emergence of 'inchoate', inarticulate claims.

Whilst this account clearly produces new insights and alerts us to features of political life to which no attention is given in deliberative accounts of democracy, it is notable that these criteria tend to be critical rather than positive. This is also a feature of Laclau's account of radical democracy, which foregrounds the articulation of demands. This account, to which I now turn, together with Mouffe's theorization of agonistic democracy, furnishes us with further criteria with which to think critically about our democratic practices.

Laclau and Mouffe: A Hegemonic Approach to Radical Democracy

The approach developed in the work of Laclau and Mouffe concentrates on the process of articulation of (democratic) political claims. In particular, they concentrate on:

> The mechanisms through which claims are made.
>
> The ways in which claims may be universalized.
>
> The forging of political subjectivity in the process.

Before looking at these aspects of their work, there are two more general points regarding their approach that I would like to make. Like Rancière, Laclau and Mouffe acknowledge the *ineliminability of power* and conflict in politics; it is not something that could be overcome, nor should we aim to do so. For them, the image of a society devoid of struggle and antagonism is precisely that of a nondemocratic order in which we are concerned with the 'administration of things', in which everything is already decided. Given this, neither political *identities* nor the *interests* that agents may hold are objectively given. They are, instead, the result of political and historical processes which have become sedimented over time, and sometimes very deeply so. Hence, politics involves acts of power and the constitution of antagonisms by actors engaged in hegemonic struggles who seek to construct political frontiers between 'insiders' and 'outsiders' through the definition of a 'core opposition' between 'friend' and 'enemy' (Howarth 2000). The achievement of *hegemony* is to be distinguished from domination; it concerns the production of 'common sense' in a particular site or sphere of the social, or indeed in society as a whole. This involves the winning of intellectual and moral leadership in society, and not just the achievement of political power. Such common sense determines what is normal and acceptable in any given terrain.

Within this general approach, Laclau (2005) argues that the minimal unit of social analysis is the category of *demand*. Demands tend to start as requests, addressed to institutions of power, and when those requests are ignored/not responded to, they are turned into claims, which may be addressed first, *to* and then *against* institutions. This process of the articulation of claims involves the constitution of the identities both of the *claimants* and of the *addressee* of the claim. The identities of neither are given in advance of the articulation of a claim. *Democratic* subjectivity, Laclau argues, emerges as a result of an articulation of *equivalences* between demands. From this it is clear that democracy is not concerned with procedures but is conceived in processual terms, the content of which cannot be specified apart from their context of articulation. This work alerts us to the fact that:

Demands, interests and identities are articulated in and through political struggle.

Attention should be given to the process of *transformation* of identities and interests, and the constitutive role of *antagonism* and conflict in politics.

The formation of any and every political site will, inevitably, involve inclusions and exclusions.

Radical democracy takes these conflicts to be part and parcel, indeed the very essence, of democracy. It is not something to be regretted, rejected or overcome. Rather, it is the very stuff of democratic contestation. In terms of our earlier example, one would have to investigate the terms in which the demand was expressed (including the claim that it was in fact religious discrimination and that it was linked to post-9/11 circumstances); the way in this particular expression allowed for the formation of alliances between different groups (inclusions) and the manner in which these alliances in turn depended on the drawing of political frontiers (exclusions).

Mouffe's Agonistic Account of Democracy

In addition to these reflections on radical democracy (and with it the role of the articulation of demands in the formation of political interests, identities and alliances), Mouffe's work sets out to develop an account of the requirements of democratic subjectivity, and this is done under the heading of agonistic democracy.[16] Mouffe develops an account of democratic relations as *adversarial* in character, which is to be distinguished from antagonistic relations. Antagonisms, Mouffe (2005, 20–21) argues, do not necessarily have to take the form of the division between 'us' and 'them' or distinctions between 'friends' and 'enemies', where the existence of the 'other' threatens the identity of the 'we'. Mouffe suggests that we can envisage agonistic relations as relations where adversaries recognize the legitimacy of their opponents. She puts it thus:

They are adversaries, not enemies. This means that, while in conflict, they see themselves as belonging to the same political association, as sharing a common symbolic space within which the conflict takes place. We could say that the task of democracy is to transform antagonism into agonism (ibid.).

This provides us with clear criteria for democratic engagement, namely, acknowledgement of one's opponent as legitimate, as sharing

---

[16] The term agonism characterizes the thinking of a set of authors who draw on Nietszche and Foucault for inspiration. Even though Mouffe does not draw on either, she situates her work within that terrain. For an account that situates Mouffe's work in relation to that of William Connoly and Ernesto Laclau respectively, see Howarth (2008).

the common space of democratic engagement and contestation.[17] Hence,

> Agonistic democracy requires of us a recognition of difference as ontological; and
>
> Respect for one's political 'enemy'/adversary.
>
> Respect for the rules of political engagement.
>
> Acknowledgement that these rules are inherently political and hence open to (re)contestation.
>
> As a result, a continued emphasis on the role of passion and identification in the fostering of democratic subjectivities.

These insights, coupled with the emphasis on the power relations as ever present and identities as contingent, offers an account of democracy as one in which disagreement, conflict and diversity play a constitutive role. Democratic outcomes will always be deeply political in character, characterized by passionate identifications as well as a respect for difference. My political enemy is an adversary, one who shares in valuing participation in a common democratic space, while acknowledging that the democratic process is always, in principle and in practice, conflictual. Hence, even when agreements are reached, they are always open to later contestation and renegotiation.

Poststructuralism and the Status of Criteria

There is one last version of a democratic grammar, to which I now turn, that has much in common with an agonistic model but which nevertheless adds depth to this account of democratic subjectivity, without falling into the idealizations of deliberative theory.[18] However, before looking at it more closely, it is necessary to reflect for a moment on the formulation of these criteria. It is abundantly clear that poststructuralist theorists tend to refrain from explicitly formulating criteria for the assessment or evaluation of democracy. This is not unimportant. Why, given the clear *critical* import of their respective accounts of democracy, is it the case? Others continually use their works to assess and

---

[17] Some commentators have argued that, in this respect, Mouffe's work is quite close to that of liberals and deliberativists.

[18] In a recent article, Fossen (2008) calls this 'perfectionist agonism'.

critically evaluate democratic practice, and these authors themselves engage in such critical evaluations. As I suggested at the outset of my discussion of poststructuralist approaches to democracy, it is my contention that this reluctance stems, at least in part, from the rejection of what is often called 'normative' approaches to democracy. In rejecting the idealizations of deliberative democracy, poststructuralists have, so to speak, risked throwing the baby out with the bathwater, as if any substantive specification of criteria would, of necessity, lead into normative idealizations. A further reason for the apparent refusal to articulate explicit criteria stems from, I would suggest, the particular form of theorizing in which poststructuralists engage (and these two reasons are of course not separable). This form of theorizing is critical in character; it tends to be deconstructive, rather than constructive. It focuses on the shortcomings and limitations of other approaches and is suggestive of alternatives but refrains from specifying them in any but the most abstract form. Hence, it tends to remain at an ontological level, where criteria of necessity have to remain empty. However, as I will argue below, these reservations need not prevent one from engaging in the elucidation of criteria, which by their very nature, play a critical role.

Aversive Democracy

The picture of aversive democracy on which I draw here is non-teleological and perfectionist, characteristics that are at the very least compatible with agonistic accounts of democracy (Norval 2007; Fossen 2008). With this picture, what is important is our ability to criticize – so as to animate – our institutions, and the imagination to change and challenge them, as crucial to the maintenance of our democratic institutions. Hence, democracy is not a matter of reaching agreement, as it is for deliberative theorists. Rather, as in the case of agonistic approaches, the emphasis is on disagreement, on 'separateness of positions', as Cavell (1990, 24–25) puts it, and on ongoing conversations and differences of position. Cavell suggests that this task of keeping our political institutions alert and alive to change and challenge is dependent on individuals having an ethic, a striving to better themselves, and so society, by overcoming habit. Such oppositional, critical thinking consists in the ability to withstand *conformism* and to respond to the inevitable failures of democracy without falling back onto cynicism (Cavell 1990,

36; Norval 2011). Following Emerson and Nietzsche, Cavell characterizes conformism in a political context as entailing a forgetting of the
need to define oneself: 'the conformist, by failing to estrange himself
from prevailing opinion (as well as from himself), lets the community
speak for him, yet without interrogating its right to do so' (Hammer
2002, 112). Hence, the picture of democracy offered by Cavell suggests
both a particular view of the individual and her relation to society, and
a particular view of democracy and its failures.

Following Emerson, Cavell draws a picture of the self that is essentially divided between a current self and a next or future self,[19] informed
by the desire for that which exceeds our current state (of self and of
society). This understanding of the self and of society as somehow
falling short of its promises deeply informs Cavell's understanding of
democracy. In this emphasis on the disappointments of democracy,
Cavell (1990, 56) is one of the few theorists who argues that it is inevitable that we will be disappointed in democracy, 'in its failures by the
light of its own principles of justice'. In this, Cavell departs from much
current writing on democracy, which tends to treat it in an unequivo-
cally triumphalist manner as an unproblematic panacea for all ills in
contemporary society. Instead, his picture of democracy emphasizes
and takes account of the multiplicity of ways in which democracy may
fail to achieve what it promises.

This has important consequences for democratic subjectivity. The
consent we give to society, on this reading, is one that recognizes and
emphasizes the existing inequities in society and our consent to them.
Mulhall (1994, 58) captures precisely what is at stake here:

Thinking of the polis as mine ensures that I am *implicated* in whatever the
polis is and does: for even if its structures and pronouncements do not embody
what I am prepared to recognize as my (political) will, my membership entails
that they are made in my name and so are one for which I am answerable.

From this it is clear that Cavell's account does not rest on a picture of
the individual self as isolated. This self – in contrast with the liberal
conception of an autonomous, self-contained self – is always already

---

[19] This search for a next self is emphatically not teleological. In this Cavell differs
sharply from theorists such as Rawls, who treat perfectionism as teleological
doctrine. There is no singular vision of what the good is that is strived for, nor
any question of imposing one's own conception of the good onto others.

divided, riven and dependent upon other human beings, since the self cannot fulfil itself without regard for others. As a result, the working out of any identity can occur only in the context of the self's relations to others.

This becomes even clearer in the account Cavell provides of community. For Cavell, as for Laclau, community is founded or *invoked* in the claims we make. Politics is the arena in which we define ourselves politically, and, this is a relational process. The political community is not given, but is *disclosive*: 'for whom you speak and by whom you are spoken for' is disclosed in the act of making and staking claims. This has important political consequences. It means that in making claims one risks rebuff 'of those for whom you claimed to be speaking,' as well as having to rebuff 'those who claimed to speak for you' (Cavell 1982, 27). Hence, to dissent is also to exercise one's political voice. Dissent seeks to investigate the extent to which my voice is in fact speaking for others, and whether others speak for me. This proposed picture of democratic claim making suggests to us that we give particular attention to the following aspects:

Political community:

Political community is disclosive.

Making a claim is an act that invokes and contests a sense of community.

It implies relations of equality.

It characterizes the place of assent and dissent as internal to the constitution of a democratic community.

It draws attention to the responsibilities we bear for the claims we make and for the claims made in our name.

The conception of the self that informs Cavell's account of democracy draws attention to and gives a clear account of the place of the individual within the community. His approach draws out and develops intuitions about the importance of not reducing our understanding of community to what we share in our exclusion of or opposition to others. In so doing, Cavell provides us with a deeper and nuanced account of what democratic subjectivity – both individually and communally – might entail.

In addition to his emphasis on the difficulties associated with the actual process of the emergence of new claims, this account of

democratic subjectivity highlights a further important aspect of democratic identification, namely, the sort of *responses* one may expect
within societies with a democratic ethos. This is particularly evident
in Cavell's treatment of the sense of injustice experienced by Nora in
The Doll's House (Cavell 1990, 108–15). His discussion highlights
the deprivation of voice Nora suffers and the difficulties she faces in
expressing her inchoate sense of injustice. His analysis makes visible
the fact that these difficulties arise from 'the work of moral consensus
itself' (1990, xxxvii). It is worth reflecting further on this reading, for
it draws out some of the complexity inherent in the making of claims
and the difficulty of expressing senses of injustice that do not fit the
parameters of current moral and political discourse. Cavell provides
useful insights to some of these issues as they arise in a contemporary
European context. It is not uncommon today for us to have a sense
that there are indeed claims of injustice addressed to our democracies that is difficult to express in terms of the available and prevailing
discourses. Think, for instance, here of the case mentioned earlier, of a
young UK Muslim woman's demand to wear a jilbab to school. What
does one make of such an experience in a context governed by a democratic grammar? What are its distinctive features and does Cavell's
understanding of democracy as aversive help us in capturing some
of them?

Let us start with the student's demand. Initially her demand was
met publicly with some incredulity if not incomprehension, given the
fact that she attended a school where there was consultation with the
community on the appropriate forms of dress for female Muslim students. In this sense she initially embodied a claim exceeding existing
discourse, one that acts as a call to open ourselves up to other, foreign
possibilities. There were no readily available responses to her and her
demands called for a response, a re-examination and re-iteration of the
dominant position, hence provoking an engagement with her claims.

The second important feature of this episode consists in the remarkable process of appeal and counter-appeal, showing the contestability
of norms and the process of argumentation and counter-argumentation
through which it is instituted. It also makes visible the contingency of
the rules and norms on which society temporarily settles. There is even
here another court of appeal, that of the European Court of Human
Rights. However, even this should not be seen as a final instance, as an
instance that can settle matters in principle and for all time. It is simply

the character of politics that even decisions by our highest courts may be and should be open to revision over time (Tully 2008b, 110).

Also notable in this respect, apart from the contestability of the norm, is the process itself. This constitutes its third important feature. A demand that initially seemed to be incomprehensible became intelligible as a result of a whole series of articulations and contestations, through which it entered into and challenged the given terms of the debate. Hence, even though the substance of the claim was later rejected by the Law Lords, it was not enough to assert that Begum simply had to accept 'the way we do things here'. As Lord Justice Brooked pointed out, the school in effect told her 'Go away, and do not come back unless you are wearing proper school uniform' (Halpin 2005), and this was not acceptable. He further argued that while the school had a right to set a uniform policy 'nobody considered that Miss Begum also had a right recognised by English law. The onus was on the school to justify any interference with that right.' He further called upon the Department for Education and Skills to issue guidance to schools so as to ensure their compliance with their obligations under the Human Rights Act. Even if she did not win the case, there is a sense in which the feeling of wrong experienced by her had been acknowledged. Society (and its representative institutions) had to respond to her demand, and had to articulate and re-articulate in explicit terms its norms as they are currently understood. At the same time, she gained a form of recognition by claiming public space in which to represent her demands on her own terms.

The fourth feature is to be found in the debate, self-examination and critical scrutiny to which different communities, institutions and policies were subjected (and subjected themselves) during this process. These included the fostering of democratic subjectivity through giving space to new voices and demands, a provocation to open and democratic debate – about issues, processes and institutions. In this sense, events such as these have the potential to initiate a process of questioning if not dislocating of a (former) self, and the need to work towards a further self. This could take many different forms, including work on history and one's account of one's own place in it, work on society and the forging of open and democratic institutions. Work on the self could, in turn, affect and inspire a different relation to others.

Events such as these opened up areas of contestation – they are practices of freedom – around the character of nationhood, national

identity, history, and justice, which may have been deeply sedimented
and resistant to interrogation. These events, through their capacity to
unsettle, also potentially open up a different, more democratic future.
And in participating in these debates, we come to take and acknowledge responsibility for our societal arrangements. This is one of the
processes through which we come to recognize 'society and its government' to be constituted as ours, as Cavell puts it. In other words, I am
not only answerable to it, but for it. Hence, an aversive conception of
democracy demands:

> Sensitivity to the expression of inchoate demands.
>
> Sensitivity to the diversity of languages that may be mobilized to express
> such demands.
>
> Responsiveness and engagement with demands.
>
> Openness to appeal and counter-appeal.
>
> Critical self-scrutiny and scrutiny of democratic procedures, processes
> and institutions.

Criteria: A Wittgensteinian Approach

'My word is my bond.'

In conclusion, I would like to return to the question of the status and
character of criteria in the different approaches explored. As should be
clear by now, the aim of this exercise, although theoretical in character,
is not to produce an account of democratic discourse that is abstracted
from the 'stream of life'. There is no presupposition here that the criteria informing our democratic life could or should be abstracted from
ordinary contexts, and from the interests and passions that inspire
engagement in democratic politics in the first instance. Those calling
for some grounding of our practices that exceeds the ordinary seeks
'to relieve us of our responsibility for our own words, for making
ourselves intelligible' (Hammer 2002, 38). This demand entails a repudiation of our criteria and a denial of the fact that in describing the
ordinary – 'what we say and imply on specific occasions' – we draw
attention to its normativity (ibid.).

It is necessary to unpack these suggestions somewhat further. In
speaking about normativity, following Cavell, I simply refer to 'our
capacity to make ourselves intelligible by projecting words into new
contexts and remain ready to declare and respect the implications of

our doing so' (Hammer 2002, 38). Whilst this may seem to affirm a purely contextual account, it is in fact rather more demanding, for it seeks to elucidate the implications of our projections of words and the fact that we commit ourselves to particular courses of action in and through such projects. My word is my bond. In dealing with democracy, this implies that certain ways of doing things imply commitments of a specific kind, which we must either defend or defend our departure from the norms implied therein. And things are never settled in a law-like fashion – they are always open to disagreement and (re) contestation.

The question remains, however, as to how, on this account, we should understand criteria? For Wittgenstein, on whom I am drawing here, criteria are closely akin to our ordinary use of the term: 'Criteria specify and thus define what it means for a thing to have (or to count as having) a given status.'[20] However, there are differences of interpretation on this point between commentators on Wittgenstein and my suggestion would be that these differences echo the differences between deliberativists and poststructuralists outlined above. Hammer (2002, 32) summarizes the issues at stake by contrasting the positions taken by two commentators on Wittgenstein, Stephen Mulhall and Stanley Cavell respectively. He argues:

For Mulhall, criteria must be structurally in place for us to be able to make judgments. Without such a framework, we would lack the grounds of mutual intelligibility in language. But for Cavell, criteria are simply functions of the judgments we (normal speakers) are prepared to make; there is no level existing independently of our actual or potential judgments by reference to which criteria regulate or justify the intelligibility of those judgments.

In other words, the *point* of criteria differs markedly for each commentator. For Mulhall, criteria provide 'standards governing the application of concepts'. For Cavell, it is 'to respond to a crisis in our

---

[20] It should be noted that whilst criteria 'allow one to determine whether an object is of a specific kind', they tell us nothing of the degree to which that object satisfies criteria (Hammer 2002, 33). By spelling out criteria we get to know what any object is. As Cavell puts it, criteria give 'a sense of how things fall under our concepts, of how we individuate things and name, settle on nameables, of why we call things as we do, as questions of how we determine what counts as instances of our concepts.... To speak is to say what counts' (Cavell, quoted in Hammer 2002, 34).

agreement'. Hence, for Cavell the need for criteria arises only under unusual, specific circumstances. We are not commonly and continuously aware of our understanding of the criteria for the use of certain concepts. It is only when some perplexity arises that we reflect upon criteria. The point of *eliciting* criteria is to *reorient* ourselves 'when we are lost with respect to our words and to the world they anticipate' (Cavell 1982, 34). As in Heidegger (1962, 105), for whom the character of equipment is revealed when it no longer functions as we expect – when the tools we use are broken, we become aware of the functions they fulfil – so for Cavell, we elicit criteria in moments of crisis, dislocation or perplexity.

This corresponds in an important sense to what occurs when we engage in practices of freedom. When a practice or norm is challenged, or questioned for some reason, we are called upon to recount the criteria, to reconsider the point of the practices in which we engage, which we value and defend or criticize. If we think about democracy in these terms, democracy could be argued to involve a process of recounting what we are prepared to say, what we are committed to, when claiming to be democrats. Yet it is crucial to note that our criteria are deeply vulnerable: 'since sharing an order of criteria depends on our agreement on an order of judgments (our attunement), they allow or even invite repudiation' (Hammer 2002, 19). They are not abstract norms that are set up over and above our democratic practices, but are embedded in the community, which is constituted only in and through the eliciting of claims.

4 Designing Democratic Institutions for Decentred Governance: The Council of Europe's Acquis

VIVIEN LOWNDES AND LAWRENCE PRATCHETT

Introduction

In the context of decentred governance, institutional design is a challenge. Chapter 1 characterises decentred governance as involving many different actors, operating across traditional boundaries of state and civil society, who act upon the meanings they ascribe to particular problems (and proposed solutions). Processes of governance are thus more varied (stretching beyond conventional institutions), actors more diverse, and outcomes more contingent and indeed conflicted. Such complexity does not, however, mean that what Gerry Stoker (2010) calls 'design thinking' is no longer relevant. The attempt to design democratic institutions just gets harder and calls for more sophistication.

Institutional design can be conceived in broad terms as the opportunity to shape practice and meaning over time, rather than in the narrow sense of creating formal rules and constitutions. If, as Norval (2007) claims, democracy is about intervening in the world to make things better (in an inevitably unfinished project), the opportunity to embed the traditions or logics (Bevir and Rhodes 2003; Glynos and Howarth 2007) that shape practice is fundamental – as is contestation over the character of such frames. Institutional design is an attempt to get certain meanings to 'stick'. It is a meta-activity that involves intervening to shape the scope of future interventions. While radical democrats will expect any framing to be contingent, with novel and contentious meanings and practices inevitably 'bubbling up', they underestimate the significance of institutional design at their peril.

In this chapter, we look at prospects for this kind of institutional design within decentred governance, focusing on the *acquis* of the Council of Europe. The concept of 'multi-level governance' is most commonly used to analyse the relationship between different players in Europe's decentred polity. Although seeming to refer only to 'vertical' levels of government, the concept has developed to include 'horizontal' interactions with non-governmental actors and to characterise the quality of relationships as well their structural arrangement. As Peters and Pierre (2001) explain, the goal is to understand 'negotiated, non-hierarchical exchanges' between diverse actors and institutions at the transnational, national, regional and local levels. Jordan (2001) uses the concept of multi-level governance to 'envisage a much more open and chaotic pattern of events' in which 'authority and power are gradually dispersing across multiple levels of governance rather [than] being retained in, and monopolised by, states'.

Research on multi-level governance has tended to focus on the role of the European Union, but in this chapter we analyse the role of another trans-European political organisation, the Council of Europe, in shaping the design of democratic institutions across the continent. As both the esteemed forebear and ugly sister of the European Union, the Council of Europe has spent sixty years seeking to frame the understanding and development of democratic practice among both the established democracies in Western Europe and, more recently, the emerging ones of Central and Eastern Europe. In many respects it is the primary European body in relation to democracy and human rights, and it provides a valuable focus for exploring the scope for intergovernmental organisations to construct shared democratic values and norms, and the mechanisms that might be applied in the pursuit of institutionalising democracy.

The ways in which inter-governmental organisations (IGOs) shape practice and encourage or even coerce their members to comply with instruments has been the subject of much academic interest (Joachim et al. 2008). Conventional accounts distinguish between rationalist and constructivist accounts of how and why members conform to international norms and practices. Rationalist approaches focus on aspects of enforcement and emphasise the capacity of IGOs to monitor member states' activities and impose sanctions for non-compliance with particular instruments (Checkel 2001). Constructivist approaches, by contrast, focus on the building of capacity among countries and emphasise the ability of IGOs to change the political preferences of countries to be more in line with international standards (Finnemore and Sikkink 1998).

The problem with existing approaches, however, is their focus on specific instruments and the extent to which they are adopted or circumvented by member states. In this chapter we offer an alternative way of understanding this relationship. Our approach is to focus on the ways in which IGOs (in our case, the Council of Europe) frame broad themes and design institutions. Rather than studying specific legal instruments or activities and the ways in which they are transposed or adopted, we focus on the wider *acquis* of the Council of Europe in relation to democracy. In this way we are able to develop the concept of institutional design and to explore both the opportunities and limitations which confront the Council of Europe in seeking to frame the democratic debate across the continent and to promote particular democratic meanings and practices.

Our argument is that the Council of Europe, since its inception in 1949, has always been concerned with framing the democratic debate in Europe and in shaping the democratic institutions of its member states. It has not sought to undertake this task through one specific mechanism, but rather seeks to continuously design democratic institutions through its ever-expanding *acquis*, that is, the collective body of treaties, policies and practices which it promulgates among members. The problem it faces in this design process is one of achieving clarity and convergence around democratic institutions while, at the same time, being flexible enough to allow for the variety of extant institutions to be found across its forty-seven member states. In this chapter we develop both a conceptual framework of how an *acquis* such as the Council of Europe's might be treated as an instrument of institutional design and an empirical analysis of its strengths and limitations in this context.

The first section of the chapter elaborates the democratic mandate of the Council of Europe and the way in which it seeks to frame democratic practice across the continent. The second section critically examines the character of democratic institutions in the context of European governance. The third and fourth sections explore the process of democratic institutional development and set out criteria for good institutional design in the context of decentred governance. Next, an empirical section assesses the council's *acquis* as an instrument of 'indirect design' (Goodin 1996) by presenting evidence on the way in which the council has sought to frame and influence the development of democratic institutions. The chapter draws here on a detailed analysis of the council's work over the last sixty years (Pratchett and Lowndes 2004). Finally, a concluding section focuses on limitations of the council's approach to shaping institutional design and reflects upon the factors that might influence future design prospects.

Designing Democracy: The Role of the Council of Europe

Debates on multi-level governance tend to focus on the European Union, to the relative exclusion of other trans-European or transnational bodies (Knodt 2004). There can be little doubt that the European Union is the primary economic and political force at a trans-European level, not only for its twenty-seven member states but also for those on its periphery or who are seeking future membership; but it is not the only important force, especially in relation to the evolution of democratic institutions and practices. To study the development of democratic governance in Europe, it is necessary to look beyond the institutions of the EU to other transnational bodies. In focusing on the Council of Europe and its attempts to shape the design of institutions for democratic governance across the forty-seven nation states that inhabit the European continent, this chapter focuses attention on an often overlooked but nonetheless important actor in the world of multi-level governance.

Despite having limited economic influence and being far less well known than the European Union, the Council of Europe has produced some important institutions that are of central importance to Europe. The European Charter on Human Rights and the European Court of Human Rights are probably its best known and most influential products, but the council also provides a forum for the development of a range of policy issues which are beyond the scope of the EU. However, it differs from the EU in at least two important ways.

First, its historical development is significantly different. While the EU has its roots in the economic goals of the European Coal and Steel Community (Warleigh 2002), the Council of Europe's roots are based more in a desire to create European unity by reference to the 'spiritual and moral values which are the common heritage of their peoples and the true source of individual freedom, political liberty and the rule of law, principles which form the basis of all genuine democracy' (Council of Europe 1949). Whereas the EU has arrived at its wider social and political roles as a consequence of its economic ambitions, the Council of Europe's point of departure was always the support and development of democracy among its member states. However, in the terms introduced in Chapter 1, the council's appeal to such fundamental principles is an act of power in itself, an attempt to foreclose an open and contingent discursive field.

Second, the territorial scope of the council has always been much wider than the member states of the EU. Countries such as Norway and Switzerland (as well as the UK up until 1973), which were not prepared to submit to the economic convergence of the EU and its predecessor institutions, have been longstanding members of the council. Moreover, virtually every Central and Eastern European (CEE) country has acceded to the Council of Europe since 1989,[1] making it the only forum where pan-European issues are debated from the basis of a shared political interest. For many of these newer democracies, Council of Europe membership is seen as a first step to wider acceptance by the EU, not least because in acceding to the council these countries must affirm their democratic credentials and submit themselves to ongoing monitoring of their democratic institutions. As Bevir and Rhodes (2003) might put it, actors from such countries are presented with a 'dilemma' in which they are challenged to modify their own political 'traditions', that is, their inherited meanings and practices.

The combination of these two differences makes the study of the Council of Europe particularly important when trying to understand the development of democracy in an era of decentred governance. While the EU, through its structural policy and other economic interventions, may have provided a catalyst for the evolution of new governance structures in Europe, it is the council which has focused particularly upon democratic institutions and their development. Its attention is as much on democratising new forms of governance as it is upon developing conventional democratic institutions. We draw a distinction, therefore, between governance arrangements which are primarily managerialist in their intention and democratic institutions which are seeking to promote and develop democratic values such as political equality and popular control in particular governance jurisdictions (Skelcher 2005). Furthermore, its wider territorial scope means that the council has had to be much more sensitive to the different contexts in which democracy is developing beyond the relatively homogenous polities of Western Europe. The importance of this wide territorial scope and heterogeneity should not be downplayed. The democratic problems facing different countries vary significantly and not all measures will have the same effect in every context. The wide

---

[1] Only Belarus has been prevented from joining the Council of Europe so far and is now a candidate country, having addressed some of its political problems.

range of countries constituting the Council of Europe encompasses significant institutional variety. Its *acquis* must contain, therefore, endless scope for flexibility and variation while, at the same time, establishing a direction of travel and convergence around core democratic institutions.

To understand the way in which the council seeks to design democratic institutions it is first necessary to elaborate its specific organisational structure. The council operates through three primary pillars: the Committee of Ministers, the Parliamentary Assembly, and the Congress of Local and Regional Authorities of the Council of Europe (CLRAE). The Committee of Ministers is the decision-making body of the Council of Europe and is comprised of the foreign ministers or their permanent representatives of all forty-seven member states. All legal instruments (Treaties and Charters) must be approved by the Committee before they are passed to member states. The Assembly is the deliberative body of the organisation, with 318 members and 318 substitutes appointed by national parliaments. It debates issues of concern to its members and makes Recommendations to the Committee of Ministers on specific instruments, as well as drawing up its own Resolutions, Opinions and Orders. The Congress represents local and regional authorities and is a consultative body of the Council of Europe. It undertakes the monitoring of democratic practices among member states and can also make recommendations. It is the published output of these three pillars which effectively constitutes the *acquis* of the council.

Governance and Democratic Institutions: Clarifying Concepts

To examine further the role of transnational bodies in the democratic design process we need to operationalise key concepts. Our starting point is to distinguish governance from democracy, a distinction which remains implicit in many accounts of governance. This distinction is important because, while the Council of Europe's *acquis* has a lot to say about democracy, it is largely unconcerned with issues of governance except where they have an impact upon democratic institutions. Next, we clarify what we understand as democratic institutions, which include not only the formal institutions of *democratic government* but also other institutions that underpin democracy in its broader, decentred sense, contributing to *democratic governance*. On the basis of this understanding we can specify the characteristics of good institutional design, providing a framework within which to elaborate and assess the contribution of the Council of Europe.

In a widely cited piece on multi-level governance, Hooghe and Marks (2003) distinguish between Type I and Type II modes of governance. Type I governance arrangements describe a formal hierarchy of multi-purpose governing arrangements in which 'every citizen is located in a Russian Doll set of nested jurisdictions, where there is one and only one relevant jurisdiction at any particular territorial scale' (Hooghe and Marks 2003). In effect, they are describing conventional, formal structures of public administration, matched by traditional forms of democratic politics. By contrast, Type II governance describes arrangements where 'the number of jurisdictions is potentially vast rather than limited, in which jurisdictions are not aligned on just a few levels but operate at numerous territorial scales, in which jurisdictions are task-specific rather than general purpose, and where jurisdictions are intended to be flexible rather than durable' (Hooghe and Marks 2003).

The obvious problem in relation to these two governance arrangements is that while Type I governance has well-established democratic institutions (albeit arguably ineffective at times), Type II governance poses real problems for conventional understandings of democracy (Sørensen and Torfing 2003). As Skelcher (2005, 97) argues, Type II bodies are often characterised by 'weak democratic anchorage ... because the policy implementation structure is designed on the principle of "governance by technocrats" who in practice act out of the interests of their own organizations' rather than the wider public interest. As Skelcher goes on to recognise, while Type II governance may enable effective and flexible structures for determining or implementing policy, these structures often lack the 'relational integrity' of consent, accountability and legitimacy that would make their jurisdiction democratic (2005, 96).

A distinction between governance and democracy, therefore, is an important first step to understanding the development of democratic institutions across Europe, especially given that Type I and Type II arrangements coexist in most countries. From our perspective, governance arrangements refer to the institutions that support policy development and implementation, irrespective of whether they satisfy any given *democratic* criteria. We understand governance in Finer's sense as 'a condition of ordered rule' (Finer 1970), which is institutionalised in diverse ways over time and space (Lowndes 2001). It is possible, therefore, to have effective governance arrangements that are remote from democracy. Indeed, as Skelcher argues, one of the big advantages of some Type II arrangements is that they exist within an 'entrepreneurial paradigm' that enables them to achieve policy goals unconstrained by the due process of democracy (Skelcher 2005, 100).

Democratic institutions exist in a constitutional paradigm and embed in the policy process different values and meanings, such as political equality and popular control (Beetham 1996). Democracy, however, is not a theoretical construct of different principles or even a specific combination of institutions. Rather, it is a dynamic complex of institutions and practices, which change over time. As the Introduction establishes, democracy is not 'reducible to', nor only occurring in, 'the sites associated with traditional representative democratic institutions'. Democratic institutions are distinct from governance arrangements but are also influenced by the particular traditions within the policy in which they exist. Among Type I arrangements may be a focus on issues such as the rules surrounding elections (ranging from electoral law through to the informal but well established canvassing practices of political parties) or the way in which representation works (including the formal role of Parliament and the informal norms and expectations of what an elected representative should do). Democratic institutions in the Type II domain may be more focused on the significance of participation, stakeholders and so on and the way in which their interests are incorporated into decision making, or upon the way in which accountability and transparency can work in an environment that is primarily technocratic in its paradigm. Essentially, democracy is constituted through practice, although more or less institutionalised forms of rule will develop over time.

The emphasis given to different modes of governance, therefore, can have significant implications for the democratic challenges and opportunities faced by countries. In some respects it relates to Scharpf's distinction between input- and output-oriented legitimacy (Scharpf 1997). While Western democracies have become increasingly concerned with the output-oriented legitimacy of network governance arrangements (attempts to re-engage citizens in political life notwithstanding) the newer democracies of Central and Eastern Europe are often still concerned with delivering the input-oriented legitimacy associated with traditional democratic institutions. In examining the Council of Europe's role in the design of democratic institutions, therefore, we are interested both in how traditional institutions are enduring and how new democratic institutions are emerging.

The Process of Institutional Design: Shaping Constraints and Opportunities

We use the term *institution* to refer to the 'rules of the game' within which democracy is played out (following Ostrom 1986; Goodin 1996). Some of these rules are formal, such as constitutions, directives and organisational structures; others are informal norms and conventions and have developed because that is the way politics operates in a particular country. The former are consciously designed and clearly specified, while the latter are unwritten codes and customs – but no less effective because of that. Democratic institutions 'work' by shaping the behaviour of political actors: politicians, civil servants, interest groups and individual citizens. The rules of the game do not determine outcomes (think of a game of football), but they do provide the framework within which actors select and pursue their strategies. Institutions provide a set of specific constraints and opportunities for the practice of democracy.

In order to understand how democracy is developing, we need an analytical framework that focuses upon the *rules of the democratic game* rather than upon the particular organisations of government. Democratic innovations involve rules and conventions that aim to shape the behaviour of many different actors and organisations, acting both individually and in partnership. Not only do formal rules have to be *created*, they also need to be *recognised* by the diverse political actors involved, and then *embedded* over time. Finally, they must be *monitored* in order to establish whether formal rules are effectively shaping political behaviour and decision making, and have achieved some measure of fit with dominant political conventions.

Democratic institutions work because they combine formal constitutional rules with informal patterns of behaviour and expectation. Democracy may be particularly effective where both the formal and informal rules are widely understood and accepted across the polity. Conversely, where the formal institutions are relatively new, informal norms and customs may still be under development or negotiation and may not have the same high level of recognition. In these circumstances, the informal norms that 'oil the wheels' of democracy are absent, posing challenges for the operation of formal institutions. But the vibrancy of democracy relates also to the potential for new, oppositional practices (akin to Tully's 'practices of freedom'; see Chapter 1) to develop 'under the radar' of formal institutional arrangements, often as a precursor to institutional reform.

There are clearly many external variables that may affect Council of Europe interventions regarding democratic institutions. These variables might include levels of education, economic conditions, social conflict, demographic developments and so on. Our concern here, however, is with the challenges that arise out of the very character of democratic institutions and it is to these that we now turn.

First, it is important to recognise that democratic institutions are nested within *complex institutional environments* (political and non-political) over which institutional designers may have very little control. Institutional arrangements that may be targeted by a particular Council of Europe intervention (local councils, regional assemblies, national governments) are located within a wider and progressively decentred governance environment. Local democratic institutions, for example, are shaped by rules that emanate from higher tiers of government, including national legislation. National governments, on the other hand, are influenced by 'institutional templates' that may not be specifically political but circulate in the wider society and economy through the media, education and business channels (inspired by, for example, commercial management styles, models of corporate governance, frameworks for digitalisation, or campaigns against sleaze and corruption). Democratic institutions are also shaped by locally specific cultures and conventions ('how things are done around here') in non-political arenas – in business or civil society, for example – whether at the national, regional or local level (Lowndes and Wilson 2003).

Second, *power relationships* shape the way that institutions develop over time. Institutions are inherently political, because rules create patterns of distributional advantage (Knight 1992). Institutional change is never a purely technical matter, because any challenge to existing institutional settlements is likely to be met by resistance. Indeed, shifting power relations may be one of the *goals* of institutional reform (e.g. empowering legislatures vis-à-vis executives, local vis-à-vis national government, NGOs vis-à-vis business lobbies, or simply citizens vis-à-vis bureaucrats and politicians). Purposive attempts at institutional change are hard to achieve. New rules may be hijacked by powerful actors and adapted to preserve their interests. New rules may exist in name only while the old rules retain their hold at an informal, but no less effective, level. For reformers, *de*-institution-alisation may present an even greater headache than the crafting of new rules, although it is an issue rarely discussed. One example from the Council of Europe's *acquis* is pertinent here. The Parliamentary Assembly, following broader trends in their member states, has shown an increasing interest in citizen participation and has issued a number of recommendations to support new mechanisms for citizen engage-ment. At the same time, however, it continues to cling to the primacy of Parliamentary sovereignty and has issued several other recommen-dations which are almost in contradiction with the desire to engage citizens more directly in decision making.

Third, *history matters* when we look at making democratic institu-tions work. The 'soft' version of this argument is simply that demo-cratic institutions are influenced by their 'inherited world'. Current practice and perceptions of future possibilities are constrained by the traditions that are expressed in both formal rules (constitutions and terms of reference, for example) and informal conventions (of pater-nalism, or deference, for example). History is a source of diversity as well as uniformity within democratic institutions, as traditions vary from locale to locale (Stewart 2000). Indeed, the very different demo-cratic structures in place across Europe are evidence of such historical legacies. The 'hard' version of the argument concerns 'path-depen-dence'. The basic idea is that, once institutional designers have started down a particular path (however arbitrary the initial choice), the costs of changing direction are high. Path dependency rests on a concep-tion of increasing returns or positive feedback. The relative benefits of sticking with one design compared with switching to another option increase over time; the costs of exit rise (Pierson 2000). Path depen-dency creates a powerful cycle of self-reinforcing activity, whether vir-tuous or vicious.

Criteria for the Design of Democratic Institutions

In the context of decentred governance, what principles should under-pin the design of democratic institutions? We argue that, for the

Council of Europe, two principles are particularly important. First, given the reality of pluralism and contingency within decentred governance, design interventions should be seen in terms of redesign rather than design, and as indirect rather than direct mechanisms for securing change. *Redesign* is important because reformers are inevitably constrained by past inheritances and the pull of path dependency (Goodin 1996). Second, an *indirect* approach is important because reformers need to steer or frame the interventions of dispersed political actors, rather than seek to impose a single set of rules. Goodin (1996, 28) counsels against 'The Myth of the Intentional Designer' and argues that the goal should be 'designing schemes for designing institutions'; that is, setting boundaries within which the 'everyday makers' of political institutions can operate (Bevir and Rhodes 2003). Institutional design depends upon influencing the behaviour of reflexive political actors on the ground. Interventions in institutional design need, therefore, to exploit rather than frustrate the creative efforts of those who make and remake democratic practice on a daily basis.

Following from these two core principles, however, are a number of other important criteria. Conventionally, good design is regarded as guaranteed by a combination of internal consistency and 'goodness of fit' with the external environment. It may be more helpful, however, to see good design as secured by clear values (the articulation of specific meanings) rather than functional necessities, and by a capacity for learning and adaptation rather than environmental 'fit'. Because institutions inevitably embody values and power relationships, institutional design is inescapably a normative project. There needs to be clarity about the values being promoted (and challenged) within institutional reform programmes. Shifting 'old' values is one reason why institutional change is hard to effect; at the same time, it is this normative dimension that makes institutional design so important and so alluring to every generation of politicians (Rothstein 1996). In institutional design, guiding values should not only be clear but 'publicly defensible'; that is, legitimate in the eyes of the wider citizenry (Goodin 1996, 41–42). The values that inform institutional design need to be understood and critically debated among the citizenry. Citizens may take issue with these particular sets of meanings, but the opportunity to 'engage across difference' (as agonists would have it) is key to democratic practice.

A 'one-best-way reflex' in institutional design should be avoided; rather than seeking the universal application of a particular model or the maximum spread of 'best practice', it is important to sustain a 'variety engine' within institutional design (Hood 1998). Tolerating, even promoting, variability within institutional design is a way of building in a capacity for innovation and adaptation to changing environments. Democratic institutions need to be flexible, not 'brittle': they need to be able to *adapt* to new circumstances, without being *destroyed* by them. As Goodin (1996, 40) notes: 'We want to have the capacity, sometimes, to bind ourselves to a certain course of action and to ensure that we (or our successors) resist any temptations to deviate from it.' As we explained at the start of the Chapter, the importance of institutional design lies in intervening to shape the scope of future interventions.

Indeed, it is a defining characteristic of all institutions that they are 'triadic' – that is, 'established and enforced by "third parties" who are not part of the institutionalised interaction'. The role of third party enforcers is to supply 'arguments as to why an institutionalised status order is to be held valid and hence deserves to be adhered to' (Offe 1996, 199, 203–04). The sophistication of these arguments is an important contribution to institutional robustness. Goodin (1996, 41) argues that institutional design must be 'sensitive to motivational complexity'. The most effective enforcement mechanisms may be those that cultivate trust and embody 'a direct appeal to moral principles', rather than those that seek simply to control the behaviour of actors assumed to be self-interested and prone to 'defection'. The success of institutional design depends as much on the 'institutional software' of persuasive arguments and convincing discourses as on the 'hardware' of rules, rights and operating procedures (Dryzek 1996, 204). This message is particularly important to the monitoring activities of the council, which can have the most impact in this area.

On the basis of this discussion it is possible to identify a framework for good institutional design with which to analyse the council's *acquis*. For our purposes, good institutional design is characterised by two competing but equally important features: *robustness* and *revisability* (Lowndes and Roberts 2013, 189–92). *Robustness* can be operationalised in relation to two criteria:

- first, the clarity of the values informing institutional design;
- second, the nature and effectiveness of 'third party enforcement'.

Because institutionalisation is an ongoing process (institutions are not once-and-for-all creations), it is not sufficient to examine the values and enforcement approach embodied in the original design. We need also to look at the extent to which value clarity is maintained over time and at the ongoing development of enforcement strategies. By 'enforcement' we mean ensuring that new institutional designs 'stick'; that they shape actors' behaviour in desired ways and give rise to new and specific 'logics of appropriateness'. Approaches to enforcement may rely more or less on direct control or on commitment building among actors, reflecting the inherent tension within decentred governance between a logic of control and a logic of collaboration (see Chapter 1).

Revisability can be operationalised in relation to two further criteria:

- first, flexibility – that is, the capacity within institutional designs for adaptation over time and for capturing the benefits of 'learning by doing';
- second, variability – that is, the extent to which there is tolerance (even encouragement) of different design variants in different locations.

In short, revisability seeks to ensure that institutional arrangements can operate in different local environments and changing circumstances, and that there is a capacity for innovation and learning.

The *Acquis* as an Instrument of Institutional Design

The Council of Europe's *acquis* in the field of democracy combines a range of formal instruments, guidelines and practices that have emerged from all three of the council's pillars (Pratchett and Lowndes 2004). A range of treaties establish the preconditions by which democracy and its wider values and principles can be realised. These treaties articulate the core principles that would be expected in modern democracies and include, among others, the council's conventions on human rights, social rights and welfare, and freedom of speech. They also include those conventions and charters which confirm the rule of law, such as treaties addressing corruption, transborder cooperation and privacy issues. Others are directly concerned with establishing particular institutional structures or practices concerned with democracy or with relationships between democratic institutions. These treaties include the European Charter of Local Self-Government and proposed charters on urban government and regional self-govern-ment. In opening a recent convention on 'access to official documents' (CETS 205) in June 2009, the council counted 207 Treaties or conven-tions within its *acquis*. In acceding to the council, member states are expected to sign and ratify many of these treaties and are encouraged to adopt others as well. In this respect, the *acquis* has the potential to be an instrument of institutional isomorphism (Lowndes and Roberts 2013, 115), as countries with very differing socio-economic, political, demographic and geographical starting points converge around the same democratic values.

Despite such convergence around core principles, the *acquis* also recognises the differences between nation states. Drawing on its prin-ciple of variable geometry, it accepts the notion that democracy will be institutionalised in different ways in different polities. The contrasts between Europe's largest country – Russia – and some of the council's smallest member states, such as San Marino, clearly requires institu-tions to develop in different ways as, indeed, do the differing histori-cal contexts and political traditions of Central and Eastern European countries compared with Western Europe.

It is also a live *acquis* which is constantly being debated and added to through its various organs. A range of other texts emerge alongside treaties including formal 'decisions' and 'declarations' on particular issues through to 'recommendations' to particular bodies or countries and 'resolutions' on particular concerns. While many of these texts do not have the authority to demand action in member states, they are nonetheless important in framing debates about democratic reform and development in different countries. As an instrument of institu-tional design, therefore, the *acquis* provides both a frame of reference for designers and a substantial resources base of ideas for democratic development.

For it to be successful, however, it has to fit the criteria for good institutional design set out in the last section. In this section we crit-ically analyse the *acquis* according to the twin criteria of robustness and revisability.

Table 4.1 summarises some of the key features of the *acquis* and analyses its robustness in relation to clarity of values and third party enforcement. This initial assessment of the *acquis* suggests it meets much of the criteria of robustness. Its evolution over a period of sixty years, and through a process of sustained debate and deliberation, has

Table 4.1. *Robustness*

Role for CoE	Examples from the acquis
Clarity of values is achieved through:	
Defining democratic values/principles	The *acquis* defines a number of the preconditions for democracy, for example: • European Convention on Human Rights (Articles 9, 10, 11 and Article 3 of Protocol 1) • Conventions on corruption (ETS173 and 174). It also seeks to define the specific values associated with democracy, for example: • European Charter on Local Self- Government (ETS 122) • Parliamentary Assembly Res800 (1983) and Parliamentary Assembly Res1353 (2003) on democracy.
Exploring potential devices	The CoE has developed a stream of work around various devices. For example, its work on e-government includes: • Committee of Ministers Rec (2004)11 on e-voting • Committee of Ministers Rec (2004)15 on e-governance. Both of these make specific recommendations on how member states should adopt new technologies in support of democracy.
Third party enforcement is achieved through:	
Promoting good practice	The CoE has a range of programmes aimed at promoting good practice. The promotional work of the Venice Commission, where it both assesses current practice and makes recommendations on how laws should be adapted is one good example. A case in point: • Venice Commission Guidelines on referendums (CDL INF (2001) 10).
Supporting democratic development	Since the accession of many CEE countries, the CoE has developed a range of programmes: • Democratic development programmes in CEE • Youth development activities.

Role for CoE	Examples from the acquis
Monitoring of democratic behaviour	The monitoring of member states takes place through a range of activities, for example: • CLRAE in relation to local/regional democracy • GRECO (Group of States Against Corruption) in relation to potential corrupt practices.
Sanctioning 'democratic' structures and vetoing 'undemocratic' behaviour	In setting out terms for accession, the CoE is able to sanction the democracy of member states, for example: • the accession criteria for Armenia (Parliamentary Assembly Opinion 221(2000)). It can also veto European states from time to time, for example: • until 2005 Belarus was not under consideration for membership. • As a political rather than an economic body, the CoE was able to act quickly in threatening to suspend Georgia in 2002.

resulted in a clear articulation of democratic values through a range of processes. The underlying values and principles that all countries are expected to sign on to are set out in a range of treaties and expanded upon in a range of resolutions and other statements. The council continues to support the exploration of different democratic devices and provides opportunities for member states to reflect on how these might be sequenced to realise procedurally legitimate democracy. In terms of framing and clarifying democratic values, therefore, the council has played an important role.

In terms of third party enforcement, the Council of Europe also has a potentially important role to play in embedding democratic institutions. It achieves this role through a number of mechanisms, some of which are in the form of 'democratic software' and others of which are more coercive. The democratic software comprises good practice frameworks and case studies on democratic devices as varied as referendums, electronic voting and the participation of denizens in local democracy. It also includes a range of resources to support the newer democracies in Central and Eastern Europe to make the transition to more developed democratic cultures, including offering extensive training opportunities to young politicians in these countries. In Bevir and Rhodes's (2003) terms, this is the terrain on which actors seek to modify their own 'traditions' in order to respond to the 'dilemma' of democratisation posed by the council.

At the same time, democratic hardware has been developed through a process of actively monitoring the behaviour of nation states and applying sanctions where relevant. Monitoring covers a range of democratic issues, from election observation activities to human rights surveillance and the sanctioning of corrupt practices. Its position as a primarily political rather than economic entity has enabled it to take a much stronger stance than the EU, for example, on activities that it sees as anti-democratic: for instance, it has been particularly outspoken on the subject of 'extraordinary renditions' and the activities of the U.S. Central Intelligence Agency in secretly detaining and interrogating terrorist suspects in Europe, and has established a formal inquiry into the allegations.

As an instrument of institutional design, however, these values are also constraining in a number of ways. First, the values suffer from an absence of dynamism and have tended to be static over a period of time. While long-established principles of the right to free and fair elections are well developed in both the European Convention on Human Rights (Article 3 of Protocol 1) and in subsequent rulings from the European Court of Human Rights (ECHR), the discussion around democratic values that reflect contemporary challenges is less well developed. The *acquis* needs to better capture the plurality of meanings ascribed by actors to democracy, especially in the non-conventional arenas to which it relates, like youth participation or social media.

Second, the *acquis* is often reactionary in nature. A tension exists between attempts to reassert the primacy of conventional democratic structures, especially parliamentary democracy, and the emergence of Type II governance structures that challenge this primacy. This defence of parliamentary democracy among parliamentarians is not wholly surprising. As Peters and Pierre recognise, we should not expect traditional democratic institutions to easily 'surrender their leverage to contextually defined and *ad hoc* models of governing' (Peters and Pierre 2004). However, this tension does present a challenge for the *acquis* in as far it creates a process of conservatism in its development. As Chapter 1 argues, democracy constantly has to be rediscovered.

As Norval (2007, 175) explains: 'Without the ability to criticise and animate our existing institutions, and the imagination to change and challenge them, democratic institutions risk to become fossilised and sclerotic.'

Third, the values contained in the *acquis* are often fragmented. The *acquis* has not emerged as a deliberate, constitutionally developed statement but is the cumulative wisdom of a range of incremental interventions, many of which reflect selectively upon past interventions. While some values (such as those around human rights) are well established, others are recognised in only some areas of the council's work. Again, aspects of what Skelcher (2005) calls 'polity forming' Type II governance are recognised in much of the council's work on local democracy but are largely ignored in other areas. Consequently, while superficially clear, the values of the *acquis* are nonetheless ambiguous in many areas. The challenge may be to make this ambiguity a source of strength, expressing as it does something of the plurality and incompleteness of interpretations of democracy, and containing within it potential raw material for the 'positive imagination' called for in Chapter 1.

On closer inspection, the third-party enforcement activities of the Council of Europe are also not always effective. The democratic software has had a big impact, especially among developing democracies outside the EU, who look to the council for guidance and support as they confront the dilemmas inherent in iterating between their own political traditions and established European 'norms'. Its hardware, however, has been less influential. Most of its monitoring activities go unreported, even in those countries that are deemed to be failing in some way in relation to the *acquis*. Although the council can be outspoken, its lack of economic position means that it has very few sanctions to impose on countries that fail to live up to its requirements. This absence of influence is particularly a problem of its visibility. Indeed, the extent to which there is any visibility of the council, it is primarily in relation to its human-rights machinery, which is perhaps, overly dominant of other democratic developments in the *acquis*.

Table 4.2 summarises some of the key features of the *acquis* and analyses its revisability in terms of the dual characteristics of flexibility and variability.

One of the strengths of the *acquis* has been its ability to be flexible. The expansion of democracy into Central and Eastern Europe has seen

Table 4.2. *Revisability*

Role for CoE	Examples from the acquis
Flexibility is achieved through:	
Being responsive to different issues as they emerge over time	• Women in political life (Committee of Ministers Rec 2003–3) • Financing of political parties and election campaigns
Supporting different speeds of democratic change in different places	• Recommendations on e-voting and e-government accept different speeds of development. • Recommendations of the Green Paper on the Future of Democracy (2004) are deliberately mixed
Reflexive development of instruments (i.e., capacity to amend conventions etc.)	• Monitoring reports are designed not only to highlight problems but also to encourage change through reflection • Charters/conventions can be added to and amended (e.g., ECHR)
Variability is achieved through:	
Supporting variable geometry	The CoE encourages local and national difference – divergence within convergence. Examples include: • Role of regions within CLRAE – only regions with legislative powers are part of the Chamber of Regions • Variability of signatories to different treaties • Development of partial agreements (e.g., GRECO) as a way of encouraging cross-country collaboration.

the membership of the council more than double since 1989, bringing in countries which share little by way of political experience and culture with the developed democracies of Western Europe. This expansion has been a major challenge for the *acquis* but it has also proven its flexibility. While some of the values have been seen as fundamental and preconditional for democracy in all member states, many other aspects of the *acquis* have been open to selective implementation. The council does not presume that democratic institutions must develop at the same pace in all European countries or, indeed, that they should converge. Instead, it has explicitly allowed institutions to emerge that are contextually sensitive and relevant to each country's circumstances.

The *acquis* has also illustrated its flexibility in the way in which it has taken on board new issues that are now affecting democracy. Its publication of a Green Paper on the *Future of Democracy in Europe* (Schmitter and Trechsel 2004) and subsequent establishment of an annual 'Forum for the Future of Democracy' is a high point in this flexibility, emphasising the council's ability to be both reflexive and responsive to democratic trends and challenges. The ability to make additions to the *acquis* through protocols, resolutions and other devices are another feature of this flexibility and demonstrate the capacity for dynamic development.

The way in which this flexibility works, however, is also a problem for the *acquis*. In effect, it is a linear, serial accumulation of knowledge, which continues to grow but not necessarily to develop in appropriate directions. The emphasis on core treaties makes the development of the *acquis* particularly path-dependent, with particular values and processes becoming increasingly locked-in over time. There is limited iteration of accepted knowledge and significant difficulty in reversing. Not only is there no mechanism for removing obsolete or redundant aspects of the *acquis* but also, once a member state has signed and ratified a particular treaty, it is especially difficult for them to withdraw from its particular terms, regardless of how inappropriate it may be to their circumstances. Although flexible in terms of taking on board new or changing contexts, therefore, the *acquis* has proven to be less responsive in relation to issues of reversibility.

The final criterion of variability is an observable feature of the *acquis*. Its defining principle of variable geometry is explicitly incorporated to ensure that the *acquis* is contextually sensitive and of equal relevance to all member states. In signing and ratifying treaties, each state is encouraged to record declarations or reservations on how or where particular provisions will be implemented, including exceptions where clauses will be ignored or overruled by domestic circumstances. Equally, membership of monitoring bodies and other organs of the council are open to selective participation by members. In this way, the principle of variable geometry ensures a high level of variability within a wider framework of consistent values.

Variability, however, poses two challenges to the success of the *acquis* as an instrument of institutional design. First, it creates a tension between a convergence around core democratic principles and a divergence around democratic institutions, as developed through the implementation of particular devices and sequences in different countries. Democratic values have substance only when they are enacted through devices and sequences (Saward 2003). Consequently, although there may be apparent consensus on democratic values across Europe and a supposed convergence around them, in reality, implementation may lead to significant divergence. As was established in Chapter 1, when we conceive of democracy as constituted in and through practices (rather than guaranteed through procedures), it is always incomplete.

Second, variable geometry may appear to support contextual sensitivity but it also runs the risk of cynical expediency. In allowing such wide institutional variety, the *acquis* makes it possible for member states to be highly selective in adopting aspects of the *acquis* that are expedient to their short-term needs but which are not addressing the longer-term values. This danger is particularly relevant to those newer democracies that see Council of Europe approval as a step on the road to closer unity with the EU. Consequently, while variability is a strength in the *acquis* it is also, potentially, a significant weakness.

Conclusions

In this chapter we have sought to understand how an *acquis* does its work by understanding it as a process of institutional design premised on the dual criteria of robustness and revisability. In applying it to the democratic mandate of the Council of Europe we are able to understand both the capacity of an *acquis* to frame and shape democratic institutions within decentred governance, and the limitations which are associated with such an amorphous instrument. As well as providing a unique empirical analysis of the Council of Europe's *acquis*, therefore, we are also able to offer new insights into how IGOs more generally are able to shape and influence institutions over time, moving beyond the rationalist and constructivist debates of recent years, to take seriously the idea that democracy is about pluralism, practice and meaning.

Thinking of an *acquis* as an instrument of institutional design offers a new way of understanding the relationship between the conscious planning of democratic standards by IGOs and the complexities of adoption and compliance among member states. It emphasises the range of instruments and processes that IGOs need to adopt to be successful. It places an emphasis upon the authority and legitimacy of IGOs, as built over many years through their *acquis*. The creation and maintenance of democratic institutions by IGOs such as the Council of Europe is not a short-term project but requires a sophisticated range of strategies to both cajole and support states to move in appropriate directions, as they confront their own dilemmas in the context of very specific and diverse political traditions. In this sense, our framework is about the development of democratic norms through an ongoing iteration of meanings and practices, as member states encounter a style of institutional design that is underpinned by a search for both robustness and revisability.

More than simply providing a framework for analysing the activities of IGOs, however, our framework also highlights their unique importance in designing and supporting the development of institutions. In terms of robustness, IGOs are uniquely placed to identify and represent the values which the international community recognises as being common goals, and to provide the third-party enforcement that is necessary to help the process along. Equally, successful IGOs are sensitive to the different institutional contexts of countries and build in responsive, variable and flexible processes to support change. In this respect, our framework offers a normative account of how IGOs should seek to design institutions among member states.

At the same time, each of the criteria poses problems of ambiguity for IGOs. For example, the council's democratic values may be robust and clear but they are also conservative and confused in places; offering flexible and variable design allows for a high level of revisability but also runs the risk of encouraging too much diversity and divergence. Empirically, the framework has highlighted tensions in the activities of IGOs, as well as drawing attention to the range of instruments that they use in seeking to design institutions. Theoretically, it has explored what institutional design means within the context of decentred governance, and considered how the tensions therein reflect Norval's (2007) 'productive ambiguity' – between the promotion of democracy and the recognition that it will always fall short of its own high standards.

5 | Assessing the Democratic Anchorage of Governance Networks

EVA SØRENSEN AND JACOB TORFING

Introduction

The first decade of the new millennium saw a growing debate among political scientists concerning the democratic quality of governance networks (Peters and Pierre 2000; Warren 2002; Sørensen 2002; Grote and Gbikpi 2002; Newman 2005; Skelcher 2005; Sørensen and Torfing 2005a; Benz and Papadopoulos 2006; Stoker 2006; Klijn and Skelcher 2007). The initial governance debate in the 1990s was mainly preoccupied with demonstrating the significant role of networks and partnerships in public governance and analysing their contribution to efficient and effective governance (Marin and Mayntz 1991; Kooiman 1993; Scharpf 1994; Rhodes 1997; Kickert, Klijn and Koppenjan 1997; Milward and Provan 2000). However, empirical studies have shown that institutionalized interaction among interdependent but operationally autonomous actors plays an important role, not only in the implementation of public policy, but also in the process of policy formulation and political decision making (Marsh and Rhodes 1992; Marsh 1998). This means that governance networks cannot be reduced to managerial arenas of effective problem-solving based on knowledge sharing, resource exchange and flexibility gains. They are deeply involved in political conflicts and power games through which the authoritative allocation of values is determined and contested. Recognizing the political character of governance networks produces an urgent need for a systematic assessment of the democratic quality of governance networks. In effect, governance researchers have begun to consider the democratic implications of governance networks, and the conclusions they reach differ. While some researchers conclude that governance networks represent a threat to democracy because they undermine the principles and institutions of representative democracy

(Mayer, Edelenbos and Monnikhof 2005; Hansen 2007), others argue that governance networks strengthen democracy because they remedy crucial shortcomings in representative democracy by enhancing participation, deliberation and contestation (Dryzek 2000; Klijn and Skelcher 2007; Sørensen and Torfing 2007).

The growing interest in the impact of governance networks on democracy is important and necessary, as it places the question of the exercise of political power and the norms and values against which it can be evaluated at the heart of the research agenda and thus helps in combating the unfortunate tendency to describe and analyse governance networks in purely managerial terms. However, the current debate about the democratic quality of governance networks is found wanting in two respects. First, there has hardly been any discussion of what democracy means in relation to network types of governance. Debates have been raised about the inclusiveness, transparency and accountability of governance networks, but the discussion has not produced any clear understanding of how we define, assess and evaluate these things, or what democracy may signify in relation to interactive forms of governance. Second, the debate on governance networks builds on the highly questionable assumption that it is possible to give a definitive, clear-cut and abstract answer to the question of whether or not governance networks are democratic. This assumption is problematic because it neglects that some governance networks are more democratic than others, and also that governance networks can be democratic in some respects but not in others. A detailed empirical assessment of the democratic problems and merits of specific governance networks in particular situations and contexts is necessary in order to increase our knowledge about the democratic quality of governance networks and our ability to develop specific, context-dependent strategies for improving their democratic performance.

A further advancement of the debate about the democratic impact of governance networks requires the development of a specific set of criteria that permits us to assess the democratic quality of specific governance networks (Agger and Löfgren 2008). In this chapter we propose a set of criteria for measuring what we have elsewhere defined as the democratic anchorage of governance networks (Sørensen and Torfing 2005b). The criteria invoke norms and values from different democratic narratives and traditions, and permit an assessment of democratic ambiguities and trade-offs. The assessment criteria will help to produce new knowledge about the democratic performance of governance networks and eventually facilitate studies of the contextual and institutional factors that condition the democratic anchorage of different types of governance networks. Such studies will be extremely valuable for crafting tailor-made strategies aiming to enhance the democratic performance of specific governance networks.

The argument proceeds in the following way: After having defined what we mean by governance networks and commented on the debate concerning their democratic impact, we present our model for the democratic anchorage of governance networks and use the basic dimensions of this model to elaborate a detailed set of criteria for measuring the extent to which governance networks are democratically anchored. Finally, we briefly discuss how the democratic anchorage model can be applied and refer to some empirical studies using the model.

Governance Networks

Governance networks are by no means a new phenomenon, but they are increasingly seen as an effective and legitimate way of dealing with complex problems that call for cross-sectoral and inter-organizational coordination and collaboration (Heffen, Kickert and Thomassen 2000; Rhodes 2000; Goldsmith and Eggers 2004; Marcussen and Torfing 2007). The current celebration of the merits of governance networks is evidenced by the persistent call for joined-up government, where public agencies form collaborative networks with one another in order to deal with horizontal problems; the proliferation of public-private networks and partnerships aiming to produce joint solutions; and the surge in networked policy interaction among actors from different sectors and levels of governance (Bache and Flinders 2004). As such, governance networks take many different forms and have many different functions. Some networks are highly formalized and mandated from above, while others are informal and self-grown from below. Some are open and inclusive, while others are closed and exclusive. Some pursue broad, society-wide policy goals, while others have a narrow focus on single issues. Some are preoccupied with knowledge sharing and coordination of programmes and activities, while others are involved in joint formulation and implementation of public policy. The plurality of forms and functions of governance networks is well documented and has led to the construction of different typologies (Marsh and Rhodes 1992; Kickert, Klijn and Koppenjan, 1997; Mandell 2008).

Of course, one might ask whether the plurality and diversity of governance networks warrant a generic study of governance networks perceived as a distinct and unified phenomenon. Does it make sense to bring all the different kinds of networks together under the shared heading 'governance networks'? We believe that it does, since there are some clearly discernable features of network types of governance that permit us to define governance networks at a generic level. Hence, governance networks can be perceived as relatively stable articulations of interdependent but operationally autonomous actors who interact with one another through negotiations that take place within a regulative, normative, cognitive and imaginary framework, which is self-regulating within limits set by external forces, and contribute to the production of public purpose (Torfing 2005). The notion of governance networks points to the existence of relatively enduring, flexible and situated ties among relevant and affected actors from state, market and civil society, who choose to pool their resources, develop shared understandings and coordinate their actions in the pursuit of joint objectives that are deemed to be valuable for the larger public. The emphasis on resource interdependency as the driving force in the formation of governance networks (Rhodes 1997) tends to privilege well-organized and resourceful actors and thus creates an elite bias. However, we should not overlook the fact that citizen groups and lay actors are often included in governance networks because they hold crucial resources in terms of local knowledge and experiences, new and creative ideas, ability to make sense of and assess governance initiatives in the light of local practices, and commitment and energy that can help to facilitate the implementation of new solutions.

There is a general belief among governance theorists that governance networks may contribute to enhancing the efficiency and effectiveness of public governance. Without governance networks we may leave out crucial information, fail to mobilize available resources and energies, face serious coordination problems and suffer from the lack of democratic ownership to joint solutions (Kooiman 2000; Peters and Pierre 2000; Klijn and Koppenjan 2004). The few scholars who have raised the question about the democratic quality of governance networks concur with these assertions and conclude that governance networks are here to stay, because they help us to govern our increasingly

complex, fragmented and multi-layered societies. Seen from this perspective, all we can do is to minimize the negative impact that governance networks might have on democracy in terms of undermining
inclusiveness, transparency and accountability (Peters and Pierre 2000).
In contrast to this rather defensive view, another group of scholars
argues that governance networks are an important tool for improving democracy in the face of the 'democratic disenchantment', which
is evidenced by declining voter turnout and party membership and
explained by the growing expectation that democratic participation
involves more than regular elections (Warren 2002; Cain, Dalton and
Scarrow 2003a; Stoker 2006). Hence, it is optimistically asserted that
governance networks can help to strengthen the interaction between
politicians and citizens between elections; supply additional channels of political influence to intensely affected citizens; mobilize and
empower private actors by enhancing their social and political capital
and developing their democratic identity; and facilitate dialogue and
collaborative decision making among multiple demoi (Young 2000;
Sørensen and Torfing 2005a, 2007; Dryzek 2007; Esmark 2007).

These different conclusions regarding the democratic implications
of governance networks suggest that the problem is not that that the
governance theorists are mistaken about the democratic problems or
merits that they are highlighting. The problem is rather the underlying
belief that it is possible to reach a final verdict about the democratic
performance of governance networks by summing up the democratic
problems or merits. Governance networks are not stable institutional
structures, but a set of contingent patterns and practices that are
shaped by the interpretations and actions of situated actors. Therefore
we must replace the abstract discussion of the democratic performance of governance networks with a concrete empirical assessment
of the democratic quality of specific governance networks in particular
political contexts. This requires the development of a criteria-based
assessment model that enables us to evaluate different aspects of the
democratic performance of networked governance practices. Such a
criteria-based assessment model is provided by the model for the democratic anchorage of governance networks, which is presented following sections in this chapter. Instead of focusing on how governance
networks might help to democratize society at large (see Sørensen and
Torfing 2005a), the democratic anchorage model facilitates a systematic, norm-based assessment of the democratic quality of governance

networks. The basic criteria of the model have already been set out (Sørensen and Torfing 2005b). However, the initial formulation of the democratic anchorage model failed to provide a detailed set of assessment criteria that can be used in empirical analyses of concrete governance networks. In this chapter we aim to compensate for this failure by translating each of the four anchorage points into a set of empirical indicators that can guide empirical analysis of the democratic quality of governance networks.

The Democratic Anchorage of Governance Networks

The democratic anchorage model claims that the democratic performance of governance networks can be ensured by anchoring the networked practices in a series of relevant political constituencies that can lend democratic legitimacy to the network and in a democratic grammar of conduct that provides a normative yardstick for assessing the more or less institutionalized negotiation among the network actors. We shall claim that governance networks as such are democratically anchored to the extent that they:

1. Are controlled by democratically elected politicians;
2. Represent the membership basis of the participating groups and organizations;
3. Are accountable to a territorially defined citizenry;
4. Facilitate negotiated interaction in accordance with a commonly accepted democratic grammar of conduct.

The first anchorage point expresses the need to establish a close linkage between representative democracy and governance networks so as to ensure that decisions made by democratically elected politicians are not undermined by mandated or self-grown governance networks. However, as persistently argued by several theorists of democracy, the institutions of representative democracy are not capable of providing an undisputed source of democratic legitimacy. This results from the fact that the link between voters and elected politicians in representative democracies has been systematically weakened by a decline in party membership and voter turnout and by the pervasive role of mass media that threatens to turn citizens into passive spectators (Barber 1984; Bobbio 1987; Hirst 1994; Pitkin 2004; Stoker 2006). Accordingly we propose that this first anchorage point be supplemented by other anchorage points that derive democratic legitimacy from the membership basis of the groups and organizations that the network actors claim to represent, from the citizens bound by the decisions made by governance networks, and from a grammar of conduct that regulates the way in which network actors interact with one another. In fact, the model builds on the assumption that none of the four anchorage points alone can ensure the democratic quality of governance networks. The four anchorage points compensate for shortcomings of the others, and only together can they provide a strong source of democratic legitimacy.

The four anchorage points invoke norms and values drawn from different democratic narratives and traditions that are encapsulated in different strands of liberal democratic theory. However, as we shall see, it is necessary to reformulate the traditional liberal democratic understanding of these norms and values in the context of governance networks and in the light of new theoretical insights. Let us consider how this is done in relation to each of the four anchorage points in turn.

Anchorage in Democratically Elected Politicians

The rationale for anchoring governance networks in democratically elected politicians takes its point of departure from the basic idea in traditional theories of representative democracy that government control within the political decision-making process ensures that these decisions are in line with the popular will expressed by the political majority of elected assemblies (Mill 1937; Schumpeter 1976; Sartori 1987). If political decisions are taken in local, interactive and deliberative arenas, then government control must be secured through delegation, oversight and upward accountability. Hence, in relation to decentred forms of governance, it could be argued that elected politicians can lend democratic legitimacy to governance networks insofar as they are capable of controlling the formation, functioning and impact of governance networks.

Now, the problem is that the very idea that elected politicians can *control* public governance is flawed. As evidenced by numerous policy and implementation studies, the actual possibility of exercising top-down political control in representative democracies is very limited (Lindblom 1968; Lipsky, 1980; Behn, 2001). Contrary to what was originally suggested by Max Weber (1920) and Woodrow Wilson

(1887), elected politicians are not capable of ensuring tight control over the outputs and outcomes of public bureaucracies, and, so far, the efforts to find new ways of ensuring the elected politicians' control of public bureaucracy have been unsuccessful. The New Public Management reform programme is the most recent attempt to enhance political control over public governance from above. It aims to control outputs and outcomes by combining delegation and decentred self-governance with target steering, performance measurement and economic incentives (Pollitt and Bouckaert 2004, 99). However, control effects are limited because of the preponderant blindness to that which cannot be measured, the surge of strategic gaming aimed at exploiting the provided incentives, and a massive crowding out of normative and professional standards as constraints on the behaviour of street-level bureaucrats (Sørensen 2007; Stoker 2008). In addition, the proliferation of quasi-autonomous public agencies and private contractors seems to make political control even more difficult.

The limits of the traditional notion of political control become even more apparent in the context of interactive forms of governance through different kinds of networks. Governance networks are defined in terms of their relative capacity for self-regulation and the attempt to control governance networks through top-down steering based on binding rules, imperative commands, narrow targets and tough sanctions will not only undermine their self-regulatory capacity (Mayntz 1991, 10), but will also be met by fierce resistance by the network actors, reduce their motivation to participate in interactive governance arrangements and prevent innovative policy solutions that imply risk taking. Hence, we need to rethink the notion of political control in order to understand how elected politicians can monitor and influence governance networks through more subtle and indirect forms of regulation that respect the self-regulatory character of governance networks.

Following this line of argument, the governance network literature has aimed to reformulate the notion of political control in terms of the exercise of *metagovernance* defined as the 'regulation of (self-)regulation' (Jessop 2002; Kooiman, 2003; Klijn and Koppenjan 2004; Sørensen and Torfing 2007). Metagovernance is a reflexive and strategic practice aiming to facilitate, manage and direct interactive forms of governance while respecting their self-regulatory capacities. In principle metagovernance can be exercised by all political actors with sufficient resources and legitimacy, but in practice metagovernance is most often exercised by public authorities at different levels of governance. A reading of the literature on metagovernance points to four main forms of metagovernance by which elected politicians can metagovern governance networks:

1. *Network design* that aims to influence the scope, character, composition and institutional procedures of networks;
2. *Network framing* that sketches out the overall political, fiscal, legal and discursive framework within which the governance networks aim to govern themselves;
3. *Network management* that attempts to reduce tensions, resolve conflicts, empower and activate particular actors, and lower the transaction costs by providing different kinds of material and immaterial inputs and resources;
4. *Network participation* that endeavours to influence the policy agenda, the range of feasible options, the decision-making premises and the negotiated outputs and outcomes.

The first and second forms of metagovernance are performed 'hands-off', that is, at a distance from the relatively self-regulating governance networks, whereas the third and fourth forms are carried out 'hands-on', that is, through a close interaction between the metagovernors and the governance networks in question. Moreover, the first and fourth forms of metagovernance are relatively interventionist as the metagovernor seeks to influence the content of what is being self-governed by the network. By contrast, the second and third forms of metagovernance are comparatively less interventionist as they merely aim to define a space for self-governance and support the governance network's self-governed activities, whatever the content might be. An overview of the basic characteristics of the four different forms of metagovernance is provided in Table 5.1.

Metagovernance of governance networks is most successful in securing well-functioning governance networks when combining all the available forms of metagovernance. In particular, metagovernors often need to combine 'hands-off' and 'hands-on' metagovernance, since the two kinds of metagovernance tend to reinforce each other. The New Public Management reforms have focussed exclusively on hands-off metagovernance in an effort to develop self-regulating quasi-markets and self-governing agencies through the design of competitive games.

Table 5.1. *Overview of the basic characteristics of the main forms of metagovernance*

	Strong intervention	Limited intervention
Hands-off	Network design	Network framing
Hands-on	Network participation	Network management

The result has been a lack of vertical and horizontal collaboration, coordination and knowledge sharing that requires hands-on metagovernance. Likewise, efforts to metagovern governance networks through the deployment of hands-on tools such as network management and network participation have proven ineffective if the governance networks in question are poorly designed and framed. These experiences suggest that hands-off and hands-on forms of metagovernance must be combined for metagovernance to be successful.

Metagovernors must also combine forms of metagovernance that differ in terms of how much they intervene in the interactions of governance networks. Combining more and less interventionist forms of metagovernance will enable metagovernors to respond to the key challenge that consists in avoiding both over-regulation and under-regulation of governance networks (Kooiman 1993, 255). There are no ways of precisely determining the tipping point where metagovernance becomes either an unbearable straightjacket for the relatively self-regulating governance networks or an insufficient means for ensuring the stability of the patterns of internal collaboration and establishing a reasonable degree of coherence between the activities of the governance networks and the goals of the democratically elected government. Nevertheless, if the metagovernors combine and balance more and less interventionist forms of metagovernance, the chances of avoiding over- and under-regulation will tend to increase.

The key question then becomes how we measure the extent to which a given governance network is metagoverned by elected politicians. Here it might help to think about when and how things can go wrong. First, the elected politicians might not be aware that a particular governance network exists. This will make it impossible for them to exercise metagovernance. Second, the politicians may not want to take responsibility for metagoverning governance networks within their jurisdiction, or they may fail to clarify whether or not a governance network is involved in 'high politics' and therefore need-ing a careful metagovernance, or whether it is engaged in 'low politics' bordering on administrative coordination, and therefore needing less, or even no, metagovernance. Third, missing or inadequate informa-tion about what is going on in a governance network will also pre-vent the exercise of effective democratic metagovernance, as will the absence of clear objectives and the lack of knowledge about how these objectives can be achieved through a combination of different forms of metagovernance. Last but not least, it is a trivial fact that politicians are overburdened and often leave metagovernance to public manag-ers. Hence, failure to cooperate with the public managers who are in charge of metagoverning governance networks and failure to discuss their metagovernance 'mandate' will seriously reduce the level of dem-ocratic control that is obtained through metagovernance.

Reversing the arguments about metagovernance failure permits us to formulate a list of positively formulated norms that can help us to measure whether governance networks are democratically anchored in elected politicians. The metagovernance norms are summarized in Proposition 1.

Proposition 1. Democratic Anchorage in Elected Politicians Can Be Measured by Paying Attention to the Following Norms:

- The elected politicians must be aware of the presence, role and character of the governance network in question, and have access to information about its processes, outputs and outcomes.
- They must assume the role of metagovernors and decide how important it is to metagovern the network.
- They must define the objectives of their metagovernance and combine different forms of metagovernance to achieve these objectives.
- They must take active part in and cooperate closely with public administrators in order to develop and perform a joint metagov-ernance strategy.

Anchorage in the Membership Basis of Participating Groups and Organizations

The rationale for anchoring governance networks in the membership basis of the participating groups and organizations takes its point of departure from the claim made by liberal theories of pluralism (Dahl 1961) and associational democracy (Hirst 1994) that the members of these groups and organizations constitute a 'demos' of directly affected people who must be represented in order for the governance network to obtain democratic legitimacy (Sørensen and Torfing 2003, 617). Governance networks provide a horizontal arena for negotiated inter-action between actors who implicitly or explicitly represent a plurality of informal groups and/or formal organizations. The interactive policy processes in governance networks are democratically legitimate inso-far as the participating actors represent the interests and preferences of the members of these different groups and organizations.

However, the classical notion of *representation* (see Pitkin 1967) is problematic, as it wrongly assumes that a pre-defined interest or pref-erence is reproduced in a passive and undistorted way at the level of representation (Laclau 1993; Saward 2005, 2006). The very idea of an unbiased one-to-one representation of a pre-given interest or pref-erence is theoretically flawed as it presupposes the presence of a fully constituted object of representation and assumes that the process of representation does not add anything to the object of representation. By contrast, we shall contend that the interests and preferences to be represented are never fully constituted, since they are formed within a particular discursive context that is constantly destabilized by dis-locatory events that reveal the ultimately undecidable character of all social and political identities. As such, the interests and preferences of political actors are always marked by the ambiguity, undecidability, and openness of the policy discourse in which they are formed (Laclau 1990, 1993).

The ultimate failure to construct a fully constituted preference or interest prior to its representation means that the performative act of representation becomes constitutive of the interests and preferences that it represents. In other words, the interests and preferences of the represented are defined by the way they are articulated by those who claim to represent them. There might be a discrepancy between how these interests and preferences are conceived and articulated by the represented and by the representatives. However, the constructed rep-resentations cannot be seen as a mere distortion of some primordial object, since there never was a fully constituted interest or preference in the first place, but rather a vague and ambiguous ensemble of con-ceptions, wants and beliefs. Therefore, the relation between represen-tatives and represented must be evaluated in terms of the degree to which the latter identify with the former (Saward 2006). Seen from this perspective, the crucial question is not whether the discursive forms of representation distort some true and original interest or preference, but rather whether those who the representatives claim to represent identify themselves with the performative act of representation (Torfing 1999, 183ff.).

The particular challenge for attempts to democratically anchor governance networks in the membership basis of affected groups and organizations through the establishment of a relation of representation is to avoid hobbling representatives with closely defined mandates. It is virtually impossible to participate in political negotiations within a governance network on the basis of a closely defined mandate. Participation in governance networks not only requires give and take in relation to a defined set of preferences or interests, but also the possibility of developing and responding to new political initiatives that modify and change the articulated preferences and interests through power-ridden forms of deliberation. Accordingly, the best way of ensuring representation is through procedures that allow for an ex post critique of the way in which representatives construct and pursue particular interests and preferences. In representative democracy such an ex post critique is institutionalized through the ballot box, but in governance networks this option is not available. Here ex post critique must take place through the creation of situations in which the network actors are forced to communicate and interact with the groups and organizations they claim to represent in order to get positive or negative feedback on their performance as representatives.

However, capacities and opportunities for ex post critique are just one among several conditions for ensuring *identification* with the representatives in governance networks. First of all, the participants in a governance network must advance more or less concrete and direct claims to represent specific groups or organizations that are affected by the negotiated interaction in the governance network (Saward 2005, 191). The advancement of such claims is important in order for the network actors to become recognized as legitimate players by the other actors in the network. However, it is not enough that the other network actors envisage these claims to represent. The represented groups and organizations must be aware of the claims to represent and must identify with the claims by constructing a 'we'-relationship to the representative. The 'we'-identity does not construct a complete identity, but rather a 'sameness' that permits disagreements up to the point where the 'we' is replaced by an 'us'-and-'them' division (Mouffe 2005). The represented groups and organizations must have the necessary capacities to critically evaluate the way in which the representatives construct and pursue particular interests and preferences and there must be regular opportunities for the represented to assess the performance of their representatives and express grievances and criticisms. Identification can be maintained despite criticisms if the representatives demonstrate their willingness to listen, learn and adjust their performance in the governance network or persuade the critics to change their views.

We can now propose a list of positively formulated norms that can help us to measure whether governance networks are anchored in participating groups and organizations. The norms are summarized in Proposition 2.

Proposition 2. Democratic Anchorage in Participating Groups and Organizations Can Be Measured by Paying Attention to the Following Norms:

- Network actors must advance claims to represent specific groups and/or organizations.
- The represented groups and/or organizations must be aware of these claims and accept their validity by constructing a 'we'-relationship to the representative(s).
- The represented groups and/or organizations must have the capacity and opportunity to critically evaluate the way that their interests and preferences are constructed and pursued by the representative(s).
- The representative(s) must be sensitive to criticisms from the represented as well as seek to persuade them to change their views.

Anchorage in a Territorially Defined Citizenry

The rationale for anchoring governance networks in a territorially defined citizenry takes its departure from the central role ascribed to the public sphere in liberal theories of participatory democracy (Tocqueville 1968; Pateman 1970; Barber 1984). Hence, we shall

claim that democratic legitimacy cannot be obtained merely by holding the network actors accountable to a demos constituted by the
groups and organizations that are directly affected by the decisions
of the network. Governance networks must also be accountable to
a wider territorially defined demos constituted by citizens who are
indirectly affected by the decisions made by the governance network,
either because the decisions made by the governance network affect
the overall allocation of resources, or because they have repercussions
for other policy areas. The citizens who live within the local, regional,
national or transnational territory in which a certain governance network is setting the agenda or making binding decisions should be able
to hold that particular governance network accountable for its policy
outputs and policy outcomes. Of course, the elected politicians help to
anchor governance networks in the territorially defined citizenry, but
it is a long way from a group of concerned and discontented citizens
to the responsible governance network, if the citizens have to seek
influence through the election of politicians who may or may not be
able to metagovern the governance network. Indeed, concerned publics should have a shorter and more direct way of holding a particular
governance network publicly accountable for its contribution to public governance.

The classical notion of *public accountability* assumes that the responsible political decision makers can be identified and held to account for
an inappropriate policy output and an unacceptable policy outcome.
However, the problem with this assumption is that the presence of
complex causalities often makes it impossible to determine the reason
why an attempt to solve a problem or exploit new opportunities fails.
There is always the possibility that contingent circumstances beyond
anyone's control caused the policy failure. Even in those cases where
the policy outcome seems to derive from a certain policy output, the
causal link between the policy output and the policy decisions that
brought it about can be highly uncertain, as political decisions are
often ambiguous, inconsistent and subject to competing administrative interpretations. As such, the idea of a one-to-one correspondence
between decision, output and outcome is problematic.

The causality problem undermines the well-established claim that
representative democracy is capable of ensuring a high level of democratic accountability. However, the difficulties with ensuring democratic accountability becomes even more outspoken with regard to

governance networks. The causal link between output and outcomes is weak, since governance networks often share responsibility for policy implementation with a variety of administrative government agencies that may affect the outcome of particular policy outputs in a negative way. The problem with tracing back policy outputs to political decisions is even bigger. First of all, it is often hard to identify clear-cut decisions in governance networks as decisions are a result of complex and informal interactions in which problems, solutions, decision-making premises and implementation strategies are loosely coupled and subject to ongoing revisions. Second, if and when policy decisions are clearly discernable, it is often difficult to establish who precisely was responsible for making the decisions. Governance networks seldom retreat to voting but tend to rely on complex negotiations that lead to the formation of a 'rough consensus' in terms of an agreement or decision that is tacitly accepted out of expediency, despite varying degrees of protest, grievance and dissent. A solution could be to hold the whole governance network to account for a particular output or outcome, but that could be seen as unfair by those who tacitly accepted the agreement or decision, not because they liked it, but because it was the best they could get under the particular circumstances. Finally, no matter whether it is the individual network actors or the whole governance network that are held to account, the attempt to sanction problematic and inappropriate decisions is exceedingly difficult. Since network actors are not elected but most often (self-)appointed, they cannot be voted out in the next election. There might be other ways of excluding failing network actors, but many private organizations tend to monopolize representation of particular groups and therefore it can be difficult to find relevant and qualified substitutes if these private organizations are excluded. Alternatively, discontented citizens may seek to cut back funding and reduce the scope and influence of governance networks responsible for clear and discernable policy failures. However, this approach will tend merely to dismantle the governance network and replace it with more hierarchical forms of top-down government that are difficult for lay citizens to control. A less drastic response would be to publicly scorn the governance networks through what is generally known as 'naming and shaming', but that is seldom very effective, as most of the network actors will plead 'not guilty'.

However, the problems related to meeting the democratic demand for public accountability of governance networks should not make us abandon the fundamental ambition of facilitating *public contestation* of political decisions taken by governance networks. The facilitation of public contestation is a must if we are to prevent governance networks from degenerating into closed and secret clubs that operate in the dark and without public approval (Fox and Miller 1995; Newman 2005; Dryzek 2007). Public contestation basically involves public debate and critical scrutiny of the ways policy problems are defined; the listing and framing of feasible options; the procedures that lead to the choice of a particular policy; and the direct and indirect results of its implementation. In other words, governance networks and the participating actors must provide public accounts of why, how and with which result they do what they do, and they must engage in public dialogue with their opponents and be sensitive to the criticisms that are raised. What we are talking about here is a new kind of narrative accountability whereby the governance network's accounts are publicly contested by critical counter-accounts (March and Olsen 1995, 141ff.).

The relevant counterpart of the governance network is the citizens within the territory bound by the decisions of the governance network, but we should not be under the illusion that all citizens will have their eyes tightly fastened on the decision making, the policy outputs and the policy outcomes of a vast number of governance networks in order to criticize what they find problematic, wrong or wanting. We will have to content ourselves with the critical engagement of concerned publics in terms of mass media, scientific and professional experts, interest organizations, social movements, competing governance networks, and politically interested and empowered individuals. Public audit and critical scrutiny of governance networks at multiple levels require a certain amount of resources, capacities and political interest, which we cannot expect always to find among ordinary citizens, and least of all in unorganized groups of citizens with low education and income. The public contestation of the narrative accounts produced by a governance network is therefore often carried out by different kinds of sub-elites (Etzioni-Halevy 1993).

There are three crucial requirements that must be fulfilled in order to facilitate public contestation of the narrative accounts produced by governance networks and the participating organizations and groups. The first requirement is transparency. Governance networks and their tasks, remit and composition should be fully visible to the general public, and networks must produce regular public accounts for why and how they arrived at particular decisions and what the results have been. The public accounts should be comprehensive, informative and accessible to lay people. Overly brief policy statements, misleading figures and arguments, and a specialized or technical jargon will leave the citizens in the dark as to what goes on in a governance network.

The second requirement is public access to dialogue with governance networks. Narrative accounts of the deeds of various governance networks can be made publicly available on the Internet or through public hearings, press conferences, mass media coverage or the presence of key network actors in accessible public spaces where they can explain themselves to citizens. If there are citizens who want to take issue with the figures, arguments and stipulations presented in the publicly available network accounts, they must have the possibility of engaging in a dialogue with members of the governance network in question. Citizens should be able to ask questions, raise concerns, advance criticisms and organize protests, and the members of the governance network should respond by giving additional accounts that address the issues citizens raise.

The third requirement is responsiveness on the part of the governance network. It does not help much to facilitate critical dialogue between the members of a governance network and a territorially defined citizenry if the former are unwilling to take eventual criticisms into consideration and, if necessary, adjust the course of action. Public contestation is reducible neither to the repressive tolerance of critical voices nor to a polite dialogue with no effect. Public contestation must be played out in a way that promotes responsiveness on the part of the governance network. Just as contesting citizens must be prepared to learn that their criticisms are ill-founded or misguided, governance network actors must be prepared to respond positively to constructive proposals, to make concessions or at least to compensate the losers. One of the ways of promoting two-way responsiveness is to ensure that the dialogue between citizens and a governance network is initiated in the early stages of the policy process and continued later on. If public contestation emerges in the final stages of the policy process where carefully calibrated compromises have already been made and political deals have been struck, the propensity of the network actors to listen to criticisms and consider new alternatives will be extremely low.

The three requirements presented in the preceding pages help us measure the degree to which governance networks are democratically anchored with indirectly affected citizens and with sub-elites who subject the outputs and outcomes of the networked policy process to public contestation. As such, we can draw up a list of norms for measuring the democratic anchorage of governance networks in the territorially defined citizenry. The norms are summarized in Proposition 3.

Proposition 3. Anchorage in a Territorially Defined Citizenry Can Be Measured by Paying Attention to the Following Norms:

- The tasks, remit and composition of a governance network must be fully visible to the general public.
- The governance network must produce regular narrative accounts that seek to justify its decisions, actions and results in the eyes of the broader citizenry.
- The participants in the governance network must engage in a constructive dialogue with those who are publicly contesting their decisions, actions and results.
- The governance network must show some level of responsiveness towards criticisms and alternative proposals raised in the public debate.

Anchorage in Democratic Rules and Norms

The rationale for anchoring governance networks in democratic rules and norms is found in deliberative theories of democracy that claim that decision makers not only gain legitimacy through their democratic linkages to a series of external political constituencies, but also through their adherence to particular democratic standards that regulate their mutual interaction (Fishkin and Laslett 2003; Gutmann and Thompson 2004). The democratic quality of a governance network depends on the degree to which the network actors follow rules and norms inherent in a democratic grammar of conduct (Mouffe 1993). In the same way as the call for 'justice' provides the basis for the deconstruction of actual 'laws' that are always found wanting in some respect (Derrida 1992), the call for a 'democracy-to-come' provides the basis for the deconstruction of historical forms and accounts of democracy (Derrida 1994). However, in order to assess the democratic character of actual forms of governance, we need to invest the ungraspable promise of a 'democracy-to-come' in a set of contingent, incomplete and deconstructable standards that can be used in concrete evaluations and assessments of democratic governance.

The democratic rules and norms that are relevant for an assessment of the structure, functioning and outcomes of governance networks can be derived from different strands of democratic theory. Some can be traced back to the aggregative and integrative strands of liberal democratic theory (March and Olsen 1989), whereas others are rooted in the new post-liberal theories of democracy (Sørensen and Torfing 2005a). The interweaving of theoretical discussions on how to define democracy and political discussions on how to institutionalize democratic forms of governance in present societies means that democratic rules and norms are subject to endless dispute. Hence, the attempt to draw up a complete or unbiased list of democratic norms and rules is doomed to fail. At best we can compile an open-ended list of relevant and commonly accepted – but ultimately contingent – rules and norms that can help us assess the democratic performance of governance networks.

However, admitting the incomplete and ultimately political character of the democratic rules and norms that constitute the democratic grammar of conduct in most Western societies still leaves us with another and even more delicate problem of what it means *to follow democratic rules and norms*. We might be able to show that some rules and norms are relevant, consistent and necessary for ensuring democratic decision making in governance networks, but we cannot expect governance networks and the political actors who inhabit them to follow such rules in a mechanical and unproblematic way, assuming that their form and content are self-evident. Ludwig Wittgenstein (1986) taught us that rule following is not as simple as it may seem. When network actors have succeeded in matching a given situation with a certain rule defined by an institutionalized logic of appropriateness (March and Olsen 1989), the real problems have only just begun. For as Wittgenstein (1986) demonstrates, rules are structurally ambiguous, since there are always numerous ways to follow a particular rule. The search for another rule that can help clarify the content of the first rule leads to an infinite regress that we can escape only by making our own constitutive reformulation of the different rules we encounter on our way. In that case, rules become merely an instance of their usage, even though there are clearly some outer limits to this usage, since actors must be able to show that they act in accordance with broadly recognized and recognizable rules (Staten 1985). This means that the democratic rules and norms can be followed only in and through a situational and contextual re-enactment, which is adjusting the rule to particular circumstances while retaining a family resemblance with other usages of the rule.

The democratic grammar of conduct that is supposed to govern the pragmatic re-enactment of rules and norms includes three kinds of normative stipulations that relate to the formation, functioning and outcome of governance networks. The *first* kind of normative stipulations relates to the democratic demand for inclusion of the affected actors. The norm that the affected actors should be able to influence decisions affecting them is inherent to the democratic idea of self-government (Rousseau 1968; Macpherson 1977). In territorially defined representative democracies, the demarcation of 'the affected' in terms of all competent citizens within the territory is taken for granted and codified by constitutional law, whereas in functionally defined governance networks the questions about who are affected and how much they are affected are subject to endless discussion. In other words, the general political consensus about how to define the voters is not matched by a similar consensus about how to define the relevant stakeholders.

Since governance networks are always predicated on the inclusion and exclusion of more or less affected actors, and since formal inclusion does not guarantee political influence, we need to qualify further the generally accepted norm about the inclusion of affected actors (Young 2000; Fung and Wright 2003; Saward 2005; Dryzek 2007; Sørensen 2012). The first rule concerns the need to ensure an ongoing debate about who should be included or excluded. The lines of demarcation that separate the included from the excluded should not be determined once and for all, but should be constantly renegotiated. The second rule is that the negotiated criteria of inclusion and exclusion must be transparent and consistently applied in relation to all relevant actors. The excluded actors should be able to understand and contest the reasons why they have been excluded. The third rule is that the admission criteria should ensure that all the intensely affected actors that can and will contribute to the networked policy process are included in the network. Of course, everything will depend on how the 'intensity' of the affectedness is defined. In any case, 'intensity' will be a matter of degree and the same goes for 'inclusion', as it is possible to distinguish the core group of participants from more peripheral groups of participants. Therefore, the rule might be that the more intensely affected an actor is, the more that actor should be involved in the core activities in the network. The final rule should be that none of the formally included actors should be marginalized in a way that systematically prevents them from influencing the network decisions (Young 2000). Hence, the political agenda and the storyline, which defines the policy problems and the range of appropriate policy solutions, should be defined in broad terms that are open for reformulation and reinterpretation, thereby facilitating actors with different views and preferences in putting forth claims and ideas that are deemed valid and not excluded a priori from the negotiation table (Hajer 1995; Torfing 2007).

The *second* kind of normative stipulations concerns the demand for democratic deliberation based on agonistic respect for other people's right to voice their opinions; commitment to reach a rough consensus based on an negotiated agreement among political adversaries; and a relatively transparent decision-making process. All the actors in the network should have an opportunity to express their views without being censored by strict demands that they be reasonable, articulate, moderate, civilized and so forth (Young 2000), and if they cannot find adequate support for their views, they should be free to leave the governance network and form or become part of another network. Moreover, network actors with conflicting views should not treat one another as enemies to be eliminated by all possible means, but rather should perceive one another as adversaries who might strongly disagree but who, nevertheless, respect each other's right to express an opinion and fight for it (Mouffe 2005). Network actors may disagree on a whole set of issues and they may attempt to influence the decision-making process by means of controlling agenda-setting, persuading and confronting one another, or manipulating opponents' subjective perception of their interests (Lukes 1974). But no matter how much they try to influence the final decisions, the network actors should be committed to reaching a 'rough consensus', where a large number of actors tend to agree on a compromise formed in the course of struggle and those who disagree tacitly accept the decision, although they reserve their right to contest it. Finally, decisions about public policy and governance should be reached through a relatively transparent process where everyone knows the terms of the debate, the options and the final decisions. Hence, standard procedures for ensuring decision-making transparency through written agendas and minutes and a clear and visible leadership should be observed.

The *third* kind of normative stipulations concerns the demand for democratic improvement of the interactive system of governance. This can be obtained by ensuring that the interactions within the governance network contribute to developing the democratic identities of the participating actors and to augmenting their political empowerment (Sørensen and Torfing 2003). It can also be obtained through self-reflexive political processes that stimulate an active search for new democratic mechanisms that can contribute to a further democratization of public policymaking processes. Democracy never reaches a final form, neither as a perfect set of institutions nor as a regulative idea. Democracy must be constantly developed through a plurality of creative, partial and experimental methods, and governance networks should be judged on their ability to facilitate such a development (Dewey 1954).

The three kinds of normative stipulations described above point to how we should measure the degree to which governance networks are democratically anchored in a democratic grammar of conduct. The relevant criteria are summarized in Proposition 4.

Proposition 4. Democratic Anchorage in Democratic Rules and Norms Can Be Measured by Paying Attention to the Following Norms:

- Inclusion and exclusion must be subject to ongoing negotiations and these negotiations should result in explicit criteria for inclusion and exclusion that should be consistently applied in relation to all relevant actors.
- The degree of inclusion in governance networks should be a function of the intensity of the actors' affectedness and the included actors should be able to influence the decisions made by the governance network.
- The deliberation within governance networks must be governed by a democratic ethos that ensures agonistic respect, commitment to reach a rough consensus based on a tacitly accepted but contestable compromise, and a relatively transparent decision-making process.
- Participation in the governance network must contribute to enhancing the political empowerment of the actors and stimulate democratic innovation through self-reflexive and experimental processes.

Applying the Model

The model for the democratic anchorage of governance networks is not an institutional model based on a set of generic criteria but an analytical assessment model that invokes norms and values articulated by different democratic traditions and theories. The norms and values are contingent upon the historical development of democratic discourse and they aim to transform this discourse by reinterpreting the traditional liberal democratic understanding of these norms and values in light of the shift from government to governance.

The four propositions outlined in preceding sections of this chapter aim to translate the key dimensions of the model of democratic anchorage into a detailed set of democratic norms that can be used in empirical assessments of the democratic quality of specific governance networks. As a general rule, the more politicized a governance network is, the more important it is that it performs well on all the different dimensions and norms. Accordingly, the first step in contextualizing the anchorage model consists in assessing the degree to which a specific governance network is operating in a highly contested terrain with major conflicts manifest and/or latent. Democratic anchorage is extremely important in governance networks operating in a highly politicized environment and contributing to the making of controversial political decisions. By contrast, democratic anchorage is less important in governance networks operating in a highly sedimented context with little disagreement. However, democratic anchorage of networked policy processes is never unimportant, since democratic anchorage is a crucial source of democratic legitimacy. It enables political actors inside and outside a governance network to problematize the taken-for-granted assumptions and appeal to relevant political constituencies and democratic principles if they think the governance network is underperforming or developing into a self-serving 'private interest government' (Schmitter and Streeck 1985).

The next step consists of assessing the conditions pertaining to the form and character of governance networks that will prevent them from doing equally well in relation to all four anchorage points. Hence, when evaluating and comparing the democratic anchorage of different governance networks, we should bear in mind that certain types of governance networks are likely to do quite well in relation to certain anchorage points while doing less well in relation to other anchorage points. In other words, we need to contextualize assessment of the democratic anchorage of governance networks in order to make sure that we focus on the most pertinent anchorage points in our empirical assessment of a particular governance network. Let us briefly consider the four anchorage points in turn.

The fourth anchorage point demanding that negotiated interaction within a governance network be anchored in a democratic grammar of conduct is relevant and important in relation to all kinds of governance networks. Hence, a governance network that fails to re-enact commonly accepted democratic rules and therefore tends to make undemocratic decisions is highly problematic and calls for some kind of political intervention. However, the relevance and importance of the other three anchorage points depend on the form and character of the governance network in question.

The third anchorage point that calls for an anchoring of the output and outcome of governance networks in a territorially defined citizenry is highly relevant for governance networks involved in making decisions with widespread repercussions for other policy areas and for large sections of the population within a particular territory. By contrast, governance networks that deal with relatively isolated problems that are of concern only to those who are directly affected by the policy output and outcome do not need this anchorage point to the same extent as governance networks with a wider impact. Governance networks that are cutting across and integrating multiple levels of governance pose a particular problem in this regard, since they invoke several territorially defined constituencies and since the evaluation of the democratic anchorage might be ambiguous or inconclusive.

The second anchorage point that aims to anchor governance networks in the membership basis of participating groups and organizations is more relevant for governance networks engaged in agenda setting or policy formulation than for governance networks engaged in knowledge sharing or policy implementation. Hence, if the governance networks pave the way for or make authoritative decisions that are crucial for the groups and organizations they are representing, or if these groups and organizations are expected to deliver active support for such decisions, then the anchorage of the network actors in their hinterland is extremely important. By contrast, if the governance networks are merely preoccupied with exchanging relevant information or coordinating the actions of different groups and organizations in order to prevent implementation problems, then a firm anchorage in their membership basis is somewhat less important.

The first anchorage point that emphasizes the need to anchor governance networks in metagoverning politicians is highly important in relation to publicly funded top-down initiated governance networks, to those that have been delegated competence to solve public tasks, and to those that tend to make political decisions of great importance to a large group of stakeholders or the wider community. In comparison, this form of democratic metagovernance is less warranted in relation to self-grown governance networks consisting of different private actors who, for example, are aiming to improve the quality of a given local community through various forms of joint action. At the least, the public metagovernors will have to rely on a tentative use of hands-off metagovernance tools because of the relatively private character of the governance network.

From a certain perspective, the democratic anchorage of governance networks in metagoverning politicians and public managers can be seen as a fundamental requirement. Public metagovernance strategies are capable of ensuring the activation of the three other anchorage points. Public metagovernors can make the influence of a particular governance network conditional on its democratic anchorage in the membership basis of the participating groups and organizations, in a territorially defined citizenry and in a democratic grammar of conduct. The public metagovernors can also use different metagovernance tools in order to improve the democratic anchorage of a particular governance network (Sørensen and Torfing 2009). Accordingly, it can be argued that metagovernance provides a privileged anchorage point. However, we should bear in mind that anchorage of governance networks in a single anchorage point is not enough to ensure democratic legitimacy.

This being said, we willingly admit that it is impossible to make hard and fast rules about the relevance of the different anchorage points. In the final instance, the relevance of the anchorage points depends on a concrete assessment of the form and character of the governance network in question. The reflections presented above serve merely to illustrate the need to contextualize the empirical application of the democratic anchorage model.

Contextualization is also needed when interpreting and acting on the results of the assessment of the democratic anchorage of a specific governance network, since the results will almost always be mixed and a matter of degree, and make sense only when the political and institutional conditions for democratic performance are taken into account. The anchorage model is not designed to produce a clear-cut answer to whether or not a governance network is democratic, since such an answer cannot be given because of the multidimensional character of democracy and the multifaceted character of empirical forms of interactive governance. Rather, the anchorage model aims to give a complex and nuanced answer that, one hopes, matches the complex and multifarious character of the empirical reality.

The democratic anchorage model and the propositions for how to measure it developed in this chapter have been tested in an empirical study of the local governance network driving the decision to build a bridge across the Femern Belt, linking Denmark with Germany (Fotel, Sørensen and Torfing 2009). The governance network is identified through a backward mapping of the social and political actors behind the local campaign to build the Femern Belt Connection. The democratic anchorage of the governance networks is based on qualitative data obtained from interviews and document studies. The qualitative assessment of the performance of the Femern Belt Network in relation to indicators set out in the propositions presented earlier in this chapter is used to score the four anchorage points, ranging from low to moderate to strong. The overall verdict is that the democratic anchorage of the Femern Belt Forum is moderate. There is strong anchorage in the membership bases of the participating groups and organizations and moderate anchorage in both elected politicians and the territorially defined citizenry. However, the anchorage in democratic rules and norms is weak and leaves considerable room for improvement. The empirical testing of the democratic anchorage model demonstrates the usefulness of the model, but also emphasizes the importance of setting boundaries in time and space on the governance network that is to be evaluated. The local governance network is also operating at the regional and national levels and has connections to Germany and the European Union, complicating the analysis of metagovernance and the assessment of whether the relevant and affected actors have been included. In addition, the democratic performance of the governance network varies over time, and this makes it extremely important to specify which period it is that is focussed on.

Another empirical study of local governance networks in the area of active employment policy shows how qualitative and quantitative data can be combined in a study of democratic anchorage using the indicators specified above (Torfing and Damgaard 2010). The focus is on the Local Employment Councils (LECs) in Denmark, and the study concludes that the LECs have a relatively strong democratic anchorage. It is only the democratic anchorage in the territorially defined citizenry that is weak, and the problem is, first and foremost, that ordinary citizens are not really interested in what is going on in the LECs and therefore do not exploit the possibility of getting information about them in order to contest their decisions.

The accumulation of case studies applying the indicators specified in this chapter will facilitate comparative analysis of the possibilities of democratic anchorage of governance networks in different countries and policy areas and at different levels of governance.

Conclusion

The elaboration and operationalization of the model for measuring democratic anchorage of governance networks have demonstrated the value of integrating insights from public administration research and political theory into the field of governance theory. Public administration research has paid increasing attention to the new decentred forms of governance that involve the formation of networks, partnerships and other forms of collaborative governance. However, the burgeoning literature on governance tends to see governance networks as a means of enhancing effective policymaking and policy implementation in an increasingly complex and fragmented world. However, a political science perspective on governance networks reveals their intrinsic political character, and, therefore, the pressing need for assessing and improving their democratic performance.

In this chapter we have presented an elaborate version of the democratic anchorage model and translated the basic dimensions of the model into a detailed set of assessment criteria that can be applied in democratic audits of governance networks. We have also reflected on the relevance of different anchorage points in relation to different kinds of governance networks operating in different political environments. It is clear that we need more empirical studies. Such studies will not only help to adjust and redefine the democratic anchorage model; they will also produce new knowledge about the democratic performance of governance networks and help practitioners design tailor-made strategies for democratizing them. While empirical studies of the democratic anchorage of governance networks will not enable us to draw any general conclusion about the democratic merits of governance networks, they might help us to produce context-sensitive knowledge about the impact of institutional design on the democratic performance of interactive governance practices.

6 | *Learning through Contested Governance: The Practice of Agonistic Intersubjectivity*

JOHN FORESTER

Introduction

A curious thing happens when we read about public conflicts and democratic contestation: we can focus easily on *'what* the conflict is *about'* or, instead, we can focus more subtly on how *those in conflict* might actually handle the issues they face. We might see, for example, conflicts over the uses of land or appropriate ways to dress in public schools or the right to marry a same-sex partner – and then taking the first view, we turn to the substantive views and perspectives, the content of the desires and wants, the arguments and rhetorical positions that each side sets out as participants understand what their 'conflict' is about. In the second view, however, we turn to the ways the land users or students or prospective marriage partners actually engage with one another and others – threatening, bargaining, trading, deferring, exaggerating, beseeching, insulting (and so on) – to press their demands, as they struggle together to transform the relationships in the world they care to change. Let us call the first of these possibilities a view of democratic subjectivity, while we call the second a view of democratic intersubjectivity.

In the first view, we see a subtle bias working to put matters of knowledge first, a bias of academic rationalism – as if conflict involves, first of all, rival claims and ideas. In this view conflicts become struggles over ideas and arguments, hopes and expectations, perhaps regarding 'what is mine' or 'proper' or 'my rights'. In the second view, we see instead a potentially more performative critical pragmatism working: we attend a bit less to what the developers or the community organizers or the religious representatives say on camera and a bit more to what they are prepared or able or willing to actually do to try to live as they wish. Depending on which view we take, we will imagine very differently the project and prospects of this book, the articulation and realization of a governance-driven democratization.

137

The first view of conflict gives us a fine feeling for the perspectives and viewpoints of the claimants, leaders and led, activists and movement members – those perhaps deeply affected whether adequately represented or not. The tribal activist says that this land is not just special or desired but 'sacred'. The gay partner unable to marry says that he feels not only disappointed and disrespected, but humiliated. We appreciate via this view the multiplicity of deeply rooted identity claims, the passionate and constitutive commitments to ways of life and traditions that make us who we are, and these declarations and professions about what matters easily lead us *to see* – to imagine and even to expect – many conflicts to be irreconcilable, intractable or incommensurable. Here we have compelling accounts of the historicity, depth, formation and articulation of democratic subjectivity (Norval 2008). Nevertheless, I will argue here, this view sells democratic action and activism short.

The second view of conflict leads us to focus more on the organizing and negotiating strategies and moves of those involved and their practical strategies of bluffing and threatening, withholding and misrepresenting, exaggerating here and making a gambit there, forming coalitions now and drawing lines in the sand then, and more. This second – critical pragmatic, performative and relational – view recognizes that many of us mere mortals walk around with multiple and conflicting deep allegiances (recognizing real obligations to parents and to children simultaneously, for example), and we seem often, nevertheless, to reconcile these non-negotiable, constitutive commitments a good deal of the time without severe angst. The second view leads us not just to be a bit less stereotyping or essentializing about any lived, potentially democratic subjectivity (environmentalist, or daughter, or Jew, for example), but also to pay more attention instead to the challenges of *engaging* practically in what we can call the *democratic interactions, the democratic dance of intersubjectivity*, of actually engaging with, facing and acting on the conflicts we find pressing (protecting open space, caring for our aging parents, resisting discrimination). Mark Warren's lucid explication of governance-driven democratization (in Chapter 2) shows us the centrality of such democratic engagements, even though he assesses the conditions of such street-level democratization more than their performances.

In the first view, then, we find the claimants' *arguments* irresistible and study those arguments about what they want, how they see the world, how their views grow out of their traditions, identities and experiences, perhaps as landless immigrants or disenfranchised people of colour or vulnerable elderly or underserved poor or alienated adolescents. In the second view, we study less the rhetorical arguments and more what those claimants and their representatives and allies do and *can do*, both in the historical present *and* – were conditions to change – in the evolving, malleable, historical future. In the first view, we consider the *content* of their claims and how their ideas might change; in the second, we consider how they might *transform and enact their actual relationships* of vulnerability or humiliation – or marginality or exclusion or domination, for example – into ones realizing more or less autonomy or community or health or security or mutual recognition. The first view appears over-theorized by academic 'theorists' keen to expose irreconcilable conflicts supposedly presenting deep challenges to liberal democracy. The second view goes begging, under-theorized and under-studied.

To explore the second, more practice-centred approach, to see how assessing practical democratic intersubjectivity can teach us about real cases of democratic conflict, this chapter will build on earlier research exploring the experience and practice of mediators of public disputes (Forester 2009, 2013b; Wagenaar this volume, Chapter 10). Those mediators have come to practical and theoretical insights about conflict the hard way – through years of assisting disputing parties in crafting inventive, productive and co-generated agreements, resolving their deep differences in workable and pragmatic ways. Those mediators can help us in surprising ways to understand that in situations that look quite bleak, possibilities for resolving differences between deeply conflicting parties may well still remain. Those mediators can help us learn to search for and construct possibilities in the real, if perhaps poorly imagined, political world where others think – believe, suspect, suppose, presume – that very little can be done (Forester 2012b, 2013a). Here, reading Wittgenstein both with and against Norval, I see obstacles as more contingent perhaps than others might, making the political 'necessity' (Cavell, as discussed in Norval 2007) more politically suspect than taken for granted by parties in any 'given' case.

We can learn a good deal from such canaries in the mines of conflict, not least of all that practical agreements between parties with deep value differences can be possible *despite their rhetoric to the contrary*. Parties can often learn about each other and better inform, and then revise, their opening demands as they learn. Dispute resolution processes often involve far more than quid pro quo negotiations, of course. Early stages of successful processes involve careful convening of the parties to enable mutual recognition not agreement, to enable surprise rather than confirmation of stereotypes, and to enable identi-fication of both joint vulnerabilities and opportunities to learn – all of which can well lead passionate parties to be no less passionate but to craft more practical proposals to serve their ends.

In a recent paper touching on these themes, Aletta Norval (2008) has contrasted three views of democratic practice: the first sees dem-ocratic politics as primarily depending on fair procedures that enable participants to make and contest claims in a public space. The sec-ond sees democratic practice as a matter of the continually fluid and evolving formation of democratic subjectivities, as claimants express previously unarticulated demands and claims on one another. The third (as I will interpret it here) sees democratic practice as a matter of sharing conventions of claims making so that we might understand claimants – immigrants, youth, gays, the underserved – as enacting relational conventions – so we can see them as appropriately included or unfairly excluded, for example, even as we recognize that politi-cal and legal claims-making activities and performances can constitute and reconstitute shifting relations between these parties and the state and with one another, and create newly oppositional and newly crea-tive public spaces as well.

Norval (2008) recognizes that a rich theoretical and practical account of democratic practice can rest upon neither formal procedure nor individual subjectivity alone. Her provocative and critical paper helps us to refine and perhaps even transform Laclau and Mouffe's account of democratic self-expression – that is, democratic subjectivity – into a rich analysis of a more critically pragmatic, performative notion of actual democratic interaction and engagement, what we might well call, 'democratic intersubjectivity'.

Laclau and Mouffe, and Norval following them, stress the omni-presence of power, of course, and the always historically contingent *expression of claims* of interests and identity, values and commitments, requests and demands, threats and inquiries, proposals and more. Agonistic theories of politics stress ineradicable differences: no mat-ter what happens in democratic debate, constitutive identities ought not be erased as if plurality could be assimilated away, as if nonwhites would be made white, as if non-Christians would be made Christian, as if gays would be made straight. What agonistic theories – or better, these theorists – tell us *less* about, though, is the performative ways in which real democratic participants, who raise claims of rights or entitlement, for example, might ever do more than 'be heard,' or worse, 'express themselves' – might ever not only express their freshly formed democratic subjectivities but also actually transform their relationships, not with each other along lines of solidarity but across those lines of presumptive deep difference vis-à-vis those with whom they critically engage for greater welfare, recognition and justice.

So we might, then, build upon the agonists – Laclau and Mouffe, Hillier and others Norval cites – to understand how in democratic practices oppositional claimants can ever make any practical differences, can as performers do more than press their wishes, make demands, take diverse subject positions. We need to understand how they can change their relationships, not only try to *be* convincing or persuasive, but convince or persuade others, not only to *ask for* (or even 'demand' or 'insist upon') gains but actually *achieve* and secure and obtain those gains. We need to assess the performative ways that real persons can not only present themselves and their subjectivities, but inter-act, act meaningfully and intersubjectively (not solipsistically or atomistically or as radically individuated subjective selves) to materially and practically get anything done, to ever, even partially, satisfy their concerns, interests or values.

If we want an account of democratic practice in which previously marginalized and activist groups actually do more than talk, do more than organize themselves and build oppositional solidarity, we need to assess how in *deed* – performatively and interactively, via intersubjective webs of conventions – at times those parties, claimants, participants, those passionately making demands, can actually transform their lived, interdependent relationships with others: with elites, politicians, the unorganized, decision makers, corporate investors, and so on.

For example, sometimes those claimants will 'put pressure' on elites or politicians by demonstrating and threatening to withdraw votes or public support; sometimes they will organize to withdraw essential services or cooperate via strikes; sometimes they will directly negotiate by contingently offering support or consent of one kind in return for procuring resources or services of another kind; sometimes they might be able to persuade political leadership via the court of public opin-ion to extend rights to previously disenfranchised persons and so on. Democratic subjectivity and 'expression' do play roles, but individual self-expression is not the point: in addition we must understand how political subjects – better, how political actors enact power as well as face power, how they can achieve results and not just talk, talk, talk about them, how they can transform relationships of political mem-bership and not just describe or pine for what a better politics might involve.

So we need an account of democratic interaction (be it struggle, organizing, mobilization, visiting, negotiation, offering, and so on) that can include *and* move beyond passionate subjectivity and ago-nistic expression to show how politically interactive performance can produce practical outcomes – produce them via real political practices in which claimants do more than express themselves. Here Norval leads us both back and forward to a sophisticated pragmatic account that Stanley Cavell develops from Wittgenstein's work. Norval sees that Cavell does not rely on any abstract account of rules and proce-dures to make sense of ordinary and even creative interaction, so he satisfies postmodernists' demands to understand social action in its actual context.

But Norval also sees that Cavell helps us to understand how one per-son can 'influence' or 'get another person to do something' or 'make a difference' or 'change a relationship' *because they interact in a conven-tional or rule-governed context*. To explore how this might work, take three ordinary if variously political examples: 'Strike three!' means the baseball batter is history. 'You're fired' means under many employ-ment conditions that a worker no longer has a job. 'I slept with your best friend' can mean a deep disruption if not the end of a relationship with one's partner, and so on.

Notice what we will lose if we see even these simple examples only as self-expression, as revealing the formation of subjectivity, rather than as intersubjective action, as performance with others. In instances such as these, saying something amounts to much more even than describing something, even if description forms one part of the action at hand.

If a spectator calls the pitch 'Strike three,' that might be mere description, but the home plate umpire's very same words do more: they invoke and express the authority of the umpire to rule the batter 'out'. Not to appreciate this difference provides an example of understanding the words and misunderstanding the institutional relationships involved, relationships of power and membership, hope and drama too.

'You're fired' uttered by a friend in the kitchen might be an ironic joke to say, 'Next time I'll make the eggs!' But uttered by an employer to an employee, these same spoken words can become not mere description but the actual act of firing someone, terminating their employment.

Just as clearly, and perhaps no less devastatingly, a lover's 'I slept with your best friend' can tear or betray a relationship, can exert enormous influence, can be a shattering action that makes change, that transforms the social and political world well beyond simply 'describing something' more or less accurately.

Of course the settings make a huge difference to just what these utterances, accomplish when we say them, but the fundamental point here is this: in making such expressions 'in context,' we are not simply *expressing* ourselves, our passions, our identities – although we may be doing all that too – we are changing relationships in the world, not just epistemically by knowing more, but ethically by acting practically as we speak.

At stake in each performance, the practical employment of each of these utterances, lies not so much a claim to knowledge (although each claim may be fallible), but a claim to practical action and practical consequence (what theorists call a perlocutionary claim). At stake in each situated performance is not so much a claim to truth or falsity – although to be sure their truth will matter! – as a claim to an altered relationship: the batter who has struck out must wait until she is at bat next to have a chance to hit; the fired employee must now look for another job, perhaps find a way to appeal the decision, or most likely no longer expect a pay cheque from this employer; the betrayed lover must do far more than 'think' about what she or he has just heard, but must re-imagine herself or himself both singly and 'together', whatever those identities may now mean.

This shows us – following Wittgenstein, Austin, Cavell and Norval and, as I myself have argued too (Forester 1999, 2012a) – that we dismiss the politics of speech at our own risk, that we dismiss what we do, what we perform more than express with words at the risk of our own blindness. So we need to understand better *how* and when such actual intersubjective performances, employing such uttered claims, can make such huge differences in our relational, political, interconnected lives.

To see 'description' or speech or even non-verbal gestures no longer as picturing or indicating objects but now as elements of action in complex contexts (the institutions above, for example, of a baseball game, a workplace, an intimate relationship) means, in political terms, that we can not only assess the democratic *subjectivity* of expressing a passionate claim and 'being heard,' but we can also recognize and explore the democratic *intersubjectivity* of being able – in a wide variety of ordinary contexts we share – to *transform* our relationships. We can bring new relationships into being, we can enact and instantiate new identities (perhaps as betrayer and betrayed, perhaps as recognizer and recognized, one who respects and is respected, and so on). But more: we can not only assess the politics of transforming relationships and identities in everyday life, we can also reveal the politics of everyday life as well, including the ways we listen to one another or fail to, the ways we attend to one another's possibilities or fail to, the ways we encourage action and recognition and kindness and care, or fail to, and so on – in the actual practices of governance-driven democratization and 'uninvited citizen participation' (Wagenaar, this volume, Chapter 10).

Subjectivity and Intersubjectivity in a Neighbourhood Redevelopment Setting

Consider a more elaborated example that we can take from the challenges of community planning and housing renovation work in order to see how our focus on democratic *subject formation* might fall short of what we can gain instead by examining the ongoing reconstitution and enactment of democratic intersubjectivity. In a small municipality near Rotterdam, in the Netherlands, Ellen Hiep faced an ordinary neighbourhood planning problem as she worked between the local Housing Association (owning and managing apartment units) and the residents who actually lived in those units. Hiep had been hired to help the Housing Association generate bottom-up plans for neighbourhood renewal and renovation, and so she soon found herself one of five 'neighbourhood coaches', each one, as we shall see, charged with learning about the wants and needs of residents in certain of the Housing Association's units in Vlaardingen.

Hiep says of her role and that of her four colleagues:

So these people had the independent role, independent from the Housing Association, to see what the residents wanted in their opinion of the neighborhood. They were independent of the Housing Association, paid by the Housing Association, but had an independent hat. We had decided who these neighborhood coaches would be; they were five people from our brainstorming group. Everyone went away for a month or five weeks, and we said, 'Go and talk to the residents in any way you want and come back with a plan about what they want.' I was one of the five people.

Continuing, Hiep explains how she went about her work:

I went to the usual suspects. I had two big, difficult apartment buildings … but I went there, and I just said, 'In what way do you want to put this straight? What do you want to do? Can I talk to you – 30 minutes or so?'

They were really glad if someone wanted to talk with them. Of course, I made a plan and said … we should have a two-way approach: first we're going to knock on doors [for] an interview – in my 'we' unit, with a hundred families or so – and afterwards we're going to have a meeting, because when we knocked on the doors we'd ask them, 'Do you want to come to a meeting to talk about all this?' and they'd say, 'OK' and we'd talk about on what day we could have the meeting. Then those people that wanted to come would come and talk more clearly on the subjects that were on the table.

She gives us a glimpse of the resulting meetings this way:

Those meetings had two parts; we had a complaining part and a positive part, because there were so many things wrong that we had a 'klaagmuur', a wailing wall, so people could write down all their complaints and put it on the wall, so that at least we'd know that all this information was captured.

This was our design in the meeting, to have a complaining wall and a positive part. It worked really well, because if you don't do that, they come and complain the whole meeting through! And we wanted to have them captured; we wanted them to complain about things, because 80% of the things were things that the Housing Association had to know anyway. So, they could drop it there; and if there would be a complaint during the meeting, I would say, 'Well, write it down and put it on the wall,' so at least it would get captured.

And then, what we'd first do was … ask, 'What would you really value and cherish that will give you that warm feeling in 10 years from now?' If you talk about it now, and if you have small kids, you might say, 'Well,

I really like the small playground' – now – but in ten years, your kids will be ten years older, so what do you think that you'll really like then?'

So Hiep set out to 'talk to the residents' and 'come back with a plan about what they want'. She'd decided to go door to door, talk to the residents, and ask if they'd be interested in coming to a meeting with other residents in their building to discuss what renovations or changes the Housing Association might work to implement. She says, for example,

[W]hen we knocked on the doors, we'd ask them, 'Do you want to come to a meeting to talk about all this?' and they'd say, 'OK' and we'd talk about on what day we could have the meeting. Then those people that wanted to come would come and talk more clearly on the subjects that were on the table.

Notice that what Hiep does by asking, 'Do you want to come to a meeting to talk about all this?' involves both issues of subjectivity and intersubjectivity. Her question probes for what the residents 'want', we might say, with respect to a particular further intention or objective, to 'talk about all this', that is, the issues concerning the building's renovation.

In probing for the residents' feelings, surely Hiep participates here in their subject formation: she sets an agenda; she asks for their evaluation of the prospect of having a meeting; she pinpoints a further intention, the object and point of such a meeting, 'to talk about all this'. Some residents said 'Yes' and some said 'No', we might surmise, and in so doing they took and adopted subject positions and refined their own subjectivities, in part because Hiep had prompted them to do so.

But more than that, if we follow Hiep's observations here, we see too that her own subject formation, her own appearing to take seriously the feelings of the residents, made a difference to the residents own subjectivities too: 'They were really glad,' characterizes several of the residents' developing sentiments and subjectivities – as they recognized Hiep's own apparent subjectivity as 'someone [who] wanted to talk with them'.

Marking these subjectivities and noticing their changes and formation seems fundamental and right, surely a deep part of the work of recognition. But such recognition, we might easily think, is not right enough, as we can now see. For in asking, 'Do you want to come to a meeting to talk about all this?' Hiep does not simply collect information about subjectivities, she *invites* those residents to such meetings. In asking if the residents want to come 'to a meeting to talk about all this', again she does not simply inventory feelings and gather data, but she acts to shape a shared future with those residents: she *promises* – and takes responsibility, then, for following through – to devote these future meetings to that purpose.

Those performances of inviting and promising, *convening and bringing together* the residents, not only produce (that is, work to form) new *relationships* and therefore form new subjectivities, as they indeed do, but they also actually *produce (work to form)* those new relationships. We see here both shifting democratic subjectivities *and* the practical action, the *inter*subjective action, through which one person's utterance can actually count as a real promise, as a real invitation, as a real question and so on.

Perhaps, we can say, a refined 'we' of the residents takes shape in these meetings, and that adds further to an evolving democratic subjectivity. But Hiep's agenda-setting, requesting, inviting and promising – in addition to *showing* that she wants to talk to the residents – these make up her practical performance, her intersubjective action, that reaches beyond any assessments of subjectivities. To make the point: if we attend only to the formation of democratic *subjectivities*, we risk losing sight of the practices and analytic possibilities of the work and actions of *forming* those subjectivities. We risk attending to evolving subjectivity and missing the action.

We risk attending to shifting subject positions but missing the intersubjective drama, the intersubjective dynamics, the intersubjective performance that makes possible the alteration or influence upon any subjectivity at all. The focus on democratic subjectivity is right, but not right enough: we need to focus as well on the constitution and enactment of democratic intersubjectivity.

In similar ways, we might make a parallel argument about Hiep's question to the residents about what they would cherish in ten years' time. Assessing their professions of what they'd cherish tells Hiep about their subject formation, but she is not doing an academic study; she needs to know far more than that, because she needs not only to learn and know but to do something more, to create a plan, one that will address and actually focus future Housing Association efforts to respond to the desires, or perhaps the priorities, of the residents. As the residents tell Hiep about what they think they will cherish in ten years, they not only tell her about their subjective feelings but they do more: they point to material conditions in the environment, in their buildings, that the Housing Association should, they argue, take into account.

Hiep goes to the residents to learn about their democratic subjectivities, to be sure, but not just that – she goes there also to *recognize* them, to *take them seriously*, to *give them confidence* that she will not only listen to them, but actually help them have instrumentally productive meetings together in the future. She seeks both to identify subjectivity and to *recognize* it, but she does even more: she tries to shape the investment of attention possible on the part of the Housing Association: that, after all, is part of what a plan for renovation would be.

So Hiep's work of recognition, of giving serious regard, of building trusted relationships, of identifying and naming and marking 'cherished objects' that the Housing Association might now address practically – all that involves careful action linking subjects, careful action made possible by and re-enacting a democratic intersubjectivity – specific *actions* (here inviting, recognizing, agenda setting, priority setting and more) that Hiep takes significantly *in addition to* gauging the residents' subjectivities.

Power, Subjectivity and Intersubjectivity

But surely, many will say, the contexts we share everyday in political-economic life, in workplaces and community settings and in personal life as well, sit riddled with relationships of power, economic power and gendered power, ideological and hegemonic power, and more. Of course, those power relationships take historical shape every day and day to day: they are neither fixed for all time (as metaphysics) nor merely imaginary (as idealizations). They form no fixed bedrock, and calling various relations of power 'ontologies' invokes a language – and a sometimes-bullying rhetoric – of metaphysics, but it clarifies virtually nothing politically. Those contexts of governance or contest, of employment or sports, community or personal lives, take shape on historical and political stages, and actors in those contexts act not as robots on those stages but as cultural, socialized, politically changing agents.

Yes, power is everywhere, and so are 'relationships' everywhere, and so are institutionally varying conditions of deference and challenge: to recognize our institutional relationships as deeply 'political' means that we see them as deeply contestable and *not static*. So the politics of everyday life and the politics of civil society and informality too involve actors and organizers, those deferring and those resisting, those rebelling and those going along, all necessarily improvising within the shifting contexts of our lives: the shifting pressures of economic ups and downs, natural disasters, personal tragedies, political machinations and movements and more.

But to see political relationships as systematically underdetermined, always contingent and in principle open to disruption and contest, does not mean that 'anything goes': it means that democratic intersubjectivity involves continuously responsive perception and interpretation, discriminating judgement and improvisation in situated contexts (Barrett 1998, 2007, cf. 2012). As improvising actors, we need to make judgements about the particulars (a joke? a threat?) and the character (irony? danger?) of the unique situations we find ourselves in, so we can act in the complex, formal and informal settings of our lives. We must navigate the ambiguities of multiple and conflicting norms; we must decipher and identify details and assess their meaning. The baseball hitter must decide with each pitch how to psych out the pitcher or catcher, how to apply the counsel of the coach, how to swing or wait for the umpire's call. The employee who has been fired must decide how or if appeal or resistance might be possible, how she or he might best now find support or new employment, how to present the news to loved ones. The jilted lover must now deal with anger or disgust or horror or denial and 'figure out' how to go on, continuing 'the relationship' in some new way or 'breaking up', and so on.

So the contexts of political (and democratic) action all have indeterminate and ambiguous and yet salient conventions, and indeterminate, ambiguous and salient rules. The contexts (or 'the rules') do not make robots of the actors however, for if they did, democratic subjectivity and democratic intersubjectivity alike would be impossible. So we see the democratic *subjectivity* of claims made upon authorities, claims made *for* civil rights, *for* freedom of religious dress, *for* rights to marry same sex partners, among endless examples. Yet we can see more too. We see the democratic *intersubjectivity* of organizers doing extraordinary work in ordinary contexts, as Charles Payne's brilliant and meticulous book on Mississippi politics shows us again and again, transforming our very understanding of the ordinary (Payne 1995). Ordinary people, Payne shows us, took risks again and again and changed their world to transform apartheid-like race relations and U.S. politics as well.

So what does this extension of democratic subjectivity into democratic intersubjectivity imply for governance, for public contestation and dispute? It means first that we can agree that agonistic theories of ineradicable conflict with ever-present power relationships are right and yet not right enough. Yes, conflicts of constitutive identities will abide, and inequalities of power will virtually always provide a setting for and partially constitute relationships at hand, but nevertheless democratic actors will have choices to make and take, to construct: how to organize, how to protest, how to build coalitions, how to invoke empowering traditions and cultural values, how to resist fear mongering, how to respond to naysayers and cynics, how to shepherd resources, how to build trust, how to focus pressure, how to negotiate, and so on.

This means that democratic actors – especially those not already empowered as full-fledged participants 'at the table' of established political institutions – must not just find ways subjectively to 'express themselves' and 'be heard' in some diffuse way, but find ways *intersubjectively to make practical and political (i.e., relational) differences*. Democratic actors and organizers, residents and claimants can practically enact that democratic intersubjectivity, that connected and engaged democratic agency, I suggest, in some combination of three distinct ways in contexts of governance challenges: through processes of dialogue that lead to greater understanding, through processes of debate that lead to more or less justified arguments, and through processes of multi-stakeholder negotiation, mediated or not, that lead to interest-satisfying action.

Consider each of these processes – and available strategies – in turn. Processes of dialogue involve conversations with all the ambiguities and uncertainties that those may involve. In dialogue with another, we try to understand 'where they are coming from', 'what the world looks and feels like to them', 'what they mean'. To get help in a dialogue, we may well ask for someone to 'facilitate' our 'conversation'. We know that a dialogue may not end in any agreement at all (or it might), and success might bring only a better sense of why we disagree as much as we do. We might want something more than dialogue – to persuade the other or to press that person to act differently – or we might be content to 'understand' more than we have. The activist organizer depends on dialogues to build relationships of trust and solidarity, to build a 'base' with which to act.

Debate, in contrast, involves not so much 'conversation' but 'argumentation'. As we debate, we are looking for who is right and who is wrong, who has the better or stronger or more persuasive argument (and who does not). Our interest in understanding is strategic: we want to win the debate, to understand our adversaries so we can find their weaknesses, so we can refute their arguments. To get help to stage a debate, we might turn not to any 'facilitator' but to a skilled 'moderator', one who will not try to bring us together across our differences but who will try to assure that contending arguments and evidence and counter-arguments can be heard fairly and effectively. Again, in social movements, for example, we may very well not engage in debate to form any agreements at all with the other, with our adversary, but we debate arguments and social costs to show an interested public or a particular audience that our account of the world – the dangers of these pollutants, the harm done by offshore drilling – provides a more plausible and coherent view of the world than does our opponents' account. The activist or organizer needs de facto debate to be able to respond to, to set right, we might say, what she or he sees as the adversary's misrepresentations or other distortions of the relevant facts at hand. Many organizers know to expect that those in power will rationalize their actions as being best for the public, as justified, as necessary – to try to continue or establish their hegemony – and so community and political organizers will have a spate of counterarguments ready to deploy and employ.

But notice that neither the processes of dialogue nor those of debate necessarily produce any further action beyond perhaps some increased understanding or clarification of the better or flimsier argument. Frustrated with seemingly endless appeals to seemingly endless dialogue in public life, some dread such talk, talk, talk and little action on the pressing problems of the day. Seeing yet again the experts on this side debate the experts on that side, we may wonder yet again, 'So what?'

So we might well be interested not so much in either dialogue or debate, primarily, but in actual materially specific negotiations. We might wish not so much to 'understand' the politicians who support shale gas drilling as to tell them as well that if they do not support greater environmental protection and job programmes, we will organize to get them out of office. We might wish not so much to debate the (de)merits of national housing policy as to negotiate with decision-making officials: in a neighbourhood perhaps, 'We'll organize neighbourhood watch programs and cleanups and voters, if you'll increase funding for neighbourhood housing services', and so on.

We negotiate not first of all to reach 'understanding' or 'justification' but to reach agreements on and commitments to concrete actions, even if those actions involve the adoption of new policies. But negotiations can go wrong just as dialogues can be chaotic and debates can be explosive. So to get help to stage complex negotiations, we may turn to skilled mediators, mediators who work to prevent and pre-empt mutually strategic, mutually punishing lose-lose agreements and who work instead to understand the breadth of parties' multiple interests so that those parties can actually find 'integrative', 'mutual gains' agreements on real actions, real options. If mediators attend – as a literature on emerging practices suggests – to inclusive representation of affected parties, to reducing missed opportunities and so maximizing mutual gain agreements, to drawing on the best available scientific information, and to making stable rather than merely convenient agreements (Susskind et al., 1999), then we can expect such mediated negotiations not only to build upon both processes of dialogue and debate, but also to provide an initial, if rough, model of an inclusive, efficient, power-sensitive, recognition-enacting governance-driven democratization (Warren, this volume, Chapter 2; Wagenaar, this volume, Chapter 10), *a working form of an astute, agonistic democratic intersubjectivity*. In such mediated negotiations – not simply any 'collaborative' or 'participatory' process (Forester 2008, 2009) – democratic actors can express deep differences and constitutively distinct identities that will be in deep conflict even as those actors may *still* negotiate practical decisions together about how to live, how not to kill one another, how to distribute food and health care, how to care for their environments and so on.

Activists and organizers, of course, need to engage with processes of negotiation unless they will stay content to express themselves and 'be heard' and not yet worry about what subsequent action anyone might take as a result. Put differently, we risk caricaturing both oppositional organizing and skilful negotiation if we see these as rivals rather than as complementary. The skilful organizer knows that by building power 'away from the table' he or she will be more able to negotiate effectively in whatever forum lies at hand: the city council or the company offices (Anguelovski 2010). Likewise, any skilful negotiator knows that much of the work of negotiation happens not 'at the table' or 'in front of the city council' at all but in building leverage or power, shaping others' perceptions of their alternatives and their needs, their risks and vulnerabilities, and more. Both organizing *and* negotiation provide instances of democratic intersubjectivity par excellence, not only because both involve the creation of new relationships, not only because both involve the exploration of new possibilities, not only because both involve building and transforming power and identities at the same time, but because both rightly refuse to reduce political action to subjective expression, to merely celebrating difference rather than also engaging it, or to 'talking' about power without engaging it practically and critically to transform the ordinary lived world.

Notice that the triad of dialogue, debate and negotiation, along with the corresponding enabling practices of facilitating, moderating and mediating, bridge the dual concerns that actual democratic participants will often have with knowledge *and* action, with epistemology *and* ethics. In dialogue we have not only a search for understanding but for expressions of recognition, if short of agreements upon action. In debate we have not only a search for the more justified argument or position, but we have the resulting nuanced warnings or threats, recommendations or assurances about possible outcomes that the debates might have covered. In negotiations, of course, we see knowledge utilized not as persuasion, not via force of the better argument, but creatively to discover mutual gains that few thought possible earlier, to probe and learn and invent so that what seemed impossible now seems only contingently so – and so that new possibilities emerge in this case – and that can sustain and strengthen a renewed democratic polity, that can give legs to the project of governance-driven democratization.

Finally, by integrating practices of dialogue, debate and negotiation we overcome the problems that Aletta Norval compellingly posed: we do not need to rely on a priori standards to define 'democratic' practices universally, nor do we fall back to accepting as democratically legitimate whatever emerges from each local context of interaction.

Each of the processes of dialogue, debate and negotiation are open to the future and ask us to respect counterfactual, hypothetical possibilities – each remains fallible and can go wrong: in dialogue we know not to be literal, we know to respect and probe ambiguity, to grapple with significance as well as fact; in debate we know that horizons of truth and justification are endlessly complex and yet not arbitrary, that argumentation depends on theories and presuppositions woven into forms of life, that debate suffers from restrictions on evidence and grows as democracy grows (Putnam 1974); in negotiation we know that astutely mediated processes can explore real political possibilities not initially visible or even imaginable to democratic participants (invited or uninvited, as Wagenaar, in his contribution in this volume, sees) coming to deal with each other practically for perhaps the first time in the same room (Forester 2009, 2013b); we know that initial opinions can give way to considered judgements, that democratic participants can not only learn about the interests and values of the other but of themselves as well, transforming not only their own democratic subjectivities but also their abilities to engage intersubjectively and democratically as well, intersubjectively and critically – where 'critically' means at least 'being sensitive to exclusions of people or data, to suppressions of feelings or arguments, to refusals to explore options and inquire into possibilities just because some may presume little to be possible'.

An account of democratic politics and governance must be equally plausible as an epistemology and as an ethics; it cannot privilege understanding at the expense of practical action to change the world. It cannot reduce democratic life to a liberal subjectivity free of interactions that actually transform relationships in the political world. Yet by building upon Aletta Norval's step backward and forward at once to the work of Wittgenstein, as appropriated by Stanley Cavell (Norval 2008), we can extend agonistic accounts of democratic subjectivity to articulate now a fresh, critical-pragmatic account of democratic intersubjectivity (Forester 2012b, 2013a). We can do that if we see that democratic intersubjectivity, as we have begun to explore it here, weaves together elements of three distinctly pragmatic yet theoretically interesting practices, those of contingently facilitated dialogues, moderated debates, and mediated negotiations (Forester 2009). These practices will undergird, I submit, any governance-driven democratization worth its name.

7 | Decentred Legitimacy in the New Community Governance

STEPHEN CONNELLY

Introduction

'The voice I can hear out there is saying: "Who the hell made you king?"'

The chairperson of a neighbourhood forum reflects on his organisation's leading role in local regeneration in a post-industrial English city. His concern points to an issue at the heart of current urban policy in Britain: what is the source of legitimacy for the new forms of governance at the level of 'the community', which in principle give citizens a leading role in steering their own affairs? The question is important: as scholars and citizens we should both care whether governance is legitimate and understand how it works, and an important element of this is the legitimacy it needs to function. But how can legitimacy be understood in the complex context of the 'new governance'?

This book is concerned with working towards an approach to governance based in a 'decentred' analysis (Bevir 2003). This approach recognises not only the complex, dynamic, multi-stakeholder nature of forms of governance which have emerged in recent decades – which I refer to as 'the new governance' (Rhodes 1996) – but also the fundamental value pluralism of the public domain in which governance occurs, and that its institutions and shared meanings are negotiated through and emerge from the myriad practices of those concerned. The concern for an actionable approach links this potentially relativistic analysis to a specific normative agenda. We are concerned about democratic governance, where 'democracy' itself is also decentred: potentially found in any governance practice and identified with the possibility of contest and claim making within an ethos of respect for deep difference (Connolly 1995). This conception of democracy is not tied to specific institutional forms but to more fundamental qualities of processes. It thus guides the analysis towards a concern with how institutions allow, or repress, Tully's 'practices of freedom', that is, challenges to existing practices of governance (Tully 2002).

The consequences for an analysis of legitimacy are profound. Orthodox accounts of British governance point to the involvement of a wider range of stakeholders than was previously the case, organised in more 'horizontal' and less hierarchical ways. (While the extent and implications of this change are contested, its existence is largely accepted. See Moran 2010). In many cases neither the involvement of these stakeholders nor the relationships between them are sanctioned by an electoral process. Unless they are to be rejected as illegitimate tout court, we need to develop criteria of legitimacy not resting on our inherited language of representative democracy (Tully 2002).

On the other hand, decentring focuses attention on processes of sense making as central to governance. As with all social practices and relations, governance is sustained by legitimation processes (Zelditch 2001), and the 'making of sense' is in part a process in which understandings and practices become collectively acceptable and thus stabilised to some extent. The legitimacy of any practice of governance is thus not a given but an achievement of those involved. Normative democratic theory matters in such processes, not as a provider of objective standards by which to judge whether a practice is legitimate or not, but as a source for some of the norms which may be drawn on by actors in the legitimising process. Of course, this does not preclude evaluation, but it does force any evaluator (whether researcher or other governance actor) to acknowledge his or her own engagement in the process.

In this chapter I elaborate this decentred approach to legitimacy, and as a case study present an analysis of how legitimacy is constructed in a northern English city, within community-based regeneration organisations working in poor neighbourhoods. The aim is not to redefine legitimacy, but rather to provide a tool for decentred analysis which is sensitive to the complexity of governance, through developing a 'provisional language' (Tully 2002, 538) – a framework within which 'local' understandings of the legitimacy of governance can be analysed without normative prejudgements. The central question of such an analysis is thus: *what norms in fact sustain and challenge the new (and old!) forms of governing under scrutiny?* Since some of these norms are likely to be democratic, a further question is: *in what ways, and to what extent, is this legitimacy democratic?* While in itself not prescribing a particular normative standpoint, this question opens up the possibility of moving towards normative judgement – a natural corollary is the final question: *in particular, is there potential here for radical democratic practice?*

Theorising Decentred Legitimacy

One widely documented aspect of the new governance in Britain has been the emergence of neighbourhood-based structures as vehicles for giving urban communities voice in regeneration initiatives and in local governance more widely (see, e.g., Taylor 2003). The general rationales for the new governance outlined in Chapter 1 are reinforced at the level of local communities by a perceived decline in the legitimacy of elected local government and the potential of increased citizen involvement simultaneously to establish more legitimate and effective local governance and to reinvigorate the representative democratic system (DETR 1998; Taylor 2003). During the 1990s a new kind of organisation emerged in Britain and elsewhere to contribute to these aims. These intermediary bodies (known as 'community forums', 'development trusts', etc.) claim to be legitimate representatives of their communities, able to speak for them in other arenas and to spend public money in line with the community's priorities. They are sites where the twin aspirations of increased community participation and governance through partnerships come together, and within British regeneration and decentralisation policy they came to be highly regarded and cast as natural recipients of responsibilities and assets devolved from the state (Quirk 2007; Rocket Science UK Ltd. 2010).

These organisations raise issues about legitimacy rather forcefully. On the face of it, they are inherently democratic in a fundamental, rather simple sense, as bodies which are at least partly constituted of 'local people' making decisions about their locality. However, they also appear to usurp some of the roles of elected local governments. Most carry out a wide range of functions, including providing services, disbursing funds to community groups, owning assets and lobbying policy makers at other levels of governance on behalf of their communities. Their own governance is complex: they are neither simply participative spaces 'claimed' by the people or, conversely, creatures of the state, but hybrids. They are community based and legally constituted, with formal governance structures centred on a board comprising members of the community and often (although not always) elected councillors and professional staff from state agencies working in their neighbourhood. Many have paid and voluntary workers, in some cases with a professional manager, all under the board's oversight. So they have no simple claim to democratic legitimacy as being 'of the people' or 'elected by the people', yet they have become familiar and apparently legitimate parts of their local governance networks. On what grounds?

Decentred Legitimacy

At a very general level, political legitimacy is a necessity for any but the most tyrannical government, being the quality which converts 'power into authority' so that 'the actions of those that rule are accepted voluntarily by those who are ruled' (Schmitter 2001, 2). While it is clear that the familiar legitimating processes of representative democracy are inadequate and inappropriate for the new governance, there is no clear replacement. This raises a prior question, however: what would such a replacement look like? A decentred perspective invites us to be open to a range of possibilities, rejecting any a priori assumptions about the grounding of legitimacy and leading to an understanding of legitimacy as constructed in and through specific practices of governance (Beetham 1991, 105).

Part of the answer will thus be that in any context, differing constructions of 'legitimacy' by actors or groups of actors are not only possible but probable, perhaps even inevitable. Democratic (and other) traditions provide many different norms, simultaneously in general circulation, which can both guide institutional design and inform contests over legitimate forms of governance. In real contexts a shared construction may (and often does) coalesce around a locally accepted 'normative yardstick' (Krell-Laluhová and Schneider 2004, 15), sufficient to stabilise a particular form of governance and against which actual practice and rhetoric are judged. Such a local norm might reflect the dominance of particular discourses in wider society or in a neighbourhood, or it might develop through the internal dynamics of a process. As Johnson and colleagues pithily expressed it in the analogous context of the legitimising of new organisational practices, 'what is becomes what is right' (Johnson et al. 2006, 57). However, such stability is never permanent: legitimacy is always in need of maintenance and susceptible to challenge (Beetham 1991), particularly when social norms and institutional structures are changing (Krell-Laluhová and Schneider 2004). Establishing new governance practices thus requires active, collective processes of sense making, as taken-for-granted routines become unworkable (Hajer and Versteeg 2005).

We need a provisional language through which to identify possible groundings for legitimacy which enables analysis of the role they play in governance without privileging any in particular (Tully 2002, 541). Here I follow Beetham (1991), whose tripartite framework is normatively neutral with respect to institutions of governance and provides sufficient 'internal' structure for the concept of legitimacy to be empirically operationalised and guide analysis. Where public authority is at stake, Beetham suggests that for power to be 'fully legitimate'

three conditions are required: its conformity to established rules; the justifiability of the rules by reference to shared beliefs [of the dominant and subordinate]; [and] the express consent of the subordinate, or the most significant among them, to the particular relations of power. (Beetham 1991, 19)

All three of Beetham's conditions have to be maintained to sustain legitimacy and each of them is open to challenge. In this they form a structure which mirrors Tully's three types of practices of freedom: in increasing order of depth of response to the provisionally legitimate status quo, these involve working within accepted rules; challenging the rules' justifiability and/or appealing to alternative justifying norms; and fundamentally challenging them by withdrawing consent from the established relations of power (Tully 2002, 540).

While Beetham's constructivist formulation is useful, it is not entirely appropriate for a decentred analysis of the new governance. Sitting within the traditions of political science as a discipline, Beetham is concerned with rather simple characterisations of whole polities, cast in binary terms of 'ruled' and 'rulers' with a power relationship between them which stands in need of legitimation. Implicit in a decentred approach is analysis of relationships between multiple stakeholders and a refocusing of attention away from the formal exercise of political power (for instance in a council chamber) and onto the legitimacy of the exercise of micropower across the entirety of diffuse governance processes affecting a locality (Hajer 2003; Healey 2006). The legitimacy question thus shifts from the simple 'does this person or institution have a justifiable right to govern us?' to 'do we currently accept this process – and its associated institutions and actors – as a justifiable way to make policy which affects us?' The answer may then shape the response to the question 'how seriously should we therefore treat it as a guide to our own actions and decisions?'(Connelly et al. 2006) These questions are not just to be asked by 'the ruled', who in the context of neighbourhood governance might perhaps be the members of 'the community' not involved directly in the institutions of governance. They are continuously relevant questions for all participants, including others who could also be considered 'rulers' – other active players in the networks of governance with decision-making powers in other arenas (Connelly 2011). Legitimacy is an issue for *all* the relationships in the networks of governance.

Given the importance of informal interactions outside the formal political arena (Lowndes and Sullivan 2008), 'rules' must be taken to include all the local conventions which guide governance practices. Further, our emphasis on practice also draws attention to how rules and their enactment in practices '*embody* justificatory beliefs' (Beetham 1991, 22, original emphasis). Thus while some governance practices relevant to understanding legitimacy may be explicit claims and counterclaims about the legitimacy of processes and actors, others are 'simply' enactments – doing the kind of things about which a legitimacy judgement, a judgement of political acceptability, could reasonably be made (Nullmeier and Pritzlaff 2009; Connelly 2011). Crucially this latter category includes both non-verbal and verbal practices: for instance, speaking in a public meeting will embody assumptions of legitimate voice justifiable by, for example, elected representative status or local resident status, even if legitimacy is not explicitly invoked.

Bringing together the preceding discussions of the discursive and contested construction of the local legitimacy of governance with Beetham's dissection of the concept, a linked series of questions provides a decentred approach to analysing governance: *What rules – formal and informal – guide governance practices? By what principles can these be justified and/or challenged? Who consents and who does not, both within the process and outside?*

Norms of Legitimacy

In practice a wide range of rules and justifying principles may underpin legitimacy. I collectively term these 'norms of legitimacy', reflecting the dual meaning of 'norms' as rules which guide action and as (moral) principles which can be used to justify practices. In British policy the norms underpinning governance have usually been treated as unproblematic and left largely implicit, as if working through partnership and participation has become an unquestionably desirable norm in itself (Atkinson 1999; Skelcher et al. 2005; and cf. DETR 1998). This seems to be particularly true at the local level, where the virtues of 'communities' and 'participation' have been promoted uncritically whatever the party political complexion of the national government (Campbell 2005; Durose et al. 2011). Of course, while partnerships may have become entirely legitimate in the corridors of central government, this is not necessarily the case for society as a whole, still less for any specific community. The new governance has been subjected to sustained critique. This has been in part on the representative democratic grounds of its lack of adequate democratic accountability and authorisation (Bekkers et al. 2007). Further, the incorporation of local communities in governance has been attacked as part of a broader neoliberal project to shift responsibility from the state to the wider population (Raco 2003; Taylor 2007), without genuinely including or empowering 'ordinary' people, despite the rhetoric (Taylor 2007).

However, although such challenges are useful correctives to the uncritical acceptance of the legitimacy of the new community governance as a whole, they are of little help with empirical analysis. A decentred analysis of possible and actual legitimising norms is necessary for understanding how specific practices might come to be (seen as) legitimate or not, and why this might vary in different contexts.

The first step in such an analysis is to note that differing – and potentially conflicting – norms are inherent in almost any governance context. Legitimacy rests on judgements both about the qualities of a process (which in a democratic polity will be pre-eminently whether it is 'democratic' or not!) and about whether it delivers adequate, and adequately distributed, benefits – that is, evaluation against 'input' and 'output' criteria (Scharpf 1999). While the two elements are to some extent separable and substitutable (Scharpf 1999), in practice they cannot be completely 'uncoupled' – perceived failures in distribution tend to lead to challenges to governance arrangements (Papadopoulos 2003, 484).

Input legitimacy is complex, and it is here that significant changes in norms have taken place in connection with the development of the new governance. In principle, stakeholders' interests can be brought into governance processes in a number of ways: through representatives legitimised by election, expertise or shared experience (often based in shared identity) or through direct presence (O'Neill 2001; Lowndes and Sullivan 2004). Representative democracy has traditionally been grounded on electoral legitimacy for its decision makers, with their advisers having a place in policy formulation on the grounds of their expertise. In contrast, the new governance involves a shift towards representation based on shared experience and direct participation by members of stakeholder groups, with the aim of policies and strategies being shaped through collaborative deliberation between stakeholders (Healey 1997; Hajer and Kesselring 1999).

Proponents argue that such approaches increase democratic legitimacy, in part by giving citizens and civil society organisations direct access to previously remote decision-making processes (Hajer and Kesselring 1999). This argument is augmented by the emphasis on deliberation, drawing on a vibrant field of political theorising which asserts a new normative criterion: that 'outcomes are legitimate to the extent they receive reflective assent through participation in authentic deliberation by all those subject to the decision in question' (Dryzek 2000, 1). However, the impossibility of such universal involvement in all but the smallest and most isolated processes forces a reliance in practice on representatives (Plotke 1997), often legitimised through arguments from shared identity (Dryzek 2001; O'Neill 2001), which are in potential competition with justifications for representation on the other grounds noted earlier in this chapter.

Given this complexity, alongside the new governance's institutional complexity, it is unsurprising that the few existing empirical studies have found a range of bases for legitimacy in practice. For instance, Skelcher and his colleagues identified three underpinning 'policy belief systems' in British partnerships, two of which justified relatively closed governance practices on the output grounds of increased effectiveness, while only the least prevalent rested on input norms of openness and inclusiveness (Skelcher et al. 2005). Similarly Häikiö (2007) showed how, in a looser governance network, actors claimed and contested legitimacy on the grounds of traditional input norms of expertise and representation and the output justification of working for 'the common good'. Connelly and colleagues (2006) show three processes involving the enactment of and (more rarely) explicit appeals to a range of conflicting legitimacy justifications. As pluralist arguments would suggest, the outcomes were fragile, partial and hybrid legitimacy, relying on shifting and often opportunistic mixes of justifications for sets of changing practices. No single norm dominated, and each process was therefore continually open to challenge.

A significant finding across these and other studies (for example Barnes et al. 2008) is the prevalence of traditional norms (perhaps less taken for granted than previously [Hajer and Versteeg 2005]) alongside the emergence of norms which take partnership as a given. This is unsurprising, as in contesting legitimacy actors draw on a limited range of norms, provided by the locally available 'repertoire of cultural resources and socially feasible discourses' (Saward 2006; Häikiö 2007, 2150). However, norms and governance practices are currently in a state of flux, with new discursive resources (for example over the value of deliberation) available to support innovations. Moreover, such innovation may well be self-reinforcing, as over time the embodiment of new principles in practices makes those principles more acceptable and thus stronger elements in actors' local repertoires (Hay 1998; Johnson et al. 2006).

Clearly the development of new practices will be context dependent – a function of local socio-political history and the nature of the process. However, 'context' is not merely local, and society is permeated by very widespread legitimacy norms – in particular norms of democracy and fair outcomes. In this sense we can see legitimacy as situated, in that its construction will always be (to some extent at least) the working out of broader (if not universal) norms through the specifics of a local situation. It is important to note, however, that alongside output and democratic process norms, local 'repertoires' may also include completely different bases for legitimacy. The recognition of 'deep pluralism' (see Chapter 1) implies that the public prevalence of democratic discourse, the dominance of democratic principles, cannot be taken for granted at the local level. Here we might find other normative foundations for governance practices such as the (unfashionable) Weberian principles of traditional and charismatic leadership, moral commitment to social justice (Brown 2001), or the place-based values characterised by Baggini as 'conservative communitarianism' (Baggini 2007). It is to the empirical investigation of the construction of legitimacy at one community's level that I now turn.

Neighbourhood Legitimacy in an English City

While the research noted above has explored legitimacy in the context of various governance settings, relatively little is known of the
processes which might create or sustain the legitimacy of community-
based organisations (Taylor 2003). Here I present findings from an
investigation conducted with the paid managers of nine intermediary
organisations in an English city to establish what legitimacy meant
'from within'.

The research was based on interviews, a round-table meeting with
the interviewees, and a subsequent meeting with a regional group of
managers and chairs from other cities, supplemented with documentary material produced by the 'development trusts' active in neighbourhood regeneration in the city.[1] The trusts, all major players in this
regeneration, had diverse origins in self-organised community groups
and local authority-convened regeneration partnerships. Their senior
managers (my interviewees) were likewise significant individuals in
local governance. Methodologically, their interpretations were important as elements of the construction of legitimacy in their own right,
but these people were also in a position to report on other discourses,
at least as they interpreted them. While the research was clearly partial
(since a more complete understanding of these organisations' legitimacy would require interviews with other stakeholders, including
the 'represented but inactive') it is nevertheless valid as an account of
legitimacy from the organisations' point of view. (It was also partial in
another sense, being largely interview-based and therefore involving
[re]interpretations of practice. A fuller understanding of the practice
of legitimacy would require ethnographic, perhaps participant, observation. See White 2009).

The core of a trust's formal governance structure is a legally required
board, at least some of whom come from the community served by
the trust in order to fulfil the criterion of being community owned
and managed. Significantly different rules for membership and election to the board existed. These ranged from universal local franchise

---

[1] 'Development trusts' are regeneration organisations whose affiliation to a
national association (Locality) commits them explicitly to being community
owned and managed, with independence and sustainability based on enterprise
(Locality 2011).

and eligibility as candidates, to the far more limited case of board members being drawn from representatives of local groups, elected by their peers at an annual general meeting. In some organisations all trustees were community representatives, while in others these were in a minority, with quotas reserved for representatives from local government and the private sector. These differences embody syntheses of input and output legitimacy concerns: democratic representation was balanced against ensuring adequate levels of management and governance skills.

Democratic quality was perceived to be important, with concerns expressed over low turnouts, unfilled board places and uncontested elections. These were addressed in part through trustees and paid staff going into the community to raise awareness and actively recruit candidates. This often involved 'cherry-picking' known individuals and 'arm-twisting', in order to get 'new people through who perhaps wouldn't automatically ever be involved in something like this'.[2] This pro-active approach was perceived as legitimate, justified variously on the input grounds of ensuring a board representative across dimensions of ethnic origin, gender, age and faith, and the output grounds of creating an effective management board and capacity building within the community. More exclusionary methods were also used in order to protect the 'community interest' from potential trustees who were perceived as being overly self-interested, representative of only a particular narrow interest, or simply destructive or incompetent. This was the principal justification for the less open election processes of some trusts, and although the interviewees were conscious that this was 'undemocratic', one typically argued that 'you have to have democracy, but you have to also protect people from themselves and protect what we are trying to achieve'.

This deliberate management of community representation was seen as essential to achieve the principal purpose of local regeneration. Giving communities some voice was important, on principled as well as instrumental grounds, but the organisations' legitimacy rested ultimately on achieving tangible outputs. Where the balance was struck in part reflected organisational purposes, with those who prioritised service delivery unsurprisingly tending towards more controlled

---

[2] Unattributed quotes in this section are from interviews and trust documentation.

processes, while at the other end of the scale the trust with the widest franchise and most open processes was established by a network of highly politicised, like-minded community development activists.

These compromises shifted over time, in response both to explicit challenges to legitimacy and to changes in trusts' sense of their own purpose. Some tended towards 'more democracy' in the quest for legitimacy in the eyes of the community, with the most politicised group recognising that their 'elections process was discredited and people were very uncomfortable with it ... there was a feeling that there was a bit of a stitch-up', and responding by introducing universal franchise for local residents. In contrast, as other organisations acquired more assets, they moved in the opposite direction, increasing community involvement through the less risky co-optation of representatives to the board and extending consultation processes. There was little evidence that these changes resulted from power struggles between individuals or factions (cf. Bevir 2003); rather, they resulted from collective and individual struggles to make practical sense from competing and almost equally valued objectives and norms.

Overall there was a notable striving for 'formal' representative democracy as the basis for being 'community managed'. However, it was clear that the boards were relatively weak, both as managers and as mechanisms for accountability between the organisations and their communities. Trustees' principal functions were to hold the paid staff to account financially and provide guidance on what they believed was right for the community, but without (in most cases) formal structures connecting them back into the community. They were 'trustees' in the political as well as the legal sense (Pitkin 1967), and their legitimacy in that role derived from their election, or simply from selection 'from the community'.

Recognition of this weakness led to two responses. First, elections were supplemented with less formal engagement processes taken from the familiar toolbox of 'public participation'. A range of justifications were presented, from service improvement to increasing legitimacy with the community, for an array of activities from almost every rung on the ladder of participation (Arnstein 1969). Some trusts used questionnaires and ad hoc 'community conferences' to consult, while others held open meetings which (partially) steered their work and provided face-to-face accountability to residents.

However, the second response overshadowed all these in ensuring that the boards' weakness did not delegitimise the trusts. The crucial element was the myriad informal mechanisms through which paid staff – rather than board members – were in continuous contact with their communities. This took place partly through staff keeping their eyes and ears open as part of their daily routine, and also through casual, ad hoc meetings between staff and residents. For example, one CEO deliberately did local voluntary work as a way of meeting people informally, because if '[you] sit for ten minutes, have a cup of tea, have a chat, you get to know an awful lot of what's really going on'. Others stressed the importance of accessible and friendly offices:

people need to know that we're here, they can walk through the door, they'll get a good cup of tea, they'll meet some nice people, they'll meet people who are just as enthusiastic about [neighbourhood X] as them.

These processes clearly follow no formal rules to deliver democratic legitimacy, but are rather guided by general social norms of communicative openness and civility. The justification for them came through a particular form of success: they enabled not only effective delivery of services but also visible responsiveness to the community. Despite the absence of formal democratic process, this justification rests on the way these practices enact core democratic functions. The communication of interests and concerns, authorisation to act on these, and accountability back to the community were all carried out informally, sometimes in single interactions in which all these legitimacy-sustaining strands were inextricably intertwined. These informal processes also gave opportunities for the challenges which are essential to democratic process and ethos: if an organisation was seen to be doing 'the wrong things' or not enough of 'the right things' then 'ears were bent' in the local pub, and no doubt elsewhere as well. Trust was central to the acceptability of these informal processes. It rested on the belief – supported by experience – that people would be listened to and that things would get done, coupled with openness and transparency to scrutiny. Several interviewees saw a trade-off between this and formal ways of guaranteeing legitimacy, with the latter only necessary where trust was lacking.

Beyond their communities, such organisations need to maintain their legitimacy with other players in the webs of local governance with whom they work in partnership, or from whom they receive funds. This legitimacy appeared to be principally output-based, resting on recognised competence and reliability in managing funds and services, rather than on community-based or explicitly democratic credentials. How widespread this 'exterior' legitimacy was lay beyond the scope of the research, and others have reported the hostility of elected councillors in particular to new, non-electoral structures for local representation (see, e.g., Häikiö 2007; Sullivan 2007). What was clear was an increased acceptance of the organisations' legitimacy over the past few years, partly earned but also an aspect of more widespread normalisation of partnership working.

As with their relations with their communities, formal links to external bodies (through partnership agreements etc.) were supplemented by more informal processes. However, these appeared to *follow* legitimacy established through demonstrating competence: once a trust had been accepted as a partner, these informal links were part of sustaining the relationship. Mutual benefit was important: for example trusts could give local authorities information about local issues, and in return were granted access to the highest levels of the administration.

The account so far has focused on the first two elements of Beetham's triad – rules and justification. I turn briefly to consent, although recognising that it is in this area that the methodological limitations noted above become more significant. The extent to which the legitimacy of the trusts' formal governance processes is grounded in *express* consent, as required by Beetham's analysis, is unclear, and was not an explicit concern of the interviewees. Given that trusts are largely sustained by external resources and policy frameworks, 'their' communities could express or withhold consent effectively only through their participation (or not) in elections and meetings. The informal processes (again) are perhaps more significant in sustaining the trusts' legitimacy, as they provided at least some channels through which dissent could be expressed. Interviewees were unaware of significant disapproval of informal modes of operation, and ongoing engagement in these processes practically demonstrated the consent of sufficient numbers of individuals and groups to sustain the trusts' legitimacy. In stark contrast, the external legitimacy derived from competence and the consent expressed through funding and invitations to join partnerships, bid for contracts and so on is clearly vital. In the six months following the fieldwork, two trusts went bankrupt as funders declined to continue support, having lost faith in the organisations' ability to manage their finances effectively.

The Complex and Informal Practising of Legitimacy

This decentred analysis suggests the perhaps unsurprising conclusion that the legitimacy of the new governance at neighbourhood scale is complex, with that of key community-based intermediary organisations hybrid and dynamic. Of course the specifics of how the researched organisations managed this complexity may not be replicated elsewhere, and further research would be necessary to determine whether their responses were at all typical. However, the general nature of the complexity, the tensions raised between different aspects of legitimacy and the significance of informal practices seem likely to be general characteristics of community governance, arising as they do from the broader institutional and discursive context within which these processes are located.

To summarise, in all the trusts there were parallel, linked sets of governance practices, justifiable overall by the sense that the organisations were working 'in the best interests of the community'. There were formal processes, aspiring to follow representative democratic rules, justified on very traditional representative democratic grounds. These were supplemented by less structured but public processes inspired more by the principles of participatory democracy. The weaknesses in these and the threats they posed (through 'too much democracy') to organisations' effectiveness in promoting a general 'community good' were addressed in part through informal processes of selecting representatives and managing community engagement. Overall, however, the organisations' legitimacy – both input and output – relied far more on a further set of informal practices of engagement between the paid staff and other stakeholders, including from the community.

These followed no rules of democratic process, but rather comprised a range of communicative practices – often simply casual conversations in commonplace settings, frequently involving cups of tea! Collectively these delivered legitimacy through the combination of being open, responsive and accountable to the community and in consequence achieving appropriate, tangible results. Such interactions are not unregulated by norms, however. Their 'rules' are assumptions about acceptable ways of behaving and communicating – the social norms of 'etiquette' and respect which govern everyday interaction (Wagenaar 2007) – which markedly contrast with the political (theoretically derived) norms by which the formal practices are justified.

The justification for all these practices is the overall purpose of the organisation – of promoting the regeneration of the neighbourhood. Like any social practice, their repetition must reinforce their legitimacy as accepted ways of doing things, *if* it contributes to a successful programme (Johnson et al. 2006): these practices are not simply acceptable 'in themselves'. Similarly, these organisations' legitimacy within local governance networks rests on norms of effectiveness and reliability. Simply being a partner in a partnership is not enough – there are broader criteria by which they are judged.

Such judgement raises the issue of consent. The consent of external funders is clearly vital, as they could, and did, withdraw both consent and funds in cases of perceived managerial incompetence. However, other stakeholders, particularly the 'local community', have little choice over governance structures or scope for effectively withdrawing consent once these are established. Although Tully (2002, 540) sees 'confrontation' or 'escape' as the deepest level of struggle, a refusal to be governed, the ability of the community to confront and sanction trusts is limited, and it is unclear that escape through non-participation would necessarily have any impact. It seems perhaps that *expressed* consent is not of great importance in practice – contra Beetham – and the absence of active, organised dissent is more significant in allowing organisations to endure (Mann 1970): legitimacy is by default, by lack of practical challenge.

Nevertheless, legitimacy in the eyes of their communities was not taken for granted and was clearly an issue for the leaders of these organisations. The importance of such individuals is unsurprising, given the importance of sense making and the active creation of meaning. The development and maintenance of organisational legitimacy through social interactions and deliberate institutional design requires work, and legitimacy emerges from the practices of individuals in doing this work.

The general features of these processes suggest the possibility for a much broader application of this decentred analysis of legitimacy to governance at scales beyond the neighbourhood. Community-based organisations are located within a broader realm of governance, organised in webs and relationships by rules of varying levels of formality which blur the boundary between the 'community' and the rest (Watson 2003). There is thus no particular reason to privilege the community sector in analysis, and other authors have shown the importance of individuals as performers of legitimacy in other governance settings (Hajer and Versteeg 2005; Häikiö 2007). Moreover, informal activities support formal representative democratic processes even in traditional, elected local government (see, e.g., Leach et al. 1994); more generally, Connelly and colleagues (2006) suggest that similar legitimacy discourses are found across both 'traditional' and 'new' governance processes. Although it is beyond the scope of this chapter, it seems the construction of hybrid, provisional legitimacies and the importance of individual practice would fruitfully bear investigation in a wide range of governance settings.

Assessing the Legitimacy of Community Governance

I turn finally to the normative questions of how to judge democratic legitimacy at this scale, and the implications of decentred analysis. Moving beyond the deliberate agnosticism inherent in starting from practice and recognising diverse interpretations of 'legitimacy', these questions are important because community-level governance is a putative site for enhancing democracy.

At first glance the findings appear problematic. In their relations with governance actors outside their communities, the democratic credentials of the community organisations appear to be intriguingly irrelevant. This echoes Skelcher and colleagues' findings (2005) about the lack of commitment to democratic process in governance partnerships – perhaps a factor in creating broader legitimacy problems for the new governance (Papadopoulos 2003). In contrast, democratic issues were certainly significant in these organisations' relations with their communities, although also not unproblematically. Their explicit governance practices draw largely on a range of recognisably democratic norms of representation and participation. However, the organisations are arguably most reliant for their local legitimacy on informal practices which have no obvious justification within these inherited languages of democratic theory, but are rather grounded only on their effectiveness in achieving 'the good of the community'.

Addressing this apparent democratic deficit would involve a privileging of the formal structures, with strengthened roles for trustees and improved 'lines of communication' to their communities, and more 'consultation' (Skidmore et al. 2006). However, the research suggests this would have significant disadvantages, since trust and informality seemed to be strongly associated, and to be important ingredients in organisations' success and local legitimacy.

Moreover, it is not clear that norms derived from representative – or even participatory – democratic theory are appropriate criteria by which to judge community governance. Disch (2006) argues that they have never been adhered to, even within the institutions of representative government. These comprise a complex mix of representation, consultation, expert advice, professional decision making and so on. To an extent these have all been subsumed within the overriding, self-justifying legitimacy of the accepted institutions of democratic government. This self-justification is also visible to some extent within the new governance, as the existence of the new structures and processes generates greater levels of acceptance. Normatively this observation is not helpful, however, as it takes the argument full circle and raises the question: are there grounds *apart from* simply 'partnership and participation are good' for making critical legitimacy judgements? Here two arguments suggest themselves, one working 'within' the inherited language of democratic theory, but applying it to practices rather than institutional forms, the other breaking away to look 'from the outside' through the lens of radical democracy.

First, the findings show that such grounds for judgement exist: there is something essentially democratic about the way that the informal processes functioned and were judged. Looking beyond practices governed by rules justified by particular strands of democratic theory, there are more fundamental principles of 'democratic responsiveness' which rest as a minimum on the existence of processes which allow accountability and authorisation (Urbinati and Warren 2008). To these must be added a *democratic* output criterion of the delivery of acceptably distributed benefits. Against these criteria the researched organisations did rather well, and their informal processes can be seen as democratically legitimate to the extent that they contribute to this. Moreover, where organisations successfully balance the competing pressures on them and create legitimacy for themselves, this may well be self-reinforcing. As with legitimacy in other innovation processes, success may breed success (Johnson et al. 2006).

However, this analysis is in turn problematic. In practice, reliance on individuals' principled and skilled behaviour is a fragile base for democratic governance. There was ample evidence in the studied organisations of skilful exclusionary practice (albeit in the name of the

community!) Furthermore, although it is rarely documented it is clear
that organisations sometimes survive despite being dysfunctional, pursuing sectional or personal interests to the detriment of both input
and output legitimacy (see, as a rare example, Wilson 2005). Even in
such cases, however, caution is needed. Attention to difference and
privileging of actors' interpretations make it hard for analysts to distinguish between the sectional and the general, particularly given that
in practice much community action arises from mobilising around single issues. We should perhaps be wary of attempting to delimit 'good'
and 'bad', 'authentic' (democratic?) and 'selfish' (undemocratic?) participation, or a singular local public interest (Armony 2004, 9) both
because of the inevitable partiality of any researcher's knowledge and
the inherent unpredictability of dynamic and contingent governance
processes. As a minimum any such judgements should come with
acknowledgement of the situatedness of the analyst's *own* judgement
and their role in the process.

A possible solution is to look elsewhere for a normative framework,
and here I return to radical democracy (see Introduction). From this
perspective it would seem natural to tie legitimacy to Tully's 'practices of freedom' – that practices are legitimate to the extent that they
recognise 'deep difference' and promote questioning and challenge.
Straightforward in theory, this is (perhaps unsurprisingly) also not a
straightforward evaluation in practice. Community-based organisations clearly have the potential to enable such practices, derived from
their position at the interface between the state and the general population. They not only have a role as arenas in which state and non-
state actors can meet, but also act as conduits for community demands
to be channelled to other, less publicly accessible parts of the web of
governance. The latter role in particular offers scope for practices of
freedom, albeit at one remove from the people themselves, through
challenging the practices of these more remote 'locations'.

However, these intermediary bodies are also themselves formal
organisations. In their heyday – before the public sector cuts of the late
2000s – the larger trusts employed many tens of workers and owned
assets worth millions of pounds. From Tully's perspective these must,
therefore, be considered as institutionalised 'practices of government',
with formalised and habitualised ways of thing and acting within relatively settled, government-sanctioned, power relations with their communities and the wider webs of local governance. Their democratic

nature cannot therefore be taken for granted. They clearly offer the possibility of democracy at the local scale, to the extent that they give local people 'an effective say and hand in how they are governed and institutionalise effective practices of freedom' (Tully 2002, 541), and all the organisations studied certainly show strong elements of this. However, there is an inherent – although not necessarily destructive – tension between a radical conception of democracy and the notion of a legitimate governance institution. While the former is fundamentally about openness to challenge and therefore to change, legitimacy is fundamentally a stabilising quality involving social recognition of 'rightfulness' in terms of a set of shared norms by a relevant community (Berger and Luckman 1967; Bernstein 2004). Thus, for a legitimate organisation to emerge and endure it must to some extent be able to limit its responsiveness to radical challenge. In practice the resolution of this tension was seen in the management of challenges – sometimes through exclusionary practices, sometimes through relegitimation through opening up structures to be *more* receptive.

It may be that the most appropriate solution to these problems with judgement is to emphasise the pragmatic aim of developing a decentred analysis of legitimacy which can play a role in critically supporting practice. To recap, decentring involves a rejection of the inherited languages of normative political theory as the only grounds for making legitimacy judgements; coupled with the concern for what is actually done rather than privileging institutional forms, this leads to the recognition of the potential for informal practices to play an important role in local democracy. Most important, however, is that the ineradicability of value differences, the ever-changing nature of policy and governance environments, and the democratic imperative of allowing significant challenges to *any* settled set of practices together push one away from being able to make static judgements about the legitimacy of any particular set of governance practices and towards embracing the dynamic nature of legitimacy as an ever-changing quality brought into being in the practices of those involved. Any settlement will only ever be local, fragile and contested.

The practical challenge, then, is to create organisations – embodiments of such temporary settlements – in ways that preserve the strengths of informality, allow the delivery of acceptable, acceptably distributed outputs and yet offer sufficient opportunities for challenge to provide the checks and balances which encourage 'democratic responsiveness'. To an extent this must involve other governance organisations with the power to sanction community-based organisations – provided *they* are committed to supporting local democracy rather than being focused on managerial efficiency. Given the doubts over this, it would be productive to nurture values and skills at the community level which underpin collective action rather than simply 'building capacity' to manage community governance. Following Pitkin (1967) this suggests a systemic approach to creating legitimate governance, nurturing not only the activists who may initiate and then manage governance institutions, but also communities of (radical) democratic subjects, empowered to be more confident and explicit in their challenging of the organisations established to govern them.

8 Designing 'the Political' in (and out of) Neighbourhood Governance

HELEN SULLIVAN

Introduction

Neighbourhoods have considerable appeal for public policymakers in countries of the global North and South as spaces for and sources of innovation in governance, democracy and service delivery (Garcia 2006; Kennett and Forrest 2006; Smith, Lepine and Taylor 2007). The basis for this appeal lies with the distinctions political theory makes between 'big' and 'small' government. 'Big' government (operating at the level of the local or the urban) is characterised by professionalism, economies of scale, heterogeneous citizenry, pluralist politics and dispassionate relationships between decision makers and citizens, while 'small' government (operating at the sub-local level) is defined by its community capacity, economies of scope, homogeneous citizenry, affective politics and proximate relationships between decision makers and citizens founded in shared identities (Lowndes and Sullivan 2008). Neighbourhood governance initiatives are frequently employed by policymakers in attempts to overcome or mitigate the adverse consequences of 'big' government, particularly the diluted connections and diminished relationships that develop between politicians, professionals and publics, resulting from the distance between decision makers and local communities. The Dutch neighbourhood council programme is a an example of a neighbourhood initiative that attempts to reduce the democratic distance between politicians and neighbourhood residents by giving residents a stronger voice in and access to decision making that affects their neighbourhood (Wagenaar 2007). Other initiatives focus on citizens as service users, giving them greater access to and choice over aspects of service delivery. For example, the United Kingdom's Sure Start programme, aimed at meeting the needs of children from birth to four years of age and their parents through neighbourhood-based flexible provision (Sullivan 2009).

These recent neighbourhood-focused interventions retain the basic commitment to combining the merits of 'big' and 'small' government, but are a product of policymakers' preoccupation with addressing contemporary governance challenges. These include the increasing complexity of societal problems, the growing interdependence between governing actors, the institutional fragmentation associated with market-orientated reforms and the implications of these reforms for democracy and participation. Complicating matters is the coincidence of, on the one hand, the imperative to involve citizens more directly in decision making and, on the other, rising levels of public disengagement with mainstream politics. The discursive power of the dominant representations of these challenges and the material consequences of actions taken in response are delineated and debated in the Introduction to this collection, and alternative theorisations are offered that draw on radical and critical democratic traditions.

This chapter explores some of these issues as they arise in the context of neighbourhood governance interventions, focusing attention on the potential and significance of political contestation of the interrelationships between different actors in the formulation of identities or the pursuit of influence in democratic decision making, and their expression through contextually contingent neighbourhood institutions and practices. A focus on political contestation in neighbourhood governance can add to our understanding of the theory and practice of governance, democracy and participation in a number of ways. It can identify the key ideas underpinning neighbourhood governance prescriptions and show how they shape the purpose, potential and limits of neighbourhood initiatives. It can illustrate how powerful actors carry and communicate these ideas in their design of neighbourhood governance institutions, manifesting them in the rules and norms that govern how these new institutions will work. Finally it can exemplify the ways in which matters of institutional design in general and rules in particular become sites of conflict in neighbourhood governance arrangements as actors seek to embed, resist or subvert proposed rules and norms.

Drawing on democratic theory and empirical evidence from recent studies in neighbourhood governance this chapter will examine how these issues and norms are politically constituted and contested in practice. I will argue that neighbourhood governance initiatives are dominated by ideas associated with liberal accounts of democracy, that these ideas valorise particular actors as institutional designers and prefer particular kinds of procedural rules and norms linked to representative democratic models and to consensual decision making. Attempts to apply these preferred designs and rules are met with a variety of responses, depending on other actors' ideas about and understanding of democratic practice. These responses point to the significance of conflict as an element in democratic practice. An alternative approach to neighbourhood governance is proposed which starts from an acknowledgement of the significance of conflict and creates a framework for interacting that allows actors to constitute each other as 'adversaries' rather than 'enemies'.[1]

Governance and Democratic Participation within Neighbourhoods

Different rationales for changing patterns of governance are observable at the neighbourhood level. Neighbourhood governance may be understood as a consequence of neoliberalisation's restructuring of relationships between state, society and market actors. Neighbourhood spaces arise from the 're-scaling' of state activity, stimulated by the application of privatisation, contracting and partnership strategies, coupled with new information and communication technologies and the privileging of consumer voices over those of professionals or elected politicians (Geddes and Sullivan 2011). However it is also possible to understand neighbourhood governance as the necessary by-product of the emergence of multi-level, multi-actor horizontal decision making that combines interdependency in governing with a loss of faith in representative democratic institutions and a reappraisal of citizens as agents in governance. This networked or collaborative governance functions across all tiers of governance but has a particular resonance at the neighbourhood level, as it is here that decisions

---

[1] The distinction between 'enemies' and 'adversaries' is one drawn by Chantal Mouffe in her work on agonistic democracy. She argues that antagonism is a struggle between enemies, whereas agonism concerns contestation between adversaries, and that the problem for democratic politics is to transform antagonism into agonism through the provision of mechanisms that facilitate 'a vibrant clash of democratic political positions' (Mouffe 2000, 103–04).

about 'choice, voice' and even control over services are most clearly described and relationships between citizens, professionals and politicians most directly experienced (Sullivan 2001). Finally neighbourhood governance may also be associated with the emergence of a 'new politics', one that may be stimulated by a combination of neoliberalisation and networked governance, but which is distinct, operating outside the conventional apparatus of party politics and representative government through new kinds of political agency and organisation, facilitating new connections between international concerns and their impact on local communities (Lowndes and Sullivan 2008). This last point emphasises the possibility of citizen-led organisation outside the contours of state-sponsored neighbourhood institutions. This in turn focuses attention on questions of institutional design in neighbourhood governance: who are the designers, what designs are prompted by different rationales, and what rules and practices operate to effect and sustain neighbourhood governance?

Working at the neighbourhood level enables close inspection of the shape and nature of democratic participation in governance initiatives and the way in which political contestation is practiced. Understandings of politics usually focus on 'who gets what and why', directing attention to the key actors in a neighbourhood setting, their resources and corresponding agency, and the means by which they exercise their agency to secure the outcomes they wish. Alternatively, one may focus on 'the political' as the foregrounding of the *constitution* of identities in and through the process of democratic exchange and the subsequent expression of those identities in a form of democratic settlement, however temporary.[2] Here the focus is also on actors, but does not predetermine who the key actors are, nor does it presume what their interests are. Rather it requires these to be formulated as part of the democratic process. Either way, at the neighbourhood level the familiarity of key actors with each other (often developed over years of living alongside

---

[2] This draws here on the distinction between 'politics' and 'the political' as it is developed in poststructuralist political theory (Lefort 1986; Laclau 1990), where 'politics' refer to a subsystem of the social order and includes the institutions and processes of that subsystem *as a given*. In contrast, the focus on 'the political' draws attention to the *contingently constituted* character of those institutions, norms and the forms of subjectivity accompanying them. Hence, the latter draws attention to the political character of a range of practices that often are presented as 'natural' and 'non-political' (Žižek, 1991, 193).

one another) and the closer proximity between decision makers and communities means that relationships and exchanges will tend to be more intimate and affective than at the urban level. The emotional intensity of such relationships means that the incidence of conflict can result in actors viewing each other as 'friends' or 'enemies', with a deep and lasting impact on their relationships (Dahl and Tufte 1973). This contrasts sharply with the more dispassionate relationships associated with actors operating at a greater distance from each other in systems of 'big' government (Newton 1982), where political conflict is experienced in a more mediated way. Powerful actors' aversion to or misunderstanding of the role of conflict in democratic participation informs many if not most of the state-sponsored neighbourhood governance programmes and influences their design and the rules that govern them, specifically the framing and regularising of exchanges between actors in ways that reify consensus but deny conflict.

Lowndes and Sullivan (2008) identify four 'ideal types' of neighbourhood governance that underpin policy and practice: neighbourhood empowerment, partnership, government and management. These ideal types are based on real-life observable structures and processes, but they offer a 'one-sided accentuation' of the central features of an institutional arrangement from which specific cases will inevitably diverge (Weber, cited in Parkin 1982, 30). According to Lowndes and Sullivan, '[T]he point of specifying ideal types is to bring conceptual order to messy realities, enabling the investigation of variation within and between institutional alternatives. Understanding the link between purpose and institutional design helps to clarify the scope for, and dimensions of, choice in governing arrangements – however imperfectly' (2008, 64). Scrutiny of these 'ideal types' reveals different manifestations of 'the political', each associated with a different democratic tradition, and offers insights into how each may inform institutional design and democratic conduct and practice.

Neighbourhood empowerment emphasises opportunities for local self-government and direct citizen involvement in decisions that affect them and their neighbourhood. It promotes the values of participative democracy. Here 'the political' is realised through the interactions of local citizens over matters of local concern independent of, as well as through, interactions with and influence over 'local experts' and decision makers.

Neighbourhood partnership focuses on the 'joining-up' of local action amongst service providers and decision makers. It is a manifestation of stakeholder democracy – a system that binds the representatives of different interest groups into a process of collective decision making in which the interactions between these (often) elite actors, based on their particular attributes and/or expertise, decide what is to be discussed and what is not. Lowndes and Sullivan (2004, 60) have referred to this trend as a 'new corporatism'.

Neighbourhood government emphasises improvements in the accessibility, responsiveness and accountability of decision making by governance units that are accountable to a smaller citizenry and are physically closer to the citizens they serve. The emphasis here is firmly on representative democracy and understandings of politics in the conventional sense: the relationship between citizen and politician hinges on the practices of election and accountability, with voting the ultimate expression of both.

Neighbourhood management promotes the neighbourhood as an efficient means of identifying diverse citizen needs, providing appropriate services as well as rooting out waste by exploiting economies of scope. It is linked to a model of market democracy, in which accountability rests on the principle that citizens are also consumers who may choose to take their 'business' elsewhere. 'Politics', in this case, is constituted narrowly within this provider/consumer relationship.

Lowndes and Sullivan (2008) acknowledge that neighbourhood governance is more messy and multifaceted than the depiction of 'ideal types' would suggest, but argue that this depiction exposes the challenges inherent in designing new governance systems by, for example, identifying the political significance of the adoption of any one of these 'ideal types' in terms of the democratic tradition that is promoted as a result: participative, stakeholding, representative and market. The selection is important both for what it implies about institutional design and the respective roles of politicians, professionals and the public, but also for the way it promotes a particular kind of politics and political conduct amongst local actors. A key issue for consideration in the context of this chapter is whether the political choices implied in this discussion are available in practice, or whether potential choices are constrained by, in the case of the UK, the pre-existence of a dominant liberal-democratic tradition that inhibits the selection or full application of designs that derive from more radical democratic traditions.

The remainder of this chapter offers a case study of neighbourhood governance in England. It explores the interaction of ideas, institutions and actors in shaping policy and practice and it highlights the political as constitutive of and embodied within these interactions. The chapter illustrates how what is possible in any given context is influenced by how ideas and power relationships combine with available institutional designs. But it also emphasises the way in which 'institutional designers' are able to shape locally contingent responses and subvert or impose particular rules. Finally the chapter reveals how the prospects for neighbourhoods as vehicles of a new politics are inhibited by the hegemony of liberal-democratic accounts and practices, which reify consensus and fail to take conflict seriously. An alternative approach is offered which situates conflict at the centre of political identity formation and democratic exchange.

Redesigning Governance: Neighbourhood Policies in the United Kingdom

The 1990s marked the beginning of a period of renewed enthusiasm for the neighbourhood amongst national and local governments throughout Europe and beyond. In England the National Strategy for Neighbourhood Renewal identified and sponsored initiatives within England's most deprived neighbourhoods; the New Deal for Communities programme supported community led regeneration; the Neighbourhood Management scheme aimed to improve the co-ordination of local services; the Neighbourhood Renewal Fund offered a resource stream to local authorities and their partners; the Community Empowerment Network targeted the building and organising of local community capacity; and the Sure Start programme focused on improving the life-chances of children from birth to four years of age. Similar initiatives in Scotland and Wales included the development of Social Inclusion Partnerships (Scotland) and the Communities First programme (Wales). Local councils also explored the potential of neighbourhood governance through decentralisation schemes, neighbourhood projects and community participation programmes (Smith et al. 2007).

These neighbourhood initiatives each provided an illustration of some of the values associated with 'small' government. All emphasised the significance of the neighbourhood as a source of shared identities and interests; some (a minority) prioritised the role of citizens making decisions for themselves, while others (the majority) highlighted the need to improve relations among the public, professionals and politicians through new participative processes and discursive practices, which sought to engage different interests in new modes and forms of interaction and exchange with the aim of identifying and addressing shared neighbourhood priorities. Neighbourhood initiatives made use of a wide variety of participative tools and methods but common amongst them was the creation of one or more 'deliberative spaces' – regularised interactions between key actors for the articulation and debate of issues and actions. These were named in numerous ways – steering groups, committees, governing bodies, forums – but each concerned itself with bringing together different interests for purposeful discussion focussed on improving local well-being.

Formally the various neighbourhood initiatives fitted into the 'ideal types' proposed by Lowndes and Sullivan. Local government initiatives tended to correspond to the 'neighbourhood government' type, emphasising the role of elected politicians and exploring the possibility of enhancing the authority and legitimacy of elected representatives by extending and enhancing their engagement with local citizens. The Neighbourhood Management and Sure Start initiatives came closest to the 'neighbourhood management' type, with its emphasis on citizens as consumers anxious to have a greater say in service design and delivery. The various community regeneration initiatives were promoted as 'neighbourhood partnerships' and attempted to recast citizens as stakeholders in the partnership, with responsibilities linked to the privileges of partnership. Finally, the New Deal for Communities and Community Empowerment Network fitted with the 'neighbourhood empowerment' type, in which the neighbourhood was a safe space for citizen and community capacity building and citizen action.

However, closer examination of the neighbourhood programmes reveals a more ambiguous picture. Despite rhetorical claims that neighbourhood initiatives would interrupt and reconstitute power relationships and patterns of influence between and among politicians, professionals, private-sector actors and the public, emergent policy prescriptions diluted political and ideological content and presented neighbourhood programmes as 'neutral' endeavours, unconnected to the conduct of politics and, indeed, somehow beyond it. For example, neighbourhood policies designed to 'put communities in the lead' (as the New Deal for Communities initiative sought to) emphasised the need for community empowerment and capacity building among community members to enable them to offer leadership in their neighbourhoods, but contained little discussion of either the ways in which existing community power relations may influence who 'took the lead' or of the implications for existing patterns of power and influence held amongst decision makers, service providers and possibly private-sector players. One way of understanding this apparent ambiguity is to reconceive neighbourhood programmes as sites of struggle for power and control among the central and local governments and the local state. The deeply political character of these programmes was made visible in the central/local exchanges that followed the centre's attempts to reduce the influence of local politicians and professionals and to enhance the role of private-sector players and consumers (Sullivan 2009). This explanation situates neighbourhood governance initiatives as expressions of a broader neoliberalisation agenda, one which emphasises the contribution of market-based approaches (as expressed in the neighbourhood management ideal type) set alongside an increasingly residual representative democratic framework.

The UK Research Council's Democracy and Participation Programme provided an opportunity to research some of the initiatives identified above. With colleagues Marian Barnes, Andrew Knops and Janet Newman, I examined neighbourhood governance as part of our Power, Participation and Political Renewal study (Barnes et al. 2007).[3] Through seventeen case studies in two English cities we explored the range and types of forums designed to encourage public participation at a local level; the membership of those forums and the motivations of individual actors; the 'rules of engagement' developed by these forums and the influence of participants over them; how the forums engaged with difference and dissent; and their impact on policy outcomes.

[3] The primary data cited in this chapter (references to interviews and fieldnotes) were collected and recorded as part of the ESRC research project 'Power, Participation and Political Renewal' (award no. L215252001).

We found that institutional design had an important impact on the nature and quality of participation and deliberation within neighbourhood governance initiatives and that pre-existing power relationships amongst and between local politicians, professionals and the public influenced the ability of different actors to contribute to the design process. We characterised the different institutional frameworks associated with the initiatives in the following way: as sources of support; as sites of challenge and opportunity; and as prisons (see Barnes et al. 2007, chapter 5 for a discussion).

In this chapter I revisit this data, focusing specifically on how politics is constituted and embodied within neighbourhood institutions and relationships,[4] and exploring the roles of actors and rules in promoting, maintaining, resisting or subverting these. In so doing, I seek to make visible the political character of processes that are usually presented as 'neutral'. I draw on two theoretical traditions to illuminate this argument: deliberative democracy and agonistic democracy. The former is selected as it is the basis for much of the 'deliberative practice' sponsored by policymakers in the 1990s (however poorly grounded in the theory much of the practice turned out to be). It was also an important element of the analytical framework employed in the study that provides the data here. The latter is selected because it highlights the role of conflict in deliberative exchanges and offers additional ways of understanding why different expressions of neighbourhood governance may be more or less functional.

Designing Democratic Procedures

Habermas's (1989) work on communicative rationality provides important insights into the ways in which institutional design may support deliberative democratic practice. Habermas prescribed a series of procedural conditions designed to promote the use of reason in argument. These require that: anyone who is competent to speak and act is allowed to take part in the process of deliberation; all those taking part are allowed to introduce any assertion they wish to make and to question any assertion made by others; all are allowed to express

---

[4] The neighbourhood institutions studied in the ESRC project included a residents' group in a regeneration programme, two Sure Start projects (neighbourhood services to support children 0–4) and two area committees.

their attitudes and wishes; and no speaker should be prevented from exercising those rights – either as a result of internal or external pressure. Participants are required to treat each other as equals, to afford each other the space to speak, to listen and to be prepared to justify positions expressed (Chambers 1996, 197–98; cf. also Norval, this volume, Chapter 3).

The residents' group in our ESRC study provided one example of the use of procedural rules to support deliberation. This resident-initiated forum represented the views of its members in negotiations with a regeneration organisation responsible for revitalising the housing estate on which they lived. Group members considered its grass-roots foundation and orientation its key strength, as resident group members were not part of the regeneration organisation's participative infrastructure and bound by its conditions. Rather, the group was led by experienced and confident individuals who were aware that they had choices in their relationship with the regeneration organisation; for example, they could work with it and develop a constitution and set of rules that suited both parties, or they could opt out of the negotiation and continue to press for change on their own terms.

The constitution of the residents' group stated that access to the group was through attending its meetings and membership was automatic for residents, who could put items on the agenda by speaking to one of the committee members or by turning up at a meeting. There was a 'code of conduct' which identified unacceptable forms of behaviour (e.g., the use of racist language) and a requirement that the group appoint a chair, a secretary and a treasurer. The chair, vice chairs and secretary drew on their own experiences as trade union representatives and committee members in voluntary organisations and on their work experiences to develop a set of rules that governed their practice in a way which they believed gave them legitimacy with their members and which acknowledged the political character of their activities and their relationship with the politicians and professionals of the regeneration organisation.

The notes of one observation of a meeting recorded the practice of these rule of democratic procedure:

Committee meetings were carefully chaired so as to ensure that everyone had the opportunity to have a say, while sticking to the agenda. There was a shared emphasis in the committee on a desire for action, and results, not merely discussion. All members took advantage of the opportunity to contribute to debate, although some did so more than others.

There was a marked difference in styles between members. The Chair was formal and considered, being very careful to explain his actions, and to emphasise the importance of openness and propriety in all the dealings of the Committee. This notion of openness extended beyond the relationship between officers and the committee, to the wider body of residents in the area covered by the Group. The rest of the committee supported this approach.

A resident participant acknowledged this openness and also described its implications for the content and conduct of deliberation:

The topics of the day are what are going on in the area, you take people's point of view and is everybody getting a fair crack of the whip and what they should be getting. At the same time it is looking out for each other, that is one of the main things. You look out for each other and if there is something available to make sure these people know and if they want it they can have it. That is the way to look at things.

This reflection highlights how group procedures facilitated what Connolly (1999) describes as an 'ethics of cultivation', respect and care for difference amongst democratic actors.

The observation notes identified two kinds of discussion at the meetings:

Firstly, between members, and secondly, between members and others who had been invited to present to the meeting. Debate within the Group focused on planning issues – in particular new proposals for alterations or improvements to the area, and a refurbishment that was underway. Deliberation was assisted by the availability of clear written policies and maps and plans, so that committee members would more readily grasp and visualise the impact of changes. With these aids, it was possible for discussions to go into considerable detail, as committee members could draw on considerable local knowledge. They also made strong use of complaints and other information that had been communicated to them, in their capacity as committee members and as ordinary residents, from other residents in their area.

The emphasis on lay or local knowledge was an important element of the deliberations and was accorded at least as much significance as technical or professional knowledge. For one resident,

[b]ecause some people think as soon as they see you're on the committee that you know everything, you've only just got on and ... you're an expert....

And I said it's not like that. I said there's a group of us, anybody can go on to it, you can sit on it and listen to what the group's talking about and what's coming across and what they're going to do. She said well they're going to do it anyway whether you say yes or no. I said I don't agree with that, you have a voice and it's listened to. I said you're going to get a bit of banter, that discussion debate, but you've gotta know the rights and wrong and we're not always in the right. That's the reason I'm on there, a voice.

The procedural elements identified by Habermas are designed to aid the transformation of views amongst participants to the deliberation, to increase the chances that they will move from positions based on self-interest to those that are more likely to deliver public purpose, as a result of their having to listen directly to others whose positions and circumstances are different from their own. The residents' group was able to create the conditions necessary to facilitate this kind of exchange partly because of the experience and skills its leading members brought to the design and conduct of the group. They also imbued the group with a 'political' perspective, one which highlighted the power relations and interests at work on the estate, located the group's own agency in its independence from the regeneration organisation and fostered the emergence of that agency in the shared identities and subjectivities that occurred through deliberative exchange.

In another example – this one a Sure Start initiative – the governance design underpinning this national programme presented all participants with a challenge: wherever they were from and whatever their background, all were at least partially outside their 'comfort zones', as professionals, experienced activists, regeneration managers and parent participants. This presented an opportunity for participants to develop the procedural rules together and to create the conditions for the agreed procedural rules to enable the transformation of views. Interviewees commented on the way in which the procedural rules emphasised the importance of listening to and taking account of the views of others. Our case study findings recorded that in one Sure Start initiative,

[t]he ability to listen to and respect others' views was a further useful skill that some interviewees identified. They were able to see the other side of arguments, or the whole picture on a particular issue. And should they voice a view, and yet the majority remain unconvinced, they felt able to accept the majority decision.

However, there were also occasions when despite the shared rules of deliberation, tensions and difficulties threatened to overwhelm the group. In one Sure Start initiative the tension between different groups of professionals spilled over into forum meetings, leaving parent participants uncomfortable and initially at a loss to know how to engage with the different professional claims being made. The Sure Start initiative also provided examples of those participants who had strong personalities that they were either unable or unwilling to rein in during discussions. Our observation notes recorded that:

In particular, some members of the board were seen as having particular views, often negative or critical, which they persistently voiced. From observation, this dynamic did occur, focusing on the concerns of some board members that the Sure Start project was not engaging with the full depth of difficulties that parents on the estate were facing – especially drugs and crime. There was some mention of party political differences between board members leading to them 'winding each other up'.

This example could be dismissed as a failure of participants to observe the rules but the 'party political' nature of the differences between key personalities highlights an important feature of the reality of local decision making. An alternative explanation is that perhaps that rules themselves were inadequate to the task, an example of an attempt to 'design out' party politics from deliberation in the pursuit of a more 'inclusive' deliberative space.

Our research also identified examples of initiatives in which the rules of procedure appeared to limit the participation of all potential contributors, including those who designed the initiative. We described these as 'institutional prisons'. What is revealing about these examples is that the design of the rules was in the hands of one powerful group of actors. The rules themselves were not necessarily contrary to the conditions suggested by Habermas, but the fact that they had been 'handed down' to all potential participants appeared to incite tensions between the designers and the rest. In one case – a council area committee – the local authority had introduced new rules into existing council institutions as a way of opening up decision making to the public. The area committee was constituted as a committee of the council but included a body of 'lay advisory members' appointed by the local authority. It also introduced a period of 'question time' during each committee meeting, when members of the public could enter into exchanges with councillors and officials, and it further created space within the meetings for focussed deliberation on a topic of local concern.

Area committee meetings were marked by conflict between and amongst politicians, professionals and the public, despite the fact that the majority of the councillors on the area committee were senior councillors, skilled at dealing with a range of people and situations; the chair of the committee was generally acknowledged to be adept at managing the meetings effectively; and the advisory members were experienced activists, voluntary organisation representatives or community leaders. Conflict took a number of forms, including members of the public refusing to ask questions in the Q&A session and using the time to make speeches about the failures of the council, members of the public shouting at council officers and politicians, and politicians arguing with one another about why the committee was not 'working'.

Our assessment of the area committee was that it failed to function partly because of the way in which the rules were designed and implemented (Barnes et al. 1997, chap. 5). For example the local authority determined the rules governing the operation of the area committee with no consultation with the public about either the size of the committees (at least three wards) or the added value of appointing lay advisory members onto the committee (most people didn't know what they were for and their presence was never explained). In addition, the meetings of the area committee were organised in such a way as to perpetuate the divide between councillors and the public. Councillors sat at 'the top table', lay members below and the public in the well of the hall. Councillors were always invited to speak first, then advisory members, then the public.

This (albeit extreme) example draws attention to the ways in which power relationships can be intensified through the construction and operation of procedural rules. One respondent summarised this in the context of the area committee as follows:

And then it's fast moving. And there is a structure; there is agenda to the meeting. We are reminded we are a committee of the council. Subject to the standing order of the council. So it's very formal and it rolls on. And in a dynamic of its own. Which is very difficult to drag back if you have an issue, you know as a member of the public or around the table. It can also result in the exchanges adopting a particular tone.

The examples described above align with Tully's (2008b) description of three general cases of practices of freedom that accompany practices of governance (as discussed by Griggs et al. in the Introduction to this collection). The Sure Start initiative is a case of professionals, services users and politicians co-operating and following the 'rules' of existing practices, modifying them in the process of reproducing them. The residents' group, independent but operating alongside a regeneration organisation, exemplifies how the governed can contest existing rules of dominant practices but do so by using existing 'language games' and institutional procedures. Finally, the area committee illustrates what happens when such institutional strategies are either not open to the governed or fail, individuals and groups in this case choosing to contest them and then 'exit' (but not attempting transformation through struggle).

Iris Marion Young (2000) and others criticise the procedural approach to deliberative democracy for failing to acknowledge the ways in which power relations shape what is possible in deliberation and act to inhibit or exclude potential participants either through the way in which rules are designed or through the privileging of certain types of speech and expression as legitimate. Young is particularly critical of the notion that 'reason' and 'rational argument' are somehow neutral terms, suggesting instead that claims to rationality may in fact reflect a dominant discourse that is not shared by those outside a particular elite. Instead, she emphasises the need for inclusive democratic practice that is capable of generating alternative discourses and transforming policymaking.

In what follows I explore ways in which an understanding of power relations and the nature of deliberation between politicians, professionals and the public, and an acceptance of conflict may offer a more productive constitution of 'the political' in neighbourhood governance.

Designing in Democratic Conflict

Norval (this volume, Chapter 3) identifies a number of features common to an agonistic analytical framework for democratic exchanges. These include: acknowledging the central role of power and conflict in politics; the importance of disagreement in constituting common deliberative spaces; the way in which political identities are constituted through political struggle; and the importance of basing democratic relations on recognition of adversarial legitimacy. I consider these in relation to the cases of neighbourhood governance discussed in the preceding section.

The practice of politics requires that power relations, conflict and contestation occupy centre stage – they cannot and should not be circumvented. Norval draws on Laclau and Mouffe to illustrate the way in which actors persist in attempting to construct a hegemonic discourse that establishes their preferred perspective as the way in which things are done and understood in specific settings. Important here is the need to construct 'political frontiers' between potential participants to deliberation, separating out 'friends' and 'enemies'. These separations are not fixed but remain in flux, open to further contestation and change.

In the residents' group discussed earlier in this chapter, the residents were clear about the separation between 'friends' and 'enemies'. At one level this was a simple distinction between 'the public', or local residents, and 'officials', whether these were politicians or professionals (public-sector planners or private-sector developers). However, the distinction was more nuanced in practice, with some officials being afforded the status of 'friends', for example, the community development workers whose job it was to support the residents' group as they required. Similarly some residents were clearly identified as 'enemies' because of the relationship they had chosen to have with the regeneration organisation. In the words of one respondent,

We had, the Chair of the [regeneration company sponsored body] on our committee, but he's never been to a meeting. I've found out he's not a bloke I'd confide in.... He's on the board. So if I had wanted something to go to the organisation I'd tell him. I'd just plant it and it would get there in the end.... At the end of the day I've got to work for the Group. As much as the regeneration organisation needs me, it can't be at the expense of my allegiance to the Group.

Norval identifies disagreement as important in constituting common deliberative spaces. She cites Rancière (1999) in arguing that shared deliberative spaces are not automatically present but require creation and that this process of creation is one based on dispute and disagreement. She argues that in the moment of disagreement following the identification of a previously unarticulated 'wrong' the possibility of 'new subjects and new spaces of commonality come into existence' (Norval, this volume, Chapter 3).

An example of this is found in the development of the relationship between politicians and resident members of a neighbourhood advisory board. Amongst the board's powers was the allocation of a small amount of money to be spent on community projects (commonly known as 'community chests'). One respondent explained,

It was a bid for someone to translate a Youth Directory – she wanted some help with the funding and it was to be translated into 12 recognised community languages. It was for some piece of research that she was doing.... The councillors, looking for value for money, were minded as a group to say 'look we'd like to be realistic about the number of people involved with these community languages who would actually use the project – maybe we could restrict it to three, because obviously it's very expensive.' I felt and several other people did as well that it wasn't very fair. Then quite a lot of people then, instead of nodding it through, said, 'no, no, no, we agree, we must publish it in all the required languages'. I think the councillors were quite surprised.

This incident did not change the formal relationship between politicians and the resident board members (the politicians still held the formal power to decide about the funding) but it did change the quality of the relationship between those politicians and those resident board members in that forum, offering an example of negotiated exchange based on difference of views that in turn offered new possibilities for how the group might operate in the future.

By contrast, in the area committee, the rules of the forum appeared to act to silence otherwise articulate and powerful individuals who had roles as lay advisory members on the forum. One respondent described meeting a fellow lay advisory member at another meeting and having the following discussion:

I think you met A yes. We happened to meet at another meeting, not connected with this. And we were just sort of chatting. Umm, I think there is a realisation that we have actually been very passive. Which is interesting cause there are some strong characters with a degree of familiarity with the issues. Really passive, sat there, and nodded. You know be respectful to the church.

Int. And why do you think that is?

(pause) I don't know really. We have never. I suppose it's quite. You come to the meetings I arrive about 20 past 6, 28 mins past 6, rushing and sweaty and everything else. Sort of sit down. Then I rush out at the end. Right think it's been a long day I want to go home. So we never see people between meetings.

I think well, are they thinking the same thing and maybe not. Maybe they are happy, maybe it's me. Umm so we never actually get the time to explore some of those issues and maybe to think about, do we have issues or ideas in common? Do we need to act as a block? I am sure the councillors will say you can't act as a block, but they do all the time. So why not us.

The political nature of the engagement between politicians, professionals and the public was rarely explicitly identified in the neighbourhood initiatives we studied. This did not mean that political identities were not being constructed nor that political struggles were not taking place; rather that participants were either consciously or unconsciously not articulating their actions in these terms. However there were times when actors did identify themselves and their actions as political, most often in one Sure Start initiative and invariably in the context of party politics (as illustrated earlier). For example one interviewee saw her participation in the Sure Start initiative as a reaffirmation of a political identity with very particular roots:

I value loyalty. Part of me is still strongly affected by the sense of betrayal by the Labour Party of what I and many like me stood for.... New Labour have completely sold us out. And that was how I lost my seat. I was on the outside. But you learn from these experiences. And I learned to value my family, and my community through that. And I see myself as returning to those values. So that is what is important to me.

This speaks to Norval's interpretation of Laclau's (2005) account of the construction of political identity – the claims actors make to and then against institutions constitute the identities both of the claimants and of those to whom the claims are made. Another example, again from a Sure Start initiative illustrates the way in which actors are able to constitute flexible political identities able to work with the fact that the focus for political action may be at once in the neighbourhood but also elsewhere. For example, for one interviewee,

I think it's important that, while we're keeping things local, we don't lose sight of the bigger picture. Because not everything is solvable locally. Like we were talking at the awayday about the benefits structure, and how there's a real disincentive for parents on benefits to take a job. It's a real disruption to their income. And that can only be addressed at a national level.

Norval's final condition pertains to what she terms 'adversarial legitimacy'. Here she draws on Mouffe's (2005) work on agonistic democracy and democratic subjectivity. This allows for actors to recognise the difference between them (that is, to be adversaries) but also to understand one another 'as belonging to the same political association, as sharing a common symbolic space' (with rules which are respected but open to challenge and change) within which to engage in conflict (Mouffe 2005, 20). So conflict is mediated or contained by the fact that all actors recognise and respect one another's right to engage in conflict through rules of engagement that all consider legitimate. The idea of legitimate adversaries is extremely helpful in distinguishing between those examples of conflict and those conflictual relationships that may be inevitable but are also counterproductive or unproductive, and those which reflect meaningful exchanges that have the potential to generate the emergence of a new route for action, a new possibility for exchange between actors.

The case studies presented here divide easily into those which reflect the expression of 'adversarial legitimacy' and those which do not. The residents' group identification of 'friends' and 'enemies' did not necessarily discount enemies from processes of productive engagement and exchange, provided they abided by the same rules as those of the residents' group.

In one of the Sure Start initiatives the importance of allowing relationships to build over time and for conflict to be managed within those relationships (not managed out of them) was highlighted. For one respondent,

In the early days, meetings were very tense, and there were some stressful issues to deal with – in particular the employment of the last co-ordinator. And people didn't know each other so well then. That's not to say that we don't still have disagreements, and different points of view. There are some strong personalities on the board. But it's more of a discussion now. Less of a fight! And I think that sort of debate is healthy.

By contrast, the area committee was a case study full of conflict and tension, none of which could be considered an expression of adversarial legitimacy because actors did not recognise one another as such and the rules of the deliberative forum did not facilitate this either.

When respondents were asked what caused conflict in the meetings, responses were very similar, regardless of who the respondent was. For example a local government employee described conflict as emanating from:

Unsatisfied members of the public. Umm, (pause). These area committees are really, I mean I am talking not just as a council worker but even as a member of the public who lives in [the area]. It's been a real stepping stone ...where people are able to come out and really voice, how they feel about certain issues that they thought they hadn't had the opportunity to voice for the last 15 years. And umm, they get a lot of people with a lot of grievances. A lot of people with a lot of anxiety. A lot of people with a lot of frustrations.

A local resident offered a similar assessment:

Int. Right. So are there particular things that cause conflict?
Respondent Yes. Whenever something isn't resolved. And that happens a lot.

The appointment of some committee members as 'lay members' because of their particular expertise or experience was considered problematic because not all of those involved in the forum – that is, the public – knew why these residents had this designation, what it meant or why they should take any notice of it. The consequence, as one lay representative described, could be more conflict:

I said I didn't want to be called a representative. Cause I didn't want to upset anybody. I am not involved in any neighbourhood stuff around here. So I couldn't bring anybody else's views.... Cause sometime it's quite frightening really, you know people questioning what you do. Any no one has ever said it yet, but you think sometimes a resident's going to say it, you know 'what are you doing, you don't represent me'.

Conclusion

It is crucial to acknowledge the political character of ideas and practices of neighbourhood governance. Different ideas and understandings of democracy underpin models of neighbourhood governance, and their adoption ensures their passage into emergent institutional designs. The empirical examples explored in this chapter reveal how the translation from idea to institution may be interrupted, usually because neighbourhood governance initiatives tend to draw on more than one model and therefore more than one democratic idea, and this results in different conceptualisations of political contestation competing with one another in the design process. In the case study described in this chapter, the dominance of liberal-democratic ideas inhibited the development of neighbourhood governance initiatives based on more radical democratic ideas, despite the rhetorical claims about 'participatory democracy' and 'shifting the balance of power between citizens and the state'.

The empirical examples offered in this chapter also demonstrate how the impact of democratic ideas and associated constitutions of 'the political' are mediated by the interventions of key actors. These actors may be those people formally designated as 'institutional designers' but they will also include those actors who can draw on their positional or personal power, authority or legitimacy in the neighbourhood to influence the design process and outcome. These interventions are themselves expressions of political attempts to secure, adapt or subvert the rules of neighbourhood governance in support of particular ideas, interests or identities.

The case study emphasises the importance of making visible the political character of procedural rules in neighbourhood governance institutions as instruments for creating the conditions in which deliberation between politicians, professionals and the public may or may not be possible. The examples in this chapter show how even apparently democratic rules privilege some actors over others in securing access to and influence over neighbourhood governance decision making, reflecting the embedded inequalities of power that exist amongst politicians, professionals and publics. This does not mean that less powerful actors cannot make their presence felt, and the chapter describes the conditions under which rules were amended, subverted or disrupted, but it also raises the question of whether there are alternative approaches to neighbourhood governance design and what they might look like.

Norval's (this volume, Chapter 3) proposal for an agonistic analytical framework for democratic exchanges is helpful in this search for alternatives, principally because it acknowledges the central role of power and conflict in politics, as a basis for defining democratic spaces, identities and relationships. The case study in this chapter demonstrates the presence of conflict in the creation and institution-alisation of new neighbourhood governance arrangements. It reveals how misguided attempts to minimise conflict are, both because of the inevitability of its emergence and because of its significance in shaping adversarial identities and relationships, opening up opportunities for more robust and meaningful deliberation.

9 Participatory Governance in Practice

THERESE O'TOOLE AND RICHARD GALE

Introduction

The decentring of contemporary forms of governance and the emergence of more participatory modes of decision making have given rise to intense debate over the extent to which this has resulted in the democratisation of governance. Much of the debate has focused on questions of institutional design in evaluating the democratic potential of participatory forms of governance, and this is particularly valuable in the context of the proliferation of a wide range of models of governance, where strategies for inclusion, mechanisms for accountability, or deliberative practices vary considerably (Chhotray and Stoker 2010). Whilst issues of institutional design are important, we argue here for the value of practice-oriented assessments of how state and civil society relations play out within participatory governance arrangements. This is important because of the possibilities for (both state and civil society) actors within governance structures to adapt or change formal rules of governance in ways which depart from institutional design – sometimes with unintended consequences – necessitating, as the Introduction to this volume makes clear, 'a larger role for contingency in understanding governance'.

In outlining a practical, critical approach to the study of politics, James Tully (2002) argues that the 'practices of governance' – that is, 'the means by which the structure of governance is held in place' – need to be understood alongside the 'practices of freedom' – that is, the responses of individuals and groups who act within systems of governance, including 'the diverse means by which subjects are able to resist, organise networks of support, bring the governors to negotiations, and hold them to their agreements' (Tully 2002, 546). Such 'practices of freedom', Tully suggests, constitute the 'democratic' side of governance, and he asserts moreover that '[p]ractices of governance imply practices of freedom and vice versa' (Tully 2002, 541). This focus on practices of governance and those of freedom foregrounds the interactive nature of governance – although, as our own account acknowledges, this interaction is typically based on asymmetric relations of power. De Certeau's (1984) distinction between the 'strategies' that institutional actors with the power to constitute the rules of the game adopt, and the 'tactics' deployed by citizens to pursue their own more autonomous objectives is a useful way of framing the asymmetric nature of the interactions between state institutions and citizens, whilst permitting consideration of the scope for citizens to exercise agency to enhance their political efficacy in their encounters with institutional power. Although state-civil society relations within participatory governance are typically asymmetrical, with state actors holding strategic power to (re)constitute the terms of engagement, we hold open the possibility that civil society actors may act tactically within them to change, modify or 'claim' governance spaces (Cornwall and Coelho 2006).

In taking a practice-based approach to assessing participatory governance, we engage with critics of participatory governance who are sceptical of its democratic potential. First, we contend that practice-oriented analyses allow identification of the possibilities for tactical appropriations of governance spaces by citizens – even where their founding rationale or design may appear to limit substantive participation. Second, we suggest that evaluation of the democratic potential of participatory governance initiatives should include not only consideration of institutional outcomes or the impact of citizens' participation on the structures of governance, but also their potential to create new political subjectivities among those who participate in them.

We develop these arguments through a case study of a youth parliament in Bradford, which reflects many of the limitations that critics identify as being characteristic of participatory governance. Whilst the terms on which young people were able to participate in this institution were initially quite constrained, we reveal how the Members of the Youth Parliament (MYPs) tactically appropriated the political space of the parliament in order to foreground a more responsive and democratic youth agenda than that envisaged by the local state. Furthermore, through their interactions and conflicts with the local authority, we also see among the MYPs the acquisition of more enduring habits of critique and action underpinning the development of a participatory habitus (Crossley 2003) and 'democratic ethos' (see Griggs, Norval and Wagenaar, this volume, Introduction).

Decentred Participatory Governance

Although the shift towards decentred and more participatory forms of governance is often portrayed as a democratising of decision making, many critics have questioned whether this shift creates opportunities for citizens' *substantive* participation in governance (Dryzek 2000, 82–83; Clarke 2010). Bang (2003) and Newman (2005), for instance, argue that participatory governance incurs particular problems of co-optation and exclusion, primarily because its rationale, typically, is not the empowerment of citizens per se, but the achievement of *effective* governance in situations of increasing social and political complexity. They suggest governments need to partner with citizens because they cannot any longer rely on old-style bureaucratic expertise to solve complex policy problems (Bang 2003; Newman 2005). The emphasis on implementation, or 'output politics' (Bang 2003), that characterises many participatory governance initiatives is criticised as falling short of substantive democratisation, constituting instead a neoliberal model of mobilising civil society actors to engage in service delivery (Beaumont and Nicholls 2008), rather than a means to empower their participation in political decision making – reducing citizens to service consumers and producers (Cornwall and Coelho 2006). Critics inspired by Foucauldian theory have analysed contemporary forms of participatory governance as an extension of 'governmentality' – a mode of disciplining citizens through increasingly refined techniques of managerialism – rather than a move to empower citizens in their interactions with the state (Newman 2005; Beaumont and Nicholls 2008). For many, the disciplining of citizens to participate in the provision of public goods and services and the 'culture governance' (Bang 2003) that attends this are integral to neoliberal governance (Burnett 2008).

Whilst these issues pose clear questions for the democratic propensities of participatory governance, we take issue with those accounts that see participatory governance simply as a mode of discipline and control. First, the practices of governing are often disorganised and contradictory, undermining their disciplinary capacity: Barnes and Prior (2009) highlight, for example, long-standing studies of unruly 'street level bureaucrats', or low-level government officials, who implement policies in ways that run contrary to centrally determined agendas or directives. Second, there is a need to attend to the agency of citizens who engage in participatory governance. Whilst appreciating the contribution of governmentality theories to the understanding of governing processes, Bevir (2011, 462) nonetheless argues that 'concrete studies of governmentality rarely examine agency as a source of discourses or as evidenced in specific instances of counter power'. Consequently 'governmentality theorists characteristically offer reified and monolithic accounts of modern power, with little sensitivity to diversity, heterogeneity and resistance within and over time.' (Bevir 2011, 462) Yet, as Newman points out, to those who see new governance practices as a disciplinary regime 'the active citizen may not act in the way envisaged by government' (Newman 2005, 134). Indeed, Cornwall and Coelho argue that participatory opportunities provided by the state, even though built on highly unequal terms, may still be 'conquered by civil society demands for inclusion' (2006, 1):

As 'invited spaces', the institutions of the participatory sphere are framed by those who create them, and infused with power relations and cultures of interaction carried into them from other spaces.... Yet these are also spaces of possibility, in which power takes a more productive and positive form. (Cornwall and Coelho 2006, 11)

Taylor (2007), following Tarrow, proposes furthermore that despite problems of co-optation and colonisation, decentred participatory governance might create new political opportunity structures that social actors can exploit. Barnes and Prior (2009) point to a range of ways in which citizens may 'subvert' government intentions, whether through obstruction, challenge, exit, ignoring or bending the 'rules', or seeking alliances with other citizens to create spaces of dialogue or deliberation. Such tactical repertoires resonate with Tully's 'practices of freedom', in which he specifies three modes of response by citizens to governance practices:

1. In the first mode, individuals and groups comply with the rules, but in so doing modify governance practices in often 'unnoticed and significant ways'.

2. In the second mode, individuals and groups challenge the rules and use the available procedures to modify governance practices.
3. In the third mode, individuals and groups resist governance practices by escaping or confronting them. (Tully 2002, 540)

De Certeau's (1984) theory of the relationship between the 'strategies' of institutions and the 'tactics' of social agents resonates with this focus on the scope for citizens to engage in autonomous political action *within* the structures and rules of participatory governance (and see O'Toole and Gale, 2008). For de Certeau, 'strategies' are the means by which institutions constitute and control the power relations in which they occupy privileged positions, both to achieve specific goals, and to maintain their positions of power. 'Tactics', by contrast, are the modi operandi of social actors who, although lacking formative roles in defining institutional parameters, are able to appropriate and utilise the formal elements and procedures of institutions to gain temporal or structural advantages. Importantly, 'tactics' often do not conform to the patterns of action anticipated by those responsible for constituting institutional 'strategies'. This distinction between strategies and tactics provides a useful approach to studying the interactions between citizens and state institutions, focussing on the practices of freedom ('tactics') employed by citizens, which may utilise the practices of governance, including language, procedures and rules ('strategies'), but in ways that create spaces for them to define their own agendas and act autonomously – perhaps in unexpected ways.

Central to our practice-based analysis of the relationship between the state and citizens, then, is the agency of civil society actors who engage in participatory governance arrangements: attending to the possibility that citizens can effect changes on the practices of the state, even where the state's purpose in including citizens in governance structures may be circumscribed.

A second key aspect of our argument for a practice-based approach to evaluating participatory governance focuses on the implications of participation for agents – as well as for the structures and practices of institutions. As Norval, Griggs and Wagenaar (this volume, Introduction) remind us: 'people are not only democrats by virtue of the existence of institutions, laws and rights, but they become so in exercising their capabilities for questioning, affirming, negotiating and contesting the regimes and micro-practices of governance that shape and limit their lives'.

We suggest that the engagement of citizens in forms of participatory governance, even if constrained by limited or tokenistic offers of engagement, can facilitate the creation of new political subjectivities, or what Crossley terms a 'radical habitus' (2003). Crossley's study of radical political movements argues that the act of participation may result in a reshaping of activists' 'habitus' (i.e., following Bourdieu, the durable dispositions informing the ways in agents respond to 'objective' social conditions) (Crossley 2003, 50). In particular, Crossley focuses on the ways in which involvement in events or movements propentiate the acquisition of: (i) questioning, criticising and distrusting perceptual-cognitive habits that facilitate challenging political elites; (ii) 'the political know-how' to turn critique into action; (iii) an ethos of action; and (iv) a feeling of pleasure and purpose from activism. These combine to create a 'radical habitus': or as Crossley describes it 'habit-busting habits'! (2003, 56) Thus, as Cornwall and Coelho remark, 'participatory sphere institutions are also spaces for *creating* citizenship, where through learning to participate citizens cut their political teeth and acquire skills that can be transferred to other spheres' (Cornwall and Coelho 2006, 8).

In the next sections, we consider these issues through exploration of a case study of the interactions between young people and a local authority in the context of a youth parliament in the city of Bradford, United Kingdom – the Bradford Keighley Youth Parliament (BKYP).[1]

The Case Study

The case study materials we present here are based on a focus group with a sub-sample of seven Members of the Youth Parliament (MYPs) between the ages of sixteen and twenty-four, comprising five women and two men, whose self-ascribed ethnicity included 'Mirpuri', 'Pakistani', 'Indian' and 'British Asian'. The focus group was followed up with six individual interviews with the focus-group participants. Additionally, we held interviews with one youth worker and two

---

[1] This case study was part of a wider, Leverhulme Trust-funded study of ethnic minority young people's political engagement, which involved twelve focus groups and fifty individual interviews, with a total of seventy-six ethnic minority young people, interviews with youth workers and council personnel, and documentary analysis. We are grateful to the Leverhulme Trust for their support for this research.

council officials associated with the Local Strategic Partnership with operational responsibility for the BKYP, and we analysed documentation and website content relating to the BKYP.

These seven MYPs in our case study were members of the first cohort of the BKYP. Our focus group with them explored their collective experiences and expectations of and reflections on the BKYP, as well as their perspectives on the city and local and national political institutions. In our follow-up individual interviews with them, we discussed their personal political biographies, exploring what brought them into the BKYP, family and peer group backgrounds, political interests and concerns and their sense of their 'future political selves'.

In the following section, we analyse the establishment and operation of the BKYP as a manifestation of participatory governance – given its role in acting as a mechanism for the Local Authority to consult with young people in its decision making across a range of policy areas.[2] We show how problems of co-optation were evident in some key aspects of the constitution and running of the BKYP. Nevertheless, we also draw attention to the interplay between institutional strategies ('practices of governance') aimed at achieving a particular set of government-determined goals, and the tactical challenges ('practices of freedom') of young people involved in these. In particular, we found ongoing recourse by the MYPs to the second of Tully's 'practices of freedom' in the form of successive challenges to and modification of institutional procedures and practices, with the effect of introducing a more responsive set of institutional arrangements than envisaged by the Local Authority. This interplay, we suggest, lends itself to a somewhat different assessment of the democratic significance of the BKYP and contributes an important dimension to existing critiques of participatory governance in highlighting the potential of 'practices of freedom' to democratise participatory governance – even where its democratic potential may have been initially circumscribed. Furthermore, analysis of young people's political habitus in relation to their participation in the parliament suggests that participation in this structure may have served to create durable patterns of critical engagement and activism

---

[2] It should be noted that not all local youth parliaments could be seen as manifestations of participatory governance, since they don't always have an ascribed role in formal structures of decision making – the Birmingham Young People's Parliament being a case in point.

among the MYPs, that is to say it has enhanced the 'democratic ethos' of the young people involved.

Practices of Governance

Before setting out our findings on these issues, let us offer a brief context to the city in which the young people lived and were politically active in 2005, at the time of the research. According to the 2001 Census, Bradford, located in the north of England, had an urban population of approximately 467,665 (Census 2001). That census showed the city had an ethnic minority population of 21.7%, with Pakistanis making up the largest group within this. Once home to a thriving textiles industry, Bradford has undergone major deindustrialisation since the 1970s and currently faces significant challenges in regenerating its local economy. As in many areas in the United Kingdom throughout the early 2000s, the local state introduced a variety of mechanisms of consultation and participation aimed at increasing citizens' involvement in local decision making. In Bradford, however, the local expression of this broader trend was shaped in significant ways by policy responses to a series of street disturbances that took place in the city (and elsewhere, in Burnley and Oldham) in the summer of 2001 – and particularly by the official report on the disturbances, the Cantle Report (2001). This report viewed the disturbances as an outcome of pronounced ethnic segregation in these areas and described communities there as living 'parallel lives'. Its ensuing policy recommendations gave pride of place to the need for value-oriented (as opposed to socio-economic) integration, couched in terms of the discourse of 'Community Cohesion' (Hussain and Bagguley 2005; Bagguley and Hussain 2006), which placed special emphasis on the cultivation of shared sets of 'core values'. As Burnett (2008, 38) argues, the community cohesion agenda posited 'unmanaged diversity' as a threat and set local authorities the goal of fostering shared core values. According to Bagguley and Hussain, this resulted in a 'blurring of the state/civil society distinction' (2006, 2), with the political connotations of the 2001 disorders giving way to the 'management' of community interaction, and elaboration of the 'managerial techniques' through which this was to be achieved (2006, 6).

    In Bradford, the community cohesion agenda took a variety of forms. Central to its delivery was the Local Strategic Partnership, known as 'Bradford Vision' (established in 2001 and replaced by the 'Bradford District Partnership' in 2008), which co-ordinated and promoted urban regeneration, neighbourhood renewal and community cohesion through partnership with the council and a variety of community and non-governmental partners. In keeping with the overall themes of the community cohesion agenda, Bradford Vision paid considerable attention to the participation and inclusion of young people in local democratic processes. Anxiety about young people's political engagement was an important point of focus in the aftermath of the 2001 disturbances, with governmental reports and media commentators suggesting young people were worryingly politically disaffected (see LGA 2002, 23). Thus in Bradford, alongside concerns with civic pride, participation and citizenship, a key strand of the community cohesion strategy focussed on encouraging young people into leadership and active citizenship. The establishment of the youth parliament was a key facet of this strategy,[3] along with the development of a system of school councils and a 'Bradfordised' Citizenship Education[4] programme for secondary schools. Arguably, Newman's (2005) contention that participatory governance initiatives are typically less concerned with the empowerment of citizens and more with the state's concern to (i) address legitimation crises, (ii) acquire the necessary expertise to solve complex policy problems, and (iii) promote social cohesion could be seen as having particular purchase in Bradford.

---

[3] Although the proposal to establish the BKYP arose prior to the 2001 disturbances, it nevertheless became an important mechanism for the implementation of the community cohesion agenda.

[4] The notion of a 'Bradfordised' Citizenship Education programme was aimed at addressing specific issues of ethnic integration and community cohesion. This was expressed as an 'Enhanced Citizenship Curriculum', which was adapted from the National Curriculum to make Citizenship Education more relevant to the local Bradford context. Four key themes were established as central to the Enhanced Citizenship Curriculum, including: (i) identity and community; (ii) diversity and cohesion; (iii) responsibilities, rights and respect; and (iv) equality. At school level this has included teaching on: concepts, knowledge, understanding, attitudes and skills necessary to promote racial harmony; local, national and global 'communities'; 'cohesion' and 'diversity'; 'responsibilities' and 'human rights'; international relations; refugees and asylum seekers; crime and its causes; and the youth justice system. Specific units were planned on the Holocaust, genocide and Islamophobia. Our information on this comes from an interview with personnel from the Community Cohesion team within Bradford Vision.

The BKYP was established in September 2002 by Bradford Metropolitan District Council (MDC), who funded and ran the parliament, with the election of 30 members (MYPs) to the parliament, representing five constituencies from across the Bradford and Keighley district. Anyone between the ages of eleven and twenty-five was allowed to stand and vote in the elections. The first cohort of MYPs was elected on a turnout of 6,417, equivalent to approximately 6.5% of the young population in the district. Whilst no specific strategies were adopted to achieve ethnic diversity among the MYPs, the elections attracted relatively proportionate numbers of white and Asian Muslim candidates, probably as a result of the area-based approach to selection, which in Bradford reflects patterns of ethnic residential concentration (Phillips 2006).

From the very beginning, the BKYP was a governmentally driven initiative: Bradford MDC established and funded the BKYP, whilst the council's Youth Service was responsible for its day-to-day running. The parliament was established to carry out the council's 'strategies' for policy implementation and service delivery in the local area. In particular, the BKYP contributed to two prominent strands of local government policy: the council's community cohesion agenda; and the Youth Service's four key objectives of 'participation', 'education', 'equality' and 'employment'. The council also drew up the parliament's constitution and expressed a formal commitment to consult the BKYP in its policymaking processes. The council's own constitution recognised the BKYP, and MYPs sat on certain council committees (such as the Neighbourhood Renewal Committee). As such, the BKYP had no institutional foundation that stood apart from its relationship to the local state: the terms on which the MYPs came together and were subsequently able to act as a coherent political body were entirely dependent on this relationship.

Encountering Practices of Governance

In a focus group, MYPs criticised the nature of their relationship with the council, suggesting that the establishment of the parliament as a democratic forum for young people in the district had been somewhat tokenistic:

> RESPONDENT I: ...as young people, you know, I felt like they'd given us responsibility with one hand, but they took it away with the other.

RESPONDENT 2: Yeah.

RESPONDENT 1: Do you see what I mean? So we were allowed to do it, because they were ticking all their boxes to say, 'oh, young people are going here, young people are getting involved here ...', you know, but it wasn't, we knew what was going on [...] And we had to stay quiet and remember we were representing the young parliament, and even though individually we all had our views.

The MYPs reported becoming increasingly dissatisfied with the dominant role that the council played in setting the Youth Parliament's agenda, with issues moved by the MYPs often overridden by the council or relegated below council issues. As the focus group discussed:

RESPONDENT 1: personally I feel that we do have difficulties, or to discuss the issues we want to discuss. It's always, like, 'talk about that, yeah, but don't go that way, talk a bit more about these issues.'

RESPONDENT 2: We were being controlled.

For example, one of the participants commented:

[T]he Bradford riots, that was one of the problems – not any more – but when we wanted to talk about that, we didn't have the chance. And that time has gone now, and it's a different issue [...] racism for example. But, they [the Council] would come back and talk about old issues, when we were trying to, maybe, get over that, you know, resolve that and move on. And I just feel like they were the ones that put the questions on the table and they pretty much controlled the agenda.

The MYPs perceived a gap between their own political aspirations and the objectives set for the parliament by the council. As another participant commented:

It's like you get told you've got the freedom, yet you haven't, do you know what I mean? You're still being controlled, it's like, you know, 'you can do this, oh go on, go on, do it' but 'oh no actually, may be not that, you can't do that'.

A significant instance of disagreement between the MYPs and the council arose at the inception of the parliament, when the MYPs proposed to hold a 'stop-the-war' rally, in opposition to the war in Iraq. This proposal was blocked by the Labour-controlled council (who had passed a motion signalling support for the New Labour government's policy on Iraq). For the MYPs, this clash illuminated at a very early stage the nature of the parliament's relationship with the council. As one participant noted:

> I personally think I was a bit naïve ... because the Council had passed a motion saying 'we support the troops in Iraq' and therefore we can't let you do this, and the young people, the kind of consensus was we wanted to do something and therefore we were just told 'finito', we can't do it, and that kind of caused a barrier, because we thought, OK, we've been elected legitimately, we've got a right to do this and we've got a Human Rights Act Article 12,[5] blah-de, blah-de, blah ... and why, and then kind of, the whole financial barrier, the whole kind of controlling the space, the whole police permission, that kind of all came into the thing, and I think that kind of woke us up a lot, in terms of, there's us guys thinking, OK, we've got the power, we're the voice, well actually you haven't because the Council controls where the money goes, and what you can do.

Additionally, the MYPs complained of a consultation overload with requests for consultation on an exceedingly broad range of council policy initiatives, which also inhibited the ability of the MYPs to forge their own agenda. Moreover, these consultations were felt to be largely tokenistic, in that the MYPs were being asked to sit on committees and read through long policy documents, with little effort having been made to ensure that the language of such documents was accessible to young people.

From the outset, the MYPs felt frustrated by the idioms and procedures (the 'strategies') adopted by the council for managing the BKYP, and the ways in which these constrained the MYPs' conception of effective youth participation. In the focus group, the MYPs continually signalled problems of co-optation within the parliament:

RESPONDENT 1: We got co-opted ....
RESPONDENT 2: Yeah, we got co-opted ...

---

[5] This refers to the UN Convention on the Rights of the Child, ratified by the UK in 1991, in which Article 12 calls for children's views to be heard in relation to 'all matters affecting the child'. This Convention forms an important frame of reference for standards frameworks in England, including *Every Child Matters* and *Hear by Right*, which reinforce the notion that children and young people should be included and consulted in relation to services and policies that affect them (Tisdall and Davis 2004).

RESPONDENT 3: At times, we may be the puppets on strings, kind of thing. Do you know what I'm saying?

Practices of Freedom

Nevertheless, once constituted as a body, the MYPs began to make 'tactical' use of the institutional arrangements available to them in the parliament, developing a more responsive youth agenda within the 'strategic' domain marked out for them by the council. For instance, rather than bow to the council's opposition to the BKYP's proposal to hold an anti-war protest march, the MYPs compromised by staging instead a 'peace walk' – ostensibly submitting to the council's position, whilst signifying their own anti-war position.

A further shift in the terms of engagement made by the MYPs was to change the name and terminology of the BKYP 'sittings'. This ensued from their experience of the first council-led sitting, which was seen to be formal and inaccessible (being housed in council chambers and conducted in the idioms of council proceedings). Instead, the BKYP sittings were dubbed 'wot's ur flava?' to better communicate to young people the purpose of the BKYP and to overcome what had been perceived as the alienating language and practices of the more formal sittings. This dissonance between the language of the council and young people was jokingly referred to in the focus group:

RESPONDENT 1: she [a city Councillor] sent me a personalised letter [following the first sitting]. I think she quite enjoyed it, really.
RESPONDENT 2: Did she?
RESPONDENT 1: Yeah. Saying I was the Chair.
ALL: Oh, you were the Chair!
RESPONDENT 3: She called you a chair?
ALL: [Laughter]
RESPONDENT 1: Insulting!
RESPONDENT 4: I know, insulting, you're an object.

The MYPs additionally took the decision to hold BKYP events in alternative venues to the council chambers, which were found to be too formal.

Another crucial development, and one significant to future cohorts of the BKYP, was the decision to rewrite the constitution of the parliament that had been drafted by the council. Changes included lowering the age range of the parliament from 11–25 to 11–21, to offset the dominance of the parliament by older MYPs, in effect to make the parliament 'younger'.

The MYPs also resisted attempts to have their workload determined by the council, diverting the consultation functions of the parliament to a 1,000-strong E-panel of young people drawn from the Bradford and Keighley district. They argued that this forum was more likely to express the diversity of young people in the district and provide a more robust mechanism for articulating youth perspectives in relation to council policies – rather than seeing the thirty MYPs as the embodiment of the voices of young people in the district.

There were a series of other changes made by the MYPs to their terms of engagement, both with the council and with young people in the area who constituted their electorate. These included strategies for determining their own political agenda, such as holding residential workshops for the MYPs and youth consultation events to facilitate more autonomous agenda-setting practices. Furthermore, the first cohort engaged in a series of mentoring meetings with the second cohort of representatives to the BKYP. These emphasised the need for the new MYPs to foreground agenda setting early on in the work of the parliament and to forge their agenda in consultation with other young people. Thus, the second cohort, under the guidance of the first, held a youth conference with 200 young people drawn from the Bradford Keighley District, in order to consult with and determine the strategic priorities of young people (these were: drugs and gun crime; racism; disability; and, significantly in relation to the BKYP's relationship with the council, the issue of the provision of youth services.

The MYPs also resisted the council's attempt to limit the parliament to service delivery and local issues. Thus, the MYPs continued consciousness-raising work in relation to international political events (such as the 'war on terror', the war in Iraq, the drop-the-debt campaign, and so on), despite their awareness that this was not seen by the council as a legitimate focus of the parliament.

RESPONDENT 1: just something that happened yesterday in the papers, about certain charities being told that they support terrorism, so therefore, and you're kind of making people aware of how that is political and what changes they can make, even if it's not a big global change.
RESPONDENT 2: Yeah, but you see, the youth parliament won't be able to do anything to do with that, because they'll say 'what's that to do with

our issues?' You know? And I think it's unfair because it affects you, do you know what I mean?

RESPONDENT 1: It does, yeah. ...

RESPONDENT 2: And the fact that we're in a transitional period, but the world the way it is, I just feel like, sometimes, this is the pretence of doing X, Y, Z, you know, we're not able to do the issues, or deal with the issues we want to deal with.

...

RESPONDENT 4: And we weren't allowed to be party political, and get a sense that, there was a big focus on, we should only do it local issues. So like ...

RESPONDENT 5: Yeah. But if that's what's affecting young people, then I don't see why we couldn't mention it. I mean, those that have got an understanding on national and international issues, they are obviously going to express those concerns. ...

Following Tully and de Certeau, the various changes outlined above can be interpreted as appropriations of the 'established language' and rules of procedure governing the activities of the Youth Parliament. Each of them, we argue, indicates that the power relations between the MYPs and the council were not static or unidirectional. Rather, they show how the MYPs threaded an alternative youth agenda through the council's existing objectives, working towards these when there was discernable overlap, yet departing from them when they were unduly constraining. A key consideration here is that the MYPs were not merely subjects of power within a given institutional set-up, but increasingly skilled and knowledgeable actors, critically aware of the constraints imposed on them by the council. When examined in this way, the nature of the MYPs' engagement with the council appears to have ranged periodically from co-operation, through negotiation and resistance, to (qualified) opposition, achieving thereby a temporal foregrounding of their own youth agenda that stood apart from (local) state imperatives. In this way, the establishment of the BKYP provided the political opportunity structure in which the MYPs developed 'practices of freedom'.

Developing a Democratic Ethos

Related to the question of the BKYP's democratic significance, we suggest, is its effects on the political subjectivities of the MYPs involved, and not only on its institutional features. Here, the focus group suggested that the shared experience of attempts by the Council to control the parliament served to increase the cohesiveness of the group and to develop its sense of a collective political identity:

[T]he Council controls how much power we have. But to be honest that was a positive as well, because it brought us all a lot more close together [agreement from other group members]. I mean, to begin with we were all like colleagues, you know like, [we] just met every now and again, but then, but *now* ... [semi-jokingly] I can safely say ... we're all like friends, do you know what I mean!

Furthermore, many of the MYPs were clearly of the view that their experiences would be of lasting importance to their future trajectories as activists. One interviewee explained how he felt his time in the BKYP had transformed his outlook and developed his political aspirations:

[J]oining the Bradford Keighley Youth Parliament – that was a big stepping stop for myself. I've overcome a lot, achieved so many things and ... I do hope to go into politics or something similar to help make a difference in the future... the youth parliament is only a stepping stone. I do like to, I would like to see myself in the future taking a very much active role to be honest.

The experience was transformative also for a female respondent, whose account of the impact of her participation exemplified the processes of acquiring the habit-busting habits that Crossley identifies (cf., questioning perceptual-cognitive habits, 'political know-how', ethos of action, and pleasure and purpose from activism):

[A]fter coming through this, I am now, I'm politically assertive ... without a doubt, not only me, but anyone else who's come through this process, right, but obviously, the more you give, the more it's going to affect you in a positive way, which it did for me.... It's changed me. Actually, it's made me excel as a person, and I will, without a doubt, and I have a whole lot of aspirations that I'm going to use out of the knowledge that I've gained now to apply to the world.

All our respondents spoke positively of their achievements in the BKYP, whilst signalling their critique of the limitations of the structure.

Through gathering biographical data, we found that respondents had often emerged as BKYP candidates from a background of school, community or anti-racist involvement, whilst participation in the BKYP had developed further their political consciousness and appetite for activism. All had either branched out into other forms of action, or were planning future activity. These included: mentoring; anti-racist peer group training; student activism (in a women's group, Black Students Society or the Federation of Student Islamic Societies (FOSIS)); international campaign activism (such as the drop-the-debt campaign, Amnesty or Tsunami relief); or community activism (including setting up a Muslim youth forum in Leeds to cover the Beeston area, where one of the 7th July London bombers had grown up). For example, one male interviewee suggested:

[I]t was the BKYP that set me up with voluntary work ... before BKYP I didn't, I didn't know where to start on, you know, becoming a volunteer or whatever, I didn't really think about it.... I was happy in my own little world, playing computer games and whatever [laughs].

If questioning engagement, political know-how, an ethos of action and pleasure in activism signal the development of a radical habitus as Crossley (2003) suggests, then these were much in evidence among our respondents and indicate the potential for the episodic involvement in the BKYP to underpin more enduring trajectories of activism.

Conclusion

In this chapter, we have posed some questions concerning the changing relationship between the state and civil society and how these relate to the political participation of citizens in participatory governance structures. Whilst the move towards participatory governance appears ostensibly to hold democratic potential, a number of theorists point to the limitations of state-sponsored initiatives to underscore a substantive increase in the democratic input of citizens into decision-making processes. In part, our case study bears out these criticisms. For example, the establishment of the BKYP clearly emanated from 'state imperatives' and was undergirded with sets of normative assumptions concerning how civil society actors, and especially young people, should enter into relationships with the state.

Nevertheless, adopting a practice-based assessment of the BKYP, we suggest that participatory governance can serve to create new political spaces and subjectivities, even when they are steered by top-down strategies. Thus the MYPs were active in reconfiguring the terms on which they interacted with the state, achieving a partial fashioning of their own agendas and creating a democratic political space for young people that did not previously exist. In this respect, their engagement in 'practices of freedom' in the face of 'practices of governance' has been significant in changing the terms of young people's engagement in the parliament – including for future cohorts. Indeed, the experience of co-optation strategies on the part of the council in Bradford was highly politicising for the members of the BKYP, and galvanised them to organise as a cohesive group in order to forge an autonomous political agenda in opposition to the expectations imposed upon them by the council. An important outcome of their experiences has been the development of more enduring dispositions of critique and activism among the MYPs.

10 The Agonistic Experience: Informality, Hegemony and the Prospects for Democratic Governance

HENDRIK WAGENAAR

Introduction: Citizens, Informality and Urban Governance

Citizens occupy an uneasy position in the major theories of urban governance and democracy, among them pluralism, elite theory and regime theory. Urban politics, at least in these three theories, is the domain of big actors and big institutions: politicians, bureaucrats, large administrative agencies, behind-the-scenes business elites, developers and construction companies, housing corporations, and pressure groups of all stripes. The one constant in this pluralist give and take is that urban policy pays heed to the requirements of a favourable business climate and, following currently popular neoliberal claims of irresistible pressures for change, to globalization and the escalating competition between 'global cities' (Lindblom 1977; Judge 1995, 28; Dryzek, 1996; Sassen 2001; Fainstein 2010). In this hard-nosed game there is hardly any room for the influence of citizens. They either sporadically combine in associations to exert pressure on specific issues or are largely indifferent to politics (Harding 1995, 43).

Citizens do play a central role in another chapter of urban theory: the informal city. Informality is a key concept in theories of planning that concern themselves with urbanization. Informality refers to 'informal modes of organizing space, livelihood and citizenship' (Roy 2010). It is usually associated with hyper-urbanization in the Global South, and it has been most extensively studied in these contexts (Roy 2003; Corbridge et al. 2005; Simone and Abouhani 2005; Chatterjee 2006; Holston 2008). In the absence of state institutions that are sufficiently strong to provide essential services to the poor, the latter have to rely

This chapter has benefitted from helpful comments from Stephen Connelly, Steven Griggs and Aletta Norval on an earlier version. Any mistakes or ambiguities are wholly mine.

on their own practical skills to create such services. Born of necessity, informality also contains hope however. Informality becomes the expression of another kind of urban politics, a 'deep democracy', a 'countergovernmentality' (Chatterjee 2006) that, informed by local knowledge of the conditions and experiences of the poor, allows them to construct an alternative 'insurgent' citizenship that destabilizes 'entrenched' forms of citizenship (Holston, 2008).[1]

As several authors have argued, informality is a 'pervasive phenomenon' that is not restricted to the Global South and should be considered an important analytical tool in understanding the different roles that ordinary citizens play in the constitution of urban space and in urban governance in general (Roy 2010; Lombard and Huxley, 2011; Devlin, 2011). First, despite their highly developed urban administrations and richly endowed policy programmes aimed at revitalizing disadvantaged neighbourhoods, citizens' distrust in urban administrations is far from uncommon in the cities of the North either. Voter turnout is declining in most of the developed democracies of the North, trust in politicians is low, politics seems detached from the problems of everyday citizens, lobbyists are seen to have undue influence over politicians, and those that vote express preferences for extremist parties on the right and left (Mathews 1999; Hay 2007). And, while elected officials pass on problems to public agencies, these agencies are themselves confronted with an urban environment that is increasingly complex, divisive, at the receiving end of global trends and low on resources (Stoker 2006; Ansell 2011, 4; Warren 2008a, 5) It is little wonder that in such an environment citizens take the initiative to manage pressing problems in their neighbourhoods, often because residents feel abandoned by city

---

[1] The optimism about informality in the cities of the South and the fear of being co-opted by the state and losing authenticity has led to a call among the deprived and some of their academic supporters for governments to 'back off'. As Parnell and Robinson describe this: 'The "abdication" of government was considered to be important in allowing the poor and their representatives in organized civil society (as opposed to elected government) to draw on their own insights and capacities to do more for themselves to end poverty. However, we should not idealize the potential benefits of informality. Informal practices in the Global South emerge in an environment where the governing elite ignores or oppresses the poor. And distinctions within communities of the poor, such as gender or caste discrimination, do not disappear with informality' (Holston 2008; Meth 2010). It is for this reason that Parnell and Robinson argue for a greater involvement of the state in 'theorizing cities from the global south' (Parnell and Robinson 2012, 603).

officials, in the process creating new 'space(s) of democratic possibilities' (Warren 2008a, 1; Wagenaar and Specht 2010; Specht 2012).[2]

Second, the concept of informality contains an implicit normative contrast with the more desirable formal procedures and institutions that are thought to comprise urbanization and urban governance. As Lombard and Huxley write: 'Such responses portray informality as a "'state of exception'" from the formal order of urbanization, in which informal sectors and areas are viewed normatively as separate from, and inferior to, those of the formal city' (Lombard and Huxley 2011, 122). In the received view, informality is seen as an 'aberration' or 'other', to some imagined ideal of western, developed, market-produced, residential development (ibid.). However, this normative contrast is misguided on two counts. First, informality is everywhere (as we will see below). Although it comes most clearly into view in situations of diversity and sharp inequality, informality is the fabric of everyday life. It is indeed the poor and ethnic minorities who, often ignored by the state and themselves distrustful of the state, have to rely on the more colourful and creative tactics of deception, evasion, subterfuge and 'playing the system' to make a living and secure shelter. But in a general sense, these informal tactics are also spaces of freedom and possibility, alternatives to the official order, where alternative understandings and practices are hatched, from which new, creative solutions to intractable urban problems may emerge. Second, and more fundamentally, informality is not outside formal systems (Porter 2011, 116). Instead, as I will argue in the second half of this chapter, in an ontological sense, formal structure and informal practices are always mutually implicated, with the formal depending on the informal and vice versa.

As a set of claims about urban governance and citizenship, the concept of informality draws inspiration from Michel de Certeau's idea of the 'everyday tactics' of citizens (Certeau 1984). These are the informal, ordinary activities and routines with which citizens lay claim to urban space and urban resources and literally create their own city, or, more precisely, a city that is adapted to their own needs, challenges and

---

[2] We should also notice a category of 'uninvited' citizen activities that go by names such as civic enterprise or social production, which emerge from a positive ideal and aim at producing social goods, such as sustainable energy and food, transportation, library services and social care, that are ignored by the market. I will discuss these in Section 3.

problems. Informality as informal citizenship contains both necessity and hope. That is, on the one hand, informality is about the imperative of obtaining the necessary means (money, information, connections, influence, space) to eke out a living in a situation in which such resources are scarce or unavailable. But it also safeguards the social ties, everyday practices and 'free spaces' (Boyte 2004, 61) with which to articulate an identity that helps one to uphold and sustain oneself in the face of the oppressive, disciplinary forces of the wider social environment (Roy 2010 96).[3] For example, listening to the stories that residents tell each other and observing the way they live and work in their neighbourhoods, the Belgian urban anthropologist Paul Blondeel was struck by the difference in tone between policymakers' reports about the neighbourhood and the residents' own stories. 'Almost all people I interviewed are confronted with serious issues, yet you don't hear tales of despair. As if these residents talk about other neighbourhoods, other worlds. As if the everyday, physical moving about in the city brings forth another reality than the distal reality of policy makers' (Blondeel 2004 6. Translation HW). To describe this effect he coined the phrase 'urban wisdom'. The informal practices of residents make the neighbourhood into a recognizable, meaningful life world, more often than not a world that does not figure in official policy reports. For example, a group of Dutch urban researchers asked residents of a 'problem neighbourhood' to draw their immediate environment. To their surprise the groups of Moroccan-Dutch youth that allegedly engaged in antisocial behaviour and figured prominently in the city's (and the media's) analyses of the neighbourhood were absent from the drawings. Asked why this was the case, the residents answered that they weren't bothered by their presence and volunteered remarkably sophisticated explanations why they were hanging out on the central square of the neighbourhood (Verloo 2012). Informal practices lead people to accept what you can't change, 'what is part of living here', not in a fatalistic sense but pragmatically, acting on opportunities where they present themselves, and seeing value where others see only problems and decay (Blondeel 2004).

In the world of urban governance, these informal civil practices form a kind of parallel world hardly noticed by urban elites; a 'low

---

[3] This is a key theme in urban sociology, of course. See for example the classic studies of Young and Willmott (2007) and Gans (1982).

game' to the 'high game' of urban politics. But although informality goes unnoticed, its effects on the everyday reality of urban life are just as potent as that of the activities of the political and economic elites.[4] In fact, the presence of a stratum of informal practices that constitutes the fabric of urban life and that is orthogonal to the imperatives of the state raises important issues for the prospects of liberal democracy and the relationship between governance and democracy. The challenge of urban complexity and diversity in combination with the inability or unwillingness of the governing and business elite to incorporate the informal world of ordinary citizens in governance strategies is not only a manifestation of what Warren calls 'pluralized ungovernability' (2008a, 5). It is also an expression of the conflicting logics intrinsic in liberal democracy; the tensions between the imperatives of the state and the demands, needs and aspirations of civil society (Dryzek 1997, chap. 3).[5] Ignoring informality in the instruments and strategies of

---

[4] I realize that I suggest a hard-and-fast distinction between urban elites and the deprived/poor here, and that I situate informality within the life-sphere of the latter. This is a simplification. But it goes to show how complex and confusing the topics of urbanization and urban governance are and how much we rely on the kind of 'compelling narratives' that we discuss in our introduction to this volume in order to chart our way through them. In the literature on the Global South, informality is usually associated with the poor, who are excluded from the official institutions of economic activity and citizenship. But several scholars recognize that informality is not restricted to the poor and that the state is implicated in informality (Porter 2011; Roy 2003, 2010, 99–100). The relationship between state and informality has been a key theme in studies of administrative discretion, a key argument of which is that discretion is necessary to reconcile the conflicting demands on administrators and to achieve a modicum of justice and responsiveness in the implementation of policy programmes (Vinzant and Crothers 1998; Maynard-Moody and Musheno 2003). Also, the state relies on informal practices in organizing the 'invited participation' and 'governance-driven democratization' that I will discuss shortly. The upshot is that in the real world of urban governance, we see a confusing jumble of criss-crossing and overlapping layers of formal procedure and informal practice from a wide range of actors. In this chapter I will focus on the implication for the state and for liberal democracy of urban informality as a mode of urban governance. Or, to be more precise, I will discuss the informal practices of deprived groups in a Western European city, as they attempt to solve pressing collective problems in their neighbourhood by gaining access to and creating working relationships with state and 'third sector' agencies.

[5] The most sophisticated argument about the tensions between state, market, civil society and democracy comes from Dryzek (1997) and Dryzek (2000, chap. 4). Dryzek sees a perennial tension between the imperatives of the state that is beholden to the demands of the business sector to secure its longevity

urban governance is not just the result of an instrumental or technical inability but also of hegemony: the radical exclusion of other possibilities to solve the tensions between the two competing logics of state and civil society (Mouffe 2000, 99). Ignoring and denying informality and elevating the self-evident legitimacy of the practices and language of urban administration is thus an instance of the constitutive and hegemonic power of governing elites to naturalize the significance of state and market assumptions over the appeal of popular sovereignty.

In the life of the city, administrative hegemony is an all-too-real issue with consequences that have a discernable impact on the life of ordinary citizens. Verloo's earlier mentioned study provides an example. In 2007, the administration of the Dutch city of Utrecht designated the neighbourhood of Zuylen-Oost an 'emergency area'. The city felt impelled to this extreme administrative measure by the anti-social behaviour of the local Moroccan-Dutch youth that drew widespread attention of the national media. The city drew up a so-called 'neighborhood action plan'. Part of the plan was to measure progress on a number of safety 'indicators', such as 'public nuisance' and 'security'. These abstract indicators have concrete consequences, such as the placement of CCTV cameras, the prohibition of public assembly in certain areas, and the assignment of youth workers to the neighbourhood. However, as Deborah Stone argues, the proclamation of such policy categories as 'emergency area', public nuisance', or 'anti-social behavior' is not a morally neutral activity. Whoever sets out to measure 'nuisance' for example, implicitly elevates nuisance to the status of a socially significant category that requires our attention. The importance of this administrative activity is its constitutive character; it operates simultaneously on the performative and the linguistic level, thereby (morally) demarcating a particular group (Moroccan-Dutch youth) and naturalizing a particular administrative domain.[6]

and stability on the one hand and those of a vital and flourishing democracy that continually improves itself along the lines of franchise, scope and authenticity on the other (1997; 2000, 86). While under certain circumstances the democratic demands of the polity can be reconciled with state imperatives, this is not a given. In fact, as Dryzek argues, a historical examination of democratization processes shows that these almost always originate in insurgent civil society (2000, 87).

[6] Those who doubt the hegemonic character of urban administration should listen to the following statement by a city official who dealt with the safety problems in Zuylen-Oost: '[Participation] is a policy that becomes more and

Yet, at the same time, the problem of pluralized ungovernability reveals the inherent limitations of administrative hegemony. The inability of urban administrations to find compelling solutions for a host of urban problems in an environment of complexity, diversity and deep pluralism leads to demoralizing and destabilizing cascades of media-fuelled 'legitimation pressures' (Warren 2008a, 5). In such an environment urban elites have a lot to gain from trying to connect with the informal practices of ordinary citizens. Ordinary citizens form ever so many potential 'publics' (Dewey 1954), and engaging these publics would improve the problem-solving, transformational potential of liberal democracy.[7] Reversely, the quality of the informal life world of citizens has a lot to gain from a responsible and committed urban administration. I do not think that we should romanticize the informal practices of ordinary citizens. Informality is a given, and although it may be hegemonically uncoupled from the world of urban politics and administration, one goal of this chapter is to find ways to make it work for a better democratic governance of cities.

Public Administration, Citizen Participation and Democracy

I have touched on urban democracy in the preceding paragraphs, and surprisingly the role of citizens in the theory and practice of urban

more important. It's no time for coddling anymore. We are going to see how we can engage them and make them co-responsible.... The public environment must be a space for play, for meeting people, where people feel good.' Perhaps I am overly suspicious of the motives of this administrator, and one statement doesn't make hegemony, but is it only me who finds this language ('coddling', public environment 'must' be a space for play) almost unbearably paternalistic? (Perhaps urban spaces serve more everyday activities than just playing, as going to work or school, grocery shopping, walking your dog, or hanging out with your friends.) Notions of 'responsibility' preceded by the suffix 'co-' and the qualifier 'making them', betray the neoliberal background to these policy intentions, particularly when the reference to 'coddling' seems to imply an ascription of blame for the neighbourhood's problems to the residents themselves. And by speaking of the residents as 'they' and 'them', the official betrays the social distance she feels to the residents of Zuylen-Oost. Particularly when later in the interview she adds: 'Participation? They are not ready for that yet.' An ideological universe contained in a short statement. (Quotes from Verloo 2012).

[7] Macpherson aptly cites Dewey on this point: '[D]emocracy is a name for a life of free and enriching communion. It had its seer in Walt Whitman. It will have its consummation when free social enquiry is indissolubly wedded to the art of full and moving communication' (Dewey 1954, 184, cited in Macpherson 1977, 73).

democracy is equally ambiguous. On the one hand in many cities in the developed world we have witnessed in the last two decades a strong drive by urban administrators to involve citizens in formulating and implementing public programmes (Fung and Wright 2003; Fung 2004). Partly this public engagement is a response to the 'pluralized ungovernability' of the preceding paragraphs, and partly to the increased demands of a better educated electorate to be more directly involved in collective problem solving (Stoker 2006; Hay 2007; Warren 2008a). The experiences with this kind of 'invited participation' are in general not too positive. Although there are carefully designed, administratively driven examples of citizen participation (Fung 2004), on the whole they fall short of their democratic promise. The reasons are many. Many invited participation initiatives are badly designed, involving citizens too far into the policy cycle for any meaningful involvement to take place and thereby disappointing the expectations that were raised. Participation often runs into the rigidities of programme rules, budgetary procedures or administrative silos. Participation also reveals deficiencies in the organizational capacity of administrative agencies to deliver services that citizens and agencies have deliberatively agreed on (Kruiter et al. 2010). In many cases, despite a rhetoric of participation, elected officials, administrators and professionals are in practice unwilling to devolve control to citizens (Kruiter et al. 2010). And, as we saw in the preceding paragraphs, more often than not agendas and problems are those of officials, not of citizens (Verloo 2012). It is perhaps for this reason that Warren speaks of 'governance-driven democratization' in terms of promises and opportunities, and Tully of 'structures of governance ... [that] place arbitrary constraints on the diverse, identity-related forms of thought and action that matter to (citizens) and by which they engage in citizen activities' (2008b, 149). It may be that we are 'witnessing a transformation of democracy as dramatic and important as the rise of mass, electoral democracies in the nineteenth century', but so far the challenges and failures outweigh the successes.

I do not want to paint an overly gloomy picture of administration-invited participation. It is perhaps hard to pin down in exact terms, but in cities that have a modern tradition of invited participation (such as the Dutch cities of The Hague and Amsterdam, which we have studied), despite all the practical hurdles and obstacles, over the years something of a participatory ethos seems to have developed – a by-now self-evident willingness among administrators and some elected officials to involve citizens in many policy initiatives. Moreover – and this I see as a theoretical breakthrough – 'governance-driven democratization' has firmly placed public administration in the centre of democratic theory. In hindsight it is hard to understand why democratic theory was, almost by default, restricted to electoral process, the extent of the franchise, protection against oppressive governments, the nature of democratic representation, and, recently, the quality of the deliberative processes (Pitkin 1967; Macpherson 1977; Held 1996; Dryzek 2000). The vast administrative apparatus that is part of every well-functioning democracy was considered as belonging to a tier of experts wedged in between the people and elected representatives that enabled the latter to realize their promises. And, although since Mill's days, an administrative bureaucracy that executes the decisions of elected officials has been an intrinsic element of liberal democracy (McPherson 1977; Held 1996, 110; Manin 1997), this layer of administrators and technocrats is generally treated as belonging to the state and is the subject of a discipline, Public Administration, in which democracy is a given more than an topic of analytical concern.

However, for most ordinary citizens it is difficult to distinguish democracy from the state. Their immediate experiences with a responsive, indifferent, effective, absent, wilful or oppressive government are mostly through their contacts with administrators, professionals, police officers and civil servants. Elective democracy is mostly experienced indirectly via the media, and, as we have seen, is more often than not regarded with considerable distrust (Mathews 1999; Macedo 2005; Stoker 2006; Hay 2007). In Anglo-Saxon countries citizens have more direct communication with elected officials in city councils or constituency offices of members of congress, but here too the picture that I painted above largely holds. In other words, for most citizens the quality of their democracy depends as much, if not more, on the behaviour of administrators and public agencies than of elected officials. As Ansell puts it: 'Public agencies are on the tail end of the chain of representation but on the front end of problem solving' (Ansell 2011, 4). Public administration is now so much an intrinsic part of the democratic process that it is fair to speak of 'electoral-administrative democracy' when we talk about the nature of contemporary liberal democracy.

However, this leaves us with the unsolved issue of how democratic governance deals with the aforementioned uncoupling of administration and informality in everyday urban life. I will argue in this chapter that one possible way to enhance the public engagement of urban administrations is for these to open up to the many examples of 'uninvited participation' in cities in the developed world. These are spontaneous initiatives of residents to manage collective problems in their neighbourhoods. Many of these take place in disadvantaged neighbourhoods, which are overwhelmed by problems of poverty, safety and (youth) crime, unemployment, high educational dropout rates, substandard housing, the negative effects of migration, and urban decay (Wagenaar and Specht 2010; Specht 2012). The argument is that locality-based communities are particularly important for the urban poor. Because the poor do not have the possibility to partake in the occupational mobility and international outlook of the better off, and are dependent on the benefits and services of local government, they are 'trapped' in their neighbourhoods and communities (Lowndes 1995, 164; Reijndorp 2004). If government fails, the poor have little choice but to unite and take the initiative to fill the void left by an unwilling or ineffective administration.

But nowadays we also see such uninvited participation in higher income neighbourhoods. These usually concern more 'middle class' issues such as sustainable energy and food, care for the elderly, transportation and even international development. And while in disadvantaged neighbourhoods residents develop informal problem-solving tactics, in higher income neighbourhoods citizens organize to produce something that is also produced, but insufficiently, inadequately or more expensively, by utilities, hospitals, transport companies or the commercial food industry (Amin et al. 2002; van der Heijden 2011). What characterizes uninvited participation is that it addresses complex urban problems, designs pragmatic and creative solutions to problems that elude the capacities of urban administrations, avoids the negative externalities of resource-intensive commercial production, manages to mobilize considerable groups of residents over long periods of time, reaches out to form effective and enduring partnerships with a wide range of institutional actors, and creates civic virtue (Warren 2001; Wagenaar 2005, 2007; Specht 2012; van der Heijden 2011). What the activism in disadvantaged neighbourhoods and the civic entrepreneurship of the higher income neighbourhoods have in common is that they both capitalize on the informal practices of everyday urban life to formulate problems, design solutions and engage in collaboration. In this sense these initiatives are textbook examples of Dewey's seminal reformulation of democracy as collective problem solving through the making of 'publics' (Dewey 1954), or the 'citizen politics' that David Mathews, director of the Kettering Foundation, eloquently argues for (Mathews 1999). But similar to the informal practices of urban life, these uninvited participatory initiatives, although they attract sympathetic attention and sporadic support from national and local government, are rarely integrated in the larger house of urban democratic governance.[8] Their potential for administrative reform and democratic transformation (Ansell 2011) remains largely untapped.

My argument in this chapter is that for 'governance-driven democratization' to succeed as a new model of urban governance, electoral politics and urban administrations must open up to the informal practices of everyday city life as well as the examples of uninvited citizen participation (Mathews 1999; van der Heijden 2011; Beunderman et al. 2012). This is in itself not a very illuminating statement, as few people would in principle disagree. It would be more productive to the development of our understanding of urban democratic governance to explore the obstacles to such a fruitful merging of public administration and informal citizen activities and to carefully delineate its potential and limits. It is to this task that I turn in the remainder of this chapter. To provide some empirical grounding for my analysis I will first introduce an extended case.

The Case of Nordmarkt, Dortmund

The origins of this case was the initiative of a the director of the local elementary school, Ms Schultebraucks-Burghardt, and a pastor of the Evangelical Church, Friedrich Laker, both of whom lived and worked near the Hannibal housing project in the Nordmarkt area of the German city of Dortmund. Over the years the housing project had deteriorated badly and a group of youngsters in the project who engaged in antisocial and criminal behaviour created fear and resentment among the residents. The pastor and the director of the local elementary school decided to address the problem by arranging a meeting of local organizations that were involved in youth services. The pastor

---

[8] The UK government has for example created a Community Shares Unit, where citizens can apply to finance local initiatives (communityshares.org.uk).

and the school director quickly learned two lessons. First, while professionals found it easy to discuss the problems of the Hannibal project with one another, residents were under-represented. Second, the appeals of the group to the city administration to deal with the youth and prostitution problem in the neighbourhood went unheeded. As the pastor said: 'It became clear to me that for the city it was preferable to have one neighbourhood in the city in which all problems were concentrated instead of having problems distributed all over the city. That at least was my impression.'

It was clear to the pastor that the group needed a powerful partner if it wanted to persuade the city administration to pay attention to the problems in the Hannibal area. He approached the housing corporation that managed Hannibal. The corporation was willing to get involved and together the new partners created a foundation, called Solidarische Nachbarschaften. The housing corporation provided an office in the building and hired a social worker, who organized youth work programmes. However, the social worker also began to organize the residents. The partners of the Solidarische Nachbarschaften realized that the residents had to be stimulated to take initiative in improving their neighbourhood. The residents became involved, but their concern was not so much the youth of Nordmarkt but the prostitution problem in their neighbourhood. In fact, as the pastor relates, residents, for reasons that will become clear later in this section, were 'quite aggressive' towards the prostitutes in their neighbourhood and were willing to violently eject them from their streets. In the evening hours clients cruised the narrow streets of the neighbourhood in their cars, in search of sex workers, violating traffic ordinances and creating a serious noise and pollution problem for the residents. However, as the pastor indicates, it was morally reprehensible and not practically useful to vent one's – understandable – anger on the women. He reasoned with the residents that 'these women lived in difficult circumstances and … were vulnerable human beings who required our compassion and help'. He therefore contacted a religious aid organization, the Mitternachtsmission, which was involved with the sex workers in Nordmarkt. In collaboration with the Mitternachtsmission, residents began to search for more positive solutions.

The residents had some prior experience in dealing with the prostitution problem. The neighbourhood contained a small walk-in centre, run by a number of young volunteers, where residents could discuss whatever bothered them in the neighbourhood. Learning about the prostitution problem in the neighbourhood, the young volunteers decided to organize a meeting with residents. At the first meeting about twenty people showed up, and it was decided that residents would start to register the license plates of clients. License plate numbers of cars that circled around the block three times or more were written down.[9] In the first week, 333 license plates were registered and sent to the police as incident reports. However, the residents ran into the same stonewalling by city administrators as the partners of the Solidarische Nachbarschaften. Despite repeated inquiries by residents, the police consistently failed to act on the reports, until, after three months, the legal period for acting on them had expired.

Residents were now exceedingly angry about the city's uncooperative attitude, and as a result the group that met at the walk-in centre grew considerably. Confronted with the city's unwillingness to act on the prostitution problem, the residents concluded that a new strategy was needed – not just protest, but also designing creative solutions. It was then, after earlier attempts to address the problem had failed, that the plea of the pastor for a more humane approach towards the prostitutes received a receptive ear. A young resident, Saïd Bouyakoub, pointed out that the city of Utrecht, in the Netherlands, had created a designated streetwalking area – a so-called toleration zone – away from any residential area, where sex workers and clients could meet and the police keep an eye on what was going on, and where the women received free social services. Saïd had learned about this on a visit to relatives who lived in Utrecht. Saïd's reaction is interesting. He told us that he had attended the meetings, but had not felt particularly engaged. He felt irritated by the attending residents who were mostly middle-aged and white and were almost exclusively focussed on protest without suggesting any possible solutions.

The toleration zone became the rallying point for the residents. A number of volunteers and residents searched the Internet for information on the Utrecht toleration zone, and managed to get in touch with a Dutch community worker who was involved with the zone. The residents invited the Dutch expert to give a talk in Dortmund. She told

---

[9] This was because the neighbourhood was a car-free zone, indicated by signs that read 'only residential traffic allowed'. Cars that drove through the neighbourhood three times or more were assumed not to belong to residents.

the residents that the Utrecht toleration zone had been studied by officers from a German police academy. However, the city administration
declared that a toleration zone was legally not possible in Germany.

With information sent by the Dutch, the Dortmund residents studied the applicability of the toleration zone solution to Dortmund. In
addition they discovered that a graduate from the police academy had
written a thesis about the legal possibility of a prostitution toleration zone in Germany, concluding that the law allowed for such an
innovation. When the residents discovered that the city administration
was unaware of this, they drew up a proposal for a toleration zone
and presented it to the city, but the city still insisted that 'the problem
couldn't be solved'. Next, the residents began a highly visible petition
campaign, while they simultaneously kept open the dialogue with city
officials. Suddenly the city reversed its position and announced that
the city's public health agency would organize a one-day study conference on prostitution to which the residents of Nordmarkt were also
invited. At the conference, the city presented a plan for a toleration
zone, backed up with expert speakers from the Netherlands. Although
the residents were mildly surprised that the city presented the zone as
its own idea, they took a pragmatic stance and expressed their desire
to work with city to implement the zone.

Even after the city administration designated a particular area to
be the toleration zone, it was remarkably reticent in making the zone
operational. As the designated area was nothing but a barren piece of
land, the women began to drift back into the streets of Nordmarkt
where they could find shops, bars and services. Residents, a local housing corporation, the Mitternachtsmission and the local police then
worked with sex workers to design shelters where the women could
work and they put forward a plan for their construction. However, the
city decided to build the shelters itself, but exhausted its budget and
skimped on sanitary facilities, so that the zone was not operational.
The collaborating partners then stepped in to provide for the sanitary facilities as well as a help post and a common space for the sex
workers. For the next ten years the collaboration of citizens, voluntary
organizations and police successfully managed the prostitution problem in Dortmund (Mais, 2011; Specht 2012).

This is one of a number of bottom-up participatory citizen initiatives
in disadvantaged neighbourhoods in a number of Western European
countries that Maurice Specht and I studied between 2005 and 2010

(Wagenaar 2007; Wagenaar and Specht 2010; Specht 2012). What do we learn from the Dortmund example? First, we see how citizens' problem definitions are shaped by everyday experiences and how they therefore hang together and modulate in unexpected ways. Although two moderators, both professionally engaged with young people, succeeded in getting residents to come together to discuss the problem of antisocial youth, at the meeting it became clear that street prostitution was considered the bigger problem. Similarly, informal practices (such as visiting a relative in another country) lay at the heart of problem solution. Second, social action emerged from acute anger with and resistance to the police and the city, which, so it was felt, had, for reasons of convenience, abandoned the neighbourhood.[10] However, resistance, and this is my third point, does not express itself as protest, obstruction or upheaval. Instead it follows the more pragmatic road of designing a workable solution to a wicked problem that had eluded the problem-solving capacities of the city, and the mobilization of experts to support and develop their proposals. Fourth, the citizens have shown themselves to be able to work on equal terms in enduring partnerships with a number of societal and institutional actors.

Fifth, and perhaps most important, to merely characterize the Dortmund case as an instance of citizen participation does injustice to the large cast of agents that played a role in it: residents (who were themselves divided into different groups), police officers, sex workers, social workers, student activists, a church official, city hall officials, administrators, and others. Each of these agents acted their part in the unfolding events, obviously to a greater or lesser extent influenced by the actions of others, but not 'determined' by or at the behest of those others. Although the actions of the residents played a central role in the solution of the prostitution problem, the Dortmund case – similar to the others that we studied – evolved into a hybrid of public administration, professional action, volunteer work and citizen participation – a new form of collaborative governance (Innes and Booher, 2010; Ansell 2011). We will see that this new form of governance is as much characterized by innovative organizational forms and roles as it is by new ways of interacting and communicating among the participants.

---

[10] That this is not an isolated case is shown by the remarkably similar experience of citizen activists in the Schilderswijk neighbourhood in The Hague (Wagenaar 2007).

In the remainder of this chapter I want to focus on two elements of this case that help us to answer the question in the preceding section of how to recognize and overcome the obstacles to a productive merging of public administration and informal citizen activities. I will focus on the creative role of distrust and the importance of practice in democratic governance. I will conclude with some thoughts about the importance of administrative organization and joint problem solving in democratic governance.

The Agonistic Experience: The Importance of Democratic Distrust

One of the most depressingly familiar features of the case is the city administration's initially reluctant attitude towards the residents of Nordmarkt. Whoever has worked with citizen activists knows that this is a common interactive dynamic: distant, stonewalling city officials who, when confronted, attempt to evade angry, distrustful citizens. In case after case, citizens talk of officials who break promises, who appear at hearings unprepared, who behave in a disinterested or arrogant way (not showing up at meetings or ostentatiously checking their smartphones at hearings, for example) (Wagenaar 2005, 2007, 2009). City officials, on their part, talk of citizens who express unrealistic desires, who engage in Nimbyism, who do not understand the constraints of governing (Verhoeven 2009). These officials then question the democratic legitimacy of these citizens' demands and appeal to the 'primacy of politics'. Yet, sometimes, out of this mutual anger and distrust, creative initiatives emerge. Two homemakers from The Hague who are enraged about the deteriorating crime situation in their neighbourhood organize a successful crime prevention project that becomes a model for the city as a whole (Wagenaar 2007). Citizens in Antwerp, who had been deceived by the city administration about the construction of an office park in their neighbourhood, seek contact with the multinational development corporation that is constructing the complex and persuade it to join with them in redesigning the project to better fit the neighbourhood's needs (Specht 2012). And the angry citizens of Dortmund formulate a workable proposal to regulate the street prostitution in their neighbourhood. I think it is no accident that this unexpected dynamic is brought about by uninvited participation – citizens who persuasively put a claim to the governing elite of a city: a claim to be heard, to be acknowledged, to have their concerns and ideas taken seriously.

On the surface level the mutual distrust is easy to understand. Citizen demands tend to disrupt the standard operating procedures of governing bodies and public agencies. Most agencies draw up their budgets and policy plans months, if not years, in advance and are beholden to statutorily prescribed, rigid work cycles. Citizen demands disrupt these bureaucratic routines. Most policy plans are the result of precarious compromises between conflicting factions within the city administration and/or the urban elite. Officials have invested their prestige in the prevailing compromise. Clearly they are reluctant to risk dearly achieved political equilibrium to respond to the demands of a group of ordinary citizens. Finally, as we have seen, citizens verbalize their concerns and ideas in a language that does not resonate with the bureaucratic or political jargon of officials. Problem formulations reflect not only the technical expertise of administrative agencies, but also elite divisions, compromises and aspirations. The direct language of citizens, on the other hand, reflects their everyday experiences, which often contradict elite aspirations. In conceptual terms we can say that uninvited citizen participation must count as a textbook illustration of the ineradicable conflictual nature of the political (Mouffe 2000, 101; Wagenaar 2011, chap. 10). When citizens voice a demand or raise an issue, they pose a direct challenge to the hegemonic equilibrium of the governing elite's problem frames and action routines. By putting their demands and ideas forward, citizens painfully expose the paradox at the heart of liberal democracy: the contradiction between market assumptions and rule of law on the one hand, versus equality and popular control over collective problem solving on the other.

Or do they? In the examples above citizens, social partners and city administrations manage to formulate creative solutions out of initial conflict. In fact, it has the appearance that workable proposals and long-standing, productive partnerships did not emerge despite but *because* of the initial conflict and distrust. Given the widespread nature of distrust and antagonism between citizens and governing elites, it is perhaps time that we begin to think differently about the role of antagonism, conflict and distrust in democratic governance.

How, practically speaking, can conflict be made productive? What can we learn from these examples, where citizens and administrators try to bridge the democratic gap that divides them? What are the prospects for an agonistic pluralism that is more than an abstract idea but instead a workable, feasible living reality? The first step, we learn from citizens, administrators, and the scholars who study conflict, is to acknowledge that there is a conflict.[11] Innes and Booher argue, for example, that the importance of agonism cannot be emphasized enough. They see awareness of conflict as 'an essential source of the creativity that allows forward movement in the face of conflict' (Innes and Booher 2010, 104). Conflict helps parties to become aware of their interdependencies. One or both of the parties realizes that the cost of denying the conflict or continuing the impasse is higher than recognizing that there is one and begins to listen to the other party. This allows the parties 'to get past the taken for granted understandings that conceal power relations and support the status quo'. (Innes and Booher 2010, 104) As Innes and Booher state:

The most creative movements typically emerge in a dialogue after an impasse is reached. It is as if the participants, in their frustration, reach deep into themselves and get past norms, platitudes, and unexamined assumptions to find an idea they did not know was there or never considered before. The group then builds on it to construct a new approach. (Innes and Booher 2010: 104)

This happened when the citizens of Antwerp sought out contact with the development corporation and discovered that the corporation had wanted to talk earlier but, thinking in a routine corporate hierarchical mode, did not know who was in charge among the citizens. In the Dortmund case this moment came when the city announced a small conference on toleration zones, to which the residents were also invited, and the surprised citizens decide to be pragmatic about the city's face-saving tactic of presenting the plan as its own and to work with the administration in implementing the plan. At that moment the conflict turned into a 'fruitful conflict': '[A] conflict that in some manner enhances or advances knowledge, understanding, meaning, or capacity between different or opposing perspectives and interests' (Ansell

---

[11] As Mouffe puts it: 'One of the keys to the thesis of agnostic pluralism is that, far from jeopardizing democracy, agonistic confrontation is in fact its very condition of existence' (2000, 103). Mouffe does not specify how such agonistic confrontation should be handled and developed to result in mutually satisfying outcomes.

2011, 168) Engaging in fruitful conflict opens up the capacity to see the complexity of an issue and design ways to successfully harness it (Wagenaar 2007; Axelrod and Cohen, 1999). In this sense, fruitful conflict has the potential to be transformational (Ansell 2011, 169).

While the ability of the actors to transform conflict is essential for navigating the intrinsic complexity and adversity of urban governance, it does not tell us how this makes decentred governance democratic. The description of the situation so far follows the orthodox bifurcation of the democratic sphere into those who rule and those who are ruled, with democracy somehow being 'produced' or 'being the natural provenance of' the first. Yet, this chapter is written in the spirit of the radical pluralism of Tully, Connolly and the authors of the Introduction. It aims at a 'redescription' of the system of liberal-democratic governance, so that the assumptions that guide the self-understandings of those who are part of it (both those who act as its as functionaries as well as those who adapt to and resist its working and outcomes), as well as those who study and theorize it, are revealed and can be made subject to critical reflection and action. The term 'redescription' is Tully's, and it will clarify my purpose to quote him more fully here: 'Rather, it [what Tully calls his public philosophy] seeks to characterize the conditions of possibility of the problematic form of governance in a redescription (often in a new vocabulary) that transforms the self-understandings of those subject to and struggling within it, enabling them to see its contingent conditions and the possibilities of governing themselves differently.' (2008a, 16) Taking Tully's cue, my argument is that we tend to see citizen participation too narrowly. Unconsciously guided by the language with which we talk about liberal democracy, we think of citizen participation as a lesser form of democracy outside the 'real' work of authoritative electoral-administrative governance. In a similar way we think of the informal tactics, understandings and meanings with which citizens and other societal actors literally create the city, as outside of and of lesser importance than the official acts of administrators and elected officials in forging a living democracy. Instead I want to argue for a broader conception of agonistic democratic governance, which aims at collectively addressing public problems and which includes constantly shifting alliances of actors, each with his or her own capacities, skills and responsibilities – and, no less important, his or her own interests, experiences, identity and perspective. Using the experiences of the residents of Dortmund, I will attempt such a redescription in the remainder of this chapter.

Practices of Freedom: The Transformative Potential of Informal Practices

In its conventional, textbook form electoral-administrative democracy is something that concerns a few, relatively small categories of actors, who follow more-or-less clearly scripted roles that are laid down by constitutional, legal and administrative procedure, the so-called Rule of Law, or Rechtsstaat. Even in the current orthodoxy of a networked polity where a broad range of mutually dependent actors engage in negotiation and bargaining to arrive at horizontal decision making, the administrative state and the procedures of electoral democracy are still the measure for our shared understanding and appreciation of democratic governance. From this perspective, it would be easy to dismiss the Dortmund case – and other instances of uninvited participation – as a mere sideshow to the 'real' work of (urban) governance, at best an interesting experiment in participatory governance but with a limited reach that applies only to small-scale local initiatives. In this view the informal practices of ordinary citizens are just an epiphenomenon of the high game of urban governance, background 'noise' to the 'signal' of official public administration.

What prevents us from easily grasping a more robust understanding of the place of informal practices in urban governance and, in line with this, a broader, more inclusive view of governance and democracy, is our adherence to a particular hegemonic way of seeing that is ingrained in the very language we use to describe the place of citizens in political and democratic theory. Tully articulates these assumptions as the three 'pillars' of conventional political theory: (1) the possibilities for citizen participation as determined by large historical forces to which citizens are haplessly subjected, (2) overarching and universal normative principles of democracy to which citizens ought to be subjected, and (3) a set of 'canonical' institutionalized background conditions that guarantee the functioning of any democratic state (2008a, 9). These assumptions, as Tully makes clear, are so self-evident, so embedded in our ordinary language and practices, that they form a conceptual horizon beyond which it is difficult to imagine an alternative legitimate conception of democratic governance. Yet, these 'naturalized' languages and practices embody and sustain structural imbalances of power and influence that curtail the current living conditions and future prospects of large groups in society.[12]

Yet a critical reading of the case will reveal that this example of citizens who spontaneously stood up to take charge of a collectively experienced problem in their neighbourhood has two important effects on our understanding of governance in the liberal-democratic state. First, it radically decentres our conception of governance. Following Dewey's lead, these citizens' activities make it difficult to conceive of governance and its manifold institutional incarnations as a domain of government separate from and in an unproblematic authoritative relation to society. Instead it invites us to widen our scope to a broader field of governance made up of countless relationships between societal agents, including political actors and administrative agencies, who, in ever-changing configurations, work on solving a variety of collective problems. To this they bring their respective understandings, meanings, interests, histories, routines, emotions and identities. A decentred approach to governance emphasizes agency as it thinks of institutions, societal problems, policymaking and democracy as created and sustained by actors who, operating within large cognitive-ideational frames (Rein 1983; Schön and Rein 1994) or traditions (Bevir and Rhodes 2003, 2010), struggle with dilemmas and dislocations.

The second effect of a critical reading of the Dortmund case is that it demonstrates the complex relationship, or perhaps it is better to speak of a field of relationships, between informal practice, agonistic freedom, governance and democracy. To understand how these elements bring each other into being, hold each other in place as it were, and add up to an ever-evolving, dynamic domain of decentred democratic governance, let's look more closely at some of its constituent elements. The driving force in this field of relationships, that which holds the whole field of forces together and moves it onward, is the notion

---

[12] As Tully puts it in somewhat uncharacteristically strong language: '[T]he economic, political and military elites and their ideologists have inherited not only much of the earth and its resources but also many of its languages, including the manipulable language of citizenship, democracy, civic goods and freedom. Yet, it is precisely this ordinary language that the oppressed and exploited of the world have always used to express their outrage at the injustices of the present and their hopes and dreams of another world.' (2008a, 10).

of *practice*. For example, if we return to the residents of Nordmarkt, the diversity of activities that they engaged in went beyond the mere expression of discontent or needs. Their 'democratic participation' involved protesting against the perceived failure of the police, registering license plates, appealing to the police, settling internal conflicts, learning about alternative solutions to street prostitution, inviting foreign experts, scanning legal information, putting a proposal together, lobbying and negotiating with the city administration, and constructing an operational toleration zone. All these activities originated in the informal, everyday practices and life forms that made up community life in the Nordmarkt neighbourhood: walking through the neighbourhood, chatting with neighbours, doing your shopping, attending church, raising children, going to work or school, having a beer in the pub, having awareness of the status of their neighbourhood in the larger urban environment, and so on. When residents felt that these quotidian practices were disrupted and threatened by the expansion of the sex trade in their neighbourhood, they began to interact – with each other, with the community organization, with the police and finally with the city administration (Snow et al. 1998).

These activities of resistance that derive their meaning from and are fused with the informality that makes up the fabric of urban life in Nordmarkt are what James Tully has called 'practices of freedom' (2008a). Practices of freedom:

[C]omprise the vast repertoire of ways of citizens acting together on the field of governance relationships and against the oppressive and unjust dimensions of them. These range from 'acting otherwise' within the space of governance relationships to contesting negotiating, confronting and seeking to transform them. The general aim of these diverse civic activities is to bring oppressive and unjust governance relationships under the on-going shared authority of the citizenry subject to them; namely to civicise and democratize them from below. (2008a, 3–4)

Practices of freedom are the engine of committed critique and permanent renewal, the ongoing developmental potential of democracy for betterment and creative problem solving (Dewey 1954; Macpherson 1977). In Tully's view the involvement of citizens should not be seen as some kind of parallel or alternative activity to the 'real' work of government, hemmed in by the normative and institutional constraints of liberal representative democracy. Tully's instead is a radically decentred theory of democratic governance, in which the actions of citizens who assert their freedom to act on situations they see as wrong, unjust or more generally as in need of improvement, form the condition of possibility of a functional and legitimate democratic regime. The concept of 'citizen', as Tully defines it, 'refer(s) to a person who is subject to a relationship of governance (that is to say, governed), and simultaneously and primarily, is an active agent in the field of governance relationship' (2008a, 3). The argument I will develop in this section is that a focus on informal, everyday practices is central to the emergence of an innovative, collaborative and transformative form of democratic governance.

A practice perspective depicts our environment as a world of becoming – open-ended and indeterminate. In their dealings with an open-ended world, agents have a fundamental forward-looking perspective in that they, as adaptive, problem-solving creatures, are continuously engaged in grasping the incompleteness of our current situation and trying to overcome it.[13] Practice, in this sense, is a move or thrust into an only partly known and knowable world. Inevitably, the world, when acted on, will throw up resistances; it 'talks back', as Schön and Rein famously said (1994). By acting, by intervening, agents – both officials and citizens – extend their intentions and understandings into this indeterminate world, without being able to predict exactly how its agency will realize itself and impact them. Knowledge of the world is obviously important, but it is only a partial, incomplete guide to our thrusts into the future. Andrew Pickering, a sociologist of science,

---

[13] The forward-looking perspective in people's dealings with the world is another of the central themes of the pragmatism of John Dewey. As Campbell, one of Dewey's most incisive interpreters, puts it: '[F]or Dewey, we find ourselves, as incomplete creatures living in changing social and natural situations, antecedently committed to lifelong attempts at overcoming difficulties.... The possibility of intelligent action thus compels inquiry; and in defending this stance Dewey embraces the "forward-looking" charge we saw above. As he writes in one of several such formulations: "[W]e live not in a settled and finished world, but in one which is going on, and where our main task is prospective, and where retrospect – and all knowledge as distinct from thought is retrospect – is of value in the solidity, security, and fertility it affords our dealings with the future." ...The function of thinking is to contribute to a life that is forward-moving, carrying with it all that matters from the experiences of the past and the present.' (Campbell 1995, 61. Dewey quote from Dewey 1980, 158).

speaks of practice as an act of extension that aims to capture the agency of the world, in his case mostly, but not exclusively, material agency:

There is no thread in the present that we can hang on to which determines the outcome of cultural extension. We just have to find out, in practice ... how the next capture of material agency is to be made and what it will look like. Captures and their properties in this sense *just happen*. This is my basic sense of emergence, a sense of brute chance, happening in time – and it is offensive to some deeply ingrained patterns of thought. (1995, 24; italics in original)[14]

There are unmistakable echoes here of Wittgenstein's rejection of a rule-oriented explanation of human behaviour. Every actor attempts to control his environment by extending his intentions and understandings into the world, only to run up against unforeseen resistances and subsequently try to adjust or adapt to these. In this way the outcomes of our actions evolve in emergent time (Wagenaar 2011, chap. 10; Cook and Wagenaar 2012). But it is precisely in the inevitable slippage between intention, action and outcome that the fundamental freedom of each actor resides, the freedom to accommodate the encountered resistance in novel and unpredictable ways. In an elemental sense, activities, even when they seem routine and institutionalized, 'are not everywhere bounded by rules' (Tully 2008a, 139). And, even where, let's say, an interaction between a citizen and a government agency is structured by legal rule and administrative procedure, the decision of which rule is applicable and how to interpret it is almost wholly dependent on taken-for-granted background knowledge and deep experience with the situation at hand (Taylor 1995; Wagenaar 2004).

No matter how strong the urge to control, the agency of the world, including the world of others, will always elude a definitive grasp of objects and subjects alike and result in a dense pattern of resistance and accommodation (Pickering 1995).[15] Initially those who intervene

---

[14] For a description of practice as cultural extension that includes more forms of agency than just material agency, see Wagenaar (2012). I draw on Pickering (1995).

[15] Practice is not all uncertainty and unpredictability. One key aspect of practice is that it is simultaneously stable, in that it embodies agents' grasp of the background knowledge that constitutes a particular situation, making it possible for them to recognize the situation as the situation it is and act on it, and it is also open-ended, so as to make it possible to creatively adapt to unforeseen developments as they unfold in emergent time. To capture practice as situated, stable, and open-ended, Cook and Wagenaar introduce three

usually meet resistance with a reaction of annoyance and irritation. Although resistance signifies insufficient understanding of the actor – inevitably, unavoidably – it is often interpreted as unwarranted obstinacy of the other and approached more often than not with the intention to force or ignore the issue. But resistance also presents an opportunity, an invitation for learning and increased understanding and for changing or transforming the situation at hand (Tully 2008a, 139; Innes and Booher 2010). In this sense resistance is not only an act of freedom of the target audience of the intervention, a performative expression of disagreement and potential, but resistance also offers an opportunity to the intervener to expand or modify a necessarily limited understanding of the situation. Practice theory thus presents a world that is both deeply equivocal *and* presents a host of opportunities for challenge and creative potential, both to agents of the state and to citizens.

One of the enduring results of our research into uninvited citizen participation was the primacy of practice in all successful citizen initiatives that we studied (Wagenaar and Specht 2010; Specht 2012). In the conventional literature on political participation, participation and non-participation are depicted as the result of a number of characteristics that citizens do or do not posses. Traditionally these are described in the well-known civic voluntarism model and consist of motivation, resources and connectedness (Verba et al. 1995). One of the key arguments against citizen participation is framed in terms of the absence of these characteristics (no motivation or social capital, no resources such as intelligence, education or democratic skills).[16] What we discovered in our research instead is that democratic participation and the resources and skills to engage in it are in themselves simultaneously the engine and the outcome of participation. Typically, citizens were triggered into action by some perceived threat to their everyday world (Snow et al. 1998; Wagenaar and Specht 2010) and then, in a truly open-ended process, developed a range of participatory skills and

concepts that, taken together, characterize practice: 'actionable understanding', 'ongoing business', and 'the eternally unfolding present'. (Cook and Wagenaar 2012)

[16] This is the famous democratic realism argument against participatory democracy, as it surfaced in the United States, after WWI, in the 1920s, and found its full expression in the famous Lippman-Dewey debate (Westbrook, 1991, chap. 9).

resources by acting on the problem at hand. For example, we found that the first years of a participatory initiative were spent in exploring the nature of the problem that triggered the initiative, with participants getting to know one another, finding out about the resources the neighbourhood had to offer, acquiring administrative skills, managing different timelines, getting informed and informing others, establishing partnerships with relevant actors and stakeholders, and acquiring communication and conflict resolution skills (Wagenaar and Specht 2010; Specht 2012). In the process, the participants acquired a variety of democratic skills and obtained self-confidence and a sense of self-worth. This dense fabric of activities was always problem centred, pragmatic, and dialectic, moving back and forth between parts and the whole, analysis and synthesis. But more importantly, this is not just a list of activities of residents of a city neighbourhood, but a remarkably complex stream of interventions in the decentred governance situation of Dortmund, a series of claims and appeals to the city administration to see and do things differently.

Let's unpack some of the activities that the actors in Dortmund – residents, police officers, administrators, voluntary organizations, community activists – engaged in. First, to escape the vicious cycle of indignation, enmity and antagonism the residents had to start to question the beliefs about the situation at hand that fuelled their initial anger and indignation. For example, the pastor convinced the residents that the sex workers were not hostile elements in the neighbourhood, but shared a fate with them: 'they are also humans'. Yet, at the same time, the residents' anger was important in challenging the conventional administrative routines and practices that defined city administration in Dortmund. By creatively looking for a solution to the public nuisance of outdoor sex work, the residents put forward the claim that the city administration was perhaps more dependent on the residents than it was willing to admit. Subsequently, by organizing a workshop on the possibility of toleration zones, the city recognized this claim of the residents, albeit in an elliptical way. Building on Dewey, Ansell asserts that collective learning occurs when actors, who are also adversaries, begin to 'explore the character and meaning of their interdependence' (2011, 176).[17] For this 'enacted interdependence' to happen,

---

[17] The argument that interdependence must be enacted is where a decentred, radically pluralist conception of democratic governance differs from standard policy network theory. In the latter, mutual interdependence is assumed (Kickert et al. 1997; Sørensen and Torfing 2008), while in the former it is

Ansell argues that two conditions should be met: stakeholders must be willing to acknowledge one another as legitimate stakeholders, and all actors must commit themselves to working together in a collaborative way (2011, 177). We now see some of the obstacles that collaborative governance encounters. In the Dortmund case, the city administration, after the initial recognition that the residents had a valuable contribution to make in resolving the prostitution problem, quickly lost interest and backed out of the implementation of the toleration zone. Nevertheless police officials and the Mitternachtsmission persevered in their commitment to work with the residents, thereby creating a remarkably successful form of collaborative governance of Dortmund's prostitution problem, which continued for more than a decade (Mais, 2011). Reversely, we now also understand why so much invited participation falters. First, the governing elite is, despite a rhetoric of collaboration and citizen involvement, often hardly willing to *performatively* acknowledge the legitimacy of citizens; that is, by actively sharing or devolving sovereignty to citizens and giving them real responsibility, or by engaging in the kind of enacted interdependence we discussed above. Second, we often encountered an exceedingly short attention span of city administrations when it came to collaborative commitment.

The Dortmund case also shows the emergent character of participatory governance. Every step in the process emerges as the result of earlier steps. In practice, emergence consists of short cycles of interactive problem exploration, design of solutions, testing of the solution, processing feedback, and exploration and possible reframing of the new situation. Wagenaar and Specht describe for example, how residents of the Belgian city of Antwerp moved through a series of problem definition/policy solution cycles this way, in trying to tackle the garbage problem in their neighbourhood (Wagenaar and Specht 2010). Angered by the relentless negative reporting on their neighbourhood, residents of Pendrecht, in the Dutch city of Rotterdam, decided on a boycott of the press. Citizens refused to give interviews to reporters or collaborate with TV crews. But instead of getting stuck in their anger they then invited journalists to a seminar in their resident university about the role of the media in urban settings.[18] And the residents of

---

an achievement, a recognition, the tenuous outcome of a series of ongoing interactive practices.

[18] The residents' university is called Pendrecht University. Its credo is: 'Where the residents are the professors and the experts the students'. Specht describes how

Dortmund, through overcoming the obstacles to collaboration with the city administration and other actors, transformed their initial hostile attitude towards the sex workers and the police into a fruitful collaboration with both groups. Outcomes can never be 'read off' from initial conditions. As Ansell puts it: '[T]ransformation is produced through a process of shifting back and forth between attention to paradigmatic reframing and attention to concrete details' (2011, 173). Emergence is thus not the passive flow of time, but a detailed and careful process of reflexive, creative and recursive joint problem solving (Ansell 2011).

There is both an instrumental, problem-driven and an identity element to this process of recursive, shared learning. Clearly one of the driving forces is the residents' budding awareness that they can affect and change for the better, a situation in which they initially felt powerless. This, again, is a slow and painstaking process of setbacks and small affirmations that gradually convince the residents that, against the odds, they can have a positive impact on their environment and on their lives. But by acting on the situation, the very activity of organizing themselves, exploring and designing solutions, resolving internal conflicts, and negotiating with authorities, by rejecting the police procedures for the handling of complaints and the city's assertion that their solutions were legally impossible, and by putting forward their own claim that the problem of street prostitution in their neighbourhood is solvable, the residents not only became better problem solvers, they also underwent a change in self-understanding. By freeing themselves from the arbitrary restraints imposed on them by traditional forms of city administration, they transformed themselves from residents to citizens. As Tully puts it: 'What shapes and holds individuals and groups together "citizens" and "peoples" is not this or that agreement but *the free agonistic activities of participation themselves*. When these activities are unavailable or arbitrarily restricted, the members of a political association remain "subjects" rather than "citizens" because power is exercised over them without their say, non-democratically' (Tully, 2008a, 147, my italics). By acting on the situation at hand the residents of Nordmarkt transformed themselves into a public, as Dewey termed it.

this reversal of traditional roles has resulted in some searching explorations of urban problems (Specht 2012). I was a 'student' myself once in the Pendrecht University, in a workshop on citizen participation, and found it one of the most challenging and rewarding meetings on this topic that I remember.

The examples cited in this section show the close and subtle association between agonism, practice, freedom and democracy. The residents
of Nordmarkt, Pendrecht and Antwerp operate in a situation of structural power differentials that characterize every governance situation.
Initially they find themselves paralysed by a host of taken-for-granted
'automatic processes' to which humans are subject and 'within and
against which free citizens "assert" themselves' (Arendt 1977, in Tully
2008a, 136). But the relationship between oppression and freedom
is more subtle than the simple negation of the first through an act
of willpower. Tully elucidates this relationship by adopting Foucault's
conception of freedom not as the antonym of power, but instead as
a *necessary* element of it. 'Power', as Foucault states, 'is exercised
only over free subjects, and only insofar as they are free' (1983, 221).
Foucault goes on to clarify his characteristically aphoristic claim in,
for our purposes, an important way: 'By this we mean individual or
collective subjects *who are faced with a field of possibilities in which
several ways of behaving, several reactions and diverse comportments
may be realized*' (ibid.; italics mine). In other words, the presence of
agents who, despite the constraints of convention, tradition or suppression, keep open the possibility of deviating from the script that
these forces impose on them is the necessary condition for power to
realize itself. Foucault then brings his argument to a conclusion by
introducing the notion of agonism: 'At the very heart of the power
relationship, and constantly provoking it, are the recalcitrance of the
will and the intransigence of freedom. Rather than speaking of an
essential freedom, it would be better to speak of an 'agonism' – a relationship that is at the same time reciprocal incitation and struggle, less
a face-to-face confrontation which paralyses both sides than a permanent provocation' (1983, 221–22). Agonism is thus the 'freedom of
speaking and acting differently' in the face of power, or perhaps more
precisely, when provoked by the negative effects of power relationships (Tully 2008a, 143).[19]
The significance of informality for democratic governance lies precisely in its potential for creative adversity. For freedom is not an act

[19] The freedom to act differently is a central insight in both Bevir and Rhodes's
interpretive political science (where it takes the form of actors reshaping
traditions when faced with dilemmas), and in poststructuralist political theory
(where it appears as the contingency that is inherent in self-definition through
the other).

of will (despite Foucault's rhetoric), the romantic notion of the sudden throwing off of the shackles of oppression, but more of an easing into or finding oneself in a series of activities with others to address a concrete issue, activities that build on the understandings and routines that make up everyday life. 'Freedom is the practice of freedom' as Tully puts it succinctly (2008a, 136), and he continues in the spirit of Arendt, 'It is neither the motive nor the goal of this kind of activity that renders it free but its spirit or character: the "principles", "virtuosity" or "ethos" (such as love or equality) the action manifests' (ibid., quotes from Arendt 1977). Informality informs practices of freedom in two ways: in the possibility of difference it projects and in its capacity for patiently persisting in collective problem solving. 'It is "a beginning" because the participants always bring something "miraculous" – new, contingent, singular and unpredictable – into the world, breaking with routine and changing the game to some extent, and they seek to carry it through, to sustain the practice over time' (ibid.) As the Dortmund case has shown us, this freedom to speak and act differently takes on the shape of exploring societal conditions that were taken for granted by officials and residents alike, in the process discovering and trying out new solutions and finding new identities. We see that residents appropriated for themselves the freedom to challenge the traditional way of governing a city. They moved between Tully's three modes of freedom – modifying, negotiating and challenging – even choosing to cooperate with city officials or granting them a face-saving tactic to bring the solution of the problem closer. In this instance of 'citizen participation', agonistic freedom seems to be problem-oriented and pragmatic, choosing a mode of freedom that seems to bring the citizens' goals closer. The freedom to speak and act differently is at the heart of democratic governance and defines it as a different transformative form of democracy, not just an add-on to conventional liberal democracy.

Democratic Governance as Civic Capacity

In this chapter I have explored some of the obstacles to a more productive role for citizens in processes of urban governance. I have concluded that an inability to acknowledge conflict and deal with it in a fruitful way was one of these obstacles. The second was a shallow and misguided understanding of informal practices and their central role in an inclusive, collaborative and creative form of democracy. The result is a radically decentred notion of democratic governance, in which both the concept and actual practice of governance transcends 'the institutional governments of states' (Tully 2008a, 3). Following Foucault, Tully exhorts us to see the actions such as those of the Dortmund citizens as an inherent element of democratic governance, and exhorts us to be attentive to the large and varied repertoire of 'participatory diversity' that societies display (2008a, 142, 150), not as a special and relatively rare decision to oppose traditional democratic institutions, let alone a form of participatory activity that is seen as an exceptional state and that requires its own justification from within conventional political theory. Instead, citizen participation, as for example practiced by the citizens of Dortmund, is bound up with and originates from the informal practices which constitute and produce neighbourhood life in Nordmarkt. Spurred by the disruption caused by extensive street prostitution and the reluctance of authorities to intervene, this informality transforms into a diversity of practices of freedom: a recalibration of the residents' attitudes towards the sex workers, the negotiation of internal conflict, the design of a solution to the problem, the collecting of information, the creation of working relationships with a host of municipal actors, and the struggle for recognition as a serious party in the governance of prostitution in Dortmund (Tully 2008a, 149).

The significance of these 'practices of freedom' is that they open up the prospect of collaborative urban governance, in which citizen participation plays an important role. The Dortmund example originated with an act of citizen protest, but quickly evolved into the kind of agonistic networked governance that we recognize in our cities today. This is not ordinary liberal-democratic 'business as usual'. In fact, the citizens of Dortmund – and all those other citizens who are triggered into forming a participatory initiative – engage in the kind of 'unusual' problem solving that urban theorists such Clarence Stone and Xavier de Souza Briggs describe under the heading of civic capacity, or Chris Ansell describes as 'pragmatist democracy'. Although these approaches differ in detail, they converge on a number of key characteristics. Civic capacity or democratic governance is problem oriented, practice driven, improvisational, and focused on arriving at 'good' outcomes, where 'good' means feasible and acceptable to those involved. This type of decentred democratic governance originates in the everyday tactics and meanings that make up the urban environment. It makes productive the inherent conflict between informality and the ensembles of administrative belief and techniques by which the administration exercises power, and it does so through a process of enacted interdependence, in which all parties begin to acknowledge their mutual dependence in harnessing the problem at hand, and formal organizations leave space for informal processes to stimulate recursive learning and collaborative rationality. In true Deweyan fashion, this agonism is an inherent and constitutive element of the relationship between citizens and policy makers, the ruled and the rulers, that makes up a working, flourishing democracy.

11 Insurgent Citizenship: Radicalism, Co-optation and Neighbourhood Geopolitics among the Palestinian Citizens of Haifa, Israel

JOSEPH LEIBOVITZ

Introduction

This chapter develops an institutional-discursive analysis of patterns and dynamics of Israeli-Palestinian neighbourhood mobilisation in the 'mixed city' of Haifa, building on the notion of 'insurgent citizenship' (Holston 1999). It highlights the often neglected symbolic and discursive facets of the political geography of urban governance and its relation to scalar dimensions of political mobilisation and collective action among ethno-national minorities. In this case, an investigation into the mobilising agendas of the Palestinian citizens of Israel (PCIs) in the northern Israeli city of Haifa is aimed at highlighting how the neighbourhood, the city and the nation are intertwined in a complex geography of citizenship and belonging.

The scalar politics of mobilisation and contestation remains a largely unexplored dimension, even in the context of a growing body of literature on urban and grassroots social movements (Afouxenidis 2006; Castells 1983; Leontidou 2006; Pickvance 2003). The quest for understanding the scaled nature of citizenship-in-practice has become increasingly pertinent in the context of the rise of 'the urban' as an important scale in and through which struggles over various facets of social and cultural rights are being worked out (Bell and Binnie 2006; Chandler 2001; Cooper 2006; Mayer 2003; Tully 1999). A focus on the scalar politics of collective action and on the strategic options available to activists in their struggle to articulate political claims is particularly illuminating as a way of gaining insights into the role of local politics in mediating identity politics in highly conflictual contexts. Seen from this prism, neighbourhood geopolitics receives its due treatment, both from a theoretical and analytical point of view, and from an empirical perspective which captures its politically constitutive role.

The 'politics of place' approach employed in this chapter highlights neighbourhood geopolitics as part of a constant and shifting dialogue between the neighbourhood, the city and the nation. The Israeli City of Haifa, often hailed in official, historiographic and popular discourses as Israel's prime model of Jewish-Arab 'co-existence', has been constructed by hegemonic discourses of majority-minority accommodation that worked to position it as a distinctive inter-ethnic and geopolitical space within the context of a highly contested society (Falah et al. 2000; Shafir and Peled 2002). At the same time, political mobilisation in its traditional Palestinian neighbourhoods has taken several forms, ranging from co-optation, to protest and resistance. From this perspective, the changing contours of Haifa's ethnic mobilisation and the relationship of ethnic elites to (local and national) state institutions reveal much about the wider context of ethno-national politics in Israel.

The chapter thus highlights how discourses of urban governance tend to structure expectations and outcomes around the appropriateness of certain political strategies of claim making. At the same time, the discussion in the chapter will point to the importance of understanding the subtle ways through which community activists can generate effective oppositional strategies, capable of enhancing local democracy and deepening citizenship.

The Neighbourhood, the City, the Nation: Territorial Constructions of Citizenship

The importance of neighbourhood political life, as representing the lived everyday experience of citizenship, has received increasing attention in the literature on governance and citizenship. As Kennett and Forrest (2006, 713) argue:

The neighbourhood provides a research vehicle to connect theoretical debates to lived experience, to engage directly with issues of participation, citizenship, exclusion and cohesion with policies formulated by governments and other bodies nationally and internationally.

Neighbourhood politics is also closely intertwined with normative approaches to local democracy, where debates have raged about the balance between responsibility and rights, and the utility of different models of citizenship, ranging from assimilation to integration (Melo and Baiocchi 2006). These emergent discussions provide a refreshing departure from the earlier generation of literature on urban governance, which tended to gravitate towards the identification of interest, power and policy outputs, but shied away from attempting to elucidate the relationship between urban institutional features and the nature of citizenship in cities. This missing element is now in the process of redressing, as increasing attention is paid to exploring the interface of governance, citizenship and participation at the level of neighbourhoods (Campbell and Marshall 2000; Yánez 2004). Not only is this a way of crystallising cross-cutting 'wicked policy issues', embodying both material and subjective concerns, and sharpening analyses of policy efficacy, but it is a fundamental building block in the deepening of citizenship. As the critical literature on participation and engagement points out, discourses of participation have a potentially dark side. They can rather easily evolve into a reincarnation of corporatism, or worse, into a coercive process which lends legitimacy to existing inequalities and power relations within and between communities, between policy experts and the public, and between marginalised groups and the state (Chandler 2001; Fagotto and Fung 2006; Fung 2006; Milewa 2004).

For this reason, it is important to expand the conceptual basis of participation to include non-traditional (and certainly non-corporatised) forms of engagement with state institutions, policy processes, and other actors. Dissent, explicit and covert forms of resistance, counter-hegemonic forces and the use of various – old and new – technologies are some of the various forms of participation in its broad sense. It seems to me, then, that analyses of neighbourhood participation and various forms of political mobilisation require at least two analytical dimensions: (1) a use of both 'hard' institutional and 'softer' discursive conceptual tools; and (2) a *relational* view of neighbourhood political activism, one that keeps a close eye on how the neighbourhood is never independent from the city, the nation and increasingly the international context. Indeed, the geography of neighbourhood politics (or what I would term 'neighbourhood geopolitics') is in itself a reflection of the varying and complex agendas undertaken by different networks of actors.

Symbolic Urban Regimes and the Scalar Politics of Citizenship

This chapter draws attention to the discursive foundations of urban regimes – an analytical perspective which emphasises how governance in cities is produced through the construction of governing coalitions, involving elected and unelected officials, business elites and – occasionally – civic groups.

Following on Stoker and Mossberger's (1994) theoretical contribution on the cross-national utility of a regime's perspective in urban politics, I wish to draw particular attention to their highlighting of a symbolic urban regime as a particular 'type' of urban governance. Symbolic urban regimes are governing arrangements that act primarily through the discursive articulation of cities. They tend to focus on the image building of cities. The political elites associated with such regimes often have limited substantive or formal powers, and as such direct their efforts to discourses of urban change and to symbolic constructions of places through flagship developments and events, marketing, cultural festivities and so on. Symbolic regimes thus involve, in their heart, a geopolitical positioning and 'imagineering' of places through storytelling and other forms of social constructions. The case of Israel would, theoretically, lend itself to highlighting the symbolic and discursive facets of urban governance, as Israeli local authorities enjoy little formal political powers in a relatively centralised system of central-local intergovernmental relations (Blank 2004).

Recent advances in discursive policy analysis offer very valuable insights on the role of discourses in framing policy problems, agendas and solutions, and in legitimating the actions of both governmental and non-governmental actors (Dryzek 2013; Fischer 2003; Hajer and Wagenaar 2003; James 2004; Torgerson 2003). In fact, discursive, and by extension symbolic, features of regime governance have been much neglected by analyses of urban politics. And yet in traditionally centralised political systems, such as that of Israel, where local government has little formal powers, local political power often expresses itself through informal, discursive and symbolic constructions, rather than through formal authority (Leontidou 1996; see also Horta 2006). Indeed, even in more decentralised political systems, discourses fulfil an important legitimating tool in the formation and actions of local regimes (Leibovitz and Salmon 1999). Local state actors can engage in processes of hegemonic construction which can then be used and recycled as resources and pillars of public policy. A city's constructed image can serve as rationale for or against intervention. It can account for policy selectivity and for policy silences (i.e., non-intervention). And it facilitates in the cementing of hard institutional features and informal relations and links, combining to produce what Lowndes (2005) has termed 'the rules of the game'.

A theoretical challenge remains in attempting to highlight the relational dynamics of urban governance and the scalar politics of citizenship. By the scalar politics of citizenship I refer primarily to the politics of making claims that is unfolding at different geographic levels: the neighbourhood, the city, the region, the nation and the transnational scale.

Neighbourhood politics can be seen as a relational practice. It is relational, first, in that it pays attention to the construction of citizenship as a lived experience of struggles, claims and engagement (Tully 1999). Secondly, it is relational in reference to geographic scale: that is, the idea that the city and its constituent neighbourhoods embed a complex layering and intermingling of the citizenship of the everyday around different levels, incorporating the household, the neighbourhood, the wider community, the national state and potentially transnational networks.

What forms of political claims and mobilisations around them are likely to occur in cases where ethnic minorities comprise an 'entrapped' segment of a larger nation? The view of the Palestinian citizens of Israel as a 'trapped minority' has originally been captured by Rabinowitz (2001), and as a subset of debates on transnationality (Bauböck 1994). A trapped minority is an ethno-national group which is divided between at least two territorial political entities, thus suffering an a priori structural subordination. This subordination is not merely in the form of various discriminatory state practices, but fundamentally emanates from the exclusion of such minorities from debate about the very nature (raison d'être) of the state.

PCIs conform to this definition, since as members of a trapped ethno-national minority within Israel, their citizenship – while 'full' in a strict political-legal sense – suffers from systematic exclusion from collective, cultural, symbolic and land-based rights (Yiftachel 1997). This exclusion compounds well-documented socioeconomic marginalisation (SIKKUY 2005). Essentially, such systemic exclusion (or 'differentiated citizenship') radiates from the definition of Israel as a national homeland for the Jewish people, as envisioned by the Jewish national movement (Zionism) (See Shafir and Peled 2002, 110–36). What forms of political mobilisation and claims to citizenship might we expect in such contexts, and how does scalar politics highlight the strategic choices evident in urban collective action? A further elaboration of citizenship is required to make sense of struggles in such circumstances.

Insurgent Citizenship

It is broadly acknowledged that citizenship consists of the rights, responsibilities and membership in a political community. While the political community has been traditionally associated with the nation-state, there are increasing challenges to the monopoly of the nation-state on civic rights and membership in society (Smith 1995; Staeheli 2003). Immigration, globalisation and cultural and economic change have brought about new dynamics so that political communities are said to be increasingly defined by members' identities, in terms of gender, ethnicity, sexuality and a range of political dispositions, rather than exclusively on the basis of their nation-states (Archibugi et al. 1998; Balibar 1995; Bauböck 1994; Krause 2003; Phalet and Swyngedouw 2002; Urry 2000; Yuval-Davis 1999). It is also commonly argued that sub-national territories and supranational institutions have become increasingly important scales through which power relations, political decisions and regulation are being reworked. Consequently, citizenship is said to be shaped and experienced through a complex geographic intersection of local, national and international engagements (Ball and Piper 2002; Ehrkamp and Leitner, 2003; Ghosh and Wang 2003; Soysal 1994; Staeheli 2003; Staeheli and Thompson 1997; Urry 2000). For instance, Purcell (2003) has recently talked of 'a new territorial openness' in which urban institutions can help to shape an alternative sense of political membership and belonging, and to even challenge current citizenship regimes. Similarly, others have identified the city as the most meaningful level – in the everyday sense – through which inter-cultural politics can be realised (Amin 2002; van den Berghe 2002; Isin 2000).

Holston (1999) has suggested that cities can be looked at as spaces of 'insurgent citizenship'. Insurgency can work as a benign force, the use of which might provide communities, activists and advocacy planners with the means of claiming rights and asserting responsibilities. For Holston, however, insurgency is mostly about resistance. His notion of resistance stems from a critical stance towards large-scale, modernist town planning, primarily in its utopian, context-less and place-detached version. In this view, planning has been one of the key tools that have supported the process of state, and often nation, building. It has sought to integrate national spaces into a cohesive whole, to facilitate the state's control over diverse localities and communities, and in turn to subject them to overarching ideals about national citizenship: loyalty to the state, the reassertion of national political institutions, conformation to national cultures, integration into the national space economy, and so on. As Holston argues: 'at the heart of this modernist political project is the doctrine ... that the state is the only legitimate source of citizenship rights, meanings and practices. I use the notion of insurgent to refer to new and other sources and to their assertion of legitimacy' (1999, 157).

To take this idea of insurgent citizenship further, the constitution of potentially new, additional or alternative sources of citizenship may refer to claims for the expansion of civil, political and social rights, and to demands for different substances and forms of recognition (such as the recognition of value pluralism and preferences, and of collective cultural rights). But what is also of importance is that participatory dynamics in politics can take different forms, from the so-called traditional elements of voting and public participation vehicles, to the presumably alternative methods of protest, resistance/insurgency, citizen jury, 'town hall meetings' and so on. Neighbourhood politics, in my view, functions as a node within fluid networks of activism, participation and concerns, around which mobilisation and the politics of claims take place. Taken together they correspond to the varied way through which the city and the rich politics of its varied communities and neighbourhoods can be read as a text of insurgent energies. Holston continues along these lines and is worth citing in this context:

These insurgent forms are found both in organised grassroots mobilisations and in everyday practices that, in different ways, empower, parody, derail, or subvert state agendas. They are found, in other words, in struggles over what it means to be a member of the modern state – which is why I refer to them with the term *citizenship*. Membership in the state has never been a static identity, given the dynamics of global migrations and national ambitions. Citizenship changes as new members emerge to advance their claims, expanding its realm, and as new forms of segregation of violence counter these advances, eroding it. The sites of insurgent citizenship are found at the intersection of these processes of expansion and erosion. (1999, 167; original emphasis)

The practice of insurgency in cities can take several forms and substances. At the personal level and among disadvantaged groups it can

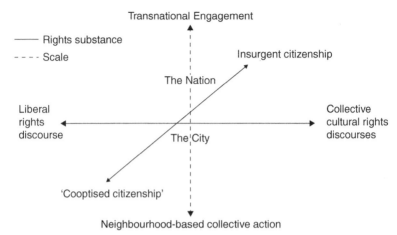

Figure 11.1. Conceptualising neighbourhood geopolitics as a relational politics of place.

take the shape of alternative storytelling and everyday practices; it may involve survival strategies and the formation of alternative economies; it can produce alternative sources of support and service provision; it can result in the creation of more or less coherent visions of the good city, of rights and obligations; and it can take the form of both informal and formal politics of claims – ranging from individual to collective action. The city in its various components thus constitutes at once a site of mobilisation practices and the very object of alternative spaces of engagement, participation, claims to rights and identity formation and maintenance (see Figure 11.1). In its radical sense – especially in the context of ethno-national territorial conflict involving trapped minorities – collective action and substances of political mobilisation would take the form of insurgent citizenship (Figure 11.1). Such insurgent citizenship is expressed in a geopolitical articulation of neighbourhood mobilisation, where the local (neighbourhood) is incorporated into claims to the city, the nation, and (at some moments) to transnational scales of reference. Secondly, the substance of such insurgent/radical citizenship would move away from 'mainstream' discourses of liberal rights that tend to individualise citizens, to discourses that would articulate and make claims to collective cultural and ethno-national consciousness. In cases where trapped minorities are subordinated not merely in terms of various discriminatory practices (important as they are), insurgent citizenship articulated in those terms represents a radical departure from co-optation, in that co-opted forms of citizenship mobilisations remain localised and conforming to incorporation discourses that frame the language of liberal rights as the only acceptable option.

In what follows I therefore consider neighbourhood geopolitics in its relational context: as part of a set of practices that form the territorialised nature of citizenship politics. Neighbourhood politics in its broadest sense is taken to mean a set of localised political practices aiming at strengthening community cohesion, living standards and participatory mechanisms, whilst articulating broader scales of reference and attachment. The prism of neighbourhood geopolitics forms part of community building and identity politics, but it also points to potential tension within and between communities (Davis 1991). It reveals intriguing and at times less than immediately visible connections between different scales of political engagement and political relevance. And it is potentially fruitful in unpacking how citizenship is experience, constructed and claimed on the basis of everyday experiences as well as through the operation of formalised legal structures.

The research on which this chapter is based was carried out in Haifa between 2005 and 2006. It included some thirty face-to-face semi-structured interviews with Palestinian and Jewish activists from the broad spectrum of political organisations and community associations. Non-participant observation of key events (policy deliberations, and events of community mobilisation and protest) was also undertaken. In addition, semi-structured interviews were carried out with residents and business owners in various neighbourhoods with significant numbers of Israeli-Palestinian residents. A further twelve interviews were conducted with local and national policymakers and representatives of non-governmental organisations in Haifa and other locations in Israel, in order to develop a picture of important urban and national policy contexts. Collection of various published and unpublished documents from various sources (government, community organisations, political party platforms and communications, etc.), and assembling of socio-economic data from the Israeli census helped to complete the picture.[1]

---

[1] It should be noted that the last formal census of the population in Israel was conducted in 1996, thus constraining the availability of good quality up-to-date data. However, the broad socioeconomic characteristics of different ethnic and social groups in Israel, including PCIs, exhibited in this census remain relevant, not least because available data suggests the deepening of inequalities and social polarisation (Svirsky and Connor-Attias, 2006).

Haifa, Israel

The Palestinian minority of Israel, which numbers some 1.2 people and accounts for about 20 per cent of the country's total population, has enjoyed full formal citizenship since 1966. Yet along a range of social, economic and cultural dimensions the citizenship experience of PCIs is far from complete. Whether one looks at economic indicators such as income levels or occupational structures, social dimensions such as educational attainment and housing conditions, or cultural aspects such as collective rights, the nature of 'differentiated citizenship' becomes almost self evident (Ghanem 1998; Jamal 2002; Ozacky-Lazar and Ghanem 2001). Having defined a priori its character as a Jewish nation-state, in accordance with the vision of Zionism (i.e., the Jewish national movement), the social and cultural aspects of Israeli citizenship contain an almost built-in uneven terrain. Thus, while some refer to Israel as an 'ethnic democracy' (Smooha 2002), others have gone even further to render its citizenship regime an 'ethnocracy' (Yiftachel 2001).

Within this context, the PCIs who live in the ineptly named 'mixed cities' of Tel Aviv-Yafo (or Yafa in its Arabic pronunciation), Lod (Lydda), Ramla, Akko (Acre), Haifa, Nazareth/Upper-Nazareth, and Jerusalem (a category in itself) remain somewhat of an enigma. They constitute 10 per cent of the Palestinian citizens of Israel, in stark contrast to the great majority of this group, which lives in completely separate towns and villages, mainly in the northern and southern peripheries of Israel. Given the ethnic, or ethnocratic, nature of the state, it is often suggested that the Palestinian minority of the ethnically fractured cities suffer from a 'double discrimination syndrome': that is, the various discriminations contained within the national political structure are re-enacted, replicated, and re-amplified through the channels of the local states in which they reside (Falah 1997). For instance, historical inequalities in budget allocations in the educational sector nationally are also replicated in municipal budget allocations (SIKKUY 2005). Similarly, national spatial planning strategies which have worked to facilitate the expansion of Jewish presence in Israel and containment of the Arab minority, would be expected to be mirrored by local planning policies in the cities of Lod, Ramla, Tel Aviv-Yafo (Yafa) and so on (Shatil 2005).

While we know increasingly more about the various national dimensions of the Jewish-Arab cleavage in Israel (and indeed of the various other cleavages which characterise Israel's ethnic, cultural and gendered mosaic; see Shafir and Peled 2002), the intersection of national and local dynamics is less evident. This issue is of wider significance, given the debates about the various, multilayered and complex nature of citizenship, and the realities of multicultural engagement in an interconnected world. These debates and discussions are echoed in numerous studies in a wide range of national contexts. In orthodox political studies, however, much of the debate about the dynamics and accommodation of inter-group relations remains located at the national scale (see for instance the special issue of *Nations and Nationalism*, 2002). The stressing of scalar politics and relational geographies of citizenship campaigns, within which political geography occupies a vantage position, offers illuminating ways of gaining a more nuanced understanding of trajectories of activism.

Constructing a City and Its Communities

Haifa grew rapidly between the two world wars, primarily due to the construction of its port, which was initiated by the British mandate authorities. Its growing economic significance was matched by its enhanced cultural role in mandatory Palestine, serving as a major centre of Palestinian theatre, printing houses, newspapers and arts. At the same time it also served as a target for Jewish immigration before the Second World War, because of its strategic location in northern Palestine. Although there were tensions between the Palestinian and Jewish communities of Haifa, there were also remarkable instances of accommodation and political and economic co-operation before and after the establishment of Israel (Goren 2006). The outbreak of inter-community hostilities during 1947 and 1948 and the war which followed Israel's declaration of independence have been subject to historiographic debate about the dynamics of the conflict and the causes, and indeed the balance of forced evacuation of Palestinians and voluntary abandonment of the city (Goren 2004; Kimmerling and Migdal 2003; Morris 2002). What is clear is that a Palestinian community of about 61,000 people was reduced to some 3,500. Since then, Palestinian immigration to Haifa from the surrounding villages, motivated by a search for economic opportunities, and natural increase have contributed to the growth of the community. In the early 1960s it constituted 5 per cent of the total population of the city, and by the mid-1990s it reached roughly 14 per cent (Israel Central Bureau of Statistics, 1995). It now accounts for 9 per cent of the population of Haifa, numbering between 25,000 and 30,000 people (City of Haifa, 2006). Close to 60 per cent of this community is defined as Christian Arab, the rest being mostly Muslim.

In terms of neighbourhoods and communities, one can identify at least three distinctive concentrations of Arab communities in Haifa, each with its own demographic, cultural and political idiosyncrasies (see Figure 11.2). One of the historical cores of Palestinian Haifa is the dense neighbourhood of Wadi Nisnas, near Haifa's old downtown area. Housing some 2,000 people, it represents the commercial, religious, political and cultural core of the Christian-Arab residents of the city. Its socioeconomic profile is well below the city's average. The neighbourhood has come to be constructed by governing discourses as 'The Arab Neighbourhood of Haifa', in a sense a showcase of Arab culture and life in the city (see further discussion in this chapter, and Figure 11.3). Its traditional affiliation has been with the Israeli Communist Party in its various incarnations. It also contains a strong element of business-owner politics, articulating an agenda which emphasises the need for business promotion in the neighbourhood. Second, there is the largely Muslim neighbourhood of Halisa, in eastern Haifa. It is one of the city's most deprived neighbourhoods, and its politics has become increasingly connected to the Islamic movement and Islamic institutions within it, as well as to more radical ethno-nationalist activism. Third, in western Haifa, in the former village of Kababir, on the slopes of the Carmel Mountain, resides one of the city's more distinctive communities, the Ahmedyyan religious sect. It is a small community, of about 1,500 people. Although connected to Islam, members of this community have developed their own identity and religious practices. Politically, the Ahmedyyans have traditionally emphasised strategies of co-optation, moderation and engagement with state institutions, both local and national. Housing needs and educational issues represent much of their claims vis-à-vis the state.

The notion of *'co-existence'* represents a major category in the official discourses related to majority (that is, Jewish) – minority

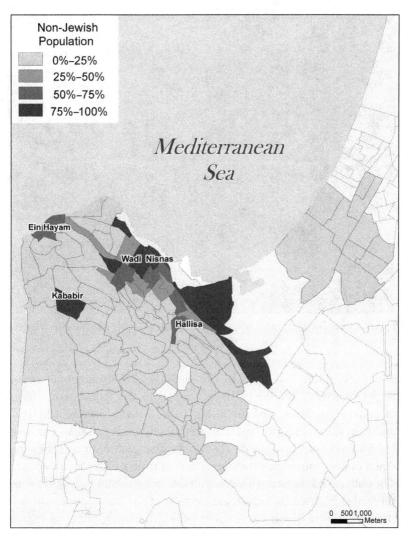

Figure 11.2. Distribution of Israeli-Palestinians ('Non-Jewish' Population) in Haifa, by census tracts, 1996.
Source: Israel Central Bureau of the Census (1996).

(i.e., Palestinian/Arab) accommodation in Haifa as a whole. It relies on historical accounts on how Haifa has long represented 'a city with a difference', and on more contemporary institutional and geographical practices. My concern is less with the historical dimensions and more with contemporary dynamics, primarily since the early 1990s, which

Figure 11.3. The orientalist imagination of the Wadi Nisnas Neighbourhood.
Source: The author.

saw a reshuffling and dramatic ups and downs in the national opportunity structures for the collective action of the Palestinian citizens
of Israel. The election of the Rabin Labour-led government in 1992
and then the Oslo Agreement between Israel and Palestinian representatives were matched with a rhetoric of changing national priorities,
equal opportunities and stronger incorporation of Israeli Palestinians.
The collapse of the peace process and the violence that followed turned
the wheel backwards, before the election of the Barak government in
the late-1990s, which again carried the promise of changed citizenship regimes and a more favourable accommodation of the Palestinian
minority. Yet, the violent events of the October 2000 uprising, which
culminated with the killing of 13 Palestinians, 12 of whom were citizens of Israel, seemed to have dramatically narrowed available opportunity structures and shifted the attitudes of both Palestinian and
Jewish Israelis towards each other and towards the state.

It is within this dramatic period that the observation of neighbourhood politics and claims-making processes takes shape and is contextualised. Here, the relational aspects of neighbourhood-city-nation

discursive constructions and political strategies offer insights into mobilisation and the nature of collective action. The neighbourhood, and by extension the city, crystallise identity politics and the territorialised nature of citizenship. They point to instances in which the local – whether the city or the local neighbourhood – is indeed exhibiting 'difference', and dynamics where neighbourhood, city and national politics gravitate towards 'sameness'.

The contours of urban regime capacity in Haifa have led to a certain combination of priorities and emphases with regard to Jewish-Arab relations in the city. The city's actual urban development policy and strategic planning coherence are weak for a range of historical, institutional and political leadership reasons. Political opportunity structures for local politics in Israel are relatively limited, given the traditionally centralised nature of the country, although this has been changing and is not the only reason for the weak nature of urban development policy and regime coherence in the city.

In the absence of formal development policy coherence and intervention in the city's various neighbourhoods, including its Arab communities, the city has developed a range of largely symbolic tools aimed at constructing the city as 'different', 'tolerant', and most particularly, the embodiment of Arab-Jewish 'co-existence' (however vaguely defined). The traditional reference to the city as 'Red Haifa', to indicate its historical dominance by Labour and the trade unions, together with its working-class ethos, hover above as an envelope of local particularism, an indication of the privileged role of Left-wing politics in the city. Its former mayor, Amram Mitzna, has stated, for instance:

I am proud to be the Mayor of Haifa, the city that has found the right balance among all ethnic and religious groups living together throughout the years in tolerance and mutual respect.... In a very complex and difficult region and in a very complicated period, Haifa remains an island of sanity, a city that has become a successful model of the possibility of living together in peace. (Mitzna 2003)

A particular institution, Beit Hagefen (meaning Vine House, an allusion to peace) has been in charge of a range of cultural initiatives celebrating Haifa's brand of inter-group accommodation. The most symbolic of these has been the invention in 1993 of the Holiday of Holidays, which aims to celebrate Christianity, Islam and Judaism, all

Figure 11.4. The visual construction of 'co-existence' in Haifa: co-existence trails in Wadi Nisnas.
Source: The author.

at the same time, in a range of festivities in the narrow streets of Wadi Nisnas (Figures 11.4 and 11.5). These celebrations combine the localisation of indigenous Arabism, with wider claims about the nature of the city and the region with which it enjoys symbiotic cultural and historical ties.

Figure 11.5. Urban institutions and the construction of inter-faith accommodation in Haifa's public discourse: The 'Beit Hagefen' Arab-Jewish Cultural Centre.
Source: The author.

The symbolic element of Haifa's regime politics also invokes a discourse which attempts to dissociate Haifa from the immediacy of the Israel/Palestine conflict and develop a supra-local and transnational identity, one that seemingly transcends local citizenship and reconnects a particular neighbourhood to broader geopolitical imaginations:

The beginning – an idea spawned by the thought and need to give a cultural and artistic expression to the uniqueness of the city of Haifa. A City which, in addition to its beauty, is special in its habitants' way of life. A city of mixed population where Jews and Arabs – of all the religions and ethnic groups – live together in mutual respect and tolerance. A city that, through its everyday life, constitutes a model of the possibility of coexistence of all people. ...

It is only natural that the *Wadi Nisnas* neighbourhood is the centre of the happening. This special neighbourhood is characterised by its originality, the beauty of its alleys and houses, the Mediterranean aroma and the connections among its inhabitants. It is a neighbourhood symbolising tolerance and hope. ...

In recent years, we have been living with the persistent sense that this project and its goals are presently more important than ever. We must carry on and prove that it is possible to live together and there is no other way but the way of the City of Haifa. (Bialik 2003)

The symbolic nature of Haifa's local regime is also well integrated into another important facet of contemporary urban politics: that of image making and urban marketing. Interviews with officials have revealed how important this image has become as a symbol of the city in its outward projection for the promotion of tourism and investment. Similarly the construction of a particular neighbourhood as symbolising a distinctive 'Haifa Model' has also been linked to the material necessity of urban economic development.

The other dimension of hegemony relates to the internal facets of Arab politics within Haifa. The symbol of 'Red Haifa' has also fitted within the identification of Haifa with the various incarnations of the Israeli Community Party, which has traditionally found its strength among the country's Palestinian citizens. The party, which is today part of the broader Democratic Front for Peace and Equality (HADASH, in its Hebrew acronyms), has been an important feature in the socialisation and activities of local Arab intellectual, economic and political elites in Haifa. Its headquarters is still located in the Wadi Nisnas neighbourhood. Historically, the party's platform has relied on Arab-Jewish co-operation on the equal footings in its leadership, its emphasis on social justice and equality, and its support of the two-state (Israel and Palestine) solution to the Israeli-Palestinian conflict. It has attempted, with varying degrees of success, to avoid ethno-nationalist discourse in favour of class-consciousness and civil rights issues. Throughout the history of Haifa, the party's informal and formal inclusion in the city council's governing coalition represented a sharp departure from national patterns of Israeli politics. It has never been part of a governing coalition in Israel's national parliamentary history.

Insurgent Citizenship: Neighbourhood Politics as Moments of Co-optation and Radicalism

Hard and soft political opportunity structures, reinforced by the ways through which discourses about the city, its neighbourhoods and communities, its various ethnic groups, and its place in the nation and wider region constitute the complex environment in which co-optation and radicalism, accommodation and dissent are forged. Neighbourhood geopolitics in Haifa, overlaid by the complexity of wider ethno-national conflict, offers us a vantage point from which to analyse strategies of collective action. Hegemonic discourses and dominant views do not go unchallenged and, in fact, in their construction they create the very substance of political mobilisation. In this context, several political projects can be discerned in Haifa.

i. Intra-minority Political Contestation and the Uncovering of 'Other' Neighbourhoods

Since the early 2000s, the dominance of HADASH over Arab politics in the city has been challenged by more radical activists, combining traditional civil rights demands around housing, education, community services, social welfare and infrastructure, with a distinctive brand of localised ethno-nationalism. This ethno-nationalism, in the form of the emergence of the National Democratic Alliance Party (BALAD), rejects both the cosy Jewish-Arab accommodation manifested in the traditional HADASH platform, and the city's projected image of co-existence. It calls for reassertions of collective cultural and ethno-national rights locally, and its infiltration into municipal politics has been a remarkable event in the landscape of ethnically fractured Israeli cities. That is, its rise in Haifa goes beyond local significance. It also rejects the projection of Wadi Nisnas as the quintessential symbol of co-existence and superficial Arab culture. It has directed attention to the multiple socioeconomic problems in which the neighbourhood is embedded (poor housing, depleted infrastructure, the lack of community services), pointed to the superficiality of the city's symbolic regime, and has been instrumental in bringing the Arab neighbourhood of Halisa into the limelight as a key example of the social and economic problems facing the Arab/Palestinian residents of the city.

In a certain sense, then, Halisa has become the counter-hegemonic locale for neighbourhood activism. Here, neighbourhood politics turns into a geopolitical question: which neighbourhood and what reality is to be highlighted, and for what political project? Essentially, the rise of radicalism in Haifa has entailed a shift in the geography of neighbourhood politics.

An even more deeply radicalised project seeks to counteract the attempt to isolate Haifa and Wadi Nisnas from the ethno-national identities of the wider Israeli and Palestinian contexts. This project contests the building of Haifa as a distinctive model. It seeks, in fact, to highlight its place squarely within the wider identity politics and territorial conflict in Israel and Palestine. It points to the replication of inequalities and discrimination in Haifa. And it seeks to revive the memory of Haifa as a lost Palestinian cultural, political and economic centre, in the context of what Israeli-Palestinians see as the *naqba,* the Palestinian disaster of 1948:

Among the Jewish population you'll find Denya [a wealthy neighbourhood] and also Neve David [a deprived neighbourhood]. But what you won't find in Haifa ... among Arab neighbourhoods you won't find a 'Denya'. There is Halisa, Abbas, Wadi Nisnas [all predominately Arab neighbourhoods which typically rank amongst the lower socioeconomic communities in Haifa]! That is, all the Arabs are actually in the same boat. So even if you see this from a class perspective, you can't ignore the *national* aspect ... and the fact that in the end the conflict is a *national* conflict. In every place there are classes, rich and poor, men and women, young and old ... but in Haifa and in Israel more generally, which were both created on the ruins of another peoples, the central element is that we're dealing with a *national* conflict. (Political activist, Haifa)

Yet, even here the fascinating altercations between the local and the national reveal complex articulations of radicalism and co-option. Radicalism in itself does not go unchallenged, but rather become submerged in the constellation of coalition politics, as discussed in sections that follow.

ii. Coalition Politics between Co-optation and Radicalism

Hegemonic discourses are not created in a vacuum but in many cases reflect long histories and traditions, and stories which then tend to then construct certain realities. They affect agenda setting, policies, elite behaviour, collective actions and political strategies. A few examples will illustrate this point.

First, there was the inclusion by the mayor of the more radical BALAD Party city council representative in the city's governing coalition, following the municipal elections of 2003. To understand the significance of this, one has to take note of the fact that at the national level Israel has mounted a constitutional challenge in an attempt to disqualify the party from running for seats in the Knesset (the Israeli parliament). The argument of state officials was that the party's platform, based on an ideology of a bi-national state, contradicted the Jewish character of the state. In the event, the Israeli Supreme Court rejected the state's claim. Nevertheless, from a national politics point of view, any thought or suggestion that the party be included in a governing coalition is beyond the realm of plausibility. Yet in Haifa, this unthinkable constellation came into being, sending a powerful signal about the viability of the Haifa model. It demonstrates the fine line between radicalism and co-optation which is interwoven into the strategies of Palestinian activists in the city:

Our entry to city council politics is already a compromise. It cannot be taken for granted. I mean, it isn't obvious that in Haifa, from which the Arabs were deported and in which a new municipality which absorbed [Jewish] immigration was established, we would eventually enter [local politics]. The same as the notion that it isn't to be taken for granted that we would enter the Knesset.... So, I will not take part in the 60th anniversary celebration for the Municipality of Haifa.... But I'm there to serve an interest.... So it's a compromise being part of the establishment that took part in [action towards the Palestinians here].... I say even more than this: when I say that I want equality I make a compromise. The fact that I have lost my homeland and now I fight to become an equal citizen, there is a compromise here; it's a value compromise.... Total equality is [for me] a compromise.... Palestine is Haifa, Akko, Jaffa.... Here, and in Jaffa and in other Palestinian cities there were more than 20 daily Palestinian newspapers, and today there's none. Newspapers are signs of cultural flourishing, the beginning of Palestinian modernisation. (BALAD activist)

Second, the social construction of 'the city of difference', or rather 'The City in Which Things are Different', as a hegemonic discourse of state and quasi-state agencies, as well as by popular media rhetoric, has found a receptive reaction among the political elite of Haifa's Palestinian community. Moreover, even the more radicalised elements of this community have come to accept the 'difference of Haifa', if only rhetorically. This difference has been accepted, at least at some moments and in some circumstances, as bearing certain obligations, particular enactments of citizenship, and distinctive ways of engaging with the state. Consequently, we can point to the building of a particular local political project, in which identity politics is mobilised in distinctive ways that incorporate higher (national) level politics, at the same time demonstrating the bifurcation of political statements and behaviour. As one of the more radical political actors has commented:

[T]he truth is that Haifa is somewhat different from the so called other mixed cities in Israel. In Haifa the atmosphere is more moderate ... more comfortable. You can even sense that the extreme right here is different from the extreme right in other places. That is, there is more friction here, but also more links [between the different communities].

The framing of Haifa as 'different', 'distinctive', 'moderate' and 'localist' has contributed to the development of certain expectations related to both state practices and mobilisation strategies. The choice of particular issues as the substance of citizenship struggles and the equally significant undertaking of particular courses of public action have been important features of the polity-building nature of identity politics and the localised terrain of urban-relational citizenship construction. Public discourses of state-minority relations, articulated by both state and Palestinian actors, have tended to gravitate towards a somewhat vaguely defined notion of acceptability, reflecting, in turn, on sets of institutional norms related to the construction of political spaces of state activity and ethnic movement politics. As one Israeli-Palestinian community activist has put it:

Even public statements are more moderate here, you can hear them [sic]. There is a feeling that, even when there is some incitements against Arabs in the country, there are always ... sort of ... attempts to exclude Haifa's Arabs from such incitement. It expressed itself during the so-called October [2000] *'intifada'* [uprising], when things not only remained more moderate here, but the Municipality also behaved differently.

iii. Neighbourhood Mobilisation as a Politically Constitutive Moment

It is perhaps in neighbourhood-based political struggles that the intricacies and complexities of movement politics reach their zenith. In the course of 2003 the predominately Arab neighbourhood of Halisa, one of Haifa's most deprived communities, became the locus of mobilisation which encapsulated the complex relations between state institutions and minority politics, as well as the internal dynamics of minority politics. The immediate trigger for the struggle was the city administration's threat to partially demolish a Palestinian-owned home (in effect, to take down a balcony), which was deemed to have been built illegally and now stood in the way of infrastructural developments that were part of a local renewal project. Beyond this, there were growing concerns over the comprehensive new master plan for the neighbourhood, which could have increased residential densities through the imposition of a new wide road at the expense of narrow tracts and through the construction of higher density housing and possible further demolitions of housing deemed substandard.

Given the suspicious attitudes of Israeli-Palestinians towards the Israeli planning system and considering its role in facilitating the project of Israeli nation building, the struggle over planning in Halisa was of particular importance. Neighbourhood residents and activists, Arabs and Jews, aided by activists and actors from the city and beyond it, were quickly able to develop into a more proactive coalition. Their protests resulted in the mayor's decision to delay the demolition and the implementation of the plan and to reopen the process to further consultation. The coalition moved rather swiftly from protest activities to proactive engagement in the planning process, and with the help of expert non-governmental organisations were able to prepare and present a comprehensive alternative plan for the neighbourhood, emphasising community integrity, housing conditions, socioeconomic challenges and participatory governance mechanisms. What started as a confrontation involving radicalised discourses about the collapse of the Haifa model seemed to have come full circle to a reassertion of the extent to which the Haifa polity of minority accommodation could claim distinctiveness.

The difference between HADASH and BALAD also expressed itself behind the veils of a collective struggle. While HADASH attempted to reassert itself as a mediating party between local residents and the city's officials, BALAD sought no such role. In contrast, it highlighted its position as representative of elements of the community vis-à-vis the machinery of local government. Conscious of its position – cementing a coalition of resistance on the one hand and wanting to retain its

legitimacy as an actor with which the state and other political actors
might engage on the other – its activists exhibited the double-bind
dilemma of radicalism and co-optation, as one of them claimed:

We're not interested in becoming the City establishment's representatives in
dealing with the residents. We're only the residents' representatives vis-à-vis
the City Council. It is a struggle ... all this attempt of the City to make use
of us, even when the intentions are good ... but our loyalty is only to the
city residents that we actually represent. We're not a linking 'chain' [which
was the situation previously].... We take a part in this struggle. We're a side
in this struggle.... We are with the people, with the Arab citizens of this city,
with the underprivileged.... I am not prepared to compromise on this, and
am not prepared to contain myself with small and cosmetic things.

At the same time, the same activist indicated that there was in the end
a return to those discursive constructions that even in the midst of
conflict, with its radicalised rhetoric and action, mediated expectations
and actions:

I know that if I should continue to live in this country, there's nowhere else
but Haifa.... And you know what? The struggle is more interesting in Haifa,
because I knew when we were sitting in Halisa that they wouldn't dare to
use bulldozers.... I mean, I took it into account, but this is Haifa! I kept
telling them: 'this is Haifa guys, they'll be afraid [to use bulldozers].' That
is, even the nature of the struggle here is more effective and more satisfying,
because you can be somewhere else all your life and achieve nothing. In
Haifa you feel that you can achieve ... and it's possible to change things....
Always too little and not enough.... But, somehow, there is some horizon
that you can see; there's a place where you can do things. This is Haifa.

The neighbourhood conflict in a sense crystallised the dilemma associated with the complexity of collective action in a deprived neighbourhood situated in an ethnically fractured city within a deeply divided
society. Radicalism would entail challenging the foundations of the
discourses of co-existence in Haifa, whereas co-option would have
led to falling in line with pre-given sets of norms and expectations.
But the dynamics of neighbourhood mobilisation and ethnic movement collective action are never likely to fall into a crude dichotomy.
Rather, the logic of coalition building in urban politics – the leading
property of regime governance – enables actors to move between and

intermingle radical action with more pragmatic steps. The imperative of coalition politics, especially from the point of view of marginalised groups, necessitates a more consensual approach at the same time that it, in fact, enables some activists to rely on coalition resources to voice more radical options. In this sense, neighbourhood mobilisation is rarely merely about the artificially constructed boundaries of the neighbourhood, but about the interweaving of neighbourhood, city and nation.

Conclusion

As we discuss, narrate and invent new ideas about democracy and citizenship in cities, it is critical to avoid ... the local trap, in which the local scale is assumed to be inherently more democratic than other scales. (Purcell 2006, 1921)

It would be tempting to simply conclude that the development of a discursive incorporation regime in Haifa has involved a dominating (hegemonic, for some) discourse of 'co-existence' and difference, supported by agents of the state and popular storytelling, and that social, community and political activism as expressed by the Palestinian political elite of the city has followed suit, 'convincing' itself and others of the cohesiveness of the Haifa model. In short, that the dominant model has been that of co-optation.

The argument is, however, more complicated than that. Griggs, Norval and Wagenaar, in the Introduction to this book, stress that a theory of decentred governance puts a premium on its practical, situated nature. As they argue, 'on the ground' (and in our case, in Haifa's neighbourhoods), it is above all a whirl of organisational routines, practical judgements, subjective voices, personal histories and improvisational practices.

In the city of Haifa, we have seen that it is the construction of a discursive political terrain, while creating certain patterns of obedience, of 'walking the line', that has served to create an opportunity structure towards which counter-hegemonic and resistance strategies could be identified. It is the complex nature of identity politics, perhaps even more so at the local level, which works to create unexpected and diverse outcomes; just at the moments when certain regimes of minority incorporation are constructed, the relational dynamics of the politics of citizenship and claim making highlight different shades of political projects.

Purcell (2001) has argued that neighbourhood activism should be seen as a multilayered political project. It is rarely that one variable – whether ethnicity, race, gender, sexuality, demography or class – can fully account for the actions of actors. Rather, neighbourhood activism is generated through and acted on an interrelated set of circumstances and constraints. Resurgent citizenship captures some of the nuances of the political projects associated with such local activism. But such projects should be understood as taking place in the context of a constant and shifting dialogue between the neighbourhood and its identities, the wider city and its projected images, and the nation-state which embodies an ethno-national territorial conflict. The politics of place in neighbourhoods is therefore, in a sense, a node in a network of multiple and at times conflicting projects of identity formation (May 1996).

In Haifa, such interconnections demonstrate how localised mobilisation in effect articulates both civic discourses of citizenship (social and civil rights) with more radical discourses of collective ethno-national identities and counter-hegemonic agendas involved in the politics of nationhood and memory. While the city's civic institutions have constructed a regime based on weak policy capacity and strong symbolic elements, it was this project that became the opportunity structure against which some actors mobilised. The intricacies of inter-minority political dynamics and rivalries are also an important element in this story, and evidence from other contexts suggests that these are important elements in understanding the collective action of minority politics in cities (Bousetta 2000).

As Table 11.1 shows, the combination of regime features and symbolic elements creates a way through which one can identity spheres within which local politics makes a difference, for better or worse (for instance, in the comparison between formal policy capacity, leadership qualities and the nature of public discourse). This is significant from a normative point of view. The expansion of progressive politics requires a local political project that is interwoven into national and transnational campaigns. By systematically controlling for those variables which account for the production of different political spaces (hence the fruitfulness of the 'politics of place' approach), the prospects for and constraints on progressive politics become more apparent.

Table 11.1. *The Constitution of Ethnic Politics Between the National and the Local: The 'Haifa Model' within the Israeli Context – Citizenship beyond the Nation-State?*

	National features: Israel	Local dynamics: Haifa
Institutional formations	Systematic exclusion of 'Arab' parties from governing coalitions	Formal and informal inclusion of Arab parties and actors in governing arrangements, including more radical elements; 'unthinkable coalitions'
Leadership apparatus	Divide and rule with periodic gestures	Attempts at co-optation; active intervention
Citizenship regime	Ethnocracy or an ethnic democracy	More fluid, episodic and spatial mixture of ethnocracy, liberal rights discourse, ethno-cultural/ national recognition, accompanied by discursive construction of specific neighbourhoods
Recognition of Palestinian ethno- nationhood	Limited to cultural features (e.g. educational system; Arabic-language signs; freedom of religion)	Discursive recognition of difference; framing of 'co-existence'
Territorial policy discourse	Judaisation; explicit territorial control and contestation	Mixture of 'liberal' planning and Judaisation by stealth
Israeli-Palestinian mobilisation	Party politics, protest, civil society, engagement and non-engagement	Party politics paramount; strong engagement with local state institutions; co-optation with undercurrents of radicalism

Finally, several questions seem to warrant elaboration by future research into the potentially constitutive geopolitical role that such ethnically fractured cities play. For instance, does minority politics tend to gravitate towards a model which mixes radical discourses with pragmatic dispositions and practices? Secondly, the search for coalition building seems to be an almost unmitigated imperative from the point of view of contemporary result-driven urban politics. Here I draw attention to the gulf between radicalised political discourse and pragmatic political action: if radical political representatives wish to achieve recognition and claim representation, then they are confronted with the dilemma of how to reach, or at least represent, outcomes and achievements. In the final analysis, does the urban political arena makes the virtues of pragmatism and the construction of 'unthinkable coalitions' more plausible?

Acknowledgements

The research which led to the writing of this chapter was funded by two Economic and Social Research Council (ESRC) grants: The Territorial Politics of Citizenship in Israel's Fractured Communities, grant number: RES-000–22–0894; and Planning Advocacies and Communicative Politics in Israel/Palestine, grant number: RES-155–25–0018. The financial support of the ESRC is gratefully acknowledged.

Bibliography

Afouxenidis, A. 2006. Urban social movements in Southern European cities: reflections on Toni Negri's The mass and the metropolis. *City* 20: 287–93.

Agger, A., and Löfgren, K. 2008. Democratic assessment of collaborative planning processes. *Planning Theory* 7(2): 145–64.

America Speaks. 2009. *Unified New Orleans Plan: How Large-Scale Citizen Engagement Laid the Foundation for Success*. americaspeaks.org/index.cfm?fuseaction=Page.viewPage&pageId=621&parentID=499&grandparentID=4&nodeID=1. Accessed 20 October 2009.

Amin, A. 2002. Ethnicity and the multicultural city: living with diversity. *Environment and Planning A* 34(6): 959–80.

Amin, A., Cameron, A., and Hudson, R. 2002. *Placing the Social Economy*. London: Routledge.

Ansell, C.K. 2011. *Pragmatist Democracy. Evolutionary Learning as Public Philosophy*. Oxford: Oxford University Press.

Ansell, C., and Gingrich, J. 2003a. Trends in Decentralization, in B.E. Cain, R.J. Dalton and S.E. Scarrow (eds.), *Democracy Transformed? Expanding Political Opportunities in Advanced Industrial Democracies*. Oxford: Oxford University Press, 140–63.

2003b. Reforming the Administrative State, in B.E. Cain, R.J. Dalton and S.E. Scarrow (eds.), *Democracy Transformed? Expanding Political Opportunities in Advanced Industrial Democracies*. Oxford: Oxford University Press, 164–91.

Archibugi, D., Held, D., and Kohler, M. (eds.) 1998. *Re-imagining Political Communities: Studies in Cosmopolitan Citizenship*. Cambridge: Polity Press.

Armony, A. 2004. *The Dubious Link: Civic Engagement and Democratization*. Stanford, CA: Stanford University Press.

Arnstein, S. 1969. A ladder of citizen participation. *Journal of the American Institute of Planners* 35(4): 216–25.

Atkinson, R. 1999. Discourses of partnership and empowerment in contemporary British urban regeneration. *Urban Studies* 36(1): 59–72.

Avritzer, L. 2009. *Participatory Institutions in Democratic Brazil*. Baltimore: John Hopkins University Press.

Axelrod, R., and Cohen, M. 1999. *Harnessing Complexity. Organizational Implications of a Scientific Frontier*. New York: Free Press.

Bache, I., and Flinders, M. (eds.) 2004. *Multi-level Governance*. Oxford: Oxford University Press.

Baggini, J. 2007. *Welcome to Everytown: A Journey into the English Mind*. London: Granta.

Bagguley, P., and Hussain, Y. 2006. Conflict and Cohesion: Official Constructions of 'Community' around the 2001 'Riots' in Britain, in S. Herbrechter and M. Higgins (eds.), *Returning (to) Communities. Theory, Culture and Political Practice of the Communal*. Amsterdam: Rodopi, 347–65.

Balibar, E. 1995. Is European Citizenship Possible? in J. Holston (ed.), *Cities and Citizenship*. Durham, NC: Duke University Press, 195–216.

Ball, R., and Piper, N. 2002. Globalisation and regulation of citizenship – Filipino migrant workers in Japan. *Political Geography* 21: 1013–34.

Bang, H. 2003. A New Ruler Meeting a New Citizen: Culture Governance and Everyday Making, in H. Bang (ed.), *Governance as Social and Political Communication*. Manchester: Manchester University Press, 241–66.

2004. Culture governance: governing self-reflexive modernity. *Public Administration* 80(2): 301–22.

2005. Among Everyday Makers and Expert Citizens, in J. Newman (ed.), *Remaking Governance. Peoples, Politics and the Public Sphere*. Bristol: The Policy Press, 159–78.

Barber, B. 1984. *Strong Democracy: Participatory Politics for a New Age*. Los Angeles: University of California Press.

Barnes, M., Newman, J., and Sullivan, H. 2007. *Power, Participation and Political Renewal: Case Studies in Public Participation*. Bristol: The Policy Press.

Barnes, M., and Prior, D. 2009. 'Examining the idea of "subversion" in public services', in M. Barnes and D. Prior (eds.), *Subversive Citizens: Power, Agency and Resistance in Public Services*. Bristol: The Policy Press, 3–16.

Barnes, M., Skelcher, C., Beirens, H., Dalziel, R., Jeffares, S., and Wilson, L. 2008. *Designing Citizen-Centred Governance: A Review of the Opportunities and Challenges of Citizen-Centred Governance*. York: Joseph Rowntree Foundation.

Barrett, F. 1998. Creativity and improvisation in jazz and organizations: implications for organizational learning. *Organization Science* 9(5): 605–22.

2007. 'Cultivating Transformative Collaboration: Actionable Knowledge as Aesthetic Achievement' in S.K. Piderit, R.E. Fry and D.L. Cooperrider (eds.), *A Handbook for Transformative Cooperation: New Designs and Dynamics*. Palo Alto, CA: Stanford University Press, 388–417.

2012. *Yes to the Mess: Surprising Leadership Lessons from Jazz.* Cambridge, MA: Harvard Business School Press.

Bauböck, R. 1994. *Transnational Citizenship.* Brookfield: Edward Elgar.

Beall, J., Crankshaw, O., and Parnell, S. 2002. *Uniting a Divided City: Governance and Social Exclusion in Johannesburg.* London: Earthscan.

Beaumont, J., and Nicholls, W. 2008. Plural governance, participation and democracy in cities. *International Journal of Urban and Regional Research* 32(1): 87–94.

Beck, U. 1997. *The Reinvention of Politics: Rethinking Modernity in the Global Social Order.* Translated by M. Ritter. Cambridge: Polity Press.

Beetham, D. 1991. *The Legitimation of Power.* Basingstoke: Macmillan.

1996. Theorising Democracy and Local Government, in D. King and G. Stoker (eds.), *Rethinking Local Democracy.* Basingstoke: Macmillan, 28–49.

Behn, R.D. 2001. *Rethinking Democratic Accountability.* Washington, DC: The Brookings Institution.

Bekkers, V., Dijkstra, G., Edwards, A., and Fenger, M. (eds.) 2007. *Governance and the Democratic Deficit: Assessing the Democratic Legitimacy of Governance Practices.* Aldershot: Ashgate.

Bell, D., and Binnie, J. 2006. Geographies of sexual citizenship. *Political Geography* 25: 869–73.

Bell, S., and Hindmoor, A. 2009. *Rethinking Governance. The Centrality of the State in Modern Society.* Cambridge: Cambridge University Press.

Bellamy, R., and Palumbo, A. 2010. *From Government to Governance.* Farnham: Ashgate.

Benz, A., and Papadopoulos, Y. 2006. *Governance and Democracy: Comparing National, European and International Experience.* London: Routledge.

Berger, P., and Luckman, T. 1967. *The Social Construction of Reality.* Garden City, NY: Doubleday.

van den Berghe, P.L. 2002. Multicultural democracy: can it work? *Nations and Nationalism* 8(4): 433–49.

Bernstein, S. 2004. *The Elusive Basis of Legitimacy in Global Governance: Three Conceptions.* Hamilton, Ontario: Institute for Globalization and the Human Condition, McMaster University.

Beunderman, J., van der Heijden, J., and Specht, M. 2012. *Meebewegen met de burger Tien acties voor de nieuwe regering.* The Hague: Ministerie van Binnenlandse Zaken en Koninkrijksrelaties.

Bevir, M. 2003. A Decentred Theory of Governance, in H. Bang (ed.), *Governance as Social and Political Communication.* Manchester: Manchester University Press, 200–21.

2010. *Democratic Governance*. Princeton, NJ: Princeton University Press.

2011. Governance and governmentality after neoliberalism. *Policy & Politics* 39(4): 457–71.

Bevir, M., and Rhodes, R. 2003. *Interpreting British Governance*. London: Routledge.

Bevir, M., and Rhodes, R. 2006. *Governance Stories*. London: Routledge.

Bevir, M., and Rhodes, R. 2010. *The State as Cultural Practice*. Oxford: Oxford University Press.

Bialik, R. (ed.) 2003. Introduction to Haifa Municipality in *Mediterranean*. Haifa: Beit Hagefen and the Haifa Arts Foundation.

Blanco, I., Lowndes, V., and Pratchett, L. 2011. Policy networks and governance networks: towards greater conceptual clarity. *Political Studies Review* 9(3): 297–308.

Blank, Y. 2004. The localisation of the 'local': local government law, decentralisation and territorial inequality in Israel. *Mishpatim* 34: 197–300 (in Hebrew).

Blondeel, P. 2004. *'Als het werkt, komt de samenhang vanzelf'. Hoe Burgers Omgaan met Wat Niet Verandert en Wat Steden Daarmee Kunnen*. The Hague: Residents 4 Regeneration.

Bobbio, N. 1987. *The Future of Democracy: A Defence of the Rules of the Game*. Minneapolis: University of Minnesota Press.

Bohman, J. 1996. Critical Theory and Democracy, in D.M. Rasmussen (ed.), *Handbook of Critical Theory*. Oxford: Blackwell, 190–219.

1997. Deliberative Democracy and Effective Social Freedom: Capabilities, Resources, and Opportunities, in J. Bohman, and W. Rehg (eds.), *Deliberative Democracy*. Cambridge, MA: The MIT Press, 321–48.

1999. Citizenship and norms of publicity. Wide public reason in cosmopolitan societies. *Political Theory* 27(2): 176–202.

2007. *Democracy across Borders: From Dêmos to Dêmoi*. Cambridge, MA: The MIT Press.

Bourdieu, P. 1977. *Outline of a Theory of Practice*. Cambridge: Cambridge University Press.

Bourgon, J. 2011. *A New Synthesis of Public Administration. Serving in the 21st Century*. Montreal: McGill-Queen's University Press.

Bousetta, H. 2000. Institutional theories of immigrant ethnic mobilisation: relevance and limitations. *Journal of Ethnic and Migration Studies* 26: 229–45.

Boyte, H.C. 2004. *Everyday Politics. Reconnecting Citizens and Public Life*. Philadelphia, PA: University of Pennsylvania Press.

Brenner, N. 1999. Globalisation as territorialisation: the rescaling of urban governance in the European Union. *Urban Studies* 36: 431–51.

Brown, L.D. (ed.) 2001. *Practice Research Engagement and Civil Society in a Globalizing World*. Cambridge, MA and Washington, DC: Hauser Center for Nonprofit Organizations and CIVICUS.

Brugnoli, A., and Colombo, A. 2012. Introduction, in A. Brugnoli and A. Colombo (eds.), *Government, Governance and Welfare Reform. Structural Changes and Subsidiarity in Italy and Britain*. Cheltenham: Edward Elgar, ix–xii.

Bullard, R. D., Johnson, G. S., and Torres, A.O. (eds.) 2000. *Sprawl City: Race, Politics, and Planning in Atlanta*. Washington, DC: Island Press.

Burnett, J. 2008. Community Cohesion in Bradford: Neoliberal Integrationism, in J. Flint and D. Robinson (eds.), *Community Cohesion in Crisis? New Dimensions of Diversity and Difference*. Bristol: The Policy Press, 35–56.

Butler, J. *Excitable Speech*. London: Routledge 1997.

Cain, B.E., Dalton, R.J., and Scarrow, S.E. (eds.) 2003a. *New Forms of Democracy? The Reform and Transformation of Democratic Institutions*. Oxford: Oxford University Press.

Cain, B.E., Dalton, R. J., and Scarrow, S.E. 2003b. *Democracy Transformed? Expanding Political Opportunities in Advanced Industrial Democracies*. Oxford: Oxford University Press.

Cain, B.E., Fabrinni, S., and Egan, P. 2003c. Toward More Open Democracies: The Expansion of Freedom of Information Laws, in B.E. Cain, R.J. Dalton and S.E. Scarrow (eds.), *Democracy Transformed? Expanding Political Opportunities in Advanced Industrial Democracies*. Oxford: Oxford University Press, 115–39.

Campbell, H. 2005. Interface: the darker side of local communities: is this the real world of planning? *Planning Theory and Practice* 6(4): 517–19.

Campbell, H., and Marshall, R. 2000. Public involvement in planning: looking beyond the one to the many. *International Planning Studies* 5: 321–44.

Campbell, J. 1995. *Understanding John Dewey: Nature and Cooperative Intelligence*. La Salle, IL: Open Court Publishing.

Cantle, T. 2001. *Community Cohesion: A Report of the Independent Review Team*. London: Home Office.

Castells, M. 1983. *The City and the Grassroots*. London: Edward Arnold.

Cavell, S. 1990. *Conditions Handsome and Unhandsome*. Chicago: University of Chicago Press.

1992. *The Claim of Reason*. Oxford: Oxford University Press.

de Certeau, M. 1984. *The Practice of Everyday Life*. Berkeley, CA: The University of California Press.

Chambers, S. 1996. *Reasonable Democracy: Jürgen Habermas and the Politics of Discourse*. Ithaca, NY: Cornell University Press.

2009. Rhetoric in the public sphere: has deliberative democracy abandoned mass democracy? *Political Theory* 37(3): 323–50.

Chandler, D. 2001. Active citizens and the therapeutic state: the role of democratic participation in local government reform. *Policy & Politics* 29: 3–14.

Chatterjee, P. 2006. *The Politics of the Governed: Reflections on Popular Politics in Most of the World*. New York: Columbia University Press.

Checkel, J. 2001. Why comply? Social learning and European identity change. *International Organization* 55(3): 553–88.

Chhotray, V., and Stoker, G. 2009. *Governance Theory and Practice*. Basingstoke: Palgrave Macmillan.

Cichowksi, R., and Stone Sweet, A. 2003. Participation, Representation, and the Courts, in B.E. Cain, R.J. Dalton and S.E. Scarrow (eds.), *Democracy Transformed? Expanding Political Opportunities in Advanced Industrial Democracies*. Oxford: Oxford University Press, 192–222.

City of Haifa 2006. *Statistical Yearbook*. Haifa: Haifa Municipality.

Clarke, J. 2010. Enrolling ordinary people: governmental strategies and the avoidance of politics? *Citizenship Studies* 14(6): 637–50.

Cohen, J., and Arato, A. 1992. *Civil Society and Political Theory*. Cambridge, MA: The MIT Press.

Connelly, S. 2011. Constructing legitimacy in the new community governance. *Urban Studies* 48(5): 929–46.

Connelly, S., Richardson, T., and Miles, T. 2006. Situated legitimacy: deliberative arenas and the new rural governance. *Journal of Rural Studies* 22(3): 267–77.

Connolly, W. 1991. *Identity/Difference: Democratic Negotiations of Political Paradox*. Ithaca, NY: Cornell University Press.

1993. Beyond good and evil: the ethical sensibility of Michel Foucault. *Political Theory* 21(3): 365–89.

1995. *The Ethos of Pluralization*. Minneapolis: University of Minnesota Press.

1999. *Why I Am Not a Secularist*. Minneapolis: University of Minnesota Press.

2005. *Pluralism*. Durham, NC: Duke University Press.

2011. *A World of Becoming*. Durham, NC: Duke University Press.

Cook, S., and Wagenaar, H. 2012. Navigating the eternally unfolding present. Towards an epistemology of practice. *American Review of Public Administration* 42(1): 3–38.

Cooper, D. 2006. Active citizenship and the governmentality of local lesbian and gay politics. *Political Geography* 25: 921–43.

Corbridge, S., Williams, G., Srivastava, M., and Véron, R. 2005. *Seeing the State. Governance and Governmentality in India*. Cambridge: Cambridge University Press.

Corburn, J. 2005. *Street Science: Community Knowledge and Environmental Health Justice*. Cambridge, MA: The MIT Press.

Cornwall, A., and Coelho, V.S. 2006. Spaces for Change? The Politics of Participation in New Democratic Arenas, in C. Cornwall and V.S. Coelho (eds.), *Spaces for Change? The Politics of Citizen Participation in New Democratic Arenas*. London: Zed, 1–32.

Council of Europe. 1949. *Statute of the Council of Europe*. ETS-001. Available at conventions.coe.int/treaty/en/treaties/html/001.htm. Accessed 3 January 2014.

Crossley, N. 2003. From reproduction to transformation: social movement fields and the radical habitus. *Theory, Culture and Society* 20(6): 43–68.

Crozier, M., Huntington, S. P., and Watanuki, J. 1975. *The Crisis of Democracy: Report on the Governability of Democracies to the Trilateral Commission*. New York: New York University Press.

Cutler, F., and Fournier, P. 2007. Why Ontarians Said No to MMP. *Globe and Mail*. 25 October.

Dahl, R. 1961. *Who Governs? Democracy and Power in an American City*. New Haven, CT: Yale University Press.

Dahl, R., and Tufte, E. 1973. *Size and Democracy*. Stanford, CA: Stanford University Press.

Dalton, R.J. 2007. *The Good Citizen: How a Younger Generation is Reshaping American Politics*. Washington, DC: CQ Press.

Dalton, R.J., Cain, B.E., and Scarrow, S.E. 2003. Democratic Publics and Democratic Institutions, in B.E. Cain, R.J. Dalton and S.E. Scarrow (eds.), *New Forms of Democracy? The Reform and Transformation of Democratic Institutions*. Oxford: Oxford University Press, 250–75.

Damgaard, B., and Torfing, J. 2011. The impact of metagovernance on local governance networks. Lessons from Danish employment policy. *Local Government Studies* 37(3): 291–316

Davis, J.E. 1991. *Contested Ground: Collective Action and the Urban Neighbourhood*. Ithaca, NY: Cornell University Press.

Davies, J.S. 2002. The governance of urban regeneration: a critique of the governing without government thesis. *Public Administration* 80(2): 301–22.
    2007. The limits of partnership: an exit-action strategy for local democratic inclusion. *Political Studies* 55: 779–800.
    2011. *Challenging Governance Theory. From Networks to Hegemony*. Bristol: The Policy Press.

Dean, M. 1999. *Governmentality. Power and Rule in Modern Society*. Thousand Oaks, CA: Sage Publications.
    2003. Culture Governance and Individualization, in H. Bang (ed.), *Governance as Social and Political Communication*. Manchester: Manchester University Press, 117–39.
    2007. *Governing Societies*. Maidenhead: Open University Press.

Denters, B., and Rose, L.E. 2005. Local governance in the third millennium: a brave new world?, in B. Denters, and L.E. Rose (eds.), *Comparing Local Governance*. Basingstoke: Palgrave Macmillan, 1–11.

Derrida, J. 1992. Force of Law: The Mystical Foundation of Authority, in D. Cornell, M. Rosenfeld, and D. Carson (eds.), *Deconstruction and the Possibility of Justice*. London: Routledge, 3–67.

1994. *Spectres of Marx: The State of the Debt, the Work of Mourning and the New International*. New York: Routledge.

DETR 1998. *Modernising Local Government: Local Democracy and Community Leadership*. London: The Stationery Office.

Devlin, R. 2011. Informal urbanism in the USA: new challenges for theory and practice. *Planning Theory and Praxis* 12(1): 144–50.

Dewey, J. 1954 [1927]. *The Public and Its Problems*. Athens, OH: Ohio University Press.

Dietz, T., and Stern, P. 2009. *Public Participation in Environmental Assessment and Decision Making*. Washington, DC: National Academies Press.

Disch, L. 2006. Rethinking 'Re-presentation'. American Political Science Association annual meeting, Philadelphia, 31 August–3 Sept.

Dowding, K. 2001. Explaining urban regimes. *International Journal of Urban and Regional Research* 25: 7–19.

Dryzek, J. 1996. *The Informal Logic of Institutional Design*, in R. Goodin (ed.), *The Theory of Institutional Design*. Cambridge: Cambridge University Press, 103–25.

2000. *Deliberative Democracy and Beyond: Liberals, Critics, Contestations*. Oxford: Oxford University Press.

2001. Legitimacy and economy in deliberative democracy. *Political Theory* 29(5): 651–69.

2007. Networks and Democratic Ideals: Equality, Freedom, and Communication, in E. Sørensen and J. Torfing (eds.), *Theories of Democratic Network Governance*. Basingstoke: Palgrave Macmillan, 262–73.

Dryzek, J.S. 2013. *Foundations and Frontiers of Deliberative Governance*. Oxford: Oxford University Press.

Duiveman, R., Wagenaar, H., and Kruiter, H. 2010. *Wijken in Uitvoering. Onderzoek naar Wijkgerichte Praktijken in Den Haag*. The Hague: Universiteit Leiden- Campus Den Haag.

Durose, C., France, J., Richardson, L., and Lupton, R. 2011. *Towards the 'Big Society': What Role for Neighbourhood Working? Evidence from a Comparative European Study*. London: CASE at the LSE.

Edelenbos, J. 2005. Institutional implications of interactive governance: insights from Dutch practice. *Governance* 18(1): 111–34.

Ehrkamp, P., and Leitner, H. 2003. Beyond national citizenship: Turkish immigrants and the (re)construction of citizenship in Germany. *Urban Geography* 24:127–46.

Elkin, S. 1987. *City and Regime in the American Republic*. Chicago: University of Chicago Press.

Esmark, A. 2007. Democratic Accountability and Network Governance – Problems and Potentials, in E. Sørensen, and J. Torfing (eds.), *Theories of Democratic Network Governance*. Basingstoke: Palgrave Macmillan, 274–96.

Etzioni-Halevy, E. 1993. *The Elite Connection: Problems and Potential of Western Democracy*. Cambridge: Polity Press.

Fagotto, E., and Fung, A. 2006. Empowered participation in urban governance: the Minneapolis neighbourhood revitalisation program. *International Journal of Urban and Regional Research* 30: 638–55.

Fainstein, S. 2010. *The Just City*. Ithaca, NY: Cornell University Press.

Falah, G. 1997. Ethnic perceptual differences of housing and neighbourhood quality in mixed Arab-Jewish cities in Israel. *Environment and Planning A* 29: 1663–74.

Falah, G., Hoy, M., and Sarker, R. 2000. Co-existence in selected Arab-Jewish cities in Israel: by choice or by default? *Urban Studies* 37(4): 775–96.

Farley, R., Danziger, S., and Holzer, H. 2000. *Detroit Divided*. New York: Russell Sage Foundation.

Finer, S. 1970. *Comparative Government*. London: Allen Lane.

Finnemore, M., and Sikkink, K. 1998. International norm dynamic and political change. *International Organization* 52(4): 887–917.

Fischer, F. 2003. *Reframing Public Policy: Discursive Politics and Deliberative Practices*. Oxford: Oxford University Press.

2009. *Democracy and Expertise: Reorienting Policy Inquiry*. Oxford: Oxford University Press.

Fishkin, J. 2009. *When the People Speak: Deliberative Democracy and Public Consultation*. Oxford: Oxford University Press.

Fishkin, J., and Laslett, P. 2003. *Debating Deliberative Democracy*. Oxford: Blackwell.

Flinders, M. 2004. Distributed public governance in Britain. *Public Administration* 82(4), 883–909.

Forester, J. 1999. *The Deliberative Practitioner*. Cambridge, MA: The MIT Press.

2008. Are collaboration and participation more trouble than they're worth? Editorial, *Planning Theory and Practice* 9(3): 299–304.

2009. *Dealing with Differences: Dramas of Mediating Public Disputes*. New York: Oxford University Press.

2012a. Learning to improve practice: lessons from practice stories and practitioners' own discourse analyses (or why only the loons show up). *Planning Theory and Practice* **13**(1): 11–26.

2012b. From Good Intentions to a Critical Pragmatism, in R. Weber and R. Crane (eds.), *Handbook of Urban Planning*. New York: Oxford University Press, 285–305.

2013a. On the theory and practice of critical pragmatism: deliberative practice and creative negotiations. *Planning Theory* **12**(1): 5–22.

2013b. *Planning in the Face of Conflict: Surprising Possibilities of Facilitative Leadership*. Chicago: American Planning Association Press.

Fossen, T. 2008. Agonistic critiques of liberalism: perfectionism and emancipation, *Contemporary Political Theory* **7**: 376–94.

Fotel, T., Sørensen, E., and Torfing, J. 2009. Democratic anchorage of infrastructural governance networks: the case of the Femern Belt Forum. *Planning Theory* **8**(3): 282–308.

Foucault, M. 1983. The Subject and Power, in H. Dreyfus and P. Rabinow (eds.), *Michel Foucault: Beyond Structuralism and Hermeneutics*. Chicago: The University of Chicago Press, 208–26.

Fox, C.J., and Miller, H.T. 1995. *Postmodern Public Administration: Toward Discourse*. Thousand Oaks, CA: Sage.

Fraser, N., and Honneth, A. 2003. *Redistribution or Recognition?* London: Verso.

Frederickson, H.G. 2007. Whatever Happened to Public Administration? Governance, Governance Everywhere, in E. Ferlie, L. Lynn Jr. and C. Pollitt (eds.), *The Oxford Handbook of Public Management*. Oxford: Oxford University Press, 282–304.

Fuller, C., and Geddes, M. 2008. Urban governance under neoliberalism: New Labour and the restructuring of state-space. *Antipode* **40**(2): 252–82.

Fung, A. 2003. Survey article: recipes for public spheres: eight institutional design choices and their consequences. *Journal of Political Philosophy* **11**: 338–67.

2004. *Empowered Participation: Reinventing Urban Democracy*. Princeton, NJ: Princeton University Press.

2006. Varieties of participation in complex governance. *Public Administration Review* **66**: 66–75.

2007. Democratic theory and political science: a pragmatic method of constructive engagement. *American Political Science Review* **101**(3):443–58.

2013. The Principle of Affected Interests, in J.H. Nagel and R.M. Smith (eds.), *Representation: Elections and Beyond*. Philadelphia, PA: University of Pennsylvania Press, 236–68.

Fung, A., and Wright, E.O. (eds.) 2003. *Deepening Democracy: Institutional Innovations, Empowered Participatory Governance*. London: Verso.

Gains, F., and Stoker, G. 2008. *How Politics Works: Understanding the New Realities of the Political Process in Public Management*. London: The Work Foundation.

Gans, H. 1982. *Urban Villagers: Group and Class in the Life of Italian-Americans*. New York: The Free Press (2nd revised edition).

Garcia, M. 2006. Citizenship practices and urban governance in European cities. *Urban Studies* 43(4): 745–65.

Gastil, J. 2008. *Political Communication and Deliberation*. Thousand Oaks, CA: Sage.

Geddes, M., and Sullivan, H. 2011. Localities, leadership and neoliberalization: conflicting discourses, competing practices. *Critical Policy Studies* 5(4): 391–413.

Gemeente Den Haag, Dienst O.C.W. 2005. *Maatschappelijke Visie: Mensen Maken de Stad*. The Hague: RIS 132471.

Ghanem, A. 1998. State and minority in Israel: the case of ethnic state and the predicament of its minority. *Ethnic and Racial Studies* 21(3): 428–48.

Ghosh, S., and Wang, L. 2003. Transnationalism and identity: a tale of two faces and multiple lives. *The Canadian Geographer* 47: 269–82.

Glynos, J., and Howarth, D. 2007. *Logics of Critical Explanation in Social and Political Theory*. London: Routledge.

Goldsmith, S., and Eggers, W.D. 2004. *Governing by Network: The New Shape of the Public Sector*. Washington DC: Brookings Institution Press.

Goodin, R. 1996. Institutions and their Design, in R. Goodin (ed.), *The Theory of Institutional Design*. Cambridge: Cambridge University Press, 1–53.

   2003. *Reflective Democracy*. Oxford: Oxford University Press.

   2007. Enfranchising all affected interests, and its alternatives. *Philosophy and Public Affairs* 35: 40–68.

Goodin, R., and Dryzek, J. 2006. Deliberative impacts: the macro-political uptake of mini-publics. *Politics and Society* 34: 219–44.

Goren, T. 2004. The Judaization of Haifa at the time of the Arab Revolt. *Middle Eastern Studies* 40:135–52.

   2006. Hassan Bey Shukri and his contribution to the integration of Jews in the Haifa municipality at the time of the British Mandate. *British Journal of Middle Eastern Studies* 33: 19–36.

Gormley Jr., W. 1989. *Taming the Bureaucracy: Muscles, Prayers, and Other Strategies*. Princeton, NJ: Princeton University Press.

Greenwood, D.J., and Levin, M. 1998. *Introduction to Action Research: Social Research for Social Change*. Thousand Oaks, CA: Sage.

Griggs, S., and Howarth, D. 2007. Airport Governance, Politics and Protest Networks, in M. Marcussen and J. Torfing (eds.), *Democratic Network Governance in Europe*. Basingstoke: Palgrave Macmillan, 66–88.

2012. Phronesis, Logics, and Critical Policy Analysis: Heathrow's 'Third Runway' and the Politics of Sustainable Aviation in the UK, in B. Flyvbjerg, T. Landman and S. Schram (eds.), *Real Social Science: Applied Phronesis*. Cambridge: Cambridge University Press, 167–203.

2013. *The Politics of Airport Expansion in the United Kingdom. Hegemony, Policy and the Rhetoric of 'Sustainable Aviation'.* Manchester: Manchester University Press.

Griggs, S. and Sullivan, H. (2012) Puzzling agency in centre-local relations: regulatory governance and accounts of change under New Labour. *British Journal of Politics and International Relations*, DOI: 10.1111/j.1467-856X.2012.00544.x.

Grote, J.R., and Gbikpi, B. (eds.) 2002. *Participatory Governance*. Opladen: Lseke and Budrich.

Gutmann, A., and Thompson, D. 2004. *Why Deliberative Democracy?* Princeton, NJ: Princeton University Press.

Habermas, J. 1975. *Legitimation Crisis*. Translated by Thomas McCarthy. Boston: Beacon Press.

1987. *The Theory of Communicative Action. Vol. 2.* Translated by Thomas McCarthy. Boston: Beacon Press.

1989. *The Structural Transformation of the Public Sphere*. Cambridge, MA: The MIT Press.

1997. *Between Facts and Norms. Contributions to a Discourse Theory of Law and Democracy* Translated by W. Rehg. Cambridge: Polity Press.

Häikiö, L. 2007. Expertise, representation and the common good: grounds for legitimacy in the urban governance network. *Urban Studies* **44**(11): 2147–62.

Hajer, M. 1995. *The Politics of Environmental Discourse: Ecological Modernization and the Policy Process*. Oxford: Clarendon Press.

2003. A Frame in the Fields: Policymaking and the Reinvention of Politics, in M. Hajer and H. Wagenaar (eds.), *Deliberative Policy Analysis: Understanding Governance in the Network Society*. Cambridge: Cambridge University Press, 88–110.

Hajer, M., and Kesselring, S. 1999. Democracy in risk society? Learning from the new politics of mobility in Munich. *Environmental Politics* 8(3): 1–23.

Hajer, M., and Versteeg, W. 2005. Performing governance through networks. *European Political Science* 4(3): 340–47.

Hajer, M., and Wagenaar, H. (eds.) 2003. *Deliberative Policy Analysis: Understanding Governance in the Network Society*. Cambridge: Cambridge University Press.

Halpin, T. 2005. Muslim girl wins legal battle over school dress. *The Times*, 3 March.

Hammer, E. 2002. *Stanley Cavell*. Cambridge: Polity.

Hansen, A.D. 2007. Governance networks and participation, in E. Sørensen, and J. Torfing (eds.), *Theories of Democratic Network Governance*. Basingstoke: Palgrave Macmillan, 249–61.

Harding, A. 1995. Elite Theory and Growth Machines, in D. Judge, G. Stoker and H. Wolman (eds.), *Theories of Urban Politics*. Thousand Oaks, CA: Sage, 36–54.

Hawkesworth, M.E. 1988. *Theoretical Issues in Policy Analysis*. Albany: State University of New York Press.

Hay, C. 1998. The Tangled Webs We Weave: The Discourse, Strategy and Practice of Networking, in D. Marsh (ed.), *Comparing Policy Networks*. Buckingham: Open University Press, 33–51.

2007. *Why We Hate Politics*. Cambridge: Polity Press.

He, B. 2006. Participatory and Deliberative Institutions in China, in E. Leib and B. He (eds.), *The Search for Deliberative Democracy in China*. New York: Palgrave Macmillan, 176–96.

He, B., and Warren, M. 2011. Authoritarian deliberation: the deliberative turn in Chinese political development. *Perspectives on Politics* 9: 269–89.

Healey, P. 1997. *Collaborative Planning: Shaping Places in Fragmented Societies*. Basingstoke: Macmillan.

2006. Transforming governance: challenges of institutional adaptation and a new politics of space. *European Planning Studies* 14(3): 299–320.

Heffen, O.V., Kickert, W.J.M., and Thomassen, J.A. (eds.) 2000. *Governance in Modern Society: Effects, Change and Formation of Government Institutions*. Dordrecht: Kluwer Academic Publishers.

Heidegger, M. 1962. *Being and Time*. Oxford: Blackwell.

van der Heijden, J. 2011. *Productie door de Burger. Democratischer dan Volksvertegenwoordiging*. Delft, The Netherlands: Eburon.

Held, D. 1996. *Models of Democracy*. Cambridge: Polity Press (2nd edition).

Hirst, P. 1994. *Associative Democracy: New Forms of Economic and Social Governance*. Cambridge: Polity Press.

2000. Democracy and Governance, in J. Pierre (ed.), *Debating Governance. Authority, Steering, and Democracy*. Oxford: Oxford University Press, 13–35.

Holston, J. 1999. Spaces of Insurgent Citizenship, in J. Holston (ed.), *Cities and Citizenship*. Durham, NC: Duke University Press, 155–73.

2008. *Insurgent Citizenship. Disjunctions of Democracy and Modernity in Brazil*. Princeton, NJ: Princeton University Press.

Honig, B. 2007. Between decision and deliberation: political paradox in democratic theory. *American Political Science Review* 101(1): 1–17.

Hood, C. 1998. *The Art of the State*. Oxford: Clarendon Press.

Hooghe, L. and Marks, G. 2003. Unravelling the central state, but how? Types of multi-level governance. *American Political Science Review* 97(2): 233–43.

Horan, C. 2002. Racializing regime politics. *Journal of Urban Affairs* 24(1): 19–33.

Horta, A.P.B. 2006. Places of resistance: power, spatial discourses and migrant grassroots organizing in the periphery of Lisbon. *City* 10: 269–85.

Howarth, D. 2000. *Discourse*. Buckingham: Open University Press.

2008a. Pluralizing methods: contingency, ethics, and critical explanation. *Working Papers in Ideology and Discourse Analysis*, University of Essex, No. 25 (July).

2008b. Ethos, agonism and populism: William Connolly and the case for radical democracy. *British Journal of Politics and International Relations* 10(2): 171–93.

2009. Policy, discourse and policy: articulating a hegemony approach to critical policy studies. *Critical Policy Studies* 3(3/4), 309–35.

2013. *Poststructuralism and After: Structure, Subjectivity and Power*. London: Palgrave Macmillan.

Howarth, D., and Griggs, S. 2012. Poststructuralist Policy Analysis: Discourse, Hegemony and Critical Explanation, in F. Fischer and H. Gottweis (eds.), *The Argumentative Turn Revisited: Public Policy as Communicative Practice*. Durham, NC: Duke University Press, 305–43.

Howarth, D., and Stavrakakis, Y. 2000. Introducing Discourse Theory and Political Analysis, in D. Howarth, A. Norval and Y. Stavrakakis (eds.), *Discourse Theory and Political Analysis*. Manchester: Manchester University Press, 1–23.

Hussain, Y., and Bagguley, P. 2005. Citizenship, ethnicity and identity: British Pakistanis after the 2001 'riots'. *Sociology* 39(3): 407–25.

Hysing, E. 2009. Governing without government? The private governance of forest certification in Sweden. *Public Administration* 87(2): 312–26.

Inglehart, R., and Welzel, C. 2005. *Modernization, Cultural Change, and Democracy: The Human Development Sequence*. Cambridge: Cambridge University Press.

Innes, J.E., and Booher, D. 2010. *Planning with Complexity: An Introduction to Collaborative Rationality for Public Policy*. London: Routledge.

Isin, E.F. 2000. Governing Cities without Government, in E.F. Isin (ed.), *Democracy, Citizenship and the Global City*. London: Routledge, 148–68.

Isin, E.F., and Wood, P.K. 1999. *Citizenship and Identity*. London: Sage Publications.

Israel Central Bureau of Statistics. 1995. *Population and Housing Census*, Jerusalem: Central Bureau of Statistics.

Jamal, A. 2002. Beyond 'ethnic democracy': state structure, multicultural conflict, and differentiated citizenship in Israel. *New Political Science* 24(3): 411–31.

James, M.R. 2004. *Deliberative Democracy and the Plural Polity*. Lawrence, KS: University Press of Kansas.

Jasper, J.M. 1997. *The Art of Moral Protest. Culture, Biography, and Creativity in Social Movements*. Chicago: The University of Chicago Press.

Jeffares, S., and Skelcher, C. 2011. Democratic subjectivities in network governance: a Q methodology study of English and Dutch public managers. *Public Administration* 89(4): 1253–74.

Jessop, B. 2002. *The Future of the Capitalist State*. Cambridge: Polity Press.
   2003. Governance and Meta-Governance: On Reflexivity, Requisite Variety and Requisite Irony, in H. Bang (ed.), *Governance as Social and Political Communication*. Manchester: Manchester University Press, 101–16.

Joachim, J., Reinalda, B., and Verbeek, B. (eds.) 2008. *International Organisations and Implementation: Enforcers, Managers, Authorities?* Abingdon: Routledge.

Johnson, C., Dowd, T., and Ridgeway, C. 2006. Legitimacy as a social process. *Annual Review of Sociology* 32: 53–78.

Jordan, A. 2001. The European Union: an evolving system of multi-level governance – or government? *Policy & Politics* 29(2): 193–208.

Judge, D. 1995. Pluralism, in D. Judge, G. Stoker and H. Wolman (eds.), *Theories of Urban Politics*. Thousand Oaks, CA: Sage, 13–35.

Kalil, A., Schweingruber, H., Daniel-Echols, M., and Breen, A. 2000. Mother, Worker, Welfare Recipient: Welfare Reform and the Multiple Roles of Low-Income Women, in S. Danziger and A. Chih Lin (eds.), *Coping with Poverty: The Social Contexts of Neighborhood, Work and Family in the African-American Community*. Ann Arbor, MI: University of Michigan Press, 201–24.

Kennett, P., and Forrest, R. 2006. The neighbourhood in a European context. *Urban Studies* 43: 713–18.

Kickert, W.L., Klijn, E-H., and Koppejan, J.F.M. 1997. *Managing Complex Networks: Strategies for the Public Sector.* Thousand Oaks CA: Sage.

Kimmerling, B., and Migdal, J.S. 2003. *The Palestinian People: A History.* London: Harvard University Press.

Kitzhaber, J.A. 1993. Prioritising health services in an era of limits: the Oregon experience. *British Medical Journal* **307**: 373–77.

Klijn, E-H. 2008a. *'It's the Management, Stupid!' On the Importance of Management in Complex Policy Issues.* The Hague: Uitgeverij LEMMA.

2008b. Governance and governance networks in Europe. An assessment of ten years of research on the theme. *Public Management Review* **10**(4): 505–25.

Klijn, E-H., and Koppenjan, J. 2004. *Managing Uncertainties in Networks: A Network Approach to Problem Solving and Decision Making.* London: Routledge.

2012. Governance network theory: past, present and future. *Policy & Politics* **40**(4): 587–606.

Klijn, E-H., and Skelcher, C. 2007. Democracy and governance networks: compatible or not? *Public Administration* **85**(3): 587–608.

Knight, J. 1992. *Institutions and Social Conflict.* Cambridge: Cambridge University Press.

Knodt, M. 2004. International embeddedness of European multi-level governance. *Journal of European Public Policy* **11**(4): 701–19.

Kohn, M. 2000. Language, power, and persuasion: toward a critique of deliberative democracy. *Constellations* **7**(3): 408–29.

Kooiman, J. (ed.) 1993. *Modern Governance: New Government-Society Interaction.* London: Sage.

Kooiman, J. 2000. Societal Governance: Level, Modes and Orders of Social-Political Interaction, in J. Pierre (ed.), *Debating Governance: Authority, Steering and Democracy.* Oxford: Oxford University Press, 138–64.

2003. *Governing as Governance.* London: Sage.

Koppenjan, J., and Klijn, E-H. 2004. *Managing Uncertainties in Networks: A Network Approach to Problem Solving and Decision-Making.* London: Routledge.

Krause, S. 2003. Lady Liberty's allure: political agency, citizenship and the second sex. *Philosophy and Social Criticism* **26**: 1–24.

Krell-Laluhová, Z., and Schneider, S. 2004. Legitimacy and the democratic quality of the political order in Britain, Germany, and Switzerland: A discourse analytical perspective. ECPR Joint Sessions of Workshops, University of Uppsala, Sweden, 13–18 April.

Kruiter, H., van Schijndel, M., and Wagenaar, H. 2010. *Bewonersparticipatie en Veiligheid. Tussen Droom en Daad ....in een Complexe Bestuurlijke Context.* The Hague: Universiteit Leiden – Campus Den Haag.

Laclau, E. 1990. *New Reflections on the Revolution of Our Time*. London: Verso.

1993. Power and Representation, in M. Poster (ed.), *Politics, Theory and Contemporary Culture*. New York: Columbia University Press, 277–96.

1996. *Emacipation(s)*. London: Verso.

2000. Identity and Hegemony: The Role of Universality in the Constitution of Political Logics, in J. Butler, E. Laclau and S. Žižek, *Contingency, Hegemony, Universality. Contemporary Dialogues on the Left*. London: Verso, 44–89.

2005. *On Populist Reason*. London: Verso.

Laclau, E. and Mouffe, C. 1985. *Hegemony and Socialist Strategy. Towards a Radical Democratic Politics*. London: Verso.

Laden, A. 2001. *Reasonably Radical: Deliberative Liberalism and the Politics of Identity*. Ithaca, NY: Cornell University Press.

Larner, W. 2000. Neo-liberalism: policy, ideology and governmentality. *Studies in Political Economy* 63: 5–25.

Latour, B. 2005. *Reassembling the Social: An Introduction to Actor–Network Theory*. Oxford: Oxford University Press.

Law, J. 2007. *Actor Network Theory and Material Semiotics*. Version of 25 April 2007, available at heterogeneities.net/publications/Law2007ANTandMaterialSemiotics.pdf. Accessed 19 November 2012.

2009. *Collateral Realities*. Version of 29 December 2009, available at heterogeneities.net/publications/Law2009CollateralRealities.pdf. Accessed 19 November 2012.

Leach, S., Stewart, J., and Walsh, K. 1994. *The Changing Organisation and Management of Local Government*. Basingstoke: Macmillan.

Lefort, C. 1986. *The Political Forms of Modern Society*. Cambridge: Polity Press.

1981. *L'Invention démocratique*. Paris: Fayard.

Leibovitz, J., and Salmon, S. 1999. 20/20 vision? Interurban competition, crisis, and the politics of downtown development in Cincinnati, Ohio. *Space and Polity* 3: 233–55.

Leontidou, L. 1996. Alternatives to modernism in (Southern) urban theory: exploring in between spaces. *International Journal of Urban and Regional Research* 20(2): 180–97.

2006. Urban social movements: from 'the right to the city' to transnational spatialities and *flaneur* activists. *City* 10(3): 259–68.

Lewis, J. 2011. The future of network governance research: strength in diversity and synthesis. *Public Administration* 89(4), 1221–34.

LGA 2002. *Guidance on Community Cohesion*. London: Local Government Association.

Lin, A.C. 2000. Interpretive Research for Public Policy, in S. Danziger, and A. Chih Lin (eds.), *Coping with Poverty: The Social Contexts of Neighborhood, Work and Family in the African-American Community.* Ann Arbor, MI: University of Michigan Press, 1–27.

Lindblom, C.E. 1965. *The Intelligence of Democracy: Decision Making Through Mutual Adjustment.* New York: The Free Press.

1968. *The Policy-Making Process.* New York: Prentice Hall.

1977. *Politics and Markets. The World's Political-Economic Systems.* New York: Basic Books.

2002. *The Market System: What It Is, How It Works, and What to Make of It.* New Haven, CT: Yale University Press.

Lipsky, M. 1980. *Street-level Bureaucracy. Dilemmas of the Individual in Public Services.* New York: Russell Sage Foundation.

Locality 2011. *Development Trusts.* London: Locality. Available at http://locality.org.uk/members/development-trusts/. Accessed 30 March 2012.

Lombard, M., and Huxley, M. 2011. Self-made cities: ordinary informality? *Planning Theory and Praxis* **12**(1): 120–25.

Lowndes, V. 2001. Rescuing Aunt Sally: taking institutional theory seriously in urban politics. *Urban Studies* **38**(11): 1953–71.

2005. Something old, something new, something borrowed…How institutions change (and stay the same) in local governance. *Policy Studies* **26**(3/4): 291–309.

Lowndes, V., and Roberts, M. 2013. *Why Institutions Matter: The New Institutionalism in Political Science.* Basingstoke: Palgrave Macmillan.

Lowndes, V., and Sullivan, H. 2004. Like a horse and carriage or a fish and a bicycle: how well do local partnerships and public participation go together? *Local Government Studies* **30**(1): 51–73.

2008. How low can you go? Rationales and challenges for neighbourhood governance. *Public Administration* **86**(1): 53–74.

Lowndes, V., and Wilson, D. 2003. Balancing revisability and robustness? A new institutionalist perspective on local government modernization. *Public Administration* **81**(2): 275–98.

Lukes, S. 1974. *Power: A Radical View.* Basingstoke: Macmillan.

Macedo, S. 2005. *Democracy at Risk. How Political Choices Undermine Citizen Participation, and What We Can Do About It.* Washington, DC: Brookings Institution Press.

Mackenzie, M., and Warren, M. 2012. Two Trust-Based Uses of Minipublics in Democratic Systems, in J. Mansbridge and J. Parkinson (eds.), *Deliberative Systems.* Cambridge: Cambridge University Press, 95–124.

MacLeod, G., and Goodwin, M. 1999. Space, scale and state strategy: rethinking urban and regional governance. *Progress in Human Geography* **24**: 503–27.

Macpherson, C.B. 1977. *The Life and Times of Liberal Democracy*. Oxford: Oxford University Press.

Mandell, M. 2008. Understanding the realities of collaborative networks in the United States, in M. Considine and S. Giguère (eds.), *The Theory and Practice of Local Governance and Economic Development*. Basingstoke: Palgrave Macmillan, 63–79.

Manin, B. 1997. *The Principles of Representative Government*. Cambridge: Cambridge University Press.

Mann, M. 1970. The social cohesion of liberal democracy. *American Sociological Review* 35(3): 423–39.

March, J.G., and Olsen, J.P. 1989. *Rediscovering Institutions. The Organisational Basis of Politics*. New York: The Free Press.

1995. *Democratic Governance*. New York: The Free Press.

Marcussen, M., and Torfing, J. (eds.) 2007. *Democratic Network Governance in Europe*. Basingstoke: Palgrave Macmillan.

Marin, B., and Mayntz, R. (eds.) 1991. *Policy Networks: Empirical Evidence and Theoretical Considerations*. Manheim: Campus Verlag.

Marsh, D. (ed.) 1998. *Comparing Policy Networks*. Buckingham: Open University Press.

Marsh, D., and Rhodes, R. (eds.) 1992. *Policy Networks in British Government*. Oxford: Clarendon Press.

Marsh, D., Richards, S., and Smith, M. 2003. Unequal plurality: Towards an asymmetric power model of British politics. *Government and Opposition* 38(3): 306–22.

Mason, A. 2010. Rawlsian theory and the circumstances of politics, *Political Theory* 38(5): 658–83.

Mathews, D. 1999. *Politics for People: Finding a Responsible Public Voice*. Urbana, IL: University of Illinois Press.

May, J. 1996. Globalisation and the politics of place: place and identity in an inner London neighbourhood. *Transactions of the Institute of British Geographers* 21: 194–215.

Mayer, I., Edelenbos, J., and Monnikhof, R. 2005. Interactive policy development: undermining or sustaining democracy. *Public Administration* 83(1), 179–99.

Mayer, M. 2003. The onward sweep of social capital: causes and consequences for understanding cities, communities and urban movements. *International Journal of Urban and Regional Research* 27(1): 110–32.

Maynard-Moody, S., and Musheno, M. 2003. *Cops, Teachers, Counselors, Stories from the Front Lines of Public Service*. Ann Arbor, MI: The University of Michigan Press.

Mayntz, R. 1991. Modernization and the Logic of Inter-Organisational Networks, Discussion Paper, Max-Planck Institut für Gesellschaftsforschung: European Centre for Social Welfare Policy and Research, 91/8.

McGoldrich, D. 2006. *Human Rights and Religion: The Islamic Headscarf Debate in Europe*. Oxford: Hart.

Melo, M.A., and Baiocchi, G. 2006. Deliberative democracy and local governance: towards a new agenda. *International Journal of Urban and Regional Research* 30: 587–600.

Meth, P. 2010. Unsettling insurgency: reflections on women's insurgent practices in South Africa. *Planning Theory and Praxis* 11(2): 241–63.

Milewa, T. 2004. Local participatory democracy in Britain's health service: innovation or fragmentation of a universal citizenship? *Social Policy and Administration* 38: 240–52.

Mill, J. 1937. *An Essay on Government*. Cambridge: Cambridge University Press.

Miller, H.T. 2012. *Governing Narratives: Symbolic Politics and Policy Change*. Tuscaloosa, AL: University of Alabama Press.

Milward, H.B., and Provan, K.G. 2000. Governing the hollow state. *Journal of Public Administration Research and Theory* 10(2): 359–79.

Mitzna, A. 2003. Mayor of Haifa introduction, in Haifa Municipality, in *Mediterranean*. Haifa: Beit Hagefen and the Haifa Arts Foundation, 2.

Mo, Y., and Chen, Y. 2005. *Democratic Deliberation: The Innovation from Wenling*. Beijing: Central Compliance and Translation Press.

Moran, M. 2003. *The British Regulatory State. High Modernism and Hyper-Innovation*. Oxford: Oxford University Press.

2010. Policy-Making in an Interdependent World, in C. Hay (ed.), *New Directions in Political Science*. Basingstoke: Palgrave Macmillan, 25–42.

Morris, B. 2002. *The Birth of the Palestinian Refugee Problems, 1947–1949*. Tel Aviv, Israel: Am Oved Press (in Hebrew).

Mossberger, K., and Stoker, G. 2001. The evolution of urban regime theory: the challenges of conceptualization. *Urban Affairs Review* 36: 810–35.

Mouffe, C. 1993. *The Return of the Political*. London: Verso.

2000. *The Democratic Paradox*. London: Verso.

2005. *On the Political*. London: Routledge.

Mulhall, C. 1994. *Stanley Cavell*. Oxford: Oxford University Press.

Nations and Nationalism. 2002. Special issue: Types of Democracy and Conflict Management in Ethnically Divided Societies, 8(4).

Newman, J. 2005. Participative governance and the remaking of the public sphere, in J. Newman (ed.), *Remaking Governance: Peoples, Politics and the Public Sphere*. Bristol: The Polity Press, 119–38.

Newton, K. 1982. Is small really so beautiful? Is big really so ugly? Size, effectiveness, and democracy in local government. *Political Studies* 30(2): 203.

2008. Trust and Politics, in D. Castiglione, J. van Deth and G. Wolleb (eds.), *The Handbook of Social Capital*. Oxford: Oxford University Press, 241–72.

Norris, P. 1999. *Critical Citizens: Global Support for Democratic Government*. Oxford: Oxford University Press.

Norval, A. 1994. Hegemony after deconstruction: the consequences of undecidability. *Journal of Political Ideologies* 9(2): 139–57.

1996. *Deconstructing Apartheid Discourse*. London: Verso.

2007. *Aversive Democracy. Inheritance and Originality in the Democratic Tradition*. Cambridge: Cambridge University Press.

2008. Beyond Deliberation: Agonistic and Aversive Grammars of Democracy, Typescript, University of Essex.

2009a. 'No reconciliation without redress': Articulating political demands in post-transitional South Africa. *Critical Discourse Studies* 6(4): 311–21.

2009b. Democracy, pluralization and voice. *Ethics and Global Politics* 2(4): 297–320.

2010. A democratic politics of acknowledgement: political judgment, imagination and exemplarity. *Diacritics* 38(4): 59–76.

2011. Moral perfectionism and democratic responsiveness. *Ethics and Global Politics* 4(4): 207–29.

2012. 'Writing a name in the sky': Rancière, Cavell and the possibility of egalitarian inscription. *American Political Science Review*: 106(4): 810–26

Norval, A., and Abdulrahman, A. 2011. EU Democracy Promotion Rethought: The Case of Egypt, in M. Pace (ed.), *Europe, the USA and Political Islam: Strategies for Engagement*. Basingstoke: Palgrave Macmillan, 10–39.

Nullmeier, F., and Pritzlaff, T. 2009. The implicit normativity of political practices. Analyzing the dynamics and power relations of committee decision-making. *Critical Policy Studies* 3(3/4): 357–74.

Nussbaum, M. 1990. *Love's Knowledge*. New York: Oxford University Press.

Offe, C. 1984. *Contradictions of the Welfare State*. Cambridge, MA: The MIT Press.

1996. Designing Institutions in East European Transitions, in R. Goodin (ed.), *The Theory of Institutional Design*. Cambridge: Cambridge University Press, 199–226.

2009. Governance as an 'Empty Signifier'? *Constellations* 16(4): 550–62.

O'Neill, O. 1997. Political liberalism and public reason: a critical notice of John Rawls, *Political Liberalism*. *The Philosophical Review* 106(3): 411–28.

O'Neill, J. 2001. Representing people, representing nature, representing the
    world. *Environment and Planning C: Government and Policy* **19**(4):
    483–500.
Osborne, S.P. (ed.) 2010. *The New Public Governance? Emerging per-
    spectives on the theory and practice of public governance.* London:
    Routledge.
Ostrom, E. 1986. An agenda for the study of institutions. *Public Choice*
    48: 3–25.
O'Toole, L.J. 1997. The implications for democracy in a networked bureau-
    cratic world. *Journal of Public Administration Research and Theory*
    7(3): 443–59.
O'Toole, T., and Gale, R. 2008. Learning from political sociology: structure,
    agency and inclusive governance. *International Journal of Children's
    Rights* **16**(3): 369–78.
Owen, D. 2001. Democracy, Perfectionism and 'Undetermined Messanic
    Hope': Cavell, Derrida and the Ethos of Democracy-to-Come, in L.
    Nagl and C. Mouffe (eds.), *The Legacy of Wittgenstein: Pragmatism or
    Deconstruction.* Frankfurt am Main: Peter Lang, 139–56.
Owen, D. 2012. Constituting the polity, constituting the demos: on the place
    of the all affected interests principle in democratic theory and in resolv-
    ing the democratic boundary problem. *Ethics & Global Politics* 5(3):
    129–52.
Ozacky-Lazar, S., and Ghanem, A. 2001. *Between Two Octobers: The
    Palestinians in Israel, October 2000 – October 2001.* Surveys on the
    Arabs in Israel, no. 27–28. Givat Haviva (Israel): The Institute for Peace
    Research.
Papadopoulos, Y. 2003. Cooperative forms of governance: problems of
    democratic accountability in complex environments. *European Journal
    of Political Research* **42**: 473–501.
Parkin, F. 1982. *Max Weber.* London: Tavistock.
Parnell, S., and Robinson, J. 2012. (Re)theorizing cities from the Global South:
    looking beyond neoliberalism. *Urban Geography* **33**(4): 593–617.
Parkinson, J. 2006. *Deliberating in the Real World.* Oxford: Oxford
    University Press.
Pateman, C. 1970. *Participation and Democratic Theory.* Cambridge:
    Cambridge University Press.
Payne, C. 1995. *I've Got The Light of Freedom.* Berkeley: University of
    California Press.
Peters, B.G. 2011. Governance as political theory. *Critical Policy Studies*
    5(1): 63–72.
Peters, B.G., and Pierre, J. 2000. *Governance, Politics and the State.*
    Basingstoke: Palgrave Macmillan.

2001. Developments in intergovernmental relations: towards multi-level governance. *Policy & Politics* 29(2): 131–35.

2004. Multi-Level Governance and Democracy: A Faustian Bargain?, in I. Bache and M. Flinders (eds.), *Multi-Level Governance*. Oxford: Oxford University Press, 74–90.

Phalet, K., and Swyngedouw, M. 2002. National identities and representations of citizenship: a comparison of Turks, Moroccans and working-class Belgians in Brussels. *Ethnicities* 2: 5–30.

Pharr, S., and Putnam, R. 2000. *Disaffected Democracies: What's Troubling the Trilateral Countries?* Princeton, NJ: Princeton University Press.

Phillips, D. 2006. Parallel lives? Challenging discourses of British Muslim self-segregation. *Environment and Planning D: Society and Space* 24: 25–40.

Pickering, A. 1995. *The Mangle of Practice: Time, Agency, and Science*. Chicago and London: The University of Chicago Press.

Pickering, A., and Guzik, K. (eds.) 2008. *The Mangle in Practice. Science, Society and Becoming*, Durham, NC: Duke University Press.

Pickvance, C. 2003. From urban social movements to urban movements. *International Journal of Urban and Regional Research* 27(1): 102–09.

Pierson, P. 2000. Increasing returns, path dependency, and the study of politics. *American Political Science Review* 94(2): 251–67.

Pitkin, H.F. 1967. *The Concept of Representation*. Berkeley, CA: University of California Press.

2004. Representation and democracy: uneasy alliance. *Scandinavian Political Studies* 27(3): 335–42.

Pollitt, C., and Bouckaert, G. 2004. *Public Management Reform. A Comparative Analysis*, Oxford: Oxford University Press.

Plotke, D. 1997. Representation is democracy. *Constellations* 4(1): 19–34.

Porter, L. 2011. Interface: informality, the commons and the paradoxes for planning: concepts and debates for informality and planning. *Planning Theory and Praxis* 12(1): 115–20.

Pratchett, L., and Lowndes, V. 2004. *Developing Democracy in Europe: An Analytical Summary of the Council of Europe's Acquis*. Strasbourg: Council of Europe Publishing.

Purcell, M. 2001. Neighbourhood activism among homeowners as a politics of space. *Professional Geographer* 53: 178–94.

2003. Citizenship and the right to the global city: reimagining the capitalist world order. *International Journal of Urban and Regional Research* 27: 564–90.

2006. Urban democracy and the local trap. *Urban Studies* 43: 1921–41.

Putnam, H. 1974. *Words and Life*. Cambridge, MA: Harvard University Press.

Quirk, B. 2007. *Making Assets Work: The Quirk Review of Community Management and Ownership of Public Assets.* London: HMSO.

Rabinowitz, D. 2001. The Palestinian citizens of Israel, the concept of trapped minority and the discourse of transnationalism in anthropology. *Ethnic and Racial Studies* 24: 64–85.

Raco, M. 2003. New Labour, Community and the Future of Britain's Urban Renaissance, in R. Imrie and M. Raco (eds.), *Urban Renaissance? New Labour, Community and Urban Policy.* Bristol: The Policy Press, 235–49.

Rancière, J. 1999. *Disagreement.* Translated by Julie Rose. Minneapolis, MN: University of Minnesota Press.

Reijndorp, A. 2004. *Stadswijk. Stedenbouw en Dagelijks Leven.* Rotterdam: Nai Uitgevers.

Rein, M. 1983. Value-Critical Policy Analysis, in D. Callahan and B. Jennings (eds.), *Ethics, the Social Sciences, and Policy Analysis.* New York: Plenum Press, 83–112.

Rhodes, R.A.W. 1994. The hollowing out of the state: the changing nature of public service in Britain. *Political Quarterly* 65(2): 138–51.

   1996. The new governance: governing without government. *Political Studies* 44(4): 652–67.

   1997. *Understanding Governance: Policy Networks, Governance, Reflexivity and Accountability.* Buckingham: Open University Press.

   2000. Governance and Public Administration, in J. Pierre (ed.), *Debating Governance.* Oxford: Oxford University Press, 54–90.

Robeyns, I. 2008. Ideal theory in theory and practice. *Social Theory and Social Practice* 34: 341–62.

Rocket Science UK Ltd. 2010. *Summative Evaluation of the Community Asset Programme.* London: Big Lottery Fund/Cabinet Office.

Rosanvallon, P. 2011. *Democratic Legitimacy: Impartiality, Reflexivity, Proximity.* Translated by Arthur Goldhammer. Princeton, NJ: Princeton University Press.

Rose, N. 1999. *Powers of Freedom: Reframing Political Thought.* Cambridge: Cambridge University Press.

Rose, N., and Miller, P. 1992. Political power beyond the state: problematics of government. *British Journal of Sociology* 43(2), 173–205.

Rothstein, B. 1996. *Political Institutions: An Overview*, in R.E. Goodin, and H-D. Klingemann (eds.), *A New Handbook of Political Science.* Oxford: Oxford University Press, 133–66.

Rousseau, J-J. 1968. *The Social Contract.* London: Penguin Books.

Roy, A. 2003. *City Requiem: Calcutta, Gender and the Politics of Poverty.* Minneapolis, MN: University of Minnesota Press.

2010. Informality and the Politics of Planning, in J. Hillier and P. Healey (eds.), *The Ashgate Research Companion to Planning Theory. Conceptual Challenges to Spatial Planning Theory*. Farnham, UK: Ashgate: 87–109.

Sanders, L. 1997. Against deliberation, *Political Theory* 25(3): 347–76.

Sartori, G. 1987. *The Theory of Democracy Revisited, I-II*. Chatham, NJ: Chatham House Publishers.

Sassen, S. 2001. *The Global City: New York, London, Tokyo*. Princeton, NJ: Princeton University Press (2nd revised edition).

Savitch, H.V., and Kantor, P. 2002. *Cities in the International Market Place*. Princeton, NJ: Princeton University Press.

Saward, M. 2003. Enacting democracy. *Political Studies* 51(1): 161–79.

2005. Governance and the Transformation of Political Representation, in J. Newman (ed.), *Remaking Governance: Peoples, Politics and the Public Sphere*. Bristol: The Policy Press, 179–96.

2006. The representative claim. *Contemporary Political Theory*, 5(3): 297–318.

2010. *The Representative Claim*. Oxford: Oxford University Press.

Scharpf, F. 1994. Games real actors could play: positive and negative coordination in embedded negotiations. *Journal of Theoretical Politics* 6(1): 27–53.

1997. *Games Real Actors Play: Actor-Centered Institutionalism in Policy Research*. Boulder, CO: Westview Press.

1999. *Governing Europe: Effective and Democratic?* Oxford: Oxford University Press.

Schatzki, T.R. 1996. *Social Practices: A Wittgensteinian Approach to Human Activity and the Social*. Cambridge: Cambridge University Press.

Schmitter, P. 2001. What is There to Legitimize in the European Union … and How Might This Be Accomplished?, in C. Joerges, Y. Mény, and J.H.H. Weiler (eds.), *Symposium: Mountain or Molehill? A Critical Appraisal of the Commission White Paper on Governance*, Jean Monnet Working Paper No. 6/01. New York: New York University School of Law. Available at www.jeanmonnetprogram.org/archive/papers/01/011401.html. Accessed 3 January 2014.

Schmitter, P., and Streeck, W. (eds.) 1985. *Private Interest Government*. London: Sage.

Schmitter, P., and Trechsel, A. (eds.) 2004. *The Future of Democracy in Europe: Trends, Analyses and Reforms*. Strasbourg: Council of Europe Publishing.

Schön, D. A., and Rein, M. 1994. *Frame Reflection. Toward the Resolution of Intractable Policy Controversies*. New York: Basic Books.

Schumpeter, J. 1976. *Capitalism, Socialism and Democracy*. London: Allen and Unwin.

Shafir, G., and Peled, Y. 2002. *Being Israeli: The Dynamic of Multiple Citizenship*. Cambridge: Cambridge University Press.

Shatil. 2005. *The Arab Citizens in the Mixed Cities*. 'Shatil' (Support Services for Social Change Organisations) Report. Jerusalem: Shatil Press (in Hebrew).

Sieber, S. 1981. *Fatal Remedies: The Ironies of Social Intervention*. New York: Plenum Publishers.

SIKKUY. 2005. *Government Policy Towards the Arab Citizens, SIKKUY Report 2004–2005*. Haifa: SIKKUY Press (in Hebrew).

Simmons, A. 2010. Ideal and nonideal theory. *Philosophy and Public Affairs* 38: 5–36.

Simone, A., and Abouhani, A. (eds.) 2005. *Urban Africa: Changing Contours of Survival in the City*. Dakar: Codesria Books.

Skelcher, C. 2005. Jurisdictional integrity, polycentrism, and the design of democratic governance. *Governance* 18(1): 89–110.

Skelcher, C., Mathur, N., and Smith, M. 2005. The public governance of collaborative spaces: discourse, design and democracy. *Public Administration* 83(3): 573–96.

Skelcher, C., Sullivan, H., and Jeffares, S. 2013. *Hybrid Governance in European Cities. Neighbourhood, Migration and Democracy*. Basingstoke: Palgrave Macmillan.

Skidmore, P., Bound, K., and Lownsbrough, H. 2006. *Community Participation: Who Benefits?* York: Joseph Rowntree Foundation.

Smith, G. 2009. *Democratic Innovations: Designing Institutions for Citizen Participation*. Cambridge: Cambridge University Press.

Smith, I., Lepine, E., and Taylor, M. (eds.) 2007. *Disadvantaged by Where You Live?* Bristol: The Policy Press.

Smith, M., and Beazley, M. 2000. Progressive regimes, partnerships and the involvement of local communities: a framework for evaluation. *Public Administration* 78: 855–78.

Smith, S. 1995. Citizenship: all or nothing? *Political Geography* 14:190–93.

Smooha, S. 2002. The model of ethnic democracy: Israel as a Jewish and democratic state. *Nations and Nationalism* 8: 475–503.

Snow, D.A., Cress, D.M., Downey, L., and Jones, A.W. 1998. Disrupting the 'quotidian': reconceptualizing the relationship between breakdown and the emergence of collective action. *Mobilization* 3(1): 1–22.

Sørensen, E. 2002. Democratic theory and network governance. *Administrative Theory and Praxis* 24(4), 693–720.

2006. Metagovernance: the changing role of politicians in processes of democratic governance. *American Review of Public Administration* 36(1), 98–114.

2007. Local Politicians and Administrators as Metagovernors, in M. Marcussen and J. Torfing (eds.), *Democratic Network Governance in Europe*. Basingstoke: Palgrave Macmillan, 89–108.

2012. Governance networks as a frame for inter-demoi participation and deliberation. *Administrative Theory & Praxis*, 34(4): 509–32.

Sørensen, E., and Torfing, J. 2003. Network politics, political capital and democracy. *International Journal of Public Administration* 26(6): 609–34.

2004. *Making Governance Networks Democratic*. Centre for Democratic Network Governance, Working Paper, 2004:1. Roskilde: University of Roskilde.

2005a. Network governance and post-liberal democracy. *Administrative Theory & Praxis* 27(2), 197–237.

2005b. The democratic anchorage of governance networks. *Scandinavian Political Studies* 28(3), 195–218.

(eds.) 2007. *Theories of Democratic Network Governance*. Basingstoke: Palgrave Macmillan.

2008. Introduction: Governance Network Research: Towards a Second Generation, in E. Sørensen and J. Torfing (eds.), *Theories of Democratic Network Governance*. Basingstoke: Palgrave Macmillan, 1–25.

2009. Improving effective and democratic network governance through metagovernance, *Public Administration* 87(2): 234–58.

de Souza Briggs, X. 2008. *Democracy as Problem Solving. Civic Capacity in Communities Across the Globe*. Cambridge, MA: The MIT Press.

Soysal, Y. 1994. *Limits of Citizenship: Migrants and Post-National Membership in Europe*. Chicago: University of Chicago Press.

Specht, M. 2012. *De Pragmatiek an Burgerparticipatie*. PhD diss., Free University, Amsterdam.

Staeheli, L.A. 2003. Cities and citizenship. *Urban Geography* 24: 97–102.

Staeheli, L.A., and Thompson, A. 1997. Citizenship, community, and struggles for public space. *The Professional Geographer* 49: 28–38.

Staten, H. 1985. *Wittgenstein and Derrida*. Oxford: Basil Blackwell.

Stewart, J. 2000. *The Nature of British Local Government*. Basingstoke: Palgrave Macmillan.

Stoker, G. 2006. *Why Politics Matters. Making Democracy Work*. Basingstoke: Palgrave Macmillan.

2008. When micro-foundations of governance matters, personally circulated working paper.

2010. Blockages on the road to relevance: why has political science failed to deliver? *European Political Science* 9: 72–84.

2011. Was local governance such a good idea? A global comparative perspective. *Public Administration* **89**(1): 15–31.

Stoker, G., and Mossberger, K. 1994. Urban regime theory in comparative perspective. *Environment and Planning C: Government and Policy* **12**: 195–212.

Stokey, E., and Zeckhauser, R. 1978. *A Primer for Policy Analysis*. New York: W.W. Norton.

Stone, C. 1993. Urban regimes and the capacity to govern: a political economy approach. *Journal of Urban Affairs* **15**: 1–28.

2005. Looking back to look forward. Reflections on urban regime analysis. *Urban Affairs Review* **40**(3), 309–41.

Stone, C., Henig, J.R., Jones, B.D., and Pierannunzi, C. 2001. *Building Civic Capacity. The Politics of Reforming Urban Schools*. Lawrence, KS: University Press of Kansas.

Sullivan, H. 2001. Maximising the contribution of neighbourhoods – the role of community governance. *Public Policy and Administration* **16**(2): 29–48.

2007. Interpreting 'community leadership' in English local government. *Policy & Politics* **35**(1): 141–61.

2009. Subversive Spheres: Neighbourhoods, Citizens and the 'New Governance', in M. Barnes and D. Prior (eds.) *Subversive Citizens. Power, Agency and Resistance in Public Services*. Bristol: The Policy Press, 49–66.

Sullivan, H., and Skelcher, C. 2002. *Working across Boundaries. Collaboration in Public Services*. Basingstoke: Palgrave Macmillan.

Sunstein, C. 2002. *Designing Democracy: What Constitutions Do*. Oxford: Oxford University Press.

Susskind, L., and Cruikshank, J. 1987. *Breaking the Impasse*. New York: Basic Books.

Susskind, L., McKearnan, S., and Thomas Larmer, J. (eds.) 1999. *The Consensus Building Handbook: A Comprehensive Guide to Reaching Agreement*. Thousand Oaks, CA: Sage Publications.

Svirsky, S., and Connor-Attias, E. 2006. *A Report on Social Conditions in Israel: 2006*. Tel Aviv-Jaffa, Israel: ADVA Centre (in Hebrew).

Taylor, C. 1985. Neutrality in Political Science, in C. Taylor, *Philosophy and the Human Sciences. Philosophical Papers 2*. Cambridge: Cambridge University Press, 58–91.

1995. Overcoming Epistemology, in C. Taylor, *Philosophical Arguments*. Cambridge, MA: Harvard University Press, 1–19.

2002. Gadamer on the human sciences, in Robert J. Dostal (ed.), *The Cambridge Companion to Gadamer*. Cambridge: Cambridge University Press, 126–42.

Taylor, M. 2003. *Public Policy in the Community*. Basingstoke: Palgrave Macmillan.

2007. Community participation in the real world: opportunities and pitfalls in new governance spaces. *Urban Studies* 44(2): 297–317.

Teubner, G. 1983. Substantive and reflexive elements in modern law. *Law and Society Review* 17: 239–85.

Tisdall, E.K., and Davis, J. 2004. Making a difference? Bringing children's and young people's views into policy-making. *Children and Society* 18: 131–42.

de Tocqueville, A. 1968. *Democracy in America*. London: Fortuna.

Torfing, J. 1998. *Politics, Regulation and the Modern Welfare State*. Basingstoke: Palgrave Macmillan.

1999. *New Theories of Discourse*. Oxford: Blackwell.

2005. Governance network theory: towards a second generation. *European Political Science* 4(3): 305–15.

2007. Discursive Governance Networks in Danish Activation Policy, in M. Marcussen and J. Torfing (eds.), *Democratic Network Governance in Europe*. Basingstoke: Palgrave Macmillan, 111–29.

Torfing, J., and Damgaard, B. 2010. Network governance of local employment policy: the Danish experience. *Journal of European Social Policy* 20(3), 248–62.

Torfing, J., Peters, B.G., Pierre, J., and Sørensen, E. 2012. *Interactive Governance. Advancing the Paradigm*. Oxford: Oxford University Press.

Torgerson, D. 1999. *The Promise of Green Politics: Environmentalism and the Public Sphere*. Durham, NC: Duke University Press.

2003. Democracy through Policy Discourse, in M.A. Hajer and H. Wagenaar (eds.), *Deliberative Policy Analysis: Understanding Governance in the Network Society*. Cambridge: Cambridge University Press, 113–38.

Tully, J. 1999. The agonic freedom of citizens. *Economy and Society* 28: 161–82.

2002. Political philosophy as a critical activity. *Political Theory* 30(4): 533–55.

2003. Wittgenstein and Political Philosophy: Understanding Practices of Critical Reflection, in C. Heyes (ed.), *The Grammar of Politics: Wittgenstein and Political Philosophy*. Ithaca, NY: Cornell University Press, 17–42.

2008a. *Public Philosophy in a New Key, Vol. 1, Democracy and Civic Freedom*. Cambridge: Cambridge University Press.

2008b. *Public Philosophy in a New Key, Vol. 2, Imperialism and Civic Freedom*. Cambridge: Cambridge University Press.

Urbinati, N., and Warren, M. 2008. The concept of representation in con-
    temporary democratic theory. *Annual Review of Political Science* **11**(1):
    387–412.

Urry, J. 2000. Global flows and global citizenship, in E. Isin (ed.), *Democracy,
    Citizenship and the Global City.* London: Routledge, 62–78.

Valentini, L. 2009. On the apparent paradox of ideal theory. *Journal of
    Political Philosophy* **17**: 332–55.

Van Til, J. 2000. *Growing Civil Society: From Nonprofit Sector to Third
    Space.* Bloomington: Indiana University Press.

Verba, S., Schlozman, K. L., and Brady, H.E. 1995. *Voice and Equality: Civic
    Voluntarism in American Politics.* Cambridge, MA: Harvard University
    Press.

Verhoeven, I. 2009. *Burgers Tegen Beleid. Een Analyse van Dynamiek in
    Politieke Betrokkenheid.* Amsterdam: uitgeverij Aksant. (published
    doctoral thesis).

Verloo, N. (in press) *Utrecht Zwanenvechtplein. Buurten, Spanningen en
    Conflicten.* Amsterdam: Amsterdam centrum voor Conflictstudies.

Vinzant, J.C., and Crothers, L. 1998. *Street-Level Leadership. Discretion and
    Legitimacy in Front-Line Public Service.* Washington, DC: Georgetown
    University Press.

Wagenaar, H. 2005. *Stadswijken, Complexiteit en Burgerbestuur.* The
    Hague: XPIN

    2006. Democracy and prostitution. Deliberating the legalization of broth-
        els in the Netherlands. *Administration and Society* **38**(3), 198–235.

    2007. Governance, complexity, and democratic participation. How citi-
        zens and public officials harness the complexities of neighborhood
        decline. *American Review of Public Administration* **37**(1): 17–50.

    2008. Introduction: dialogical meaning in policy analysis. *Critical Policy
        Studies* **1**(4): 311–34.

    2009. Commentary: recovering public ethos; critical analysis for policy
        and planning. *Planning Theory and Practice* **10**(3): 414–21.

    2011. *Meaning in Action: Interpretation and Dialogue in Policy Analysis.*
        Armonk, NY: M.E. Sharpe.

    2012. Dwellers on the threshold of practice: the interpretivism of Bevir
        and Rhodes. *Critical Policy Studies* **6**(1): 85–99.

Wagenaar, H., and Cook, N.S. 2003. Understanding Policy Practices: Action,
    Dialectic and Deliberation in Policy Analysis, in M. Hajer, and H. Wagenaar
    (eds.), *Deliberative Policy Analysis: Understanding Governance in the
    Network Society.* Cambridge: Cambridge University Press, 139–71.

Wagenaar, H., and Specht, M. 2010. *Geëngageerd Bewonerschap.
    Bewonersparticipatie in Drie Europese Steden.* The Hague: Nicis
    Institute.

Waldron, J. 1999. *The Dignity of Legislation*. Cambridge: Cambridge University Press.

Walzer, M. 1989. *In the Company of Critics: Social Criticism and Political Commitment in the Twentieth Century*. London: Halban.

Warleigh, A. 2002. Introduction: Institutions, Institutionalism and Decision-Making in the EU, in A. Warleigh (ed.), *Understanding European Union Institutions*. London: Routledge, 1–22.

Warren, M. 1992. Democratic theory and self-transformation. *American Political Science Review* 86(1): 8–23.

1996. Deliberative democracy and authority. *American Political Science Review* 90: 46–60.

2001. *Democracy and Association*. Princeton, NJ: Princeton University Press.

2002. What can democratic participation mean today? *Political Theory* 30: 677–701.

2003. A Second Transformation of Democracy? in B.E. Cain, R.J. Dalton, and S.E. Scarrow (eds.), *Democracy Transformed? Expanding Political Opportunities in Advanced Industrial Democracies*. Oxford: Oxford University Press, 223–49.

2008a. Citizen Representatives, in M.E. Warren, and H. Pearse (eds.), *Designing Deliberative Democracy: The British Columbia Citizens' Assembly*. Cambridge: Cambridge University Press, 50–69.

2008b. Governance-Driven Democratization. Working paper 2008:3, Centre for Democratic Network Governance, Roskilde University.

Warren, M., and Castiglione, D. 2006. Rethinking Democratic Representation: Eight Theoretical Issues. Prepared for delivery to Rethinking Democratic Representation, Centre for the Study of Democratic Institutions, University of British Columbia, 18–19 May.

Warren, M., and Pearse, H. (eds.) 2008. *Designing Deliberative Democracy: The British Columbia Citizens' Assembly*. Cambridge: Cambridge University Press.

Watson, V. 2003. Conflicting rationalities: implications for planning theory and ethics. *Planning Theory and Practice* 4(4): 395–407.

Weber, M. 1920. *Makt og byråkrati: Essays om politikk og klasse, samfunnsforskning og verdier*. Oslo: Gyldendal Norsk Forlag.

Wenling Department of Propoganda 2003. *Democratic Sincerely Talk: The Innovation from Wenling*. Wenling: Wenling Department of Propaganda.

Wenman, M. 2003. 'Agonistic pluralism' and three archetypal forms of politics. *Contemporary Political Theory* 2(2): 165–86.

Westbrook, R.B. 1991. *John Dewey and American Democracy*. Ithaca, NY: Cornell University Press.

White, J. 2009. The social theory of mass politics. *The Journal of Politics* **71**: 96–112.

Wilson, N. 2005. The dark side of community development. *Planning Theory and Practice* **6**(4): 519–26.

Wilson, W. 1887. The Study of Administration. *Political Science Quarterly* **2**: 197–222.

Wittgenstein, L. 1986. *Philosophical Investigations*. Oxford: Basil Blackwell.

Yánez, C.J.N. 2004. Participatory democracy and political opportunism: municipal experience in Italy and Spain (1960–1993). *International Journal of Urban and Regional Research* **28**: 819–38.

Yanow, D. 1996. *How Does a Policy Mean? Interpreting Policy and Organizational Actions*. Washington, DC: Georgetown University Press.

Yiftachel, O. 1997. The political geography of ethnic protest: nationalism, deprivation and regionalism among Arabs in Israel. *Transactions of the Institute of British Geographers* **22**(1): 91–110.

2001. Centralised power and divided space: 'fractured regions' in the Israeli 'ethnocracy'. *GeoJournal* **53**(3): 283–93.

Young, I.M. 2000. *Inclusion and Democracy*. Oxford: Oxford University Press.

Young, M., and Willmott, P. 2007 [1957]. *Family and Kinship in East London*. London: Penguin Books.

Yuval-Davis, N. 1999. The multi-layered citizen: citizenship at the age of 'glocalisation'. *International Feminist Journal of Politics* **1**: 119–36.

Zelditch, M. 2001. Theories of Legitimacy, in J.T. Jost and B. Major (eds.), *The Psychology of Legitimacy: Emerging Perspectives on Ideology, Justice, and Intergroup Relations*. Cambridge: Cambridge University Press, 33–53.

Zerilli, L. 1998. This universalism which is not one. *Diacritics* **28**(2): 3–20.

Žižek, S. 1991. *For They Know Not What They Do*. London: Verso.

Index

action research, 13
agonistic democracy, 74, 75–76,
    75n16, 178n1, 191–96, 232–36.
    See also aversive democracy
agonistic intersubjectivity, 34,
    137–54
    contextual conventions, 149–50
    continuously responsive perception
        and interpretation, 149
    debate, 151, 153–54
    dialogue, 150–51, 153–54
    implications of, 150
    ineradicable differences, 140–41
    interaction in rule-governed context,
        142–43
    need for account of interaction that
        produces practical outcomes,
        141–42
    negotiation, 151–54
    neighbourhood redevelopment
        example, 144–48
    power relationships and, 148–54
    subjectivity versus, 137–39
agonistic pluralism, 25–26, 234
agonistic respect, 25, 26–27, 32,
    129, 130
America Speaks, 54
Ansell, Chris, 225, 242, 247
area committees, 189–91,
    193–94, 196
area-based governance, 4–5, 8, 208
aversive democracy, 13, 77–82.
    See also agonistic democracy;
    Cavell, S.; conformism;
    democratic grammar; democratic
    subjectivity; Emerson, R.;
    non-teleological perfectionism;
    Norval, A.; Rancière, J.

Baggini, J., 163
Bagguley, P., 206
Bang, H., 201
Barnes, M., 184, 201–2
Beetham, D., 159, 168
Begum, S., 60–61, 60n2, 80–81
Belgium
    garbage problem, 243
    redesign of construction project,
        232, 234
    urban wisdom, 220
Bevir, M., 3, 9, 102, 202, 243–44n18
Blondeel, P., 220
Bohman, J., 22–23, 46–47, 67, 68
Booher, D., 234
Bouyakoub, S., 229
Bradford Keighley Youth Parliament
    (BKYP), 200–1, 204–16
    community cohesion, 206–8, 207n3,
        207n4
    developing democratic ethos,
        213–15
    practices of freedom, 211–13
    practices of governance, 206–11
    relationship with council
        government, 208–11
    shifts in terms of engagement,
        211–13
Brazil, 41–43
Briggs, X., de Sousa, 247
Burnett, J., 206
Butler, J., 69

Campbell, J., 239n13
Canada
    citizens' assemblies on electoral
        reform, 55
    judiciary and policymaking, 41–43

Cavell, S., 13, 77–80, 78n19, 82, 83–84, 83n20, 142, 154
de Certeau, M., 200, 203, 213, 219–20
Chambers, S., 22–23, 65–67
China
  experiments in democracy, 39
  Zeguo township experiment, 50–51
circumstances of politics, 18, 62–63, 63n4. *See also* Waldron, Jeremy
civic capacity theory, 19, 36, 246–48
civil societies. *See also* collaborative governance and decision making
  as domain of governance-driven democratization, 41, 42, 43–44
  harnessing capacities of, 57–58
  increased political and organizational capacity, 48
  rapid development of dense, 47–48
Coelho, V. S., 202, 204
collaborative governance and decision making, 39, 178–79
  community engagement, 4, 5, 242–43
  conflict and consensus, 242–43
  democratic anchorage, 113–36
  network governance, 2, 4, 5, 110–12
community cohesion, 35, 206–8, 207n3, 207n4, 257
Community Empowerment Network, 182, 183
community governance, legitimacy and
  assessing, 171–75
  complexity of, 169–71
  consent as condition of, 159, 168, 170
  consequences for analysis of legitimacy, 156
  criticism of community governance, 161
  formal links to external bodies, 167–68
  informal practice of, 166–68, 169–72
  input and output-oriented legitimacy, 161–62, 165
  justifiability as condition of, 159–60, 165, 166, 167, 169–70
  neighbourhood-based structures, 157–58, 164–68

norms of legitimacy, 160–63
practices of governance and freedom, 173–74
problematic nature of analysis of, 172–73
processes of sense-making, 156
replacement for legitimating processes of representative democracy, 158–59
rules as condition of, 159, 160, 164–65, 167, 169–70
conflict
  creative role of, 232–36
  fruitful, 234–35
  neighbourhood governance and, 178, 178n1, 191–96
conformism, 77–78
Connelly, S., 162–63
Connolly, W., 25, 26–27, 70. *See also* ethos of engagement
contested governance, 137–54
  contextual conventions, 149–50
  debate, 151, 153–54
  dialogue, 150–51, 153–54
  implications of intersubjectivity, 150
  interaction in rule-governed context, 142–43
  intersubjectivity versus subjectivity, 137–39
  negotiation, 151–54
  neighbourhood redevelopment example, 144–48
  sharing conventions of claims-making, 140
Cook, S., 240–41n15
Cornwall, A., 202, 204
Council of Europe (CoE), 87
  acquis, defined, and number of treaties and conventions within, 33, 87, 98–99
  acquis, flexibility, revisability and variability in, 103–7, 104
  acquis, robustness in, 99–107, 100
  acquis as instrument of institutional design, 98–106
  compared to European Union, 88–89
  complex institutional environment of, 94
  core principles, 98–99

democratic mandate of, 88–90
historical development of, 88
monitoring, 102, 103
organisational structure of, 90
power relationships and, 94–95
reactionary nature of, 102–3
role of third party enforcers,
  101–2, 103
territorial scope of, 89–90
values that inform, 99–101, 102–3
criteria used in evaluating democratic
  practices, 32–33, 60–84, 83n20
abstraction and idealization, 64,
  64n6
aversive democracy, 77–82
deliberative theory, 65–69
poststructuralist theory, 69–77
Wittgensteinian approach to, 82–84
critical responsiveness, 26–27
Crossley, N., 202–3, 214, 215
culture governance, 6, 201

Davies, J. S., 5
decentred governance
defined, 9
hegemony, 11–12, 14–15
implications of acceptance of, 9–11
interaction between practices and
  conditions, 14–15
meaning and, 11, 12–15
political nature of, 9–10
practical, situated nature of, 10–11
decentred legitimacy, 34–35, 155–75
assessing at community-governance
  level, 171–75
complexity of, 169–71
consent as condition of, 159,
  168, 170
consequences for analysis of
  legitimacy, 156
criticism of community
  governance, 161
formal links to external bodies,
  167–68
informal practice of, 166–68,
  169–72
input and output-oriented
  legitimacy, 161–62, 165
justifiability as condition of, 159–60,
  165, 166, 167, 169–70

neighbourhood-based structures,
  157–58, 164–68
norms of legitimacy, 160–63
practices of governance and
  freedom, 173–74
problematic nature of analysis of,
  172–73
processes of sense-making, 156
replacement for legitimating
  processes of representative
  democracy, 158–59
rules as condition of, 159, 160,
  164–65, 167, 169–70
deliberative theory, 22–25, 27–28, 63
in context of inequality, 67–68
criteria used in evaluating
  democratic practices, 65–69
democratic anchorage model, 126
ideal and non-ideal theory, 67n9
proceduralism, ideal of, 67
democracy, 30–31. *See also* aversive
  democracy; conflict
agonistic pluralism, 25–26
deliberative theory, 22–25, 27–28
ethos of engagement, 26–27
ethos of non-teleological
  perfectionism, 27
governance-driven democratization,
  32, 38–59
incompleteness of, 30n8
intrinsic fallibility of, 27
narrowing of meaning of term, 30
participatory, 23–24
as practical and processual, but not
  procedural, 30–31
as practices of governance and
  freedom, 22–28
redescription of, 235–36
reframing, 29–32
tensions between liberalism and, 29
democratic anchorage model, 33–34,
  113–36
accountability to territorially defined
  citizenry, 113–14, 121–26, 132
applying model of, 131–35
democratic rules and norms,
  113–14, 126–30, 132
democratically elected politicians,
  113, 114–18, 133
empirical studies, 134, 135

democratic anchorage model (*cont.*)
  evaluating and comparing, 131–32
  importance of, 131
  membership basis of participating
    groups and organisations, 113–14,
    118–21, 132–33
democratic demands
  articulation and universalization
    of, 73–75
  emergence of, 72–73
  management of, 12
Democratic Front for Peace and
    Equality (HADASH), 266,
    267, 271
democratic grammar, 28, 33,
    113–14, 126–30, 132, 133.
    See also agonistic democracy;
    aversive democracy
democratic realism argument,
    241n16
democratic subjectivity. *See also*
    disclosive community
  bias of academic rationalism, 137
  formation of, 31–32
  intersubjectivity versus, 137–39
  neighbourhood redevelopment
    example, 144–48
  power relationships and, 148–54
Denmark
  distrust of versus involvement in
    government, 47
  Local Employment Councils, 135
Derrida, J., 30n8
Dewey, J., 30n8, 223n7, 226–27, 237,
    239n13
dialogical meaning, 12–13, 15
Disch, L., 172
disclosive community, 79
Dryzek, J., 22–23, 221–22n5

electoral democracy
  governance-driven democratization
    as delinked from, 50–51
  limitation of democracy to, 225
  overtaxed nature of, 38–39
  policymaking under, 46
  political complexity and, 46–47
Emerson, R., 25, 77–78.
    See also aversive democracy;
    conformism

ESRC Democracy and Participation
    Programme, 184–85, 184n3,
    185n4
Essex School of poststructuralist
    discourse theory, 11–12
ethos of engagement, 26–27.
    See also Connelly, S.
European Union (EU)
  compared to Council of
    Europe, 88–89
  internal differentiation within
    constitutional regimes, 41–43
  judiciary and policy-making, 41–43
  multi-level governance, 88

Finer, S., 91–92
Forester, J., 143
Forrest, R., 250
Foucault, M., 7, 27, 245, 247
freedom, practices of
  decentred legitimacy, 155–56, 173–74
  democracy as, 22–28
  modes of response to, 159,
    202–3, 246
  neighbourhood governance and, 191
  participatory governance, 199–200
  practices of governance and, 7–9
  transformative potential of informal
    practices, 236–46
  youth parliament, 211–13
Fung, A., 55

Gains, F., 18
Germany
  governance network and bridge
    construction, 134
  street prostitution in housing
    project, 227–32, 234, 242–43, 247
Glynos, J., 13
Goodin, R., 96, 97
governance
  critique of orthodox, 5
  defined, 39
  hegemony as form of, 11–12
  micro-economic narratives of, 3
  narrowing of meaning of
    term, 29–30
  network narrative of, 4
  networked polity, 2
  political nature of, 9–10

popularity and ambiguity of, 2–3
practices of, and freedom, 7–9,
 199–200
practices of, democracy as, 22–28
shift from government to, 1–7
Type I and Type II modes of,
 91–92, 103
governance narratives, 1–7
governance networks, 2, 3–5, 5, 108–36
 causal link between policy output
  and policy decisions, 122–23
 debate over democratic quality of,
  108–10
 defensive view of, 111–12
 democratic anchorage of, 108–36
 empirical studies, 134, 135
 input and output-oriented
  legitimacy, 92–93
 legitimacy, 159–60
 as means to address limits of
  representative democracy, 4–5
 metagovernance, 115–18
 norms of inclusion and exclusion,
  128–30
 optimistic view of, 112
 plurality of forms and functions of,
  110–11
 political control, 113
 proliferation of, 110
 public accountability, 122
 public contestation, 123–25
 representation, 118–21
 resource interdependency, 111
 as tool to advance short-term policy
  goals, 4–5
governance orthodoxies, 1, 2–3, 5, 6–7
governance-driven democratization,
 32, 38–59
 administration-invited participation,
  223–27
 assessing fit between processes and
  issues, 59
 broad judgments of, 52
 challenges to, 55–56
 characteristics of, 40, 45–52
 civil society as domain of, 41,
  42, 43–44
 civil society, harnessing capacities
  of, 57–58
 defined, 38, 39

deliberation, new forms of, 56–57
 as delinked from electoral
  democracy, 50–51
 democratization, defined, 40
 direct democracy as domain of, 42
 direct participation, opening new
  venues of, 54–55
 economy as domain of, 41, 42, 43
 elite-driven nature of, 48–49, 53–54
 identifying potentials of, 58
 need for theoretically-organized
  knowledge for process
  conception, 58–59
 non-elected institutions as domain
  of, 42
 opportunities and challenges
  brought by, 40–41, 53–58
 reflexive institutions, 42, 44
 representation, altering forms
  of, 55–56
 as response to democracy
  deficits, 45–48
 state as domain of, 41–43, 42
 territorial constituencies,
  51–52, 53–54
government
 characteristics of, 7
 interdependency with other
  actors, 3–4
 intertwining of activities of thought
  and, 1
 narrowing of meaning of
  term, 29–30
 networked polity, 2
 new canonical beliefs in, 1
 shift to governance, 1–7
Griggs, S., 203, 273
group theory, 18

Habermas, J., 29, 65, 68, 68n12, 72,
 185–86, 188, 189
Häikiö, L., 162
Hajer, M., 62
Hammer, E., 82–83
Hart, D., 61
hegemony, 11–12, 14–15
 approach to radical
  democracy, 73–75
 domination versus, 74
 urban governance, 221–23, 222n6

Heidegger, M., 84
Hiep, E., 144–48
hermeneutic meaning, 12
Holston, J., 254–55
Hooghe, L., 91
Howarth, D., 11–12, 13
Hussain, Y., 206
Huxley, M., 219

informality concept
    decentred legitimacy, 166–68, 169–72
    defined, 217–18
    distrust in urban administrations,
        218–19
    everyday tactics of citizens, 219–20
    hegemony, 221–22
    normative contrast with formal
        procedures and institutions, 219
    pluralized ungovernability, 221, 223
    transformative potential of informal
        practices, 236–46
    uninvited participation, 219n2,
        225–27
    urban elites versus deprived/poor,
        221n4
    urban governance, 217–23, 236–46
Innes, J. E., 234
institutional design, 33, 85–107.
    See also Council of Europe
    character of democratic institutions
        in context of European
        governance, 90–93
    complex institutional environments
        and, 94
    criteria for good, 95–98
    history and, 95
    indirect approach to, 96
    neighbourhood governance, 180,
        181–82, 185
    participatory governance, 199
    power relationships and, 94–95
    process of, 93–95
    redesign, 96
    revisability in, 98, 103–7, 104
    robustness in, 97–98, 99–107, 100
    role of third party enforcers, 97,
        101–2, 103
    rules of the democratic game, 93–94
    values that inform, 96, 99–101
    variability within, 96–97

insurgent citizenship, 36–37, 254–73
    coalition politics, 268–70
    co-optation and radicalism, 266–73
    forms and substances of, 255–57
    intra-minority political contestation,
        267–68
    neighbourhood mobilisation as
        politically constitutive moment,
        270–73
    resistance, 254–55
    symbolic urban regimes, 251–54
    territorial constituencies, 249–76
inter-governmental organisations
    (IGOs). *See also* Council of
    Europe
    institutional design and, 106–7
    rationalist and constructivist
        approaches, 86–87
interpretive methods.
    See also pluralism; practice,
    philosophy of
    interpretive policy analysis, 17–18
    meaning, 12–14
interventionism, 16
Israeli-Palestinian neighbourhood
    mobilisation, 36–37, 249–76
    changes in Palestinian population of
        Haifa, 259–60
    'city of difference' concept for Haifa,
        249–50, 260–63, 265–66, 269–70
    coalition politics, 268–70
    co-optation and radicalism, 266–73
    discourses, 252–53, 265–67, 268–70
    distinctive Arab concentrations in
        Haifa, 260
    ethnocracy, 258
    image making and urban
        marketing, 266
    intra-minority political contestation,
        267–68
    overview of Haifa, 258–66
    as politically constitutive moment,
        270–73
    radicalised projects, 267–68
    relational dynamics, 253, 262–63
    symbolic elements and regime
        features, 263–66, 274, 275
    symbolic urban regimes, 251–54
    territorial constituencies, 249–76
    trapped minority, 253

Johnson, C., 157–58
Jordan, A., 86

Kennett, P., 250
Klijn, E-H., 2
Knops, A., 184
Kohn, M., 24

Laclau, E., 25, 64n6, 69–70, 73–75,
    140, 194–95
Laden, A., 64n6
Laker, F., 228, 242
language games, 8–9
Lasswell, H., 10
Lewis, J., 3
liberalism, tensions between
    democracy and, 29
Lombard, M., 219
Lowndes, V., 6, 179, 181–82

Macpherson, C. B., 29, 30
market-based approaches
    neighbourhood governance as, 184
    public sector subjected to, 3
Marks, G., 91
Mason, A., 64n6
Mathews, D., 227
meaning, 12–15
metagovernance, 115–18, 133
    defined, 115
    failure of, 117–18
    hands-on versus hands-off forms of,
        116–36, 117
    interventionism, 116, 117–36
micro-economic (neo-liberal) version
    of governance, 3, 5
minipublics, 56–57
Mitzna, A., 263
Moore, S., 60n2
Mossberger, K., 252
Mouffe, C., 10n5, 22, 25–26, 69–70,
    73–74, 75n16, 140, 178n1, 195,
    234n11
Mulhall, S., 78, 83–84
multi-level governance, 85–86

National Democratic Alliance Party
    (BALAD), 267, 268–69, 271
National Strategy for Neighbourhood
    Renewal, 182

neighbourhood governance, 35,
    176–98
    ambiguous nature of, 183–84
    appeal of, 176
    as by-product of multi-level,
        collaborative decision making,
        178–79
    as combination of neoliberalisation
        and networked governance, 179
    conflict and, 178, 178n1, 191–96
    constructing political
        frontiers between potential
        participants, 192
    creation of deliberative spaces, 183
    democratic participation in, 178–82
    democratic procedural design,
        185–91
    emphasis on local knowledge,
        187–88
    empowerment as type of, 180, 183
    ethics of cultivation, 187
    government as type of, 181, 183
    ideal types of, 180–82, 183
    inadequate or unobserved
        procedure, 189
    institutional prisons, 189–90
    Israeli-Palestinian neighbourhood
        mobilisation, 249–76
    management as type of, 181, 183
    openness, 187
    partnership as type of, 181, 183
    political contestation in, 177
    political versus politics, 179, 179n2
    power relationships and, 191–96
    as rescaling of state activity, 178
    resdesign of governance, 182–96
Neighbourhood Management scheme,
    182, 183
neighbourhood regeneration
    development trusts, 164–68, 164n1
    deliberate management of
        community representation,
        165–66
    democratic quality of, 165
    formal governance structure, 164–65
    formal links to external bodies,
        167–68
    informal practice of legitimacy,
        166–67
    weakness of, 166–67

Neighbourhood Renewal Fund, 182
Netherlands
  crime prevention project, 232
  negative press reports, 243–44n18
  neighbourhood council
    programme, 176
  neighbourhood redevelopment,
    144–48
  'People Make the City' (policy
    report), 4–5, 5n2, 8
  prostitution toleration zone, 229–30
  residents' view of alleged anti-social
    behaviour by youth, 220, 222
  safety problems, 222–23n6
New Deal for Communities
  programme, 182, 183
New Public Management reform
  programme, 115, 116–17
Newman, J., 184, 201, 202, 207
non-teleological perfectionism, 27
Norval, A., 13, 25, 27, 85, 102–3,
  107, 140, 142, 153, 154, 191–93,
  194–95, 203, 273

Offe, C., 3
O'Neill, O., 64n6

Parnell, S., 218n1
participatory governance, 35–36,
  199–216
  administration-invited participation,
    223–27
  characteristics that citizens
    possess, 241
  creation of radical habitus,
    202–3, 215
  decentred, 199–216
  developing democratic ethos,
    213–15
  emergent character of, 243–44
  enacted interdependence, 242–43,
    242n17
  extent of democratisation
    through, 199
  modes of response to practices of,
    202–3
  non-traditional forms of
    engagement, 251
  practices of, 206–11
  strategies versus tactics, 203

substantive participation
  in, 201
uninvited participation, 219n2,
  225–27
youth parliament case study, 200–1,
  204–16
path dependency, 95, 96
Payne, C., 149–50
'People Make the City' (Dutch policy
  report), 4–5, 5n2, 8
perlocutionary claims, 143
Peters, B. G., 2, 86, 102–3
Pickering, A., 239–40
Pierre, J., 86, 102–3
Pitkin, H. F., 175
pluralism, 9–10
  acknowledging, 14, 17–22
  agonistic, 25–26, 234
  power, 20–21
  radical, 21–22, 24, 25, 28, 30,
    235–36
  standard, 20–21
pluralized ungovernability, 221, 223
policy analysis, 10–11, 29–30
  discursive, 252–53
  performative, 16–17
  problem-oriented, 10
  qualitative, 12
policymaking, 2
  causal link between policy output
    and policy decisions, 122–23
  critique of orthodox governance, 5
  under electoral democracy, 45–48
  generation of legitimacy, 48–49
  governance-driven
    democratization, 38
  mutual dependency and
    collaboration, 3–4, 5
  unitary solutions in, 17–18
political communication, 19, 68
politics. *See also* conflict
  acknowledging pluralism of
    society, 17–22
  conventional versus radical meaning
    of, 9, 17
  dystopian view of citizen
    participation, 20
  realist notion of, 19–20
  restricted conception of
    power, 20–21

poststructuralist theory, 11–12, 13, 28, 63
  articulation and universalization of demands, 73–75
  constitution of subjectivity in processes, 75–76
  contingency, 70–71
  criteria used in evaluating democratic practices, 69–77
  emergence of democratic demands, 72–73
  failure to formulate criteria, 76–77
  historicity of democracy, 70
  ontological emphasis, 69–70
  policy analysis and, 10–12, 13
  universalization, 69–70, 70n14
Power, Participation and Political Renewal study, 184–85, 184n3, 185n4
practice, philosophy of
  analysis of democratic governance and, 16–17
  field of relationships between informal practice, agonistic freedom, governance and democracy, 237–38
  interaction between conditions and practice, 14–15
  interpenetration of human and material in, 16
  interventionism, 16
  practices of governance and freedom, 7–9, 22–28, 155–56, 191
  primacy of, 15–17
  resistance and accommodation, 239–41
  as situated, stable, and open-ended, 240–41n15
  temporal emergence, 16
pragmatist governance, 16, 30, 247
Prior, D., 201–2
prostitution toleration zones, 229–30, 234
public accountability, 122, 123–24, 161
public contestation, 123–25
  access to public dialogue, 125
  responsiveness, 125
  transparency, 124–25
Purcell, M., 254, 274

qualitative policy analysis, 12

Rabinowitz, D., 253
radical democracy, 27, 73–75, 173–74
radical pluralism, 21–22, 24, 25, 28, 30, 235–36
Rahman, S., 60n2
Rancière, J., 28, 72–73, 192–93
rationality, condition of, 66
reciprocity, requirement of, 66
reflexive institutions, 42, 44, 129
Rein, M., 239
religion
  in Haifa, Israel, 260
  religious language and worldviews in public dialogue, 67, 67n10
  religious symbols and dress in schools, 60–62, 60n1, 60n2, 72–73, 80–81
representation
  altering forms of, 55–56
  closely defined mandates, 120
  constitutive of interests and preferences, 118–21
  democratic anchorage model, 118–21
  ensuring identification with representatives, 120–21
rhetoric
  agreement in spite of, 34, 139–40
  bullying, 148
  inhibition of collaboration in spite of, 183–84, 197, 224, 243
Rhodes, R.A.W., 102, 245n19
Robinson, J., 218n1
Rosanvallon, P., 43, 49
Rose, N., 1

Sacranie, I., 62
Sanders, L., 24, 62
scalar politics, 249, 251–54, 259
Scharpf, F., 92
Schön, D. A., 239
Schultebraucks-Burghardtand, G., 227–28
Skelcher, C., 91, 92, 103, 162, 171
Specht, M., 230–31, 243
Stoker, G., 9–10, 18, 85, 252
Stone, C., 247
Stone, D., 222

Sullivan, H., 6, 179, 181–82
Sure Start programme, 176–77, 182,
    183, 188–89, 191, 194, 195
symbolic urban regimes, 251–54
    defined, 252
    discourses, 252–53
    relational dynamics, 253
    scalar politics of citizenship, 253

Taylor, M., 202
temporal emergence, 16
territorial constituencies, 51–52, 53–54
    accountability to territorially defined
        citizenry, 113–14, 121–26, 132
    demarcation of 'the affected', 128
    Israeli-Palestinian neighbourhood
        mobilisation, 250–51
trapped minorities, 253
Tully, J., 7–9, 27, 29–30, 155–56,
    159, 170, 173–74, 191, 199–
    200, 202–3, 213, 224, 235,
    236–37, 237n12, 238–39, 244,
    245–46, 247

UN Convention on the Rights of the
    Child, 210n5
United Kingdom
    demands against airport
        expansion, 12
    medical research tissue-banking, 49
    neighbourhood governance, 176–77,
        182–96
    neighbourhood regeneration
        development trusts, 164–68
    partnership working, 6
    religious symbols and dress in
        schools, 60–62, 60n1, 60n2,
        72–73, 80–81
    youth parliament, 200–1, 204–16
United States
    distrust of versus involvement in
        government, 47
    empowerment in public school
        governance, 55
    examples of governance-driven
        democratization in, 50
    judiciary and policymaking, 41–43
    legislation of public processes, 50
    Mississippi politics, 149–50
    New Orleans after hurricane
        Katrina, 54

secret detention of terrorist
    suspects, 102
stem-cell research, 49
universality, condition of, 66
universalization, 69–70, 70n14
urban governance, 36, 217–48
    administration-invited participation,
        223–27
    creative role of distrust, 232–36
    democratic governance as civic
        capacity, 246–48
    distinguishing democracy from the
        state, 225
    distrust in urban administrations,
        218–19
    enacted interdependence, 242–43,
        242n17
    hegemony, 221–23, 222n6
    informality concept, 217–23
    pluralized ungovernability, 221, 223
    symbolic urban regimes, 251–54
    uninvited participation, 219n2,
        225–27
    urban elites versus deprived/poor,
        221n4
urban wisdom, 220

Verloo, N., 220, 222

Wagenaar, H., 12–13, 154, 203,
    240–41n15, 243, 273
Waldron, J., 18, 62–63, 63n4.
    See also circumstances of politics
Ward, M., 61
Warren, M., 22–23, 221, 224
Wenman, M., 25
Wittgenstein, L., 82–84, 127–28,
    154, 240

Young, I.M., 22–23, 191
youth parliaments, 205n2, 210n5
    community cohesion, 206–8, 207n3,
        207n4
    developing democratic ethos,
        213–15
    practices of freedom, 211–13
    practices of governance, 206–11
    relationship with council
        government, 208–11
    shifts in terms of engagement,
        211–13